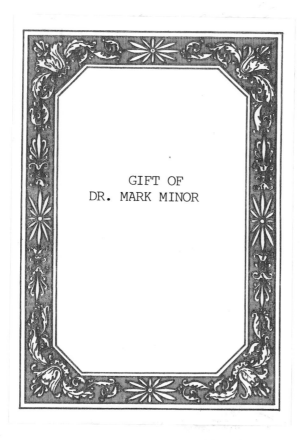

Pulpits, politics and public
order in England
1760–1832

Pulpits, politics and public order in England
1760–1832

ROBERT HOLE

Principal Lecturer, Polytechnic South West

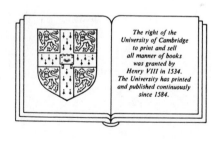

The right of the
University of Cambridge
to print and sell
all manner of books
was granted by
Henry VIII in 1534.
The University has printed
and published continuously
since 1584.

CAMBRIDGE UNIVERSITY PRESS

Cambridge
New York   Port Chester
Melbourne   Sydney

Published by the Press Syndicate of the University of Cambridge
The Pitt Building, Trumpington Street, Cambridge CB2 1RP
40 West 20th Street, New York, NY 10011, USA
10 Stamford Road, Oakleigh, Melbourne 3166, Australia

First published 1989

Printed in Great Britain at the University Press, Cambridge

British Library cataloguing in publication data
Hole, Robert.
Pulpits, politics and public order in
England, 1760–1832
1. England. Christian church. Relations
with state, 1760–1832
I. Title
322'.1'0942

Library of Congress cataloguing in publication data
Hole, Robert.
Pulpits, politics, and public order in England, 1760–1832 / Robert
Hole.
p.   cm.
Originally presented as the author's thesis (Ph.D.), Exeter
University
Bibliography.
Includes index.
ISBN 0–521–36486–8
1. Church and state – England – History – 18th century.   2. Church
and state – England – History – 19th century.   3. Christianity and
politics – History of doctrines – 18th century.   4. Christianity and
politics – History of doctrines – 19th century.   5. England – Church
history – 18th century.   6. England – Church history – 19th century.
I. Title.
BR758.H65 1989
941.07'3 – dc20   89–31422 CIP

ISBN 0 521 36486 8

WV

*To my Father
and in memory of
my Mother*

Contents

Contents ix

Acknowledgements

The bulk of the research for this book was done in the Bodleian Library, Oxford, the British Library, London, and Exeter University Library. I am deeply indebted to the staff of these institutions, and to those of the other libraries and archives in which I have worked on this study, namely: Bristol Central Library; Buckfast Abbey Library; Devon and Exeter Institution; Devon Record Office; Exeter Cathedral Library; John Rylands University Library of Manchester; Lambeth Palace Library; National Registry of Archives; Rolle College Library, Exmouth; and University College, London, D. M. S. Watson Library. I am grateful to the Governors and Staff Development Committee of Rolle College, Exmouth, for granting me study leave and supporting my research.

This book began life as an Exeter University Ph.D. thesis and I owe an immense debt of gratitude to my supervisor, Michael Duffy, who has guided and encouraged my studies at every stage. I have also benefited greatly from the comments of my examiners, Harry Dickinson and Bruce Coleman. In its later stages, parts of the manuscript were read by my colleague Nick Smart, and all of it by A. M. C. Waterman. Jonathan Clark has provided me with detailed comments on it which have proved stimulating and valuable and I am pleased to be able to record my gratitude for his generosity and encouragement. My friend and ex-colleague John Highfield has contributed to its development at every stage, from that evening, on the beach at Mombasa, when I outlined my initial thoughts on the project, to the final stages of preparing the manuscript; from challenging my arguments to correcting my syntax. On a personal level, my aunt, the late Miss Meta Hole, provided invaluable domestic support; it was her care of my cocker spaniel, Beatrix, which allowed me the necessary freedom to live in libraries and archives for long periods. My greatest debt, however, is to my parents, to whom this work is dedicated, for their careful attention to my upbringing and my early education.

Abbreviations

MANUSCRIPT COLLECTIONS

BL	British Library, Department of Manuscripts
Bodl.	The Bodleian Library, Oxford
DRO	Devon Record Office, Exeter
LPL	Lambeth Palace Library
UCL	University College, London, D. M. S. Watson Library, Manuscript Room

PRINTED BOOKS

Barrington, *Sermons*	Shute Barrington, *Sermons, Charges and Tracts* (London, 1811)
Burke, *Corr.*	*The Correspondence of Edmund Burke*, 10 vols. (Cambridge, 1958–78)
Burke, *Works*	*The Works of the Right Honourable Edmund Burke*, 6 vols. (London, 1877–83)
Burke, *Writings*	*The Writings and Speeches of Edmund Burke*, vols. 2 and 5 (Oxford, 1981)
Coleridge, *Works*	*The Collected Works of Samuel Taylor Coleridge* (London and Princeton, 1976–)
Fletcher, *Works*	*The Works of the Rev. John Fletcher, Late Vicar of Madely*, 7 vols. (London, 1825)
Hall, *Works*	*The Works of Robert Hall*, 6 vols. (London, 1832)
Horne, *Works*	*The Works of the Right Reverend George Horne DD Late Lord Bishop of Norwich*, 4 vols. (London, 1818)
Horsley, *Charges*	*The Charges of Samuel Horsley, LLD, FRS, FAS* (Dundee, 1813)
Horsley, *Speeches*	*The Speeches in Parliament of Samuel Horsley* (Dundee, 1813)
Hurd, *Works*	*The Works of Richard Hurd DD Lord Bishop of Winchester*, 8 vols. (London, 1811)

Jenyns, *Works*	*The Works of Soame Jenyns Esq.*, 4 vols. (London, 1790)
Jones, *Sermons*	William Jones, *Sermons on Various Subjects and Occasions*, 2 vols. (London, 1830)
Jones, *Works*	*The Theological, Philosophical and Miscellaneous Works of the Rev. William Jones MA, FRS*, 12 vols. (London, 1801)
Knox, *Works*	*The Works of Vicesimus Knox, DD*, 7 vols. (London, 1824)
More, *Works*	*The Works of Hannah More*, 11 vols. (London, 1853)
Paine, *Writings*	*The Writings of Thomas Paine*, edited by M. D. Conway, 4 vols. (New York, 1894–96; reprinted New York, 1967)
Paley, *Works*	*The Works of William Paley*, 7 vols. (London, 1825)
Parl. Deb.	*The Parliamentary Debates from the Year 1803 to the Present Time* (London, 1812–)
Parl. Hist.	*The Parliamentary History of England from the Earliest Period to the Year 1803*, 36 vols. (London, 1806–20)
Priestley, *Works*	*The Theological and Miscellaneous Works of Joseph Priestley LLD, FRS*, edited by J. T. Rutt, 25 vols. (Hackney, 1817–31)
Robinson, *Works*	*Miscellaneous Works of Robert Robinson, Late Pastor of the Baptist Church and Congregation of Protestant Dissenters at Cambridge*, 4 vols. (Harlow, 1807)
Toplady, *Works*	*The Works of Augustus Toplady AB, Late Vicar of Broad Hembury, Devon* (London, 1794)
Watson, *Misc. T.*	Richard Watson, *Miscellaneous Tracts on Religious, Political and Agricultural Subjects*, 2 vols. (London, 1815)
Watson, *SPO*	Richard Watson, *Sermons on Public Occasions and Tracts on Religious Subjects* (Cambridge, 1788)
Wesley, *Works*	*The Works of the Rev. John Wesley AM, sometime Fellow of Lincoln College, Oxford*, third edition, 14 vols. (London, 1829–31)

JOURNALS

AHR	*American Historical Review*
BIHR	*Bulletin of the Institute of Historical Research*
CH	*Church History*
ECS	*Eighteenth Century Studies*
ED	*Enlightenment and Dissent*

EHR	*English Historical Review*
Hist.	*History*
HJ	*Historical Journal*
JBS	*Journal of British Studies*
JEH	*Journal of Ecclesiastical History*
JHI	*Journal of the History of Ideas*
JMH	*Journal of Modern History*
PP	*Past and Present*
PPN	*The Price-Priestley Newsletter*
PT	*Political Theory*
SCH	*Studies in Church History*
TRHS	*Transactions of the Royal Historical Society*

Introduction

It is no uncommon foible with those who are honoured with the acquaintance of the great, to attribute national events to particular persons, particular measures, to the errors of one man, to the intrigues of another, to any possible spark of a particular occasion, rather than to the true proximate cause, (and which alone deserves the name of a cause) the predominant state of public opinion. And still less are they inclined to refer the latter to the ascendancy of speculative principles, and the scheme or mode of thinking in vogue. I have known men, who with significant nods and the pitying contempt of smiles, have denied all influence to the corruptions of moral and political philosophy and with much solemnity have proceeded to solve the riddle of the French Revolution by ANECDOTES! Yet it would not be difficult, by an unbroken chain of historic facts, to demonstrate that the most important changes in the commercial relations of the world ... had their origin not in the cabinets of statesmen, or in the practical insight of the men of business, but in the closets of uninterested theorists, or in the visions of recluse genius. To the immense majority of men even in civilised countries speculative philosophy has ever been, and must ever remain, a terra incognita. Yet it is not the less true, that the *epoch-forming* Revolutions of the Christian world, the revolutions of religion and with them the civil, social and domestic habits of the nations concerned, have co-incided with the rise and fall of metaphysical systems. (S. T. Coleridge 1816)[1]

Just as it is essential to study the history of ideas in the context of the society which produced them, so is it necessary to relate changes in that society to the beliefs, values and basic assumptions of its members. The secularisation of political thought is one of the most fundamental developments in the intellectual history of England in the last three hundred years. It has been, in part, the result of changes in the social and economic organisation of life and in the nature and function of government, but it has, itself, contributed to those changes through its effect on the basic attitudes to society and government of both subjects and rulers. The period from 1760 to 1832 saw crucial changes in the way the English related their religious beliefs to their

---

[1] 'The Statesman's Manual', *Works*, vol. 6, pp. 1–114 (pp. 13–15). (In all cases, where emphases appear in quotations, these are in the original work.)

1

views of politics and society. Those changes form the basis of this study.

Any student of the history of ideas in this period works today in the context of two recent scholarly traditions; one that of Sir Lewis Namier and his critics, the other that led by J. G. A. Pocock and Quentin Skinner. Namier would certainly have incurred Coleridge's wrath; for all his immense gifts to historical scholarship and methodology, he underestimated the importance of ideas and ideals in determining human conduct. His critics, most notably Herbert Butterfield, rightly re-emphasised the importance of the role of principles and beliefs. But Namier's exposition of the structure of politics and the pursuit of power was such that now we must look at men's professed values and the use they made of principled arguments in a new and more sceptical light.[2]

The old study of the history of political theory as a set of timeless abstract ideas largely divorced from the clamour of political debate which produced them has been criticised by Skinner and Pocock with considerable effect.[3] They apply a degree of Namierite scepticism to the classic expressions of political philosophy and urge a study of ideas based on a wider range of sources and more aware of the significance of language. They warn against the construction, through extrapolation, of a complex philosophy from the random and unconnected comments of an individual, which imposes a false coherence on his thought. Rather, the historian of ideas must seek to understand the lack of coherence by examining the precise circumstances which led men to select and use specific arguments at particular times.

This book is, of course, influenced by these two major traditions. It takes, however, two more specific exemplars. The first is Christopher Hill's Ford Lectures of 1962.[4] In his introduction to these, Hill outlines in broad and telling brushstrokes an understanding of the complex role of ideas in history which later scrutiny has done nothing to diminish. He recognises that 'ideas were all important for the individuals whom they impelled into action; but the historian must attach equal importance to the circumstances that gave these ideas their chance'. However, like Marx, Hill avoids 'the error of

---

[2] Namier's approach is reflected not only in his classic works, *The Structure of Politics at the Accession of George III*, second edition (London, 1957), and *England in the Age of the American Revolution*, second edition (London, 1961), but also, in miniature, in his review of Norman Sykes's *Church and State*, 'Church and State in Eighteenth-Century England', in *Crossroads of Power* (London, 1962), pp. 184–6. H. Butterfield, *George III and the Historians*, revised edition (New York, 1957), 'George III and the Namier School', *Encounter*, 43 (April 1957), 70–6.
[3] Q. Skinner, 'Meaning and Understanding in the History of Ideas', *History and Theory*, 8 (1969), 3–53; 'Motives, Intentions and the Interpretation of Texts', *New Literary History*, 3 (1972), 393–408. J. G. A. Pocock, *Politics, Language and Time: Essays in Political Thought and History* (New York, 1971); 'Virtues, Rights and Manners: A Model for Historians of Political Thought', *PT*, 9 (1981), 353–68.
[4] C. Hill, *Intellectual Origins of the English Revolution* (Oxford, 1965).

thinking that men's ideas were merely a pale reflection of their economic needs, with no history of their own'.[5]

The second exemplar is H. T. Dickinson's study of political ideology in eighteenth-century Britain.[6] Dickinson seeks to combine the Butterfield and the Skinner-Pocock critiques of Namier. He argues that, while there is no need to abandon the realism of Namierite historians, we must recognise that 'political agents both act *and* think'. If the historian 'does not understand the values of a particular society, then he will not understand the political agents of that society. To understand these political values, he must examine the political rhetoric, the arguments, prejudices and assumptions of the age.'[7]

Neither Hill nor Dickinson goes as far as Coleridge in alleging that ideas were the predominant cause of political and social change; nor will this book. The links between the arguments set forth and the specific political circumstances in which they were used will be explored. But it will not be assumed that the ideas were merely a reflection of those circumstances. As Hill argues, ideas have a history of their own. Certainly, however, their history was much influenced by the political circumstances surrounding them. Traditional ideas and customary ways of thinking interacted with events in a dialectical fashion to produce new arguments and emphases and even, in the long term, new values and assumptions. To understand those changes it is necessary to examine both the political and social history of the period under study and the history of ideas within it.

Religion is something of an umbrella concept. Its major concerns are spiritual, eternal and soterial. It is important always to remember that its political and social dimensions examined in this study are secondary and incidental to its major purpose. However, many of its multifarious aspects do relate to political and social life. In its Christian form it incorporates a set of spiritual beliefs, ranging from creation to judgment and life after death, which deeply influence man's view of the purpose of life and his perception of his real interests. Its scriptures contain specific moral precepts set out in general principles with a number of illustrative examples but do not provide a sufficiently comprehensive code to preclude some variety of interpretation. Religion assumes epistemological criteria which transcend the merely rational and human and provide man with a source of authoritative knowledge through divine revelation either in the form of written scriptures or through the teaching of the church. It also involves a number of ecclesiastical organisations which vary in their hierarchical structures, their

---

[5] *Ibid.*, p. 3.
[6] H. T. Dickinson, *Liberty and Property: Political Ideology in Eighteenth-Century Britain* (London, 1977).
[7] *Ibid.*, pp. 6, 7.

geographical extent and their relation to the state. These churches provide a professional clergy who, as well as carrying out spiritual duties, may also teach the laity and perform various social and political functions in the community.

Hill is well aware of the importance of religious ideas in seventeenth-century England. 'The Bible', he noted, 'especially the Geneva Bible with its highly political marginal notes, came near to being a revolutionist's handbook, not for the last time in history.'[8] Dickinson pays less attention to religious arguments in the eighteenth century and so reflects in part the great degree of secularisation which had taken place in political thought in the intervening period. In a wide-ranging general survey this is, perhaps, understandable, but in fact a considerable number of religious arguments were still being used in the political debate of the period. Moreover the nature of those arguments and the use to which they were put were changing significantly in the last years of the century.

Those changes reflected the social and political events of the period, not only the French Revolution, but also the American struggle and the riots, unrest and political demonstrations at home. They also reflected, in Coleridge's words, 'the ascendancy of speculative principles, and the scheme or mode of thinking in vogue'. The effect of a century or so of rational-cum-empirical thought on Christian metaphysics and the influence of critical, scientific methodology on the study of the scriptures significantly changed the way some Christians applied religious ideas to the issues of their day. Their arguments were also greatly influenced by ecclesiastical politics. The privilege and status of the Church of England, the wish to defend the alliance between church and state, the desire for toleration by Catholics and Unitarians and for full civil rights by trinitarian Protestant Dissenters were all reflected in the varied reactions of men of different denominations. The history of Christian political thought needs to be set in the political and social context of events, the intellectual context of developments in philosophy and theology, and in the ecclesiastical context of the denominations' concern with toleration, civil rights and church politics.

The major areas of scholarship upon which this work touches and which form its context and foundation are reviewed below.[9] In attempting to analyse the changing ways in which religious arguments were used in the formation of political and social theory, it seeks to fill a gap left by all of these studies. Most ecclesiastical historians concentrate upon one or a few denominations and largely neglect theoretical arguments. This book considers the political ideas of Catholic priests, Anglican clergymen, Dissenting

---

[8] Hill, *Intellectual Origins*, p. 2.
[9] See the Bibliographical appendix below, pp. 259–69.

ministers, laymen of all Christian denominations, trinitarian and unitarian, deists and atheists.

Social historians concentrate upon the churches' response to change and attitudes to social problems and policies, but have not fully considered the relationship between the theories of society inherent in these attitudes and the development of political thought in general.

Intellectual historians and students of political theory and ideology have tended until recently to ignore religious arguments in this period in a way that would have been unthinkable in sixteenth- or seventeenth-century studies. In an intellectual version of the Whig interpretation, the progressive triumph of rationalist scientific thought over supernatural and metaphysical beliefs is traced as an inevitable and laudable process. The concentration on natural religion is seen as progressive, the reassertion of the revealed nature of the Christian faith as retrograde.

The recent publications of Dr Jonathan Clark have focussed attention on religion as a significant element in the ideology of the ancien regime, and to some extent this book needs to be seen in the light of his work.[10] It seeks to explore in detail a number of issues and attitudes which Clark touches upon only briefly in his pioneering and important work. Many of the conclusions it reaches are consistent with Clark's broad thesis, others dissent from it in significant ways. But this book has its own problematic and it should not be read simply in terms of the new agenda which Clark has proposed. In one sense, it seeks to be broader than Clark by giving a more balanced attention than he attempted to the views of those of all religious denominations, and of none.

But in other ways, of course, Clark's work is far more wide ranging. As the sub-titles of his books make clear, he is concerned with 'ideology, social structure and political practice', with 'state and society'. This book is concerned with the use of religious arguments in political and social theory. In Clark's work, religion constitutes only one theme, and it is not necessary to accept his arguments concerning the nature of political parties and the growth of radicalism to value what he has to say about the central position which religion occupied in eighteenth-century political ideology. This book should be seen neither as 'supporting' nor 'opposing' Clark in crude terms, but rather as an attempt to refine one area of his analysis. The implications of that refinement for Clark's wider purpose are, properly, beyond the scope of this book; to allow them to distort the analysis attempted here would be to capitulate to Clark's agenda; but where significant differences emerge,

---

[10] Principally, *English Society 1688–1832: Ideology, Social Structure and Political Practice during the Ancien Regime* (Cambridge, 1985), and *Revolution and Rebellion: State and Society in England in the Seventeenth and Eighteenth Centuries* (Cambridge, 1986).

these are established in the main body of the text, and summarised in the bibliographical appendix.

This book seeks to combine insights provided by the studies of political philosophy and the history of ideas, of popular ideology and political history, of theology and ecclesiastical history, and of sociology and social history. While it will attempt to examine the whole range of religious political thought, it will seek to redress existing imbalances in two ways. First it will pay no more attention than is absolutely necessary to the much-studied Evangelicals, though it will take their ideas seriously. Secondly it will give full weight to Catholic thought, which most Protestant writers tend to ignore.[11] It will not try to assess the practical effects of the ideas and theories it analyses nor will it consider social policies as distinct from social theory. The study is centred upon English and Welsh ideas, and Scottish and Irish thought will generally be excluded.[12] Only if a Scot, like David Hume, or an Irishman, like Edmund Burke, made a major impact in England is their work considered in any detail.

Another important and closely related issue that will be excluded is the religious reaction to developing economic theory. The relationship of Protestantism and capitalism, Christian attitudes to economic self-interest and acquisitiveness, religious attitudes to Mandeville in the early eighteenth century and Smith and Ricado later, the economic theories of Dean Tucker and the Rev. Robert Malthus require a book, or rather a series of books, to themselves.[13] Professor A. M. C. Waterman's forthcoming work on Christian Political Economy from 1798 to 1833 is eagerly awaited.

This work is based on the mass of published sermons, speeches, pamphlets and longer discourses which poured off metropolitan and provincial presses in these years and is now held by the Bodleian and the British Library. While some use of manuscript material has been made, the desire to examine those arguments employed in the public domain has led to a concentration upon printed material. This study centres upon the effect of the French Revolution, and an analysis of the changes of emphasis in Christian political and social theory in the 1790s constitutes the heart of its argument. These changes are set in context by a study of the thirty years before and thirty years after that critical decade. The reaction to events in France is thus placed in the fuller setting of English conservative and radical thought, of the growing alarm over riots and disorder, the dislocation arising

---

[11] Edward Norman and David Hempton are honourable exceptions. See also J. M. Turner, '"Of Methodists and Papists Compar'd"', *Proceedings of the Wesley Historical Society*, 41 (1977), 37–8.

[12] On Scotland see W. M. Kirkland, 'The Impact of the French Revolution on Scottish Religious Life and Thought with Special Reference to Thomas Chalmers, Robert Haldane, and Neil Douglas' (unpublished Ph.D. dissertation, University of Edinburgh, 1951).

[13] On these issues see the works by M. M. Goldsmith, T. A. Horne, S. Rashid, W. G. Shelton, J. Viner and A. M. C. Waterman cited in the bibliography below.

from economic and social change in the countryside and from the growth of industrial towns, the movements for religious rights and parliamentary reform, for spiritual revivalism and moral improvement, the development of popular education and the rivalry between the established and Dissenting churches to provide it, and the growing awareness of the need for social control.

All the concerns of this book could be described as political thought in its widest sense. However, the terms political theory and social theory will be used in a narrower way to identify two aspects of that wider field. The term *political theory* is used to denote the traditional, central concerns of political philosophers relating to the origin of political society, the nature of governmental authority, the sources of political obligation, and the circumstances in which revolutionary changes in the form of government are permissible. The term *social theory* is used to denote theories of the nature of society, the importance of a clearly defined social hierarchy, the means by which social order and unity are maintained, the importance of effective social control, the nature of man and the need for restraints and sanctions on human behaviour. It will be claimed that there was a fundamental change of emphasis in Christian argument from political theory to social theory in the 1790s. This was accompanied by a decline in the use of religious arguments in political theory in favour of secular ones. The term *religious argument* is used here to denote an argument which consciously depended for its effectiveness on a belief in God and an acceptance of the authority of the scriptures or the church. The term *secular argument* denotes one which either did not make reference to God or things divine at all, or which did so only in a cosmetic way. When the name of God was invoked but the structure of the argument remained intact whether or not one believed in His existence, that is regarded here as a secular argument.

It will be argued that the secularisation of political thought was more something that occurred within the churches by a change of emphasis in clerical sermons and speeches than something that was imposed from outside by deists and atheists. However, the growing concentration on secular rather than religious arguments in political theory from the early 1790s was counterbalanced by an increasing emphasis on Christian social theory and on arguments of sanction and restraint.

Part I
Pre-Revolution, 1760–1789

1

Christian political theory

Christianity has acted as a prop of the state since the conversion of the Emperor Constantine. The connexion of religion and political theory has a long history. A sacerdotal concept of the anointed monarch survived the Protestant Reformation in England, and the constitutional conflicts of the seventeenth century had an important religious element. The restoration of Charles II was celebrated with Anglican sermons which spoke unequivocally of divine hereditary right, passive obedience and non-resistance. James II's adherence to the Catholic faith posed a cruel dilemma to the Church of England, and desperate steps were taken to clothe the ensuing settlement in the language of Holy Writ by Whig and Tory alike. The dispute between Benjamin Hoadley and Francis Atterbury, and the trial of Dr Sacheverell established both the crucial differences between Whig and Tory views, and the common arena within which their positions stood.[1] Between 1679 and 1719, abstract and normative principles relating to political authority and obligation and the possibility of revolution, which are fundamental to any scheme of political values, were related to a specific set of constitutional arrangements. Like those arrangements, the principles on which they were based had a long life, but neither were immutable.

In the period from 1760 to 1789 religion continued to be used to support and defend the constitutional principles upon which British government was founded, but noticeably more so by clerics than by laymen. The records of parliament from 1760 to 1789 show that religion was rarely invoked in purely secular debates.[2] Only when matters relating to the church and its

[1] Richard Schlatter, *The Social Ideas of Religious Leaders 1660–1688* (London, 1940); Gerald Straka, *The Anglican Reaction to the Revolution of 1688* (Madison, Wisconsin, 1962); G. V. Bennett, *The Tory Crisis in Church and State 1688–1730: The Career of Francis Atterbury, Bishop of Rochester* (Oxford, 1975); Geoffrey Holmes, *The Trial of Doctor Sacheverell* (London, 1973); J. P. Kenyon, *Revolution Principles: the Politics of Party 1687–1720* (Cambridge, 1977); Margaret Jacob, *The Newtonians and the English Revolution 1689–1720* (Hassocks, 1976).

[2] Even the Saints used largely secular arguments. Sir Richard Hill's speeches, containing quotations from scripture and prayers, were exceptional and led to his being rebuked by a constituent. In the early 1830s, the Recordites were less inhibited and contemporaries noted that this was unusual. See Ian Bradley, 'The Politics of Godliness: Evangelicals in Parliament

relationship to the state were under discussion were religious arguments employed there.[3] Such occasions showed that Members of Parliament could produce detailed religious arguments, appeal to scripture, and discuss theological niceties with some erudition, though these debates tended to be dominated by a limited number of well-informed members. But such arguments were largely reserved for church–state issues. This is hardly surprising given that most parliamentary discussion was of detailed practical issues, while religion relates to fundamental principles and basic values which were often assumed, or even ignored. Even when secular issues arose which did involve basic religious principles, there is rarely any record of a theoretical discussion of them in parliament.

Clerical writings of the period, on the other hand, had a high political content. Sermons, charges, tracts, memoirs, letters, pamphlets and books by clergy and some clerically inclined laymen frequently related the fundamentals of government to religion in a theoretical way and cited the scriptures to justify the political order.

This chapter analyses the use made of religious arguments in political theory by various Christian groups: first by the main parties in the Church of England, then by Methodists, Catholics, Old Dissenters and Unitarians. These arguments varied somewhat according to the religious beliefs of the writer, the immediate political climate at the time of writing, and the philosophical and ideological assumptions of the author. These variations will be considered in detail in the following three chapters, which place the arguments outlined here in their religious, political and constitutional contexts.

The established church

Authority and obligation

Almost all agreed that the authority of government was decreed by scripture and that Christians were obliged to recognise, and to submit to, that authority. A number of biblical texts were appealed to, but two stood pre-eminent and provided the inspiration of hundreds, indeed thousands, of sermons. St Paul's Epistle to the Romans 13.1–7 reads,

Let every soul be subject unto the higher powers. For there is no power but of God:

1784–1832' (unpublished D.Phil. dissertation, University of Oxford, 1974), pp. 72–3 and 257–9.
[3] Notably: the vexed question of subscription to the thirty-nine articles by Anglican clergy, university students, and, to the theological articles, by the Dissenting clergy; the efforts to relieve Catholics from the penal laws and grant additional rights to Protestant Dissenters; and the regular attempts to repeal the Corporation and Test Acts.

the powers that be are ordained of God. Whosoever therefore resisteth the power, resisteth the ordinance of God: and they that resist shall receive to themselves damnation. For rulers are not a terror to good works, but to the evil. Wilt thou then not be afraid of the power? do that which is good, and thou shalt have praise of the same: for he is the minister of God to thee for good. But if thou do that which is evil, be afraid; for he beareth not the sword in vain: for he is the minister of God, a revenger to execute wrath upon him that doeth evil. Wherefore ye must needs be subject, not only for wrath, but also for conscience sake. For for this cause pay ye tribute also: for they are God's ministers, attending continually upon this very thing. Render therefore to all their dues: tribute to whom tribute is due; custom to whom custom; fear to whom fear; honour to whom honour.

The first epistle general of St Peter 2.13–18 reads,

Submit yourselves to every ordinance of man for the Lord's sake: whether it be to the king as supreme; or unto governors, as unto them that are sent by him for the punishment of evildoers, and for the praise of them that do well. For so is the will of God, that with well doing ye may put to silence the ignorance of foolish men: as free, and not using your liberty for a cloke of maliciousness, but as the servants of God. Honour all men. Love the brotherhood. Fear God. Honour the king. Servants, be subject to your masters with all fear; not only to the good and gentle, but also to the froward.

These two texts provided the crucial foundation of most of the pre-1789 writings considered in this book. They were, as will emerge, interpreted in different ways by different people at different times, but their fundamental authority and centrality was never questioned. They had, in the past, been used to justify passive obedience and non-resistance, but these ideas were now rejected, with varying degrees of fervour, as 'exploded theories' by every significant writer. In this period each interpretation of these texts succeeded in reconciling them to the Revolution Settlement and to the existing constitution, but the exact nature of that reconciliation varied significantly between different members of the Church of England. The positions adopted reflected the parties in the church, and the views of the high-church patriarchalists and the latitudinarian contractarians will be considered after those of the bishops.

The *Book of Common Prayer* at this time provided for four political feasts or fasts during the year, giving forms of service for Gunpowder Day (5 November) which also served to mark the arrival of William III, Martyrdom Day (30 January) to commemorate the execution of the 'Blessed King Charles I', Restoration Day (29 May) to celebrate the return of Charles II, and Accession Day (25 October) marking the start of the current reign. All of these gave rise to political sermons, those preached on 30 January in particular directed thoughts towards the fundamental issues of government.[4] This fast had been instituted by Act of Parliament during the reign of Charles II, and the rubric directed that, after the creed, parts of the homily against Disobedience and Wilful Rebellion should be read, or the minister should preach a sermon of his own on the same theme. At Westminster, if parliament were in session, the Commons attended service in St Margaret's and heard a sermon from a priest, usually an academic or one of the chaplains to the House, while the Lords assembled in Westminster Abbey to listen to one of the bishops.

The views expressed in any sermon were, or course, those of an individual bishop, not the collective view of the whole episcopate at the time. But they do reveal the attitudes of new arrivals on the bench. No bishop preached the Abbey Martyrdom Day sermon more than once, and the task normally went to a newly consecrated man. Between 1761 and 1788 thirty-seven men were elevated to the episcopate. Apart from the three appointed to the see of Sodor and Man (who did not sit in the House of Lords), and three others, all of them preached an Abbey Martyrdom Day sermon almost as soon as was practical – eight in the first year following their consecration, nine in the second year, six in the third year, three in the fourth and one in the fifth. Only three men appear to have been unreasonably delayed, having to wait seven, ten and eleven years respectively. This meant that, as well as rapidly reflecting changes in the ideological complexion of the episcopal bench, the sermons were also the work of men still seeking preferment. Almost invariably they occupied junior sees and looked to those in political power to elevate them to more lucrative livings. Not once was the sermon preached by a bishop of Winchester or Durham, while a bishop of Bristol appeared three times and one of St David's on five occasions. The changes discernible in these sermons over the period will be discussed in Chapter 3, here the broad orthodoxies which dominated at least the first two decades of George III's reign will be considered.

When discussing the question of political authority the bishops faced something of a dilemma. It was important for them to deny that monarchy, or any other form of government, had a divine origin otherwise all rebellion which sought to change the *form* of government (including the 1688 Revolution) would be impermissible. On the other hand, there was a

---

[4] For a useful general survey of the fast from its inception to its removal in 1859, see Helen Randall, 'The Rise and Fall of a Martyrology: Sermons on Charles I', *Huntington Library Quarterly*, 10 (1946–7), 135–67. Her section on the late-eighteenth-century sermons (pp. 152–67), however, does not identify the important changes of attitude in this period analysed below, here and in Chapter 3. B. S. Stewart, 'The Cult of the Royal Martyr', *CH*, 38 (1969), 175–87, concentrates on the sermons before 1750, mostly before 1715. Some of the sermons between 1720 and 1760 are discussed in J. A. W. Gunn, *Beyond Liberty and Property: The Process of Self-Recognition in Eighteenth-Century Political Thought* (Kingston and Montreal, 1983), pp. 150–6, and J. C. D. Clark, *English Society*, pp. 158–60.

reluctance to consign political obligation to merely secular injunctions. Unlike the Hobbesian concept that right arose from power, Christians considered that there was an important distinction between authority and power. The former was a normative term implying obligation, while the latter was merely an empirical one. No sacred obligation could arise from a secular authority, so if the origin of government was human, how could obligation to it be divine? The orthodox answer was clear and undisputed. St Paul's reference to government as the ordinance of God and St Peter's reference to it as the ordinance of man provided a neat scriptural basis on which to draw a distinction between a divine obligation to submit to government in general, and the freedom of a society to determine for itself what form that government should take.

Robert Lowth, Bishop of Oxford, in 1767 expressed the argument succinctly and precisely:

Government in general is the ordinance of God: the particular Form of Government is the ordinance of man . . . The form of government therefore has not an absolute, but only a relative, goodness; all forms considered in themselves are indifferent; all are lawful; all have even the sanction of divine authority. It follows that it is the duty of every individual to acquiesce in that form of government, under which Providence hath placed him.[5]

This crucial point was made time and again by other bishops in the Abbey Martyrdom Day sermons.[6] The emphasis which accompanied the point varied somewhat. John Moore, the Bishop of Bangor (who was later translated directly to Canterbury), stressed the duty of submission and the obligation to support every political constitution by the powerful sanctions only religion could impose. Bishop Markham, on the other hand, stressed the distinction between the human and the divine spheres; while God had left worldly arrangements to man, salvation was achievable under any government.[7] But these were merely variations of emphasis; on the basic formula all were agreed.

This formula was accepted not only by the bishops but virtually unanimously within the Anglican church. It was, however, often hedged about by so many qualifications that it is almost meaningless to talk of genuine agreement. Acceptance of the broadest formula allowed diverse views on matters of detail and so accommodated a wide range of political opinions within the church. The Assize sermons preached in the two University cities within seven days of each other in March 1769 revealed the extent of this range. Both took the opportunity to consider the origins of

[5] *A Sermon* . . . (London, 1767), pp. 14–15.
[6] Notably by Bishops Green 1763, Lamb 1768, Hinchcliffe 1773, Markham 1774, North 1775, Moore 1777, Ross 1779, Thurlow 1780, Warren 1781.
[7] Moore, *A Sermon* . . . (London, 1777), p. 6; Markham, *A Sermon* . . . (London, 1774), p. 11.

government, but, while the Oxford sermon stressed the divine nature of monarchy, the Cambridge one insisted upon the concept of popular sovereignty.[8]

The Oxford sermon was preached by George Horne, who, together with his close colleagues William Jones and William Stevens, formed a small group of Hutchinsonian patriarchalists.[9] George Horne was, clerically, the most successful of the three, though for a man whose friends included Charles Jenkinson and John Moore, Archbishop of Canterbury from 1783 to 1805, his advancement was less than dramatic. A fellow of Magdalen, Oxford, since 1750, he was elected its president in 1768. He served as chaplain-in-ordinary to the King for a decade from 1771, and in 1776 became vice-chancellor of the University of Oxford, adding its chancellor, Lord North, to his powerful patrons. He was appointed Dean of Canterbury in 1781, but it was not until after the outbreak of the French Revolution that he was elevated to the episcopate as Bishop of Norwich in 1790, just two years before his death. William Jones was Horne's undergraduate friend and life-long acolyte. He held a number of livings, but was best known as perpetual curate of Nayland in Suffolk. He became chaplain to Horne when the latter became Bishop of Norwich and outlived his old friend by eight years. As well as going on to play a leading role in the propaganda war of the 1790s, he edited Horne's works and prefaced them with a biography. Jones's own works were edited and his biography written by William Stevens. Stevens, the Treasurer of Queen Anne's Bounty, was George Horne's first cousin. He made his money in the hosiery trade and devoted his leisure time to theology. He bitterly attacked liberal churchmen who supported the American rebels in 1776 and consistently supported and defended William Jones. In his public utterances, at least, he was the most extreme of the group, but this may well have been because his lay status gave him greater freedom to express his true views.[10]

---

[8] G. Horne, 'The Origin of Civil Government', 2 March 1769, *Works*, vol. 2, pp. 434–49. R. Watson, 'Christianity Consistent with Every Social Duty', 9 March 1769, *SPO*, pp. 5–26. The range of opinion was acknowledged by John Gordon in his Accession Day sermon at Cambridge on 25 October 1771, *The Causes and Consequences of Evil Speaking against the Government* (Cambridge, 1771) p. 1, when he urged obedience whatever the source of government authority.

[9] For a qualification on the use of this term see below, pp. 61–2.

[10] On Horne see W. R. Ward, *Georgian Oxford, University Politics in the Eighteenth Century* (Oxford, 1958), W. Jones, *Memoirs of the Life, Studies and Writings of . . . George Horne* (London, 1795); on Jones see Stevens 'Life' in Jones, *Works*, vol. 1 pp. i–lv; on Stevens see *Memoirs of William Stevens Esq.* (London, 1812). This high-church group became known as the Hackney Phalanx. For a highly sympathetic account see A. B. Webster, *Joshua Watson, the Story of a Layman 1771–1855* (London, 1954), pp. 18–32. For more critical assessments of the high churchmen see Nancy Murray, 'The Influence of the French Revolution on the Church of England and its Rivals, 1789–1802' (unpublished D.Phil. dissertation, University of Oxford, 1975), pp. 44–79, and P. B. Nockles, 'Continuity and Change in Anglican High Churchmanship in Britain,

The Cambridge Assize sermon was preached by Richard Watson. Unfairly dubbed 'the Republican Bishop' by his enemies, he referred to himself on the title page of an anonymous pamphlet in 1772 as 'a Christian Whig'. He saw himself as a disciple of John Locke. He became Professor of Chemistry at Cambridge in 1764 and Regius Professor of Divinity in 1771. He became bishop almost by accident. Shelburne appointed him to the see of Llandaff in 1782, hoping to draw his patron, Lord Rutland, closer to the ministry.[11] After Shelburne's fall, Watson took an independent line. Having already offended the crown in 1776, he was never translated from this extremely poor see, which he held for thirty-four years until his death in 1816.[12]

Although Horne and Watson represented the extremes of Anglican political attitudes, they both accepted the basic formula. Watson was the readier to adopt the old Court Whig position. In his 1776 Accession Day sermon to the University of Cambridge,[13] he insisted that the form of government was the ordinance of man, but agreed that, once established, any form of government was ordained by God and, providing that government was conducive to the benefit of society, men were obliged by God to submit to it. The high-church patriarchalists were generally reluctant to admit that the form of government was open to human choice, but on occasions George Horne was prepared to concede the point. In his 1788 Accession Day sermon in Canterbury Cathedral[14] he accepted that the different modes by which rulers came to power in different constitutions were indeed an 'ordinance of man' but he insisted that, once so established, submission to them was a religious duty which allowed of no exceptions.

However, these highly qualified acceptances of the basic formula were almost the only points of contact between two quite different views of political society. Watson, the advocate of popular sovereignty, believed that universal consent was the only legitimate source of civil power. God, he argued, did not give some men power over others; rather, he made all men equal – all had been given largely the same natural advantages. Such equality and individual independence was inherent in the Creation. There-

1792–1850' (unpublished D.Phil. dissertation, University of Oxford, 1982), pp. 1–87. Compare Gunn, *Beyond Liberty and Property*, pp. 164–93, and J. C. D. Clark, *English Society*, pp. 216–35.

[11] T. J. Brain, 'Some Aspects of the Life and Work of Richard Watson, Bishop of Llandaff, 1737 to 1816' (unpublished Ph.D. dissertation, University of Wales, 1982), pp. 26–8. Watson's political theory however is not one of the aspects given detailed consideration in this sympathetic study.

[12] Watson, *Anecdotes of the Life of Richard Watson* . . . (London, 1817), *passim*, but esp. p. 59; *A Letter to the Members of the Honourable House of Commons*, second edition (London, 1772); Assize Sermon (1769), in *SPO* (Cambridge, 1788), p. 26; 'Answer to Jenyns' (1782), *Misc. T*, vol. 2, pp. 331–64 (p. 333); Letter to the Bishop of Ely (1786), in *Anecdotes*, p. 86.

[13] Watson, *SPO*, pp. 83–104 (pp. 93–4).

[14] 'The Duty of Praying for Governors' (1788), *Works*, vol. 2, pp. 560–73 (pp. 563–64).

fore any government which made one man, or a group or succession of men, superior to the others 'must spring from their express appointment and free consent'. Watson was not hostile to the concept of monarchy, but he insisted that the king's power was a fiduciary not an arbitrary one, a trust committed to him by the community which must be exercised in the public interest according to the law of the land.[15]

Horne rejected absolutely the concepts of a pre-social equality and of the necessity of popular consent to government. Such views were reasonable enough for a pagan to adopt, but Christian revelation, he argued, clearly showed that there was

> an intimate connexion between religion and government; that the latter originally flowed from the same divine source with the former, and was, at the beginning, the ordinance of the most High; that the state of nature was a state of subordination, not one of equality and independence, in which mankind never did, nor ever can exist, and that the civil magistrate is 'the minister of God to us for good'.[16]

Political authority was based, not, as Watson argued, on the sovereignty of the people but upon the prescription of God. William Jones, in a sermon of June 1778, stressed the distinction between political authority and physical power. The people may indeed have power in the physical sense that a gang of robbers do, but legitimate authority can come only from God. All power inherently belongs to Him and 'is a talent committed by him to man'. This divinely appointed authority of the magistrates had as its corollary a sacred obligation on subjects to obey and honour their governors.[17] Moreover, the high-church patriarchalists were clear that it was specifically monarchy which was the divinely appointed form of government. Horne was scathing about the alternatives. Aristocracy and democracy were recent and 'illegitimate' forms of government. Christianity and monarchy stood together, whilst a republic, he suggested, would be accompanied by a cold and empty classical religion which lacked clergy, services, sacraments and salvation.[18]

By their qualifications Horne and Watson effectively rendered the basic formula meaningless; there was no agreement on where the line demarcating the ordinance of God and the ordinance of man should be drawn. The degree of unity it afforded the Anglican church may have been spurious, but it was eagerly welcomed. The range of political opinion it was able to embrace was wide. Secular-minded clerics like Josiah Tucker, Dean of

[15] 'Sermon' (1785, 1793), *Misc. T*, vol. 1, pp. 448–93 (p. 478); 'Answer to Jenyns', *Misc. T*, vol. 2, pp. 338–44; Restoration Day sermon (1776), *SPO*, pp. 59–79 (pp. 65, 74); *Anecdotes*, p. 203.
[16] Assize Sermon (1769), *Works*, vol. 2, pp. 444–5, 448.
[17] *The Fear of God, and the Benefits of Civil Obedience, Two Sermons* (London, 1778), pp. 20, 24–7.
[18] Horne, Restoration Day sermon (1760), *Works*, vol. 3, pp. 115–36 (p. 133); Martyrdom Day sermon (1761), *Works*, vol. 3, pp. 398–421; 'God the Preserver of Princes' (1780?), *Works*, vol. 3, pp. 277–92 (pp. 280–2); 'The Duty of Praying for Governors', *Works*, vol. 2 (pp. 564, 571).

Gloucester, and religiously inclined laymen, like Edmund Burke, used it to reconcile their political stance to their faith.[19] But, although politically convenient and comfortable, the formula obfuscated rather than clarified the real nature of political authority and obligation.

The right of rebellion

The basic formula (that government *qua* government was of divine ordinance and that normally political obedience was a religious duty, but that the specific form of government was left to human determination) had a corollary – that rebellion was permissible in certain circumstances. This too was widely accepted in broad principle. Moreover, almost everyone agreed that the Revolution of 1688–9 was justified and accorded with the will of God. But thereafter, there was widespread disagreement about the circumstances necessary to justify such actions at other times. Because the basic formula had blurred the relationship between the ordinance of God and the ordinance of man in its definition of authority and obligation, the limits of that authority were unclear, and Anglicans defined them according to their political, not their theological, beliefs.

The bishops had moved from their role of personal advisers to the monarchy, and now saw themselves as members of the House of Lords and supporters of the king's ministers and the balanced constitution.[20] The political views which arose from this Court Whig position were set out in their Westminster Abbey Martyrdom Day sermons. When Brownlow North opened the 1775 sermon with the words 'Christianity hath left untouched the civil rights and liberties of mankind', he was expressing a common and often repeated sentiment.[21] Twelve years earlier, John Green had set out the theory clearly. While Christianity did enjoin submission to the legally constituted authority in the state, in whatever form it took, it must not be used to justify slavery or tyranny. If the magistrate failed to defend the laws and liberties of the people and to pursue the good ends for which he was appointed, he should not be obeyed.[22]

The problem remained, however, how to judge when such a situation had arisen. Thomas Newton, in 1764, made a plea for moderation, stressing the need to avoid the extremes of anarchy on one side and absolute passive

---

[19] J. Tucker, *A Treatise Concerning Civil Government* (London, 1781), pp. 85–6, compare pp. 417, 422–6; E. Burke, 'Thoughts on the Present Discontents' (1770), *Writings*, vol. 2, pp. 241–323 (p. 292).

[20] Episcopal support for ministers was not however automatic. See W. C. Lowe, 'Bishops and Scottish Representative Peers in the House of Lords, 1760–1775', *JBS*, 18 (1978), 86–106 (pp. 87–97).

[21] North, *A Sermon . . .* (London, 1775), p. 5; see also: Hinchcliffe, *A Sermon . . .* (London, 1773), p. 4; Markham, *A Sermon . . .*, p. 11; Moore, *A Sermon . . .* (1777), p. 6.

[22] *A Sermon . . .* (London, 1763), pp. 6–7.

obedience on the other. But he had no solution to the problem of how to make the subjective judgment of where the line should be drawn.[23] A decade later William Markham reflected that the church was committed to the support of two conflicting principles: one of resistance which arose largely from the Old Testament; the other of obedience drawn chiefly from the apostolic epistles. Both principles were reasonable in themselves, but each had limits which were often ignored. The proper balance between them was to be decided, Markham argued, not according to any religious principle, but by means of secular wisdom. He warned against theoretical maxims which, even when true, could mislead men, and suggested that they should turn, not to mere expediency, but to the empirical principles of the constitution.[24] The issue was to be decided by legal not theological means. The right of rebellion was justified in the eyes of God only when the constitution was being violated.

Most bishops probably agreed with Markham, but more widely in the church there was little consensus. Beyond the fact that there was a theoretical right of rebellion which occasionally obtained, and that 1688 was one of those occasions, there was little agreement and no real orthodoxy. Horne and Watson again represented the extremes of Anglican thought. Having argued that it was universal consent which gave governments the authority to exercise power, Watson insisted that, by definition, government had no authority to act contrary to the interests of the people. Oppression was an act of vice, for government was subject to the laws of nature, known to men either through reason or revelation. Passive obedience was subversive of those natural rights and resistance to a king or a government acting contrary to the interests of the people was almost a sacred duty. While he agreed that Christians were obliged to obey lawfully established government, Watson held that the only valid title was appointment by the people; he told Pitt in a letter of 12 May 1784, '. . . it is part of my political creed that the voice of the people, whenever it can be clearly known . . . *is* and ought to be supreme in the state'. If the people decided that the crown had increased its powers beyond the point where it served the best interests of the people, it was proper for the Christian to offer resistance.[25]

Horne was less forthright than Watson. He chose the context of the

---

[23] *Of Moderation: A Sermon* . . . (London, 1764), p. 15. Compare Hinchcliffe preaching on the same text, p. 6.

[24] Markham, *A Sermon* . . ., pp. 8–13. On this attitude to the constitution see H. T. Dickinson, 'The Eighteenth Century Debate on the Sovereignty of Parliament', *TRHS*, fifth series, 26 (1976), 206.

[25] Watson, Restoration Day Sermon, *SPO*, p. 74; *Anecdotes*, p. 203; *Letter to the Commons*, pp. 10–11; Assize Sermon (1769), *SPO*, p. 23; Accession Day Sermon (1776), *SPO*, pp. 83–104; Letter to Pitt, 12 May 1784, in *Anecdotes*, p. 129.

ancient world to declare that, if aristocracies and democracies were founded on a compact, it was a compact of rebels who had betrayed their allegiance to their natural rulers. But if, as Horne appears to have believed, kings were divinely appointed and obedience to them enjoined by God, were there any circumstances in which resistance was permissible? This was a delicate question which demanded a balanced answer from any cleric seeking preferment. After a youthful denial of the possibility, Horne maintained a judicious silence, and even Jones was somewhat muted.[26] It was the layman William Stevens who was prepared openly to argue the case for passive obedience. Government, he insisted, was always for the benefit of mankind for it could never be so badly administered as not to be preferable to anarchy. But this practical argument was superseded by a moral one – non-resistance was a Christian duty. God's teaching must be obeyed. He rejected the assumption of some Christian thinkers that the will of God should be equated with human wisdom; it was, he argued, an objective truth revealed to man in the scriptures: 'If the doctrine of non-resistance is to be rejected because repugnant to our nature, we may, upon the same principle, reject all the distinguishing doctrines of the gospel . . . the word of God may forbid, what the voice of depraved reason allows.'[27]

Horne and Jones never committed themselves so far towards passive obedience, but clearly their sympathies lay in that direction. A church which could comprehend both their views and Watson's concept of popular sovereignty and universal consent encompassed an extremely wide range. Certainly all Anglican political views could be accommodated within such parameters. Probably most of the country clergy stood somewhere between Horne and the bishops. Almost all accepted that the form of government could be changed. But since enthusiastic support for the existing constitution was near universal in the Church of England, and (at least after the first few years) George III was widely regarded as the best of kings,[28] the issue was only a theoretical one and could be discussed in a dispassionate way. Although the range of views in the Anglican church was wide, the various parties avoided open warfare.

The other Christian churches

The basic formula, that government in general was the ordinance of God, while specific forms of government were the ordinance of man and in certain circumstances could be changed, was accepted not only by members

---

[26] Horne, *Restoration Day Sermon* (1760), *Works*, vol. 3, p. 133; Jones, *Fear of God*, p. 21.

[27] Stevens, *The Revolution Vindicated and Constitutional Liberty Asserted* (Cambridge, 1777), pp. 15–16.

[28] Linda Colley, 'The Apotheosis of George III: Loyalty, Royalty and the British Nation', *PP*, 102 (1984), 94–129.

of the Church of England but also by almost all non-Anglican Christians. Because it could be interpreted very freely and so subsume a wide variety of political views, it allowed a considerable range of opinion within a denomination, and it is misleading to speak too definitely of a sect having a specific political position. How far rank-and-file members of a church shared their leaders' political theory is difficult to assess.[29] Moreover, sometimes different leaders within a denomination took different political stances. It is with these crucial qualifications in mind that the theoretical political views of the leaders of the non-Anglican churches must be considered.

The Methodists

The political and social effects of Methodism have been extensively discussed.[30] The political theories of its protagonists have received somewhat less attention.[31] This analysis will seek to place their ideas in the context of the thought of other Christians rather than rework ground already well tilled. Wesley dominated Methodism in the years before 1789. His political position was close to that of George Horne, though unlike Horne he

---

[29] J. E. Bradley argues that nonconformity in general was much less radical than the study of its leadership has suggested: 'Whigs and Nonconformists: Presbyterians, Congregationalists and Baptists in English Politics, 1718–1790' (unpublished Ph.D. dissertation, University of Southern California, 1978); 'Whigs and Nonconformists: "Slumbering Radicalism" in English Politics, 1739–89', *ECS*, 9 (1975), 1–27; 'Religion and Reform at the Polls: Nonconformity in Cambridge Politics 1774–1784', *JBS*, 23 (1984), 55–78.

[30] The classic texts in the controversy, É. Halévy, *The Birth of Methodism* (1906), translated and edited by B. Semmel (Chicago, 1971), *A History of the English People in 1815* (London,, 1924); J. L. and B. Hammond, *The Town Labourer 1760–1832* ; (London, 1917); E. R. Taylor, *Methodism and Politics 1791–1851* (Cambridge, 1935); E. Hobsbawm, 'Methodism and the Threat of Revolution', *History Today* (February 1957), 115–24; and E. P. Thompson, *The Making of the English Working Class* (London, 1963; revised edition, Harmondsworth, 1968), are summarised by E. S. Itzkin, 'The Halévy Thesis – A Working Hypothesis? English Revivalism: Antidote for Revolution and Radicalism 1789–1815', *CH*, 44 (1975), 47–56. They should now be read in the light of B. Semmel, 'Élie Halévy, Methodism and Revolution', Introduction to É. Halévy, *Birth of Methodism*; of John Kent's scepticism in 'Methodism and Revolution', *Methodist History*, 12 (1973–4), 136–44; and of David Hempton's wide-ranging analysis in *Methodism and Politics in British Society, 1750–1850* (London, 1984). For sound sense in a brief compass see I. R. Christie, *Stress and Stability in Late Eighteenth-Century Britain: Reflections on the British Avoidance of Revolution* (Oxford, 1984), pp. 200–9.

[31] W. J. Warner, *The Wesleyan Movement in the Industrial Revolution* (London, 1930), pp. 74–122, remains the fullest analysis. Maldwyn Edwards, *John Wesley and the Eighteenth Century: A Study of his Social and Political Influence* (London, 1933; revised edition, 1955), pp. 13–53, is superficial by comparison. Leslie Stephen's discussion of Wesley's thought largely ignores his political ideas, *History of English Thought in the Eighteenth Century*, 2 vol. (1876; third edition 1902; reprinted New York, 1949), vol. 2, pp. 409–24. Dickinson, *Liberty and Property*, neglects him. The two best recent discussions are B. Semmel, *The Methodist Revolution* (London, 1974), which relates Wesley's political ideas to his theology and to the influence of the European Enlightenment and American Revolution, and D. Hempton, *Methodism and Politics in British Society, 1750–1850* (London, 1984), which suggests Wesley lacked a clear ideology and merely reacted to events.

regarded politics as being of only peripheral importance in life. Wesley was deeply devoted to the monarchy. He fasted on the thirtieth of January, considered 'a King, a lovely, sacred name' and defended George II and George III when they were accused of weakness.[32] But it would be wrong to describe his views as 'the politics of divine right'.[33] If by divine right one means simply that royal authority, like any other form of governmental authority, came from God, then that was indeed Wesley's position, but so was it that of most Anglicans and many Dissenters. But if one means that monarchy is the only legitimate form of government and that royal power cannot be limited by any rights of the people, that was not Wesley's position. He noted in a tract *On Obedience to Parents* that God had given parents a right he had not given the king of England, who had no power except to execute the law of the land: 'The will of the king is no law to the subject.'[34] Indeed, Wesley appeared to accept the basic formula about government in general and its specific forms when, in his pamphlet *Thoughts Concerning the Origin of Power*, he argued that, whereas in England the fountain of power was the king, in the United Provinces it was the states, and that both derived their authority from God.[35] Certainly Wesley's sentiments of devotion to the monarchy were more fervent than most men's, but when that sentiment is stripped away, the hard dogma beneath is more conventional.

Wesley deeply deplored the secularisation of life in many fields, including that of politics, and this led him to exaggerate the difference between his views and those of most of his contemporaries. He suggested that most people were advocates of popular sovereignty and universal consent and that his view that all authority came down from God was then a rare one.[36] In fact, the majority of Anglicans, at least, and some others shared his view. Wesley's arguments against equality, universal consent and popular sovereignty were eclectic. He attacked equality on logical grounds, insisting that such a theory should include women and minors over eighteen – which he assumed everyone would agree was self-evidently ridiculous. He attacked the theory of a social compact on historical grounds, demonstrating that the British people patently had not chosen most of their kings. He attacked the concept of consent on religious grounds. A ruler cannot take the life of a subject without consent, but that consent must come not from the subject, but from God. No man had the right to take his own life, so he could not alienate to his governor a right he never possessed. Only God can

---

[32] Wesley, *The Works* (Oxford, 1975), vol. 11, p. 62; *Works*, vol. 11, p. 197.
[33] Thus Bernard Semmel sub-titles a section on Wesley's politics in *Methodist Revolution*. The section is, however, more judicious than its title.
[34] *Works*, vol. 7, p. 101.
[35] *Ibid.*, vol. 11, pp. 47–8.
[36] *Ibid.*, p. 48.

give magistrates rights over life and death, and such authority is essential to governments if anarchy is to be prevented.[37] But such views were neither so extreme nor so rare as Wesley chose to make out.[38]

It is, perhaps, hardly surprising that Wesley's supporters believed his views were more extreme than was the case. William Mason, a Methodist lay-preacher, argued that rebellion against the established powers was always sinful and led to damnation. Like William Stevens, he insisted that, if this was passive obedience and non-resistance, so be it, God's will must be done. Even someone highly educated and much closer to Wesley could be confused on the issue, as was John Fletcher. When defending Wesley against his critics in 1775 and 1776, Fletcher made three attempts to define Methodist views on the nature of authority before getting them right. Initially, he adopted a position which was almost undiluted Filmer: power came from God to Adam and so to his royal descendants; national governments grew out of family government. A few months later, he qualified this view in two ways. He explained that the heirs of Adam might not only be monarchs but could include other forms of government – king and parliament, doge and senate, emperor and diet. That was in line with Wesley's view, but Fletcher went beyond this to argue that God-given authority was operative and binding only if the government 'retains that power by the consent of the majority'. Only in his third attempt did Fletcher describe Wesley's position accurately. Government is the creation of God, not of the people. Its authority is of divine not human origin. Its right to govern is independent of the people. However, the consent of the majority is necessary to support civil government, as is the consent of soldiers in an army. It is a tacit, not a formal act of consent, and it is not the source of authority, merely the requisite without which that authority cannot be exercised.[39] Wesley, like Horne, had little taste for rebellion. While his theory may have allowed the possibility, it was not a possibility he chose to explore. What was really significant about Wesley's political theory was not its royalist sentiments, nor its fairly conventional substantive dogma, but its emphasis. At a time when many Anglicans were stressing the autonomy of man in determining the form of government, Wesley placed his emphasis on the divine source of authority.

---

[37] *Ibid.*, pp. 48–53.

[38] The suicide argument, repeated *inter alia* by William Jones, *Fear of God*, p. 27, and W. Paley, 'Principles of Moral and Political Philosophy' (1785), *Works*, vol. 4, p. 264, was drawn from Sir Robert Filmer, *The Anarchy of a Limited or Mixed Monarchy* (1648), p. 8. Locke's views on the argument are discussed by John Dunn, *The Political Thought of John Locke* (Cambridge, 1969), pp. 88–93, and in G. Windstrup, 'Locke on Suicide', *PT*, 8 (1980), 169–82.

[39] J. Fletcher, 'A Vindication of Mr Wesley's "Calm Address . . ." . . .' (1776), *Works*, vol. 5, pp. 1–68 (pp. 40–3); *American Patriotism Farther confronted with Reason, Scripture and the Constitution* (Shrewsbury, 1776), pp. 37–8, 58–9.

The Catholics

Members of the Catholic church in England also accepted the basic formula but their interpretation and emphasis were both different from the Anglican and Methodist ones and varied from Catholic to Catholic. Traditionally, Catholics had stressed the right of the people to determine the specific form the government took and had accepted the theory of popular sovereignty since the sixteenth century. In 1759 Richard Hurd, later Anglican Bishop of Lichfield and then of Worcester, suggested that this was because, when Pius V excommunicated Elizabeth, the Jesuits argued that the origin of the royal power lay in the people because they believed that, if it could be shown to come from a human source rather than from divine right, the deposition of monarch by pope would seem less invidious.[40]

While most eighteenth-century Catholics did indeed follow St Robert Bellarmine in believing that monarchy as a form of government was an ordinance of man, they still accepted that government *qua* government was divinely instituted. The support some Catholics had, naturally, given James II both before and after 1688 made them appear, to many, advocates of despotic government. But most were anxious to establish their political loyalty and lay the ghosts both of Jacobitism and of the sixteenth century. Repeatedly in their writings Catholics assured their fellow countrymen that 'The odious doctrine of deposing power, transferring crowns and dispensing with oaths has long been exploded in every Catholic university.'[41] This led some to play down the belief in popular sovereignty, but many Catholic priests, trained in the continental seminaries, brought back with them ideas from the French Enlightenment tradition of popular rights, and so reinforced the declining thesis.

Anglicans saw the Catholic dual allegiance to pope and king as a problem, but in fact it made Catholics see and explain the spiritual nature of governmental authority much more clearly than Anglicans could.[42] It was the establishment of the Church of England and its relationship with the state which really confused that issue. Since the Reformation, the supreme governor of the established church had been the head of state and so political and spiritual power were combined. Any attempt to disestablish that church and make a clear separation between spiritual and political

[40] R. Hurd, 'Moral and Political Dialogues' (1759), *Works*, vol. 4, p. 61. He went on to argue that the Anglican reaction to this (and to the puritan theories of the seventeenth century) led to an exaggeration of the sanctity of the king and an undervaluing of popular rights. Priestley made largely the same point in 'Essay on the First Principles of Government', *Works*, vol. 22, pp. 1–144 (p. 20). The comments on this idea in J. N. Figgis, *The Theory of the Divine Right of Kings* (Cambridge, 1896), pp. 173–85, 204, remain of value.
[41] [Alexander Geddes], *Letter to a Member of Parliament* (London, 1787), p. 29.
[42] J. Berington, *The State and Behaviour of English Catholics* (London, 1780), pp. 152–3; *An Address to the Protestant Dissenters* (Birmingham, 1787), pp. 25–6, 52; *The Rights of Dissenters* (Birmingham, 1789), pp. 53–4.

power might be seen, and would certainly be represented, as a secularisation process which weakened the sacerdotal underpinnings of the civil magistrate. Any attack upon the privileges of the established church could be seen as an attempt to secularise the state. But, as Catholics saw clearly, that was to misunderstand the nature of the theological and spiritual support for government. The Catholic subject was prepared to submit wholly to the civil, the political authority of the magistrate. What he would not concede was that the magistrate had any spiritual authority over him, for that was entrusted to Christ's vicar on earth, the pope. But, while he denied that the king had any spiritual authority over him, he could well concede that the king's political authority had a spiritual origin – that it was ordained of God, as St Paul had argued was the political authority of the pagan Roman emperors.[43] The crucial distinction was between the source and the nature of royal authority. Therefore the separation of political and spiritual authority, the denying of spiritual authority to the king, the disestablishment of the national church, need not in any way be secularising the state or weakening the spiritual source of political authority and the consequent obligation of the Christian to obey.

The most articulate and prolific Catholic controversialist of the period was Joseph Berington. He grew up in Shropshire within the English Catholic community which centred on the country houses of those gentry who had maintained the faith during the years of persecution. The complex conflict of fidelity and patriotism of those years was part of his inheritance. He felt his Englishness strongly, but inevitably his education and training for the priesthood took place abroad, at St Omer. He returned having imbibed the vibrant ideas of the French Enlightenment, and soon made contact with radical Dissenters in Britain. While priest at Oscott in the 1780s he regularly met not only Boulton and Watt but also Joseph Priestley, whom he admired and respected as 'an enemy to every species of restraint on conscience'.[44]

But in some ways Berington was atypical of the community he served.[45]

---

[43] This was clear in the teaching of the doctrine of subordination by the Catholic hierarchy in Ireland. See S. J. Connolly, *Priests and People in Pre-Famine Ireland, 1780–1845* (Dublin, 1982), pp. 220–9. But Connolly suggests that some parish priests may have dissented from this official church policy. See below, pp. 121–2.

[44] Berington, *State and Behaviour*, Preface, p. xi. Samuel Parr (Anglican clergyman) remembered dining with Priestley (Unitarian minister), Berington (Catholic priest), Robinson (Baptist minister), Galton (Quaker), and Pound (minister of the New Jerusalem Church); see Anne Holt, *A Life of Joseph Priestley* (London, 1931), p. 143.

[45] Most Catholics who published their ideas on political theory in the thirty years before the French Revolution adopted the popular sovereignty stance. However, the dispute which emerged in the early 1790s showed that such ideas were more characteristic of the Cisalpine party than of the church as a whole. Some gentry, like Sir John Throckmorton, supported Berington, but many did not. Some clergy, such as Thomas Potts, later president of Oscott, took a populist line, but others – most notably John Milner – did not. See Eamon Duffy,

He was a leading member of the Cisalpines, who asserted national independence in the church and urged acceptance of oaths limiting the powers of the pope which would restore to English Catholics their civil rights and enable them to play once again an active part in political life. Most of the vicars general, however, took an ultramontane stance, feeling that too many concessions and compromises were being made and that important spiritual principles were being sacrificed in the desire for political justice.

Berington was also atypical in that he spoke the philosophical and political language of the Enlightenment, talked of the rights of mankind and described himself as a thoroughgoing Whig. His political views were close to those of Richard Watson. He insisted that the limitation of absolute monarchy was part of the Catholic tradition. Allegiance was based on the 'sacred compact' the king made with his people. If he broke it, as Berington alleged James II had done, he was no longer entitled to the people's allegiance. If kings violated the laws they could properly be replaced. But behind this secular autonomy of the people to adopt the form of government which best protected their interests, Berington recognised there lay a divine obligation to submit to a properly established order.[46]

A number of leading Catholic laymen, such as Lord Petre, Lord Stourton and Sir Robert Throckmorton, shared Berington's opinions. Others, like the Welds of Lulworth, followed the more conservative views of the hierarchy. Perhaps most characteristic were men like Christopher Stoner, who remained faithful to the hierarchy, but showed tolerance to the Cisalpines. Most English Catholics before 1789 were less radical than Berington, both politically and theologically. They were Burkean Whigs who combined an acceptance of Bellarmine's theory with a natural conservatism – but in this period their views found no major theoretical exponent either clerical or lay.[47]

The Old Dissenters

Protestant Dissenters too accepted the basic formula, but again their interpretation of it allowed a wide range of political positions to be adopted within their ranks. Many of their leaders occupied a fairly radical position close to Watson's place in the political spectrum, and sometimes more extreme than his. Others, like John Clayton the Congregationalist minister,

'Joseph Berington and the English Cisalpine Movement, 1772–1803' (unpublished Ph.D. dissertation, University of Cambridge, 1973), pp. 194–5, 231, 300–1.

[46] Berington, *State and Behaviour*, pp. 16–17, 20, 26–7, 42–3, 73, 136, 139; *Address to the Protestant Dissenters*, pp. 49–50; *Rights of Dissenters*, pp. 7, 51–2.

[47] It was only later that John Milner emerged as the scourge of the Cisalpines. See Eamon Duffy, 'Ecclesiastical Democracy Detected', *Recusant History*, 10 (1970), 193–209 and 309–31, and 'Doctor Douglas and Mister Berington – an eighteenth-century retraction', *Downside Review*, 88 (1970), 246–69 (pp. 246–7, 249–50).

took a firmly conservative position. Even men like Andrew Kippis, pastor of the Westminster Presbyterian Meeting from 1753 to 1796, while arguing staunchly for religious rights and supporting some reform of parliament, adopted a conservative stance on a number of issues.[48] Moreover, it is far from clear how many of the Old Dissenters followed the lead of their more radical ministers.[49] In examining briefly the views of two eminent Baptist ministers, Caleb Evans and Robert Robinson, we must bear these qualifications in mind and not blithely assume that they spoke for the whole sect. Evans was a tutor in theology at Bristol Baptist Academy until 1781, when he succeeded his father as principal of the Academy and minister of Broadmead Baptist Church in Bristol. He was regarded as one of the leaders of the radical Dissenting community. He was a staunch Calvinist and an opponent of the Methodists. Robinson was the pastor of a congregation of Baptists in Cambridge from 1761 until his death in 1790. He too had Calvinist leanings, but towards the end of his life moved towards a unitarian position.[50]

In 1775 Evans told Wesley in an anonymous *Letter* that, until he was presented with hard evidence for the *de jure divino* position, he would 'consider the origin of all power, under God, to be the people'. The phrase 'under God' brought him within the basic formula, but the full weight of his interpretation was on the side of popular rights. In Gunpowder Day sermons both in 1775 and 1788 his argument was the same. Government was an ordinance of God, in St Paul's eyes, only when it acted for the people's good. When it ceased to do so it could be lawfully resisted. Constitutions were determined by men and the people had an undoubted right to take power back into their own hands if their safety and happiness were violated by the government. Resistance to injustice was a positive duty.[51]

Robinson was in broad agreement. He adopted the basic formula when he

[48] A. Kippis, *Observations on the Coronation* (London, 1761); *A Vindication of the Protestant Dissenting Ministers* (London, 1772); *The Excellency of the Gospel* (London, 1777); *A Sermon Preached at the Old Jewry* (London, 1788).

[49] Traditional authorities like C. Robbins, *The Eighteenth-Century Commonwealthman* (Cambridge, Massachusetts, 1959), need now to be read in the light of Bradley's work, see above, p. 22, note 29. Much more work on a local level needs to be done.

[50] Norman Moon, 'Caleb Evans, Founder of the Bristol Education Society', *Baptist Quarterly*, 24 (1971), 175–90. Also on Evans, G. W. Hughes, *Robert Hall* (London, 1943), pp. 28–38. Hughes, *With Freedom Fired: The Story of Robert Robinson, Cambridge Nonconformist* (London, 1955), pp. 41–53, 88–107. For a somewhat more rigorous analysis of Baptist political ideas see O. C. Robison 'Particular Baptists in England, 1760–1820' (unpublished D.Phil. dissertation, University of Oxford, 1967), pp. 401–39. On Robinson's influence on the Cambridge Dissenters see J. E. Bradley, 'Religion and Reform'.

[51] C. Evans, *A Letter to the Rev. Mr John Wesley* (Bristol, 1775), p. 10; *British Constitutional Liberty* (Bristol, [1775]), pp. 20–1; *British Freedom Realized: A Sermon* (Bristol, [1788]), pp. 24–5. The political context of these works is discussed below, pp. 44–9.

argued that St Paul meant that government not governors was divinely appointed. This text, he claimed, had been much exploited in the past by those who misrepresented St Paul as 'a conspirator against the rights of mankind'. For Robinson the form of government was a strictly secular business:

> The truth is, the best mode of governing is a matter of reasoning and not of faith, and the divine spirit has not wasted the noble gift of inspiration upon unnecessary subjects. Mankind are here left to the use of their reason, and reason is sufficient on this article without revelation, as we have seen in many pagan governments.

Government had divine authority only when it protected men's natural rights effectively. If it contravened those rights, that authority was forfeit and it could properly be resisted.[52]

The Unitarians

So far, Christians of all denominations were able to agree on the basic formula so clearly expressed by Bishop Lowth in 1767. Although their qualifications may have made it meaningless to speak of any true meeting of minds, and despite the fact that agreement may have been spurious, at least superficially Christians occupied common ground. It is only when one gets to the Unitarian borderland between Christianity and deism that the consensus was strained to breaking point.

The two best known of these heterodox Dissenters were the Arian, Richard Price, and the Socinian, Joseph Priestley.[53] Although their philosophical and theological positions were significantly different, their substantive political views were similar.[54] Responding to Burke's exposition of the basic formula, Richard Price took a significantly more secular stand, denying a positive, active role for God in instituting government. Government was a divine institution, he argued, only in the way any other expedient of human prudence against injury could be considered divine. Certainly anything which came immediately from man's foresight and industry could ultimately be ascribed to God, as all things could, but it was

---

[52] Robinson, 'Christian Submission to Civil Government', Martyrdom Day sermon 1780, *Works*, vol. 3, pp. 290–307 (pp. 291, 293–4). See also 'Arcana' (1774) and 'A Political Catechism' (1782), *Works*, vol. 2, pp. 1–139 (pp. 59–70) and pp. 257–362 (pp. 267, 283).

[53] On Price see D. O. Thomas, *The Honest Mind: The Thought and Work of Richard Price* (Oxford, 1977); there is no comparable, definitive intellectual biography of Priestley. The works by Thorpe, Holt, Lindsay, Gibbs and Schofield, cited in the bibliography below, are all partial or inadequate. On Price, Priestley and their context see the journal *Enlightenment and Dissent*. The millenarian dimension of their thought is discussed by Jack Fruchtman, 'The Apocalyptic Politics of Richard Price and Joseph Priestley . . .', *Transactions of the American Philosophical Society*, 73, part 4 (1983), pp. 1–125.

[54] M. R. Watts, *The Dissenters: From the Reformation to the French Revolution* (Oxford, 1978), pp. 474–6.

only in this extremely tenuous form that Price would regard government as being of divine ordinance.[55]

Priestley, though never quite so explicit, clearly occupied a similar position. Although, like Price, he supported government and expected Dissenters to obey and live as good and honest citizens, he never argued that men were under a divinely imposed obligation to obey government, even in general. Although he frequently came to a point at which such an assertion could indeed have been consistent with his argument, he never made it. Rather, his secular view of politics led him to suggest that God willed the greatest happiness of the greatest number, and so implied divine approval of a utilitarian approach.[56]

Price's view of politics was less secular than Priestley's, and he did not share the latter's utilitarian bias. But his belief in God-given individual rights led him to an advocacy of minimal government which was close to Priestley's. For both, government was an evil, albeit a necessary one, which should be restricted as much as possible, not a divine ordinance for which God should be praised.[57]

On these questions of the source of authority, political obligation and the right of rebellion, all trinitarian Christians occupied ground within the ideological arena already established by the Anglican church. Most Anglicans took a position between the episcopal centre and the high-church patriarchalists, and were there joined by most Methodists. Many of the Protestant Dissenters and some Catholics tended towards the popular sovereignty views of the Bishop of Llandaff and a few stood alongside the Unitarians in a position more extreme than Watson's. Such a picture is still, in some ways, crude and oversimplified. The views held were far too complex to be accommodated on a single spectrum and the ideas of the leaders may have been uncharacteristic of the bulk of the lay members of the denomination. However, it does reflect, roughly, the position of the

---

[55] R. Price, *The General Introduction and Supplement to the Two Tracts on Civil Liberty* (London, 1778), pp. iv–v; *A Sermon Delivered . . . at Hackney*, 10 February 1778 (London, 1779), postscript p. 2, where, replying to Bishop Lowth's Ash Wednesday sermon, Price insisted civil government was not 'the appointment of heaven' but 'the contrivance of man'.

[56] J. Priestley, *An Essay on the First Principles of Government* (London, 1771), pp. 55–7, 85; 'A View of the Principles of the Protestant Dissenters' (1769), *Works*, vol. 22, pp. 335–79 (pp. 351–2); 'An History of the Corruptions of Christianity', Appendix to Parts 10 and 11, *Works*, vol. 5, pp. 426–36; 'A Letter to the Right Hon. William Pitt', *Works*, vol. 19, pp. 111–34 (pp. 115, 119, 131); 'The Present State of Liberty in Great Britain and her Colonies' (1769), *Works*, vol. 22, pp. 380–98 (pp. 388–9).

[57] R. Price, *Britain's Happiness* . . . (London, 1759), p. 9; *Observations on the Importance of the American Revolution* (London, 1784), p. 14; *Additional Observations on the Nature and Value of Civil Liberty*, second edition (London, 1778), pp. 25–6, 31. J. Priestley, *Lectures on History and General Policy* (1761) (London, 1840), pp. 221–2, 226, 305, 321–2, 403, 408; *First Principles*, pp. 57–8, 119, 174–5.

leading churchmen of the age – the Anglican bishops, Horne, Watson, Wesley, Fletcher, Berington, Evans, Robinson, Price and Priestley. Before proceeding to see how these positions were changed by Paley's utilitarianism and by the political and social crises of the 1780s, it is necessary to analyse these basic attitudes more fully, by placing them in their religious, political and philosophical contexts.

2

The religious context

To what extent were the political ideas outlined in the previous chapter influenced by the religious beliefs of the denomination, or the party within the Anglican church, to which they belonged? Denominations may be distinctive in a number of ways, including a specific set of theological dogmas, an attitude to scripture and its interpretation, a form of ecclesiastical organisation, social composition and the legal and political rights its members enjoyed. To place the arguments in their full religious context the influence of each of these must be considered.

Theology

Few based their political theory directly on their theology and even fewer on a brand of theology peculiar to a denomination.[1] The Methodist Arminians claimed to find the political implications of Calvinism unacceptable as well as its soteriology. John Fletcher insisted that what he regarded as the antinomian nature of Calvinism led directly to political subversion:

the transition from ecclesiastical to civil Antinomianism, is easy and obvious, for, as he that reverences the law of God, will naturally reverence the just commands of the King; so he that thinks himself free from the laws of the Lord, will hardly think himself bound by the statutes of his sovereign.[2]

But despite the Methodist alarm, most Calvinists did not deserve the antinomian tag.[3] The best-known Calvinist in the Church of England was Augustus Toplady, the incumbent of Broadhembury in Devonshire, and on the rare occasions when he expressed political views they were of the most

---

[1] Guy Swanson, *Religion and Regime; A Sociological Account of the Reformation* (Ann Arbor, 1967), pp. 229–32, discusses the connexion between theology and political and social order. Robbins, *Commonwealthman*, pp. 231–2 argues it was unimportant, but see also Nockles, 'Continuity and Change', pp. 7, 30.

[2] J. Fletcher, 'Vindication', *Works*, vol. 5, p. 43. For the context of the debate see below, pp. 46–7, and Semmel, *Methodist Revolution*, pp. 56–71.

[3] P. Toon, *The Emergence of Hyper-Calvinism in English Nonconformity 1689–1765* (London, 1967), pp. 49–69, 143–52, and Robison 'Particular Baptists'.

conventional and moderate kind. He praised the balanced constitution and stressed that both excessive liberty and despotism were to be deplored. He rejected republicanism, strongly supported the constitutional monarchy and was closely in line with episcopal political thinking. His political views reflected his membership of the established church, not his Calvinist theology.[4]

Wesley, however, shared Fletcher's opinion that there was a connexion between Calvinism and republicanism, and he stressed that the divine authority in political matters passed directly from God to the supreme power in the land and could be delegated to others only through that power. In the sixteenth century the Calvinists had used the argument that inferior magistrates also had divine authority directly from God, to justify their rebellion against the supreme power. Wesley insisted that this was theologically unsound as well as politically subversive and dangerous.[5] But such connexions between theology and political theory were rare. Generally there was little coincidence between the political spectrum of views and the theological one.

Some writers argued that there was no link at all between theology and political theory. In 1774 William Markham, Bishop of Chester, asserted that Christianity gave no directions which were 'merely political'.[6] Robert Robinson argued that the separation between religion and politics was so great that there was no need for a ruler even to be Christian so long as he understood government and kept his public word.[7]

Others argued that, while there might be some connexion, it was not with those aspects of theology distinctive of a denomination. Richard Watson distinguished between practical and speculative religious opinions. He cited five examples of practical religious views which would make a man unfit to serve as a public minister of religion: atheism, which rendered oaths useless; Catholicism, which he believed could depose monarchs and absolve subjects from their allegiance; deism, which undermined the bulwark of revealed religion against vice; passive obedience, which led to tyranny and subverted men's rights; and immorality. But of speculative opinions he demanded only two: that Jesus was Messiah and that He rose from the dead. All the other theological niceties seemed to him to be politically unimportant and no reason to exclude men who would teach morality and support

---

[4] A. Toplady, 'Moral and Political Moderation Recommended', Fast sermon 1776, *Works*, vol. 3, pp. 297–306. Compare 'The Church of England Vindicated from the Charge of Arminianism', *Works*, vol. 5, pp. 82–5.

[5] Wesley, 'Thoughts Concerning the Origin of Power', *Works*, vol. 11, pp. 47–8. For inferior magistrates see Quentin Skinner, *Foundations of Modern Political Thought* (Cambridge, 1978), vol. 2, pp. 204–6. See also below, p. 47.

[6] Markham, *Sermon . . .*, p. 12.

[7] Robinson, 'Political Catechism', *Works*, vol. 3, p. 26.

civil society.[8] For the latitudinarian Watson, the links between theology and politics were loose, broad and general, not specific, detailed, or precise.

Joseph Berington took up the distinction. He agreed it would be proper to exclude from civil rights any group with practical opinions subversive of public order, though he denied that Catholics held the views Watson attributed to them. The theological difference between Catholics and Protestants, he argued, was not in their practical but in their speculative opinions, which were phantoms 'too unsubstantial for legislative discussion'. Such spiritual views had no connexion with the subject's civil conduct. How, he asked, could one's allegiance be affected by whether one believed there were seven or only two sacraments? Why should the magistrate forbid you to wear a sword because you chose to pray for the repose of the soul of your dead father? There was nothing special about Anglicanism which made it alone suitable to support the state; its doctrine was purely spiritual, and its morality common to all enlightened men. The speculative opinions on which the denominations were divided were, Berington insisted, politically irrelevant; all Christians were agreed on the practical ones which provided the divine source of political authority and obligation.[9]

Edmund Burke shared this unconcern with theological differences. He was concerned with the body and substance of religion, not its sectarian forms and dogmas. He could see no significant difference between the *Directory* of 1645 and the *Book of Common Prayer* of 1662, or between the Roman Articles and the thirty-nine Anglican ones. Burke was a lifelong supporter of toleration for the traditional Christian sects. In a speech on the 1773 Toleration Bill he compared 'those great dangerous animals' of atheists and deists to the Christian Dissenters' 'poor fluttering silken wings of a tender conscience'. Atheists posed a political threat to society, but theological differences between the Christian sects were of no significance at all.[10]

Scripture

The theory of a divine source of political authority and obligation rested upon the texts of SS Peter and Paul.[11] To what extent did the interpretation

---

[8] Watson, *Letter to the . . . Commons*, pp. 8–15.

[9] Berington, *Rights of Dissenters*, pp. 11–17, 20–1; *State and Behaviour*, p. 141.

[10] Burke, 'Speech on Clerical Subscription', 6 February 1772, *Writings*, vol. 2, p. 364; Letter to Richard Burke, 23 March 1792, *Corr.*, vol. 7, p. 118; Letter to Unknown, 26 January 1791, *Corr.*, vol. 6, pp. 216–17. Burke held such views from at least the age of 15; see Letter to Richard Shackleton, 15 October 1744, *Corr.*, vol. 1, p. 33. 'Speech on Toleration Bill', 17 March 1773, *Writings*, vol. 2, pp. 381–90 (p. 386).

[11] See above, pp. 12–13.

of scripture in general and of these texts in particular vary along denominational lines and what effect did this have on denominational political views?
The well-established differences between the attitudes of Catholics, Anglicans and more extreme Protestants towards scripture seem largely
unrelated to the way the critical texts were interpreted. While it is true that
Berington did not discuss them in detail and Robinson stressed that each
man could interpret them for himself,[12] those who did interpret them did so
in a way which reflected their political views rather than any denominational attitude to scriptural exegesis. Many complained that others, though
never themselves, perverted the texts' real meaning to suit their own
political ends. Such complaints were heard from such diverse characters as
Bishop Markham, Soame Jenyns, a lay Anglican convert from deism,
Joseph Priestley and Robert Robinson. Thomas Paine, in 1775, before he
abandoned Christianity fully, lamented how some men used scripture to
justify even slavery.[13]

. Most men of all religious and political persuasions took a straight-
forwardly literal approach to the texts, stressing whatever words or phrases
best suited their purposes. The high-church patriarchalists concentrated on
St Paul's central theme and ignored his qualifications; the contractarian
Whigs emphasised the phrase 'for good'. Bishop Newton, seeking a central,
balanced view, emphasised both 'for good' and 'for conscience sake'.[14]
Some, however, adopted a more modern and critical approach. Dean
Tucker refused to bandy around scriptural quotations at all. He criticised
John Cartwright, the parliamentary reformer, for setting out what he
regarded as Lockean doctrine in *The People's Barrier* (1780) and claiming it
was scriptural. But instead of re-interpreting these texts himself, Tucker
concentrated on the logical inconsistencies in Cartwright's case, and so dealt
with the scriptural challenge by a secular argument.[15]

A few men made a real attempt to set SS Peter and Paul's injunctions in
the first-century context which evoked them. John Green, Richard Watson
and Richard Hurd all stressed the historical circumstances in which the
epistles were written, and those attitudes of their recipients which the

[12] Robinson, 'Hauxton Discourse', in *Sixteen Discourses . . . to Christian Assemblies in Villages near Cambridge* (London, 1786), pp. 41–60 (p. 52).
[13] Paine, 'African Slavery in America' (1775), *Writings*, vol. 1, pp. 4–9 (pp. 5–6). Perhaps Paine had in mind the Rev. Thomas Thompson; see below, pp. 43–4. For the debate on Paine's religion see R. R. Fennessy, *Burke, Paine and the Rights of Man* (The Hague, 1963), pp. 12–14; S. Newman, 'A Note on *Common Sense* and Christian Eschatology', *PT*, 6 (1978), 101–8; W. Christian, 'The Moral Economics of Tom Paine', *JHI*, 34 (1973), 367–80 (pp. 368–9).
[14] For the high-church patriarchalists, see [W. Stevens], *Strictures on a Sermon . . .*, second edition (Cambridge, 1777), pp. 28–9; for the contractarian Whigs, J. Greene, *A Sermon . . .* (Norwich, 1764), p. 9; for the Court Whigs, J. Gordon, *Causes and Consequences*, pp. 5–6, and Newton, *Of Moderation*, p. 15.
[15] Tucker, *Treatise*, pp. 357–62

apostles sought to amend.[16] In each case these rudimentary exercises in hermeneutics limited the extent of the obligation under which Christians in eighteenth-century England found themselves. While it is true the interpretation suited their political purposes, there was a serious academic argument behind it. All three men were in the old Court Whig tradition, two were already bishops and the third, Richard Watson, was a noted biblical scholar who became regius professor of Divinity at Cambridge two years later and bishop in 1782. Others, like Soame Jenyns and Robert Robinson, also set the texts in an historical context, but in a much less rigorous and incisive way.[17] Approaches to scripture did vary, but that variation was not due to denominational differences.

Ecclesiology

Yet there was a widespread belief that denominations did represent political positions. In 1775, Brownlow North, Bishop of Worcester, offered no supportive evidence but expressed a commonly held view when he said that 'if the doctrines of popery incline us to the obedience of slaves, the doctrines of the independents are as ill-calculated to render us good subjects'.[18] In part the argument was an historical one which associated the Dissenters with the Independents of the middle of the seventeenth century and the Catholics with the alleged despotic policies of James II. But it was also an argument about forms of ecclesiastical government. Extrapolating secular political theory from ecclesiology, it was assumed that Catholics, who accepted the spiritual supremacy of the pope and the authority of the church, looked to absolute monarchy, whereas extreme Protestants, who stressed the individual interpretation of the Bible and personal contact with God, tended to favour an extreme democracy and anarchy.[19]

In his youth, even Joseph Priestley held that view. In the lectures he wrote at the age of twenty-eight, he suggested a religion without a visible head suited the spirit of liberty and independence prevailing in northern Europe, whereas 'superstition' was more suited to monarchy, though even then he admitted that some of the evidence contradicted that view. Later, however, he became anxious to deny, not only that there was any causal connexion between a denomination and a political theory, but also that there was any contingent one either. In 1769 he disputed Blackstone's

---

16 J. Green, *Sermon*, pp. 2–6; Watson, Assize Sermon (1769), *SPO*, p. 14; Accession Sermon (1776), *SPO*, pp. 87–93; R. Hurd, 'A Sermon . . .' (1786), *Works*, vol. 8, pp. 38–40.

17 Robinson, 'Christian Submission' (1780), *Works*, vol. 3, pp. 291–307; Jenyns, 'Short and Cursory Observations on . . . the New Testament', *Works*, vol. 4, pp. 245–7.

18 North, *Sermon* (1775), p. 27.

19 Contrariwise, for the influence of secular political theory on ecclesiastical government, especially in Methodism, see E. R. Taylor, *Methodism and Politics*, pp. 38, 62–4, 72–87.

allegation that the 'spirit and doctrines of the sectaries' did not make good subjects. Partly this was because his definition of a good subject differed from that of Blackstone, but in the same year he also specifically denied either that Protestant dissent inclined one to any particular form of government, or that any Dissenter was an enemy to government in general or to monarchy in particular. Dissenters were, he argued, about as much divided as the rest of the nation in their political views, which owed nothing to their religious principles.[20] By 1780, he also denied that Catholicism led men to favour arbitrary government, a point his new acquaintance Joseph Berington frequently made, and which the Anglican parson and parliamentary reformer Christopher Wyvill also accepted.[21]

The fact that many patriarchalists, from Horne to Watson, regarded themselves as high churchmen and some at the popular sovereignty end of the Whig spectrum, like Watson and Wyvill, were low churchmen, should not lead us to think there was any direct correlation between ecclesiology and political theory. The Court Whig bishops, who espoused the Warburtonian concept of the alliance of church and state, should not in this sense be called high churchmen. Moreover, the Anglican Evangelicals who took a 'low' view of the church and stressed men's individual relationship with God, as opposed to the Hackney Phalanx's emphasis on an authoritative and mediating church, were on the conservative end of the political spectrum along with the high churchmen. If one is to identify a correlation between Anglicans' political theories and their religious beliefs, it must be with their views of the nature of man, not with their concept of the church.[22]

Civil and religious rights

Soame Jenyns was more sophisticated than many observers of the denominational scene. He argued that hostility between groups usually arose because of their different material interests, but suggested that religious and political opinions were so inextricably combined that material interest groups were often defined by the religion they shared. When this

[20] Priestley, *Lectures on History*, p. 361; 'Remarks on ... Dr Blackstone' (1769), *Works*, vol. 22, pp. 320–1; 'Principles of Dissenters', *Works*, vol. 22, pp. 354–7.

[21] Priestley, 'A Free Address to Those Who Have Petitioned for the Repeal of the Late Act of Parliament in Favour of the Roman Catholics', *Works*, vol. 22, pp. 499–516 (p. 505); Berington, *Address to Protestant Dissenters*, pp. 21–2; 'Wyvill's Answer to ... the Committee of Correspondence', in *A Collection of Letters .... Addressed to the Volunteers of Ireland on a Parliamentary Reform* (London, 1783), pp. 21–45 (pp. 33–4); M. Fitzpatrick, 'Joseph Priestley and the Cause of Universal Toleration', *PPN*, 1 (1977), 3–30.

[22] A. Russell, *The Clerical Profession* (London, 1980), p. 39. Compare V. Kiernan, 'Evangelicalism and the French Revolution', *PP*, 1 (1952), 44–66 (p. 46). See also Charles Daubeny, *A Guide to the Church* (London, 1798), in the preface of which he considers his social and political agreement and ecclesiastical disagreement with Wilberforce.

led them to take collective action, government must be concerned 'for every religious sect holds principles more or less productive of arbitrary power, liberty or anarchy, which must necessarily affect the civil constitutions under which they are professed'.[23]

Certainly, if the bulk of the members of a denomination came from one social and economic class, there would then be a coincidence with a material interest.[24] Priestley suggested as much when he noted that, as Dissenters rarely had large fortunes, their ministers looked to the political interests of the people at large, just as, he alleged, the established clergy favoured the interests of the Court which disposed of sees and benefices.[25] However, the Catholics were more heterogeneous socially and perhaps even the social composition of Protestant denominations was a reflection of the opportunities and the civil rights they enjoyed.[26]

It seems likely that the political theory adopted by members of a denomination was influenced, not so much by theology, scripture, or even ecclesiology, as by the legal and civil rights they enjoyed or were denied. Trinitarian Protestant Dissenters were tolerated but, in theory if not always in practice, excluded from office by the Test and Corporation Acts. Catholics and Unitarians were not even fully tolerated in law. They all had a vested interest in changing the constitution in the church, and so intimately were the two parts of the constitution linked that this meant they had to recognise that a change in the constitution in the state was also a possibility.[27]

The fact that it was civil rights and not theology or ecclesiology which led to the different political views of the denominations is well illustrated by considering the position in Scotland. Here it was the Presbyterian church which was established, and it is noticeable that the political views of its leading figures were in accord not with those of Presbyterians in England, but with those of the Anglican establishment. George Campbell, the principal and professor of Divinity at Marischal College in Aberdeen, preached a fast-day sermon in 1776 which could well have come from any

[23] 'Disquisitions on several subjects' (1782), *Works*, vol. 3, pp. 279, 281.

[24] On the influence of economic groupings on religious sects, see H. R. Niebuhr, *The Social Sources of Denominationalism* (Hamden, Connecticut, 1929), esp. pp. 26–9, 57–72; and B. R. Wilson, 'An Analysis of Sect Development', in *Patterns of Sectarianism: Organisation and Ideology in Social and Religious Movements*, edited by B. R. Wilson (London, 1967), pp. 22–45. See also I. Kramnick, 'Religion and Radicalism: English Political Theory in the Age of Revolution', *PT*, 5 (1977), 505–34.

[25] J. Priestley, 'A Free Address to Protestant Dissenters' (1771). *Works*, vol. 22, p. 263. R. E. Richey, 'The Origins of British Radicalism: The Changing Rationale for Dissent', *ECS*, 7 (1973–4), 179–92, suggests a connexion between radical political ideology and the self-identity of Dissenting groups.

[26] Berington, *State and Behaviour*, pp. 109–27.

[27] For the view that schism in the church was equated with faction in the state, see J. A. W. Gunn, *Factions No More: Attitudes to Party in Government and Opposition in Eighteenth Century England* (London, 1972), pp. 16–20.

episcopal pulpit in England.[28] He discouraged change, allowed rebellion only in very exceptional circumstances, and steered a middle course between passive obedience and anarchy; generally government was appointed by providence and 'obliged us in conscience to obedience and submission'. He rejected any notion of a social compact, condemned both Charles I *and* parliament, denounced the American rebellion and argued that Rousseau's notion of republican government was incompatible with Christianity. His letters to his friend John Douglas, Bishop of Carlisle and later of Salisbury, showed his warmth to the established church in England, although he considered the Scottish establishment superior in its avoidance of a religious test. Like many Anglicans, he supported the abolition of the slave trade, but insisted his opinion was not founded on 'the modish philosophy of *unalienable right*. That is a language I do not understand'.[29]

There is no reason to think that, if Dissenting ministers in England had been part of the established church, they would have argued very differently from their Scottish co-religionists. Indeed, Joseph Berington recognised as much when he confessed that he suspected that, if the Dissenters or the Catholics had been in power in England, they would have acted little differently from the Anglicans. Men were all too prone, he reflected, to see the splinters in others' eyes, and not the beam in their own.[30]

The differences between the political theories of the various Christian denominations and parties were, of course, reflected in their use of religious arguments. Those different arguments were not employed, however, because men were inexorably driven by their faith to use them. Rather, men were led to select them from the wide range of religious arguments and interpretations available to the Christian by the legal and political position in which their denomination was situated.

---

[28] G. Campbell, *The Nature, Extent and Importance of the Duty of Allegiance* (Aberdeen, 1777).
[29] BL, Add. MS Eg 2185, ff. 191–2, 194–5; BL, Add. MS Eg 2186, ff. 5–7, 10–11.
[30] Berington, *Address to the Protestant Dissenters*, p. 26.

3

The political context

Secular politics and the constitution in the state

For most educated Englishmen political theory was not some etiolated branch of philosophy, but a living ideology which informed their attitudes to political institutions and contemporary debates. Most of the statements of Christians, clerical and lay, were made in response to the stimulus of events, and the various arguments outlined in Chapter 1 need to be set in their contemporary political contexts. These events rarely changed those men's fundamental beliefs, but they did determine which aspects of a wide and complex ideology should be emphasised and vigorously argued. Disputes within and between denominations were also focussed and clarified as controversialists on all sides answered each other's arguments.

This chapter does not attempt to provide a comprehensive review of all religious reactions to the political events of the period, but rather to set the body of theory examined in Chapters 1 to 6 in the general context of contemporary political events by examining some of the crucial points of contact between theory and practice. The major ideological debate of these years centred around the revolution in America, but there were also domestic matters which involved basic issues of principle – the role of the king in the constitution, the Wilkes affair, parliamentary reform, and slavery. The main analysis attempted here relates to the politico-religious reactions to the dispute and war with the American colonies, but first, to set this controversy in context, some brief snapshots of a few of the contributions to domestic debates are offered.

The attitudes to the constitution of the new king, George III, and his tutor the Earl of Bute were misunderstood by contemporaries almost as much as they have been by historians. Samuel Squire and John Green preached the 1762 and 1763 Abbey Martyrdom Day sermons respectively. Both were appointees of the new reign, being consecrated in 1761, but they were in the old Court Whig tradition. Both men used their Abbey sermons to warn the king of the limitations of his constitutional position. Squire suggested that the anniversary of Charles I's execution was a reminder that kings were only men and susceptible to fortune. Those who sought to recommend themselves to a king by 'magnifying his prerogative' were merely spreading a net in which he could become entangled. The king's advisers should remember that royal power and popular liberty were so intimately united that any attempt to tear them apart was in serious danger of destroying both.[1]

Green went further and so interpreted St Paul as to stress that rebellion was perfectly permissible against a king who exceeded his powers and threatened the rights and liberties of his people.[2] By the following January, however, the cry of 'Wilkes and Liberty' had been heard in the streets of London, and Bishop Newton contented himself with a perfectly balanced constitutional sermon which urged moderation on all sides and condemned factional politics. By 1767, Bishop Lowth was preaching on the text 'fear thou the Lord and the king and meddle not with them that are given to change'.[3]

Wilkes was to become the new target for condemnation in political sermons, but in 1763 the attack amounted to little more than the traditional cries for stability, order and restraint.[4] It was only after the Middlesex election of 1768 that the important constitutional issues were established and debated. John Wesley made a pugnacious defence of the king and his mother, denouncing the press as one-sided and suggesting that French gold lay behind Wilkes. Most of all he disliked the way that now 'every cobbler, tinker, porter and hackney-coachman' thought he knew about the complex world of politics; Wesley stressed his own very limited knowledge. His defence of the Commons' declaration of Colonel Luttrell as MP for Middlesex reflected the overall lack of serious argument in Wesley's case, which rested more on passion than understanding.[5] George Horne, who shared Wesley's attitude to monarchy, put forward a much more informed theoretical argument in early March 1769, between Wilkes's second expulsion and third election. Horne used the Oxford Assize sermon to argue at length against the concepts of a state of nature, a social compact and

---

[1] *A Sermon* . . . (London, 1762), pp. 9–10, 12–15; on Squire's concern with maintaining the balance of the constitution see Robbins, *Commonwealthman*, pp. 288–92; on Squire generally see R. Browning, *Political and Constitutional Ideas of the Court Whigs* (Baton Rouge, 1982), pp. 117–50.

[2] *A Sermon* . . . (London, 1763), pp. 5–7, 17–18. By contrast, Horne was, characteristically, uncritical of the king – 'The Christian King, a Sermon Preached before the University of Oxford', 30 January 1761, *Works*, vol. 3, pp. 398–421.

[3] T. Newton, *Of Moderation*; R. Lowth, *A Sermon* . . . *1767*.

[4] See, for example, the Archdeacon of Wells, Francis Potter's Charge, *The Nature, Guilt and Consequences of Murmuring* (Oxford, [1763?]), pp. 3–5, 14–15.

[5] 'Free Thoughts on the Present State of Public Affairs' (1768), *Works*, vol. 11, pp. 14–33 (pp. 15–16, 22–4, 26–7, 31–2).

government founded on the consent of the people, and he argued his case on religious grounds.[6]

By then, virtually the whole establishment was behind the king.[7] Bishop Moss's Martyrdom Day sermon in the same year had roundly denounced the press's allegations that there was a deliberate plot to overthrow the constitution, and that liberty was on her death-bed. Now there was no danger from the executive, he declared, only the danger of anarchy from factional politics. These topical observations were juxtaposed with a statement of the basic formula on the religious grounds of political authority and obligation, but no direct links were explicitly made, nor was the orthodox statement at all amended in the light of current events.[8]

Others made a much cruder use of religion in the debate. Wilkes declared he 'firmly and sincerely' believed that the voice of the people was the voice of God, and promised to obey it as a 'divine call', while the pseudonymous 'Steady' accused the Wilkites of introducing God into the argument only out of self-interest and private ambition.[9] Wesley's further contribution in February 1772, which bitterly satirised the union of Wilkes and Liberty, brought no more in the way of genuine spiritual argument.[10] For all the sound and fury, the Wilkes case advanced serious debate in this field very little.

In many ways the waters around the question of parliamentary reform had been muddied by the complex of issues in the Wilkes case. As they cleared, some eminent reformers argued their case on Christian principles. James Burgh's *Political Disquisitions* devoted a great deal of attention to the role of religion in society in establishing morality and the manners necessary to a stable order. Burgh combined these conventional views of the social role of religion with a call for liberty and a reformed franchise.[11] John Cartwright also stressed the Christian basis of the case for equality. All had an equal title in Christ to the Holy Spirit, and he founded his argument for political equality on the Christian assumption of the spiritual equality of all

---

[6] 'Origin of Civil Government', *Works*, vol. 2, pp. 434–49.

[7] The rhetoric was largely, but not entirely, reflected in actions. Of 42 clergymen, ministers or Doctors of Divinity whose votes are recorded, only 4 in any contest voted for Wilkes or Glynn. But, although 38 supported Proctor in March or December 1768, only 9 voted for Luttrell in April 1769. Apart from Buckinghamshire and Devonshire, the clergy gave only limited support to the petitions of 1769. See G. Rudé, *Wilkes and Liberty: A Social Study of 1763 to 1774* (Oxford, 1962), pp. 77, 82, 143–4, 178.

[8] C. Moss, *A Sermon* . . . (London, 1769), pp. 3–4, 6, 8–9, 18–19.

[9] *The Controversial Letters of John Wilkes* (London, 1771), pp. 7–8, 293.

[10] 'Thoughts on Liberty' (1772), *Works*, vol. 11, pp. 34–46 (p. 35).

[11] *Political Disquisitions* . . ., 3 vols. (London, 1774). On morality and order see vol. 3, pp. 30–1, 203–9, 223–5, 322–3; on Reform see vol. 1 *passim*. See also, Carla Hay, 'The Making of a Radical: The Case of James Burgh', *JBS*, 18 (1979), 90–117; *James Burgh: Spokesman for Reform in Hanoverian England* (Washington DC, 1979) which stresses his religious convictions and the moralistic basis of his political thought.

men.[12] Thomas Northcote, a chaplain in the Royal Artillery, as well as a writer of tracts for the Society for Constitutional Information, argued that only parliamentary reformers truly sought a constitution in keeping with the will of God.[13] However, most Christian writers opposed the reform of parliament, though they rarely used religious arguments in doing so. Moreover, most parliamentary reformers, including the Anglican clergyman Christopher Wyvill, relied on secular arguments for the justice of reform.[14]

The campaign against slavery and the slave trade was quite different in nature. It drew support from a much wider range of Christians, including Bishop Porteus, Thomas Bradshaw, William Paley and John Wesley, as well as radicals like Robert Robinson, John Cartwright and Richard Price.[15] Certainly some men used the scriptures to try to justify slavery, but generally these were men with a vested interest, only rarely the clergy or active lay Christians. The Rev. Thomas Thompson argued that slavery was consistent with humanity and revealed religion, citing evidence of Jewish bondservants both from the Old and New Testaments.[16] But his argument was slender and uncharacteristic of most clergy who published their views on the issue, many of whom attacked such arguments as specious and misleading. In doing so, Granville Sharp based his argument on the need to love one's neighbour and show humanity and compassion to a brother-in-Christ, not on any God-given right of liberty the slave possessed.[17] While he argued firmly on scriptural evidence, and declared that slavery was an

---

[12] *Take Your Choice!* (London, 1776), pp. 2–6. See also the footnote added to the second edition (1777), pp. 40–1.

[13] 'The Constitution of England', in Society for Constitutional Information, *Tracts Published and Distributed Gratis* (London, 1783), pp. 123–34 (pp. 125–8, 132–4).

[14] See below, pp. 229–32, and I. R. Christie, *Wilkes, Wyvill and Reform* (London, 1962), chaps. 3 to 6.

[15] LPL, MS 2098, f. 37 (Porteus Notebook, 1777–80); T. Bradshaw, *The Slave Trade Inconsistent with Reason and Religion* (London, 1788), pp. 6, 8–9; W. Paley, 'Moral and Political Philosophy', *Works*, vol. 4, pp. 148–51; J. Wesley, 'Thoughts on Slavery' (1774), *Works*, vol. 11, pp. 59–79; R. Robinson, 'Slavery Inconsistent with the Spirit of Christianity', *Works*, vol. 4, pp. 60–103; J. Cartwright, *American Independence . . .* (London, 1774), p. 7; Price, *Observations on the American Revolution*, pp. 83ff.

[16] *The African Trade for Negro Slaves* (Canterbury, n.d.). He cited Leviticus 25.39 and I Corinthians 7.20.

[17] D. B. Davis, *The Problem of Slavery in the Age of Revolution 1770–1823* (London, 1975), pp. 375–85, suggests that Sharp converted anti-slavery into a defence of traditional authority. Roger Ansty, 'A Re-interpretation of the Abolition of the British Slave Trade, 1806–1807', *EHR*, 87 (1972), 304–32, stresses the empirical nature of the argument and the importance of the latitudinarian tradition of benevolence, but argues that the concept of liberty was also important in the pre-1780 debate. Seymour Drescher, 'Two Variants of Anti-Slavery: Religious Organization and Social Mobilization in Britain and France 1780–1870', in *Anti-Slavery, Religion, and Reform: Essays in Memory of Roger Ansty*, edited by Christine Bolt and Seymour Drescher (Folkestone, 1980), pp. 43–63, suggests theoretical stances had little effect on attitudes. On the wide range of support from various Christian groups see G. M. Ditchfield,

abomination in the sight of God, he based his argument on paternalist and humanitarian grounds, not ones of abstract political and human rights. Certainly Sharp agreed that, while Christianity enjoined submission to authority, it did not authorise the oppression involved in slavery. Indeed, a slave master was being sacrilegious in claiming to own another human being whom Christ Himself had purchased by His sacrifice on the cross.[18] Many Christians who would have denied the abstract principles of natural rights were happy to support the claim against slavery, and Sharp did nothing to alienate them.[19]

The American Revolution

The Wilkes case and the debates on parliamentary reform and slavery were contemporaneous with the development of the dispute with the American colonies. This involved many of the same principles of liberty, consent and popular sovereignty. Horne's 1769 Assize sermon was directed as much against the rebels in Massachusetts as against the men of Middlesex who demonstrated for John Wilkes. But not all Christians were hostile to the American cause. The unitarian John Cartwright put forward a strong religious argument in favour of the American rebels in 1774. He insisted that liberty was the universal gift of God, original, inalienable and inherent in all men. To deny the Americans their God-given rights, Cartwright insisted, weakened the moral base of society, a point also made in James Burgh's *Political Disquisitions* of the same year.[20]

As the conflict developed into war, the stream of pamphlets became a flood. Many men dealt, at least in part, with the religious foundations of government and considered the rights of the struggle in spiritual terms. Richard Price was at the centre of the storm.[21] His *Observations on the Nature of Civil Liberty* was based on a religious concept of the nature of political society – the classic popular sovereignty, universal consent thesis – but the main tenor of his argument was secular. It was only after the barrage of replies

'Repeal, Abolition and Reform: A Study of the Interaction of Reforming Movements in the Parliament of 1790–6', in *Ibid.*, pp. 103–18 (pp. 107–8).

[18] *The Just Limitation of Slavery in the Laws of God* . . . (London, 1776), pp. 17–19, 37, 39, 47–9, 55, 62; *An Essay on Slavery, Proving from Scripture its Inconsistency with Humanity and Religion* (Burlington, West Jersey, 1773; London, 1776), pp. 19–21, 27, 32; *The Law of Liberty* . . . (London, 1776), pp. 8, 10–11, 18, 39; *The Law of Passive Obedience* . . . (London, 1776), pp. 7–14, 40–2, 85–6 (p. 18).

[19] Sharp did assert that Natural Law had a divine origin in *A Declaration of the People's Natural Right to a Share in the Legislature* (London, 1774), pp. xxi–xxiv.

[20] Cartwright, *American Independence*, pp. 7, 39, 45; Burgh, *Political Disquisitions*, vol. 3, pp. 30, 209, 223–4.

[21] Price's role is discussed in Carl Cone, *Torchbearer of Freedom: The Influence of Richard Price on Eighteenth Century Thought* (Lexington, 1952), pp. 69–90, and P. Brown, *The Chathamites* (London, 1967), pp. 148–56.

dragged in all manner of religious arguments that Price considered the spiritual underpinnings of his case in more detail in *Additional Observations* of 1777 and his *General Introduction . . . to the Two Tracts on Civil Liberty* in 1778. 'Civil Liberty' he argued,

must be enjoyed as a right derived from the Author of nature only, or it cannot be the blessing which merits this name. If there is any human power which is considered as *giving* it, on which it depends, and which can invade or recall it at pleasure, it changes its nature, and becomes a species of slavery.

His critics, Price insisted, were wholly wrong in asserting that civil governors derived their powers immediately from God and were accountable to Him only.[22] The issue was clear. The popular sovereignty thesis justified American actions whereas the British government's case rested on the argument that political authority was given by God to established governments and only rights granted by those governments could be enjoyed by subject peoples.[23]

The criticisms on religious grounds which greeted the *Observations* were both wide ranging and predictable. They varied from the crudely abusive to the thoughtful and intelligent. One critic ironically lamented that St Paul was a high churchman and Tory, while Dr Price dissented from the apostle and was a staunch Whig.[24] Others described Price's upbringing as being 'in the very bosom of sedition', Dissenters as secret enemies to government – an *imperium in imperio* – and the sects as leading the country into anarchy and atheism.[25] But Dissenters also challenged Price and suggested his politics were far too secular. One alleged that he excluded God entirely from civil government, another that the Americans perverted religion to justify rebellion. Their principles were less connected with the gospels than with 'Aristotle's Categories'.[26]

The predictable points about liberty and licence, God-given inequalities and the need to submit to providence were all made and the divine nature of

[22] *Additional Observations*, pp. 4, 23.

[23] These contrary religious interpretations split the episcopal church in America. See, David Holmes, 'The Episcopal Church and the American Revolution', *Historical Magazine of the Protestant Episcopal Church*, 47 (1978), 261–91. The ideas involved are more fully analysed in John Berens, ' "A God of Order and Not of Confusion": The American Loyalists and Divine Providence, 1774–1783', *Ibid.*, pp. 211–19 and Glenn T. Miller, 'Fear God and Honour the King: The Failure of Loyalist Civil Theology in the Revolutionary Crisis', *ibid.*, pp. 221–42. On the influence of American religious arguments on English writers see C. C. Bonwick, 'An English Audience for American Revolutionary Pamphlets', *HJ*, 19 (1976), 355–74.

[24] James Stewart, *The Total Refutation and Political Overthrow of Doctor Price . . .* (London, 1776), p. 63. Stewart went on to argue the patriarchalist case, pp. 68–74.

[25] *Remarks on Doctor Price's Observations . . .* (London, 1776), p. 68; *The Duty of the King and Subject on the Principles of Civil Liberty . . .* (London, 1776), p. 5.

[26] John Martin, *Familiar Dialogues between Americus and Britannicus . . .* (London, 1776), pp. 54–55; *Obedience the Best Charter . . .* (London, 1776), pp. 61–2.

political obligation repeatedly stressed.[27] But inevitably the sections of the Gospels Price's critics kept returning to were those relating to Christ's payment of tribute and his injunction to render to Caesar the things that were Caesar's.[28] John Gray expanded Christ's succinct nine-word statement into a two-hundred-and-forty word paraphrase which equated Price with the Pharisees, Judaea and the Roman empire with America and the British empire, rejected passive obedience, endorsed religious toleration, but insisted on the acceptance of imperial authority, and urged men not to waste time on political questions, 'which have a tendency to foster discontent and sedition'.[29]

Most of Price's critics argued on a crude and popular level. Only a few came close to the heart of the matter. Price's political theory rested on his concept of the nature of man and on his belief in human perfectibility.[30] A few critics challenged those assumptions on theological grounds. Price's rejection of the doctrine of original sin was quite contrary to traditional Christian theology, which argued that the nature of man required government and the evil elements in human character needed to be restrained by religious sanctions.[31] Price's most perceptive critics shifted the emphasis from the political theory of obligation and rights to the social theory of the nature of man and society and the need for restraint and sanctions.[32] The major movement of emphasis which took place in the 1790s in the context of the reaction to the French Revolution was thus anticipated in the debate on the American Revolution in the middle of the 1770s.

Most of Price's critics mingled their religious arguments with secular ones. John Fletcher was unusual in presenting a case almost wholly religious in nature. He insisted that the American controversy was closely connected with Christianity, and examined in great detail the scriptural teaching on authority and political obedience, on taxation and the rights of

---

[27] *Ibid.*, p. 6; John Gray, *Doctor Price's Notions of the Nature of Civil Liberty* . . . (London, 1777), p. 16; *A Letter to the Rev. Dr Price* . . . *by a lover of Peace and Good Government* (London, 1776), p. 18; Martin, *Familiar Dialogues*, p. 20; *Three Letters to the Reverend Dr Price* . . . (by a cobbler) (London, 1779), p. 17; *Licentiousness Unmasked; or, Liberty Explained* (London, 1776?), p. 16.

[28] *Duty of King and Subject*, p. 19; Fletcher, *American Patriotism*, Preface, p. iii, and pp. 12–14; 'Vindication', *Works*, vol. 5, pp. 8, 10–11; *Licentiousness Unmasked*, p. 13; Stewart, *Refutation and Political Overthrow of Dr Price*, p. 66.

[29] *Dr Price's Notions*, pp. 51–2.

[30] Carl B. Cone, 'Richard Price and the Constitution of the United States', *AHR*, 53 (1948), 726–47 (p. 730), argues that Price's political thought was an extension of his moral philosophy. See also Bernard Peach's introduction to *Richard Price and the Ethical Foundations of the American Revolution*, edited by B. Peach (Durham, North Carolina, 1979), and the responses by D. D. Raphael and S. R. Peterson cited below, Chapter 4, note 11, p. 63.

[31] *Remarks on a Pamphlet Lately Published by Dr Price* . . . (London, 1776), pp. 22–3, 43; *Licentiousness Unmasked*, p. 16; *Duty of King and Subject*, p. 5.

[32] *Remarks on a Pamphlet*, p. 5; Richard Hey, *Observations on the Nature of Civil Liberty* . . . (London, 1776), p. 27; *Licentiousness Unmasked*, pp. 8–10; *Three Dialogues Concerning Liberty* (London, 1766), pp. 96–8.

property. He employed a recurring metaphor equating government with marriage; once the initial choice had been made it was binding; those already under government were not free to choose a new master. Men had no right, he argued, to live under any specific form of government: 'a *direct* and *adequate* representation in parliament is no more essential to British Liberty, than circumcision to true Christianity'. He defended, moreover, the propriety of Christians going to war against the rebels.[33]

Before the outbreak of war, John Wesley had joined in a dispute with Caleb Evans on the American cause which mixed secular and religious arguments. Wesley's *A Calm Address to our American Colonists* was straightforwardly secular in argument because it was largely plagiarised from *Taxation no Tyranny* by Samuel Johnson who, while a devout Anglican, took a strictly secular approach to political questions.[34] But Wesley also developed his theological argument concerning inferior magistrates, thus implicitly depriving the colonies of any God-given right to rebel.[35] Evans insisted that taxation and representation had been joined by God, and that American action was compatible with Pauline teaching.[36] When Wesley came to respond to Price he quoted extensively from his own earlier arguments. He discussed the nature of liberty and of government, and much of his argument was in secular terms.

But unlike Josiah Tucker, Dean of Gloucester, who issued statements which were consciously and deliberately secular in argument,[37] at the critical juncture Wesley's case was based on his faith; government was not a trust from the people but a delegation from God.[38] In *A Calm Address to the Inhabitants of England* (1777), Wesley concentrated much more closely on spiritual arguments in advancing the same case. For all his passion, these were clear, fixed and precise. While some of his minor lieutenants let their

[33] Fletcher, 'Vindication', *Works*, vol. 5, pp. 3, 6–11, 24–8, 39–43, 47–50; *American Patriotism*, pp. 58–61, 65–8, 114; 'The Bible and the Sword', *Works*, vol. 5, pp. 196–9.

[34] Wesley, 'A Calm Address to our American Colonies' (1775), *Works*, vol. 10, pp. 80–9. On Johnson's secular approach see Donald Greene's Introduction to Johnson, *Political Writings* (New Haven, 1977), pp. xxxii–xxxv, and his *The Politics of Samuel Johnson* (New Haven, 1960), pp. 54, 236, 300–1; C. F. Chapin, *The Religious Thought of Samuel Johnson* (Ann Arbor, 1968), discusses Johnson's Christian politics (pp. 118–40), but is at times rather naive (p. 138).

[35] 'Free Thoughts on Public Affairs', *Works*, vol. 11, pp. 14–33 (p. 24); 'Thoughts on Liberty', *Works*, vol. 11, pp. 46–53 (pp. 47–8); on inferior magistrates see above, p. 33. A. Raymond, '"I fear God and honour the King". John Wesley and the American Revolution', *CH*, 45 (1976), 316–28, sets Wesley's views on America in the context of his fears of revolution in Britain.

[36] *Letter to Wesley*, pp. 5, 10; *British Constitutional Liberty*, pp. 8–10, 20–8.

[37] Wesley, 'National Sins and Miseries', *Works*, vol. 7, pp. 402–5; J. Tucker, *Four Tracts on Political and Commercial Subjects* (Gloucester, 1776); *An Humble Address and Earnest Appeal* ... (Gloucester, 1775); *The Respective Pleas and Arguments of the Mother Country and the Colonies* (Gloucester, 1775); see also Wesley, 'Some Observations on Liberty ...' (1776), *Works*, vol. 11, pp. 90–118, and compare *The Voice of God: Being Serious Thoughts on the Present Alarming Crisis* ... (London, 1775), pp. 7–13.

[38] Wesley, 'Observations on Liberty', *Works*, vol. 11, pp. 90–118 (p. 105).

feelings run riot and explicitly advocated passive obedience and non-resistance to government,[39] other Methodists took a much more moderate stance, and it was these who were in step with Wesley himself.

While Methodists opposed Old Dissenters, a battle was also being waged within the Church of England. Beilby Porteus's 1776 fast-day sermon before the king led to his being rewarded with the see of Chester,[40] while opponents of the American policy lost favour. By chance, it was Richard Watson's turn to preach both the Restoration Day and Accession Day sermons at the University of Cambridge in 1776, and he used the sermon in May to make a classic restatement of his political views in essentially secular and rational terms. His October sermon concentrated on the religious authority which underlay his argument. Watson devoted the heart of it to an exposition of Romans 13, which had in the past, he said, too often been used to defend tyranny. He sought to combine this exegesis with a re-affirmation of his support both for the balanced, mixed constitution in Britain and the rights of the colonists.[41]

Watson's sermons were answered by bitter and unsubstantial pamphlets by William Stevens,[42] but it was William Jones who presented the classic exposition of the high-church patriarchalist case in a sermon on *The Benefits of Civil Obedience* two years later. Like Watson in 1776, Jones stood back from the colonial conflict and set out his case in general terms. He discussed the divine source of authority and the absolute nature of obligation, stressed the duties not the rights of the people and argued the scriptural case for this emphasis. He denounced wilful rebellion and false ideas of liberty and, in perhaps his closest reference to America, warned that destruction was near for a country which put natural rights before positive law.[43]

The bishops charted a predictable course through these troubled waters. On the theoretical level they continued to occupy a position somewhere between Watson and the high-church patriarchalists. On a practical level they condemned the American rebellion. Men should not interfere in matters above their rank. Moreover, scripture, reason and revelation all

---

[39] For an extreme view see W. Mason, *The Absolute and Indispensable Duty of Christians* . . . (London, 1776), pp. 9–20. Thomas Coke contributed a preface to this, but he was then only a youthful curate and later withdrew from the position: see John Vickers, *Thomas Coke: Apostle of Methodism* (London, 1969), pp. 103, 129. For a satirical, malicious and occasionally witty attack on Mason see John Towers, *A Friendly Dialogue between Theophilus and Philadelphus* . . . (London, 1776), esp. pp. 14, 17.

[40] Henry P. Ippel, 'British Sermons and the American Revolution', *The Journal of Religious History*, 12 (1982), 191–205 (p. 194).

[41] Watson, Restoration Sermon, *SPO*, pp. 78–9 and Accession Sermon, *SPO*, pp. 83–104 (p. 87).

[42] W. Stevens, *Strictures on a Sermon* and *Revolution Vindicated*.

[43] W. Jones, *Fear of God*, p. 29; compare W. Jones, 'An Address to the British Government . . .', *Works*, vol. 12, pp. 335, 355–8, 362.

taught the duty of submission to properly constituted authority, and not even the pursuit of liberty should lead men to break this divine law.[44]

Richard Price had praised the number of fast days the Americans had before the war, but others saw these as sinister. Like the English sectaries between 1641 and 1660, the Americans, they claimed, were misusing religion to persuade the people that their cause was that of God.[45] However, calls for the British to follow the colonists' practice and to call a fast day to pray for success in the struggle grew and were acceded to on 13 December 1776.[46] Some complained, however, that the fast was ill kept and ridiculed by those who supported the American cause.[47] On later occasions the regular February fasts demonstrated the division of opinion and produced fast-day sermons condemning the war as well as those supporting it.[48] In sermons on 21 February 1781, Bishop Moore, George Horne and Samuel Parr were rephrasing their arguments to accommodate the fact of defeat, while Richard Price was reflective and restrained in victory.[49] All that remained was for controversialists on all sides to consider what had been learned from the dispute.[50] None of them came out of the debate with significantly different views from those with which they had entered it, but the issues of moral and political principle involved had led them to articulate

---

[44] J. Yorke, *A Sermon* ... (London, 1776), pp. 9–11; J. Moore, *Sermon* ... (1777), pp. 6–7; B. Porteus, *A Sermon* ... (London, 1778), pp. 12–13.

[45] Fletcher, *American Patriotism*, p. 98; *Experience Preferable to Theory* (London, 1776), pp. 87–8.

[46] Part of Bishop Hurd's sermon to the House of Lords on that day anticipated Burke's argument in the *Reflections on the Revolution in France* (1790) that abstract theories of government should not be applied 'directly to the correction of established governments'. Hurd, *Works*, vol. 8, pp. 5–6. For a useful general survey of fast days from 1563 to 1857 and a discussion of their increasing use for political purposes, see Roland Bartel, 'The Story of Public Fast Days in England', *Anglican Theological Review*, 37 (1955), 190–200, and on sermons on the American War, Ippel, 'British Sermons'.

[47] Fletcher, 'Bible and Sword', *Works*, vol. 5, p. 193; Wesley, 'A Calm Address to the Inhabitants of England' (1777), *Works*, vol. 11, 134.

[48] For example, on 10 February 1779, compare the establishment sermons from G. Stinton, *A Sermon* (London, 1779), R. P. Finch, *A Sermon* (London, 1779), and the doggerel patriotic poem in *The Arminian Magazine*, 2 (1779), 566, with Richard Price, *A Sermon* (London, 1779), esp. p. 26; or, on 4 February 1780, the establishment offerings of G. Horne, *A Sermon* (Oxford, 1780), J. Warren, *A Sermon* (London, 1780), J. Cornwallis, *A Sermon* (Canterbury, [1780]), and T. Seddon, *A Sermon* (Liverpool, 1780), with R. Watson's in *SPO*, pp. 113–15, 125–9, 134–5.

[49] John Moore, *A Sermon Preached before the Lords* ... (London, 1781); G. Horne, *A Sermon Preached before the University of Oxford* ... (Oxford, 1781); S. Parr, *The Works*, 8 vols. (London, 1828), vol. 2, pp. 353–5; R. Price, *A Discourse* ... *at Hackney* ... (London, [1781]).

[50] Wesley, 'How far is it the Duty of a Christian Minister to Preach Politics?' (9 January 1782), *Works*, vol. 11, pp. 154–5; J. Cornwallis, *A Sermon Preached before the Lords* ... *January 30 1782* (London, 1782), pp. 10–18, 22; J. Tucker, *Four Letters* ... *to* ... *the Earl of Shelburne* (Gloucester, 1783), Letter I; Watson, 'A Sermon Preached before the Lords' (30 January 1784), *SPO*, pp. 139–60; Price, *Observations on the American Revolution*; Robinson, 'Political Catechism', *Works*, vol. 2, pp. 259–354.

much more clearly and explicitly than they had done hitherto the fundamentals of their political faith.

The use and interpretation of history

The reactions of Britain's religious leaders to current political events were occasionally open and explicit. More often they were coded and indirect and reflected in the emphasis and selection they employed in making general points about political theory. These reactions were also revealed in the use men made of history and the way they interpreted it. On certain points they were in broad agreement.

1688 was the fundamental point of reference.[51] Almost all agreed that in certain circumstances men had a right to change the form of government; the basic formula tended to obscure the fact that there was no real agreement about what the preconditions for such a change were. On one thing only were all agreed – that the Revolution of 1688 was such an occasion. Some saw it as a unique event, others as an exemplar and model. Men disagreed about the theoretical nature of what had happened, but almost everyone accepted that the events of that time were not only just in the eyes of God, but the undisputed workings of divine providence.

While Protestants dated most of their arguments from 1688, Catholics looked back to the Reformation of the sixteenth century and, while 1688 remained important for them, it was seen in that longer context. For Berington, at least, 1688 posed no problem. He insisted that the history of England in the sixteenth and seventeenth centuries was the history of Catholic loyalty, and the only Catholic villain he denounced was James II.[52] Although not all Catholics felt the same, in general the reverence in which 1688 was held was near universal.

However, the events of the earlier seventeenth century posed greater problems and the reactions to the Civil War provided a more telling insight into men's thinking. Were Englishmen morally justified in taking up arms against Charles I; how far were they entitled by God's law to take their resistance to his rule? Many of the reactions were, of course, predictable. George Horne and John Wesley condemned the Revolution without reservation, while Joseph Priestley sought to defend the sectaries from the charge of sedition, and Robert Robinson declared them 'stern asserters of

---

[51] 1688 was invoked usually in general terms; the specific details of the settlement were discussed less often. See H. T. Dickinson, 'The Eighteenth Century Debate on the Glorious Revolution', *Hist.*, 61 (1976), 28–45 (pp. 29, 40–5). As he suggests (p. 33), the clergy urged loyalty to the whole constitution, not just to the crown. See also Nockles, 'Continuity and Change', pp. 10–13.

[52] *State and Behaviour*, pp. 16–17, 26–7.

the civil and religious rights of mankind', who made a brave stand against tyranny and did the will of God.[53]

But it was the attitude of the episcopate to those events which provided the most interesting insight. The Westminster Abbey Martyrdom Day sermon directed the thoughts of a newly appointed bishop to the events of the 1640s every year throughout this period. The political crisis of the early 1780s was reflected in a marked change of emphasis in the 1780s both in the general political tenor of the sermons and in the specific interpretation of the Civil War. This crisis had many causes: defeat in the war and the loss of the American colonies, the trebling of the national debt and the consequent high taxation, the war with France, Spain and Holland, the imperial problems in Ireland and India, all combined with the growth of faction at home between the decline of Lord North's government and the establishment of the Younger Pitt's to produce a situation of considerable political instability. In the spring of 1780 the County Associations of propertied radicals turned their attention from economical to parliamentary reform and the Society for Constitutional Information was established.[54]

In this situation, the sermons became noticeably more conservative and authoritarian. Generally, at least from 1782, they stressed much more than before the rights of government, its divine authority and the duty of obligation. The insistence on balancing the royal rights with those of the people, and the reiteration of the right of men to change the form of government, which characterised the sermons in the 1760s and 1770s, were heard less and less.

The most marked change, however, was in the attitude to Charles I. Just over four months after their father's execution, Prince Charles and Princess Mary heard a sermon at Breda in which the parallels between the deaths of Charles Stuart and Jesus Christ were strongly drawn.[55] By the reign of George III there was no hint whatsoever of such an interpretation; by then it would have been considered not only blasphemous but also politically heretical. Then, the orthodox line was laid down time and again. Charles I was at fault. He was badly educated and ill advised and had an extravagant idea of the royal prerogative and almost divine authority 'derived from the pedantry of mere bookish, and the ambition of mere worldly men'. The prevailing opinions of divine hereditary right meant that many of the king's sentiments were incompatible with the 'liberal principles' on which they believed the constitution was founded. But the king's opponents went

[53] Horne, 'Christian King' (1761), *Works*, vol. 3, pp. 407–8, 'Praying for Governors' (1788), *Works*, vol. 2, p. 569; Wesley, 'Free Thoughts on the Present State of Public Affairs', *Works*, vol. 11, pp. 14–33 (pp. 28–30); Priestley, 'Principles of Dissenters' (1769), *Works*, vol. 22, pp. 358, 362–9; Robinson, 'Christianity a System of Humanity' (1779), *Works*, vol. 3, pp. 280–1.
[54] For a discussion of the parallel economic and social problems see below, pp. 85, 91.
[55] *An Explanation of Some Passages in Dr Binke's Sermon* . . . (London, 1702).

much too far in their reactions and the advocates of freedom became immoderate rebels who abridged the liberties of the people even more than the king had done. When bishops expressed some personal sympathy for Charles, as did Robert Lamb in 1768 and Thomas Thurlow in 1780, they had to combine that sympathy with a clear condemnation of his constitutional excesses.[56]

Indeed, in 1772 there had been a major row in the Lower House when Thomas Nowell, principal of St Mary's Hall, regius professor of Modern History and public orator in the University of Oxford, preached the Martyrdom Day sermon in St Margaret's before the House of Commons. He implied that Charles I was blameless and that the usual excuse that the king's despotic government in part justified the rebellion, was 'as groundless as it is base'.[57] The Commons, when the members eventually read the published version of the sermon, rescinded the vote of thanks which had been passed as a matter of course. One member declared that those who took up arms against the king were 'not only blameless but praiseworthy'; another alleged that the form of service for the day had been drawn up by Father Petre, James II's confessor.[58] A motion to abolish the annual ceremony was lost by only 125 votes to 97.[59] Nowell received no further preferment. No bishop in the 1760s or 1770s adopted a position even remotely like that of Nowell.[60] All accepted that Charles I had governed improperly and had provoked the reaction against himself. Although that reaction had gone far beyond what was permissible, the king and his advisers were initially to blame.

However, only eleven years after Nowell's censure, Lewis Bagot, Bishop of Bristol, was able to speak of Charles as 'a great and good man' who maintained his integrity and the purity of his conscience through many calamities. He argued that

Concessions one after another were extorted from the peaceable and forgiving temper of the King, till at length the hand of civil government was so weakened, that the Laws and Liberties of the Nation had nothing left to protect them. The great forces once broke through, a total subversion of all Order, Religion and Government presently followed.[61]

---

[56] S. Barrington, *A Sermon* . . . (London, 1772), p. 12; Yorke, *A Sermon* . . ., p. 10; R. Lamb, *A Sermon* . . . (London, 1768), p. 10; T. Thurlow, *A Sermon* . . . (London, 1780), p. 13.

[57] *A Sermon* . . . (London, 1772), esp. p. 19.

[58] It was in fact the work of Sancroft.

[59] *Parl. Hist.*, vol. 17, cols. 245, 312–19; vol. 18, cols. 183–4. On the poor attendance at the annual sermons see vol. 20, col. 245.

[60] The difference of climate between Oxford and Westminster is shown by the fact that Nowell had preached the same sermon in St Mary's in 1766 without comment. See Ward, *Georgian Oxford*, p. 251.

[61] *A Sermon* . . . (London, 1783), pp. 12, 15.

Never in the reign of George III had the Lords heard such sentiments expressed on this occasion, but they heard them again in 1787 from John Butler, Bishop of Oxford. He also argued that Charles I had done nothing to justify the acts against him, and he insisted that the person of the king was sacred. He argued that it would be a mockery to celebrate Martyrdom Day as a fast if it were recognised that the people had a right to murder their sovereign.[62] These statements provoked no dissenting comments from the House of Lords. They were in line with the general change in ideological tone of the sermons from 1782 onward, which reflected both the political crises in Britain and the empire and an increased concern with the growth of Enlightenment irreligion in Europe.

Religious politics and the constitution in the church

The Restoration and Revolution Settlement fixed the form of the constitution not only in the state, but also in the church. Dreams of a comprehensive national church were abandoned. Episcopal Protestantism, in the form of the Church of England, was established by law and that church and its members enjoyed a wide range of privileges. The Toleration Act of 1689 recognised some of the rights of trinitarian Protestant Dissenters but excluded Catholics and unitarian Protestants from its provisions. Even the tolerated Dissenters were, in theory, excluded from public office by the Corporation and Test Acts. While agitation for a reform of parliament was limited, that for reform in the constitution in the church was wider. Many Dissenters of conservative political views thus supported reform in at least one part of the constitution, and, in practice, once the constitutional position of the church had been changed, the path to the reform of the constitution in the state lay open.

There were a number of occasions in the first three decades of George III's reign when matters of toleration, or of civil and political rights, arose,[63] notably when moves were made to repeal the Test and Corporation Acts and to relieve Catholics from the penal laws. Although questions of theology were raised, and sometimes discussed in detail, the basic division was a political not a doctrinal one.[64] Some Catholics and Protestant Dissenters supported each other's cases against the privileges of the Anglicans,

---

[62] *A Sermon* . . . (London, 1787), pp. 11–13.

[63] For a useful discussion of the distinction see J. Dybikowski, 'David Williams and the Eighteenth Century Distinction between Civil and Political Liberty', *ED*, 3 (1984), 15–35 (pp. 17–22).

[64] J. Tucker, *Letters to the Rev. Dr Kippis* . . . (Gloucester, 1773), discussed fully the theological difference between Calvinists and Arminians in the light of the toleration debate.

although traditional hostility kept others apart despite their coincidence of interest.[65] At the heart of the debate, from the perspective of political and social theory, was the role, function and propriety of a church establishment in a state, and it was around this issue that the debates centred. Anglicans, of course, had a vested interest in defending their privileges, but many used apparently disinterested theoretical arguments to support their case. Dissenters also had an interest, in showing those arguments to be specious and win a share in the privileges themselves, but in some cases their arguments too transcended the merely selfish and appealed to issues of principle. Here, the debate surrounding the question of subscription from 1772 to 1779 will be concentrated upon, for this led to clear and detailed expositions of the arguments on all sides.[66]

In February 1772 a petition from unorthodox ministers of the Church of England seeking relief from the requirement to subscribe to the thirty-nine articles was debated in parliament. This arose immediately from a meeting of the discontented clergy at the Feathers' Tavern and embodied principles set out in 1766 by Francis Blackburne in *The Confessional*. The petition was rejected but the issue was debated again in May 1774 when the motion was negatived without a division. The February petition for the Anglican clergy led, in April 1772, to the introduction of a bill to relieve Dissenting ministers and schoolmasters from the need to subscribe to the doctrinal articles in order to be exempt from the penal laws, to which they were otherwise liable. This passed the Commons, but was defeated in the House of Lords in May, as was a similar bill in 1773. The matter then lapsed until March 1779 when, in the aftermath of the Catholic Relief Act of 1778, another attempt was made – only to meet the same fate.[67]

The case for the abandonment of subscription was clearly articulated. Both sets of petitioners stressed their loyalty and their awareness of the need for government to provide order, stability, peace and security, but argued that the just state should make distinctions between its citizens only on virtue and merit. There was no reason to think Dissenters would preach political sedition if subscription were abandoned. Dissenters were good citizens and had much to offer the state. Houghton described them in the House of Commons as 'quiet, inoffensive and useful citizens', while outside

---

[65] Priestley, 'Free Address to . . . Catholics', *Works*, vol. 22, pp. 499–516; Berington, *Address to Protestant Dissenters*, the second edition of which included a supportive letter from Priestley to Berington. See also M. Fitzpatrick, 'Joseph Priestley and the Cause of Universal Toleration', *PPN*, 1 (1977), 3–30.

[66] The best account of the controversy is in R. B. Barlow, *Citizenship and Conscience* (Philadelphia, 1962), pp. 132–220, though Sir Leslie Stephen, *History of English Thought*, vol. 1, pp. 421–6, remains of interest. For the view from Oxford see Ward, *Georgian Oxford*, pp. 239–55. See also John Stephens, 'The London Ministers and Subscription, 1772–1779', *ED*, 1 (1982), 43–71.

[67] *Parl. Hist.*, vol. 17, cols. 245–95, 431–46, 742–91, 1325–7; vol. 20, cols. 239–48, 305–22.

of the House others stressed that relief from subscription would make them *more* loyal.[68]

The exposition of the Dissenters' case in 1774 found Robinson much more circumspect and cautious than was usual for him. Occasionally others allowed their resentment freer expression.[69] But beneath the bitterness and specific complaints was the long and widely held view that politics and religious faith were quite separate things, that a government had no jurisdiction over men's consciences, that a man's faith was no business of the state and that civil and ecclesiastical institutions should be completely separate.[70] This argument was developed in two distinct, though connected, ways. The first argued the case on a secular concept of human rights. Robinson suggested liberty was the proper end of government and Priestley explained that, while as a Christian all he wanted was toleration, as a man he wanted full civil rights as well.[71] Wilkes argued that the law, especially as it regarded schoolmasters, was not just a persecution of Dissenting ministers, but also a direct invasion of the natural rights of the laity – the right of a father to educate his children as he wished. The magistrate was justified in interfering only to preserve peace, social order and civil rights, but the doctrinal points of the thirty-nine articles had no connexion with any of these.[72]

The second argument was a religious one, against having an established church as part of the state constitution. St Paul's injunction to obey the powers that be, it was argued, related only to secular not religious matters. Even if one accepted that he meant that Nero's civil excesses should be submitted to, he obviously never intended that the emperor's paganism should be embraced. Moreover, when Christ instructed men to render to Caesar the things of Caesar, he added that the things of God should be rendered to God, thus excluding religion from the power of the magistrate. Robinson, though a believer in popular sovereignty as his other writings made abundantly clear, set out in *Arcana* to show that, whatever men considered the origin of government to be, natural, popular or divine, an established church could not be justified.[73]

---

[68] E. Radcliffe, *A Sermon . . . Respecting Subscription* (London, 1772), pp. 1–6, 14–15; Kippis, *Vindication*, pp. 72–3; *Parl. Hist.*, vol. 20, col. 239; Priestley, 'Letter of Advice' (1773), *Works*, vol. 22, p. 455.

[69] Robinson, 'Arcana' (1774), *Works*, vol. 2, p. 64; Priestley, 'Address to Protestant Dissenters' (1774), *Works*, vol. 22, pp. 483–98 (p. 490); *Parl. Hist.*, vol. 17, cols. 246–8, 265, 294; vol. 20, col. 310; Priestley, 'Letter of Advice', *Works*, vol. 22, p. 453.

[70] For the general theory of toleration which lay behind these specific arguments see U. R. Q. Henriques, *Religious Toleration in England, 1787–1833* (London, 1961), pp. 18–53.

[71] Robinson, 'Arcana' (1774), *Works*, vol. 2, p. 66; Priestley, 'Letter of Advice', *Works*, vol. 22, pp. 450–1.

[72] *Parl. Hist.*, vol. 20, cols. 309–19.

[73] *Works*, vol. 2, Letter IV, pp. 57–70 (p. 59).

There was, however, no shortage of defenders of establishment privileges. Thomas Nowell in his controversial Commons Martyrdom Day sermon in 1772 linked the Dissenters to the seventeenth-century regicides. Thomas Balguy, Archdeacon of Winchester, whose 'consummate assurance' Priestley found so inadequate and irritating, saw the Feathers' Tavern petition as an attack on the Anglican church which could lead to the end of establishment. In the House of Commons, Sir Roger Newdigate, MP for Oxford University, opposed both petitions, but Edmund Burke distinguished between the two.[74]

While Burke supported greater toleration of Dissenting ministers, he strongly opposed the petition of the Anglican clergy.[75] Because of his lack of concern with forms and dogmas, Burke had no conception of a 'true church' which must be defended from imposter sects by establishment. Any church was an artificial construct, man made and capable of change. An established church was only a system of religious doctrines and practices which were fixed by some law; parliament could change the religious establishment simply by changing that law. Different laws established different churches in different places. As he was later to point out to Lord North in 1778, the Presbyterian faith was established in Scotland, the Independent Congregational in New England and the Catholic in Canada, all with perfectly satisfactory results for the state.[76]

The purpose of establishment was not to benefit the church, although advantages did accrue, especially financial ones. Its purpose was to support the state, but in his speeches on clerical subscription in 1772 and 1774 he did not explain the precise mechanism whereby it did so. He merely suggested that its teachings should be congruent with state interests. He was unconcerned what doctrines Anglican clergymen believed within the privacy of their rectories, but in the interest of public peace and social order they must teach from their pulpits only the state-approved religion which was practised by those in public life, officially taught and supported by tithes. Parliament undoubtedly had a right to require the clergy to comply with the doctrines and ceremonies it established. He implied that this rigorous test might be more likely to exclude the politically undesirable than a merely biblical one would do. The state would be foolish to pay men 'of

---

74 Nowell, *A Sermon . . .*, pp. 11–12, 15–17; Priestley, 'Letter of Advice', *Works*, vol. 22, p. 453; T. Balguy, *A Charge Delivered to the Clergy of the Archdeaconry of Winchester . . .* (London, 1772); *Parl. Hist.*, vol. 17, cols.. 255, 743; vol. 20, col. 246.

75 'Speech on Clerical Subscription, 6 February 1772', *Writings*, vol. 2, pp. 359–64, 'Speech on Toleration Bill, 3 April 1772', *ibid.*, pp. 368–70. Norman Sykes suggested it was Burke's eloquence which led the Commons to reject the petition: *From Sheldon to Secker, Aspects of English Church History, 1660–1768*, The Ford Lectures (Cambridge, 1959), p. 222.

76 Burke 'Speech on the Relief of Subscription . . . for Church of England Clergy', *Works*, vol. 6, p. 96; Letter to Perry, 18 July 1778, *Corr.*, vol. 4, p. 7.

distempered imaginations' to preach, simply because they believed the scriptures; such subversives could undermine both church and state.[77]

Burke argued on empirical principles and on the pragmatic ground of the need to maintain 'order and decorum and public peace'. This led him to support the Dissenting petition while opposing the Anglican one. His speech in the House of Commons in March 1773 in favour of toleration developed ideas he had already set out in his *Tract* on the popery laws in 1765 and reflected the same preoccupation with the connexion between religious toleration and civil order.[78] A state must avoid making any of its subjects justly discontented and so providing cause to revolt. If men were free to practise their faith they would, he believed, see that no change would be to their advantage. Disorder came from misery and persecution, not quiet and prosperity; so, toleration was a means to security in the state. Burke's popery laws tract was in part an attempt to counter the Protestant case in Ireland. Both he and his wife were the offspring of mixed marriages, and he was always favourably inclined to the old faith which had supported so many governments for so many centuries. But, as his 1773 speech made clear, his argument was much more fundamental than a piece of special pleading for Catholics. Intolerance could be dysfunctional in two ways. As well as providing potential rebels with a cause, it also incited other groups to hatred of the persecuted, leading them to civil disorder. In 1779 he detected signs of this antagonism in Scotland and Ireland; in the following year he attributed the Gordon Riots to the hatred of Catholics encouraged in England by the penal laws before the First Relief Act.[79]

His 1773 speech made clear that, while all Christian denominations could reconcile men to government and order, atheism did the opposite. He combined his defence of the rights of Dissenters with a bitter attack on atheists who posed the real threat to the state and under whose systematic attacks he could see 'some of the props of good government already begin to fail'.[80] Burke's position was clear and consistent. Anglicans should be kept

---

[77] Burke, 'Speech on Clerical Subscription', 6 February 1772, *Writings*, vol. 2, pp. 359–64; 'Speech on Clerical Subscription, 5 May 1774), *ibid.*, pp. 465–7.

[78] This was Burke's position in the 1770s. It changed somewhat later (see below, pp. 122, 124). On Burke's views on toleration in general see Henriques, *Religious Toleration*, pp. 99–135; on his attitude to the Irish Catholic Relief Act see A. Paul Levack, 'Edmund Burke, his friends, and the Dawn of Irish Catholic Emancipation', *The Catholic Historical Review*, 37 (1952), 385–414 (pp. 389–90, 399–400). See also Robert Donovan, 'The Military Origins of the Roman Catholic Relief Programme of 1778', *HJ*, 28 (1985), 79–102.

[79] Letters to Rockingham, 9 May 1779, *Corr.*, vol. 4, p. 70, and to Dermott, 17 August 1779, vol. 4, p. 120; 'Thoughts on the Approaching Executions' (1780), *Works*, vol. 5, p. 518.

[80] Burke, 'Speech on Toleration Bill, 17 March 1773', *Writings*, vol. 2, pp. 381–90 (p. 389); 'Tract on Popery Laws in Ireland' (1765?), *Works*, vol. 6, pp. 5–48 (pp. 34–5, 45–6); Letter to Dermott, 17 August 1779, *Corr.*, vol. 4, pp. 120–1; 'Thoughts on Executions', *Works*, vol. 5, p. 518.

doctrinally orthodox and be supported fully by the state, Dissenters should be tolerated and atheists proscribed, all in the interests of public order.

Some Anglicans agreed with Burke,[81] and a few went even further. These were mainly men influenced in some way or other by Enlightenment thought. Dean Tucker and Archdeacon Paley, although not politically radical, represented new ways of thinking and both supported the greater degree of toleration of Dissenters advocated in 1772 and 1773. Richard Watson and Christopher Wyvill went further and supported the Feathers' Tavern petition as well,[82] although neither of them signed it. This was the occasion when Watson made his distinction between practical and speculative religious opinions.[83] While he argued strongly in favour of a religious establishment, he denied that subscription was necessary to preserve it.[84] Christopher Wyvill insisted that subscription to the Bible was sufficient in an enlightened age. He argued that religion was useful to the state only if it could be believed with sincerity. But retaining the articles, which he claimed most of the clergy were known to disapprove of, made the established church appear 'a political engine'. Like Burke, Wyvill saw the political and social function of religion as being the preservation of order, and argued that the freer religion was of divisions, the more politically useful it would be. Subtle differences in theology which divided men should be excluded from any test. To insist on one system or interpretation rather than another was impolitic since all systems were consistent with the general aims of religion and government. Religion was most socially beneficial if it was understood rationally.[85]

But these 'enlightened' thinkers who stressed the social function of religion were in a minority. Most Anglicans agreed with Balguy that the constitutional privileges of the established church must be reserved for the doctrinally orthodox. The fundamental change of emphasis to social theory did not happen until after the outbreak of the French Revolution, and when it came it led inexorably to the reform of the constitution in the church in 1828–9 and that, as Balguy feared, led on in turn to the Reform Act of 1832.

Before 1789 most Christian reaction to political events, both of a religious and a secular nature, continued to concentrate upon the constitutional and

---

[81] Bishop Shipley sacrificed his hopes of preferment by his support (see P. Brown, *Chathamites*, pp. 329–30).

[82] Paley, 'A Defence of the Consideration on . . . Subscription' (1774), *Works*, vol. 3; J. Tucker, *An Apology for the Present Church of England*, second edition (Gloucester, 1772); Watson, *Letter to the Commons*; C. Wyvill, *Thoughts on our Articles of Religion . . .*, third edition (London, 1773). See also I. R. Christie, 'The Yorkshire Association, 1780–4: A Study in Political Organisation', *HJ*, 3 (1960), 144–61, and T. Brain, 'Richard Watson and the Debate on Toleration in the Late Eighteenth Century', *PPN*, 2 (1978), 4–26.

[83] See above, pp. 33–4.

[84] Watson's view is fully discussed in Brain's dissertation, 'Richard Watson', pp. 88–107.

[85] Wyvill, *Articles of Religion*, pp. 9, 15.

philosophical themes established during the Revolution Settlement. Those events did not change the arguments fundamentally, but their nature made men concentrate upon certain crucial issues: the origin of political authority and obligation, the importance of representation and consent, and the nature of political, civil and religious rights. These issues were fundamental to any political philosophy, and therefore the final context in which the ideas outlined in Chapter 1 must be set is the philosophical one.

4

The philosophical context

If it is true, as has been suggested, that even John Locke began with his conclusions, then worked out arguments to support them,[1] it would not be surprising if lesser thinkers did the same. The fact that some of Filmer's theories had been refuted by Locke, and some of Locke's by Hume, was irrelevant to men who sought philosophical arguments to support their political convictions. The reasons men held the convictions they did depended more upon the intellectual and social experiences and backgrounds of individuals than any rigorous or logical thought. It is more likely to be explained by some process of intellectual prosopography than one of philosophical analysis. Yet part of any individual intellectual biography was the current intellectual climate, the bag and baggage of ideas.

In this period, as in most others, few ideas in current popular use were new, though men were aware of the new way of thinking and questioning in Enlightenment France. The traditional British debate ranging between patriarchalist and contractarian justifications of government remained an important source from which arguments, supporting whatever prejudices a man held, could be selected. It is, finally, impossible to say how far such ideas influenced men's opinions and how far they merely reinforced existing convictions. What is certain is that their influence was neither precise, rigorous nor straightforward, for most men did not think in such ways. Yet, clearly, philosophical ideas did influence men's political thought in broad, general terms.

The changing use of religious ideas in that political thought reflected both the growing fashion for rational arguments and the English taste for an empirical foundation to abstract theory. Those who based their thought on revelation and the supernatural found themselves increasingly on the defensive, and a wide range of Christian thinkers from Catholics to Unitarians stressed the rational nature of their belief.

---

[1] G. J. Schochet, *Patriarchalism and Political Thought* (Oxford, 1975), p. 273.

Patriarchalist and contractarian thought

One of the most important themes of J. C. D. Clark's *English Society* is the continuing importance of Filmer, and the relative neglect of Locke in the eighteenth century; the pervasion of patriarchalist and the rarity of contractarian thought. These are difficult matters to quantify, but Clark's assertion is a persuasive one. It might be helpful to draw a clearer distinction than Clark does between patriarchal political theory and social theory. Most of the evidence Clark cites related to an hierarchical theory of *society*, and here undoubtedly the familial model ruled supreme. But it is another matter to infer from this a justification of monarchy and a theory of political obligation. What Clark describes as patriarchalist accounts of the state were often patriarchalist accounts of society. The fact that one might flow logically from the other does not mean that most eighteenth-century men who thought about these matters followed that logical path, or found where it led an acceptable destination.

Of the thinkers examined above, Horne, Jones and Stevens have been described as 'high-church patriarchalists'. This is more a convenient label than a precise statement of an exact philosophical position. The differences between the three men and the chronological development of their attitudes make precision impossible, and they themselves probably regarded Hutchinson as a much greater intellectual influence than Filmer.[2] Moreover, Filmer's name was too closely associated with theories of passive obedience and non-resistance for men openly to invoke it. However, Horne's 1769 Assize sermon 'On the Origin of Civil Government' followed aspects of Filmer's argument closely. The human race sprang from a single common parent – first Adam, then Noah – whose power was supreme. Horne conceded that power had not uniformly been handed down from father to son, sometimes it was dropped by one and seized by another, but it had never descended to the people.[3] William Stevens adopted an even more extreme patriarchal line. He saw

the foundation for civil authority in the sentence passed on Eve, *Thy desire shall be to thy husband, and he shall rule over thee.* From that time, at least, the natural equality and independence of individuals was at an end, and Adam became (Oh dreadful sound to republican ears) universal monarch by divine right.

That charter to Adam – authority over all the rest of the human race at that time (Eve) – was the foundation of all civil governments thereafter.[4]

---

[2] On the wider philosophical and theological influences on this group see N. U. Murray, 'Influence of the French Revolution', pp. 44–55, and on Hutchinsonianism, Nockles, 'Continuity and Change', pp. xxvi–xxvii.

[3] Horne, 'Origin of Civil Government' (1769), *Works*, vol. 2, pp. 439–42. Compare Jones, *Fear of God*, pp. 32–3.

[4] *Strictures on a Sermon*, pp. 9–10.

But these views were at an extreme end of a spectrum; such explicit patriarchal arguments for political legitimacy and political obligation were unusual. Whilst Clark is quite right to stress the widespread and common nature of patriarchalist social theory, a strictly political philosophy drawn from Filmer, and those who thought like him, was relatively rare, at least after 1760.

At the other end of the Anglican political spectrum, Richard Watson was also unusual in acknowledging John Locke as his intellectual master. Watson described Locke as 'our best philosopher', defended him from his critics and invoked him as an authority.[5] Although he made little reference to the social compact and did not regard the state of nature as an historical period, Watson did consider the latter a useful theoretical concept. He considered pre-governmental man as being in a Lockean social state, not a Hobbesian solitary one. He argued that the law of nature was too vague and its sanctions too weak to overcome man's self-love and restrain his passions in the absence of government and religious revelation. However, Watson argued, the liberty which man enjoyed in this natural state could, in a social state, be limited only by law enacted by the general will of society. Universal consent was 'the only legitimate source of civil power'.[6]

Although Clark is right to suggest that this position was relatively rare, Watson was not alone in adopting a contractarian and consensual view of government. Hume's demolition of the social compact thesis did not deter men like John Greene, a parish priest in Norwich, from telling a Guild Day congregation in the cathedral that 'the general sense of mankind' told men that government was founded on a general compact.[7] Nor was Watson alone in his admiration of Locke. Enough other thinkers shared that position to make Josiah Tucker consider it worthwhile to make a number of very explicit attacks upon the 'Whig Philosopher'.[8]

Lockean views were, however, very far from being the norm in this period. Rather, they occupied one extreme end of the political spectrum. Most men adopted a political theory which was neither pure Locke, nor pure Filmer. Patriarchalism largely ruled the day as far as social theory was concerned, but on the central political issue of the divine or popular source of governmental authority and the right of resistance, Filmer and Locke

---

[5] 'Christianity Consistent . . .' (1769), *SPO*, p. 26; 'Answer to Jenyns', *Misc. T*, vol. 2, p. 333; Letter to the Bishop of Ely, 1786, *Anecdotes*, p. 86.

[6] Watson, 'Christianity Consistent . . .', *SPO*, p. 6; 'Sermon to the Stewards of the Westminster Dispensary' (preached 1785, published 1793), in *Misc. T*, vol. 1, p. 478. The phrase quoted was added in the 1793 Appendix, but is wholly consistent with the position taken in 1785.

[7] *A Sermon . . .* (Norwich, 1764), p. 8.

[8] Tucker, *Letters to Shelburne*, p. 109; *The Notions of Mr Locke and his Followers . . .* (privately printed, Gloucester, [1778]); *Treatise*.

provide the two philosophical poles between which Christian thought ranged.

Moral epistemology and the nature of man

On a more profound level, philosophical influences were limited. Any serious theory of politics and society needed to be founded on some understanding of moral epistemology, but this received little extended discussion in this period. There were two major traditions. One, the materialist view, led from John Locke's sensationalist epistemology to a utilitarian conception of morality. The view was well expressed by Joseph Priestley. Morality was learned by experience. As a child was checked and controlled, so he learned the concepts of right and wrong and of obligation.[9] This explained to Priestley why different men adopted different moral principles. There was for him no absolute morality, merely relative ones which different circumstances taught to different men. If men defined as moral those things which brought the greatest happiness, then different conceptions of human happiness would lead to different moral standards. In essence, this was only slightly removed from the position adopted by Paley and the generations of Anglican clergy who studied him.[10]

Priestley's necessarianism and materialism had, however, many contemporary critics, including his colleague Richard Price. Price expressed the other main tradition, that human morality was innate. His *Review of the Principal Questions in Morals* (1757) was the philosophical foundation of all Price's later political writings.[11] He argued that to extend Locke's sensationalist epistemology from physical to moral operations logically led men into 'an extravagant and monstrous scepticism'. Morality arose, he argued, neither from sensation and reflection, nor from experience and education. Rather, man had within him a moral sense which existed independently of his faith, opinion or will. Rectitude, he argued, was the primary and supreme law which gave all others their force and obliged men to obey them. The law of rectitude was God's own nature, and man's obligation to obey it was therefore infinitely greater than any obligation which arose

---

[9] Priestley, *Hartley's Theory of the Human Mind* (London, 1775), Introductory Essay, pp. xlii–xliii.

[10] See below, Chapter 5.

[11] To this extent I agree with S. R. Peterson, 'Richard Price's Politics and his Ethics', *JHI*, 45 (1984), 537–47, but the case against D. D. Raphael's charge of inconsistency between Price's politics and his ethics ('Review of Peach's *Richard Price and the Ethical Foundations of the American Revolution*', *PPN*, 4 (1980), 70–4) is less conclusive than she suggests; see above p. 46. The best discussion of Price's ideas set in the context of his life is Thomas, *Honest Mind*. On Price's philosophy, see also W. D. Hudson, *Reason and Right: A Critical Examination of Richard Price's Moral Philosophy* (London, 1970).

simply out of human will or any merely human perception of individual or public utility.[12]

The political implications of Price's belief in this universal law of rectitude *per se* could be seen in very traditional theological terms and could have been used to establish an obligation to obey even a despotic government. Price used it, in fact, to support a firmly libertarian position. His logical argument rested upon his theological heterodoxy. Price set his face against the high Calvinism of his father, but, unlike the orthodox anti-Calvinist position which reconciled free-will with original sin, Price denied entirely the doctrines of original sin and the Fall of man. Instead of seeing man as inherently sinful and needing to be restrained by church and state, Price argued that man's natural state was virtuous. Sin was not something immanent in man's fallen nature but an avoidable individual fall from a nature which was rational and good. If man were absolutely free, he would obey the universal law of rectitude. The role of government therefore should be not to restrain man but to give him complete liberty. Society and government were man-made, but individual liberty was God-given.[13] While most Christians denied Priestley's necessarianism, and many, especially Evangelicals, agreed with Price about the divine nature of the sense of morality, few followed him into the realms of perfectionism and minimal government.

Civic virtue and Christian meekness

Our understanding of the complex interrelationship between the classical and the Christian which dominated eighteenth-century English education, perception and values has been immeasurably enriched by the work of J. G. A. Pocock on civic humanism. In *The Machiavellian Moment* (1975) he argues that in the Renaissance the Aristotelian concept of man as *zōon politikon* was revived 'in a paradoxical though not a directly challenging relation' to the Christian view of man as a spiritual being, a member of a transcendent and eternal community whose true interests could never be achieved during his brief earthly life. Machiavelli saw the two worlds, civic and Christian, and the two moralities which applied to them, as quite separate. But Protestantism, especially in its puritan manifestation, led to a merging of the two and an equation of civic and religious liberty, and of civic virtue and spiritual salvation. This, however, led to a secularisation of the personality and to a concept of society which was seen in an historical rather

---

[12] *Review of the Principal Questions in Morals* (1757; third edition, London, 1787), pp. 64, 171–96.
[13] Price, *Sermons on the Christian Doctrine* (London, 1787), pp. 74, 231–8; *Additional Observations*, pp. 4, 11–12, 23, 26.

than a soterial framework. This led, in turn, both to man becoming more self-regarding, and to a more materially based society.[14]

The humanist concept of man as a citizen – rational, virtuous and desirous of liberty – was conceived by Machiavelli as contradictory to the Christian ethos. He considered Roman paganism as being far superior as a state religion. It embodied ferocity, courage, pomp and magnificence, and strove for worldly glory. It made men bold to fight, defend and exalt the state, whereas Christianity 'glorified humble and contemplative men, rather than men of action'. The Christian preference for the *vita contemplativa* produced weak citizens who handed over the world 'as a prey to the wicked'.[15]

The elimination of much of the spirituality from eighteenth-century Christianity by the Latitudinarians and the 'rational Christians' partly concealed the paradoxical nature of the value system which arose from the mixture of classical and Christian studies. In the 1790s there was a renewed emphasis upon a Christian concept of the nature of man which was in open conflict with the view of the civic humanists. Also, the secular view of human society in an historical context was challenged by a transcendent vision of society as part of a divine community with an eschatological dimension. In the thirty years before the outbreak of the French Revolution, however, the contradictions between civic and Christian concepts of man and society were allowed to rest largely undisturbed – the voices raised were light or unregarded.

Soame Jenyns was no philosopher. Samuel Johnson was rightly contemptuous and dismissive of his *Free Inquiry into the Nature and Origin of Evil* (1757).[16] But Jenyns, like a dog at a bone, worried away at the uncomfortable fact that Christ had taught his followers to despise the world, not govern it. Government, he argued, must involve violence, fraud and corruption; while Christians must show peace, forbearance, good-will and benevolence.[17] Alone among religions, Christianity was completely unconnected with government, and was concerned solely with the preparation of the soul for death and life eternal. The nation state demanded active virtues of its citizens, but the Christian could show only the passive courage of patience, resignation and suffering. Patriotism was forbidden him:

A Christian is of no country, he is a citizen of the world, and his neighbours and countrymen are the inhabitants of the remotest regions, whenever their distresses demand his friendly assistance: Christianity commands us to love all mankind,

---

[14] Pocock, *The Machiavellian Moment* (Princeton, 1975), p. 462.
[15] N. Machiavelli, *The Discourses* (Harmondsworth, 1970), p. 278. Compare J. J. Rousseau, *The Social Contract* (Harmondsworth, 1968), pp. 180–4.
[16] Johnson, 'Review of Jenyns *Origin of Evil*', in *The Literary Magazine*, 2 (1757), 306.
[17] Jenyns, 'Origin of Evil' (1757), *Works*, vol. 3, pp. 27–175 (pp. 145–9, 162–3).

patriotism to oppress all other countries to advance the imaginary prosperity of our own.

The humility of the Beatitudes was so new and so opposite to their own values that the pagan moralists thought such a way of thinking criminal and contemptible. This, Jenyns insisted, was also the view of most so-called Christians of his own day, who rejected Christ's teaching on meekness and self-sacrifice in practice and often denied it in principle. Although Christian and pagan values were diametrically opposed, English education was based on the classics and British government on the pagan virtues of valour, patriotism and honour. No governor or politician could be a Christian, for Christianity, if truly practised, would subvert the state.[18]

The historian, Edward Gibbon, saw Christianity not only as incompatible with government but also as a force for evil in the world. He deplored the influence of Christian values on citizens and rulers. He conceded that the doctrine of predestination might encourage martial courage, but in general Christianity denied the manly virtues and encouraged servility and pusillanimity. The Emperor Theodosius was 'chaste, temperate, liberal and merciful', but these virtues were seldom beneficial to him and were sometimes mischievous to mankind. The practical result of Christian teaching was to encourage passive obedience and non-resistance to the emperor. This had two effects. It led to despotism and weakened the courage and resolve of the people. Patience and cowardice replaced the active virtues of the pagan world – heroism, courage and glory – and so contributed to the decline and fall of the empire. Gibbon suggested that the faith most in accord with strong government was Islam. He praised Muhammad and showed how Islamic law sustained and strengthened the state, while Christianity only weakened it.[19]

This awareness of the incompatibility of the active *virtù* of civic humanism and the sacrificial virtue of Christian theology was potentially the most radical philosophical solvent of the age. But in England between 1760 and 1789 the issue was little discussed. This part of Gibbon's argument was overshadowed, in his critics' minds, by his suggestion that the growth of

---

[18] Jenyns, 'A View of the Internal Evidence of the Christian Religion' (1776), *Works*, vol. 4, pp. 1–121 (pp. 23, 39, 43, 59–61, 85–7); 'Disquisitions on Several Subjects' (1782), *Works*, vol. 3, pp. 177–299 (pp. 292–8).

[19] Gibbon, *The History of the Decline and Fall of the Roman Empire*, 6 vols. (1776–88) (reprinted London, Dent, n.d.), vol. 1, pp. 468–9; vol. 3, p. 389; vol. 4, pp. 1–2, 20, 106; vol. 5, pp. 207–92. Gibbon's attitude to religion changed over time and is the subject of much discussion. The debate is reviewed by P. Turnbull, 'The "Supposed Infidelity" of Edward Gibbon', *HJ*, 25 (1982), 23–41. The complexity of Gibbon's views is established in J. G. A. Pocock, 'Gibbon's *Decline and Fall* and the World View of the Late Enlightenment', *ECS*, 10 (1977), 287–303. D. D. Smith, 'Gibbon in Church', *JEH*, 35 (1984), 452–63, reads perhaps too much between the lines.

Christianity should be explained in human secular terms rather than as an act of divine providence, and that Constantine's conversion was a cynical policy based on his perception of the use of Christianity to the state.[20] Jenyns's comments on patriotism evoked far more replies than did his suggestion that no Christian could be a politician. Wilberforce tussled with the latter problem in his conscience, but it was not until 1797 that he publicly dealt with Jenyns's argument in print.[21]

Richard Watson, who replied to Gibbon in 1776 and to Jenyns in 1782, had already anticipated the argument in 1769. He described the Gospel precepts as being 'short, instructive, sublime and figurative, according to the genius of the Eastern languages'. It was quite wrong to interpret these as enjoining humiliating principles which would be inconsistent with the existence of civil society and so subversive of human happiness.[22] Bishop Porteus noted the argument, but did not seem unduly perturbed by it. He discussed it with Jenyns, and, although he found the replies to his objections unsatisfactory, he still felt the work may have won some converts from young people of fashion who would not have read a graver book.[23] The secularisation of Christian thought which Pocock has identified can be seen clearly in the responses to Jenyns and Gibbon, but the paradox remained.

Hume and the Enlightenment

The influence of the Enlightenment on English Christian thinkers was complex, their attitude to it ambiguous. In one sense the response was negative against a movement which challenged the role of religion as a prop of the state. '*Écrasez l'infâme*' was Voltaire's watchword, and the French Enlightenment was characterised by an explicit critique of Christianity unparalleled in European history. Most *philosophes* saw religion as a barrier to rational progress because of its dogmatic attitude to knowledge.[24] In attacking superstition, they attacked the blind acceptance of authority which could lead to enslavement in political terms. There were two major traditions in the French Enlightenment: a deist one led by Voltaire, and an

---

[20] *Decline and Fall*, vol. 1, pp. 430–500; vol. 2, pp. 1–69, 218–59.

[21] R. I. and S. Wilberforce, *Life of William Wilberforce*, 5 vols. (London, 1838), vol. 1, pp. 381–4. Comments from Pocock on Wilberforce would be very welcome. His reference to the Evangelical terms in which the co-incidence of civic and Christian virtues could be expressed suggest he would see Wilberforce's personality as more secularised that the 'Saint' would have cared to admit. See *Machiavellian Moment*, p. 463. See below, p. 148.

[22] Watson, *An Apology for Christianity* (Cambridge, 1776); 'Answer to Jenyns' *Misc. T*, vol. 2, pp. 331–64; Assize sermon 1769, *SPO* (pp. 8–16, 23).

[23] LPL, MS 2098, f. 9 (Porteus Notebook, 1777–80).

[24] S. Gilley, 'Christianity and Enlightenment: An Historical Survey', *History of European Ideas*, 1 (1981), 103–21, warns against exaggerating the irreligion of the Enlightenment.

atheist one led by d'Holbach.[25] Most English thinkers conflated the two traditions and regarded the *philosophes* simply as atheists. Even Priestley, whose rational Christianity was not far from the deist position, showed hostility to the apparent godlessness of the French Enlightenment. In 1774 he visited Paris with his patron Shelburne and was much dismayed at the irreligion of the *philosophes*. Prior to that visit all his references to Enlightenment thinkers, especially Montesquieu and Beccaria, had been positive and admiring. After that visit, every reference was, to some extent, hostile. And yet Priestley was clearly deeply influenced by Enlightenment ways of thinking.[26]

This ambiguous attitude to the Enlightenment was not limited to rational Dissenters like Priestley. John Wesley's distaste for the irreligion of the *philosophes* was clear, but his acceptance of many aspects of Enlightenment liberal thinking, on toleration, slavery and so on, has been demonstrated.[27] Beilby Porteus, Bishop of Chester from 1777 to 1787, and later of London, shared many of these liberal views, notably on slavery, and admitted in 1777 in a private notebook that Voltaire's writing delighted him. However, he suggested that Christ had had a higher view of the poor than Voltaire did because He considered them capable of a reasonable religion. Moreover, he described the Abbé Raynal's *Histoire Philosophique* as one of the most 'seducing and pernicious Books' ever to appear in Europe. Writing of Voltaire he argued, 'No man ought to break through the order that is established.' He had no objection to men thinking as they pleased, providing they did not publish any thoughts which might disturb the social peace. This point, he observed, also applied to Hume and Gibbon.[28] Other bishops were also well aware of the danger. In 1783 Lewis Bagot, Bishop of Bristol, warned explicitly that Enlightenment philosophy was a threat to the human personality, social manners and sound government.[29]

Because of this equivocal relationship to Enlightenment ways of thinking, no Englishman of this period can be numbered among the *philosophes*. But there was one considerable British thinker who can be so regarded, the

---

[25] Voltaire saw the importance of some form of religion to maintain social stability and control the *canaille*. See *Philosophical Dictionary* (New York, 1962), pp. 251, 605, and R. I. Boss, 'The Development of Social Religion: A Contradiction of French Free Thought', *JHI*, 34 (1973), 577–89.

[26] Priestley, *Letters to a Philosophical Unbeliever*, Part I, second edition (Birmingham, 1787), Preface, p. xiii. The point is more fully argued in my unpublished MA thesis, 'Joseph Priestley and the Enlightenment', University of Manchester, 1978, pp. 4–6, 53–4.

[27] Semmel, *Methodist Revolution*, but see Hempton, *Methodism and Politics*, pp. 22–3, for a cautionary note. It seems likely that Wesley shared a common climate of opinion with the *philosophes* rather than being directly influenced by them.

[28] LPL, MS 2098, ff. 19–20, 37, 44–5, 51–2 (quotation ff. 19–20). On Raynal, compare Wesley's *Journal*, 27 April 1778, *Works*, vol. 4, p. 120.

[29] Bagot, *A Sermon* . . . , pp. 14–15.

Scot David Hume. The Scottish Enlightenment, although taking a decidedly secular approach, was not on the whole irreligious on the French model, but Hume emerged clearly as an infidel.[30] The critique of religion which Hume developed in his *Essays* (1742) and his *History of England* (1754–62) was based upon the philosophical principles he established in his *Treatise of Human Nature* (1738–40), *Enquiry Concerning Human Understanding* (1748) and *Dialogues Concerning Natural Religion* (1779). His critique was, essentially, twofold. First, he denied that religious injunction was a valid source of political obligation. Secondly, he denied that religion was an effective source of restraint on man's behaviour; it was, rather, a positive source of harm to society.

Both of these arguments arose from his epistemology. Adopting a position of 'mitigated scepticism', Hume denied not only that revelation, but also that traditional rationalism and empiricism based on sensational experience were valid sources of knowledge. This meant that a number of the traditional arguments upon which political and moral philosophy had been based were ruled out of court. As well as divine injunction, so also was any concept of natural law rejected. Justice, Hume insisted, was not a natural quality, but an artificial and voluntary invention of man. He stressed the importance of the human passions and recognised the power of self-interest which itself would act as a source of restraint. Restraint was, for Hume, not something that needed to be imposed on man by the moral injunctions of religion and the threat of Hell (which assertions he held to be epistemologically invalid), but rather by the secular operation of the human passions themselves. The passion of self-interest became aware it was better served by its restraint than by its liberty; an individual could acquire more in the peace and security of society than in the violence and licence of the solitary state. The whole process operated on a human level, government was merely an invention of man, and natural and civil justice were artificial constructs. Religion had no place in the process.[31]

Hume regarded religion as being more than philosophically irrelevant; it was also socially and politically harmful. It led men to be factious, ambitious and intolerant. It diverted attention from human, social values towards spiritual concerns which distorted men's perceptions of their own interests.[32] A constant theme of Hume's *History* was the deleterious effect of religion on society. The power of the Druids, the Anglo-Saxon conversions, the medieval church, the Protestant reformers and the seventeenth-century

---

[30] E. C. Mossner, 'The Religion of David Hume', *JHI*, 39 (1978), 653–63, argues he was neither theist nor atheist but an anti-Christian sceptic.
[31] Hume, *A Treatise of Human Nature* (1738) (London, Dent, n.d.), vol. 2, pp. 197–8, 228, 243.
[32] Hume, *Dialogues Concerning Natural Religion* (1779) (Indianapolis, 1980), Section XII, pp. 214–28 (quotation p. 222).

sectaries were all condemned in turn for corrupting society. If religious principles were in opposition to the human passions, they had little effect; the passions invariably triumphed. But when religious principles allied themselves with the passions and became 'symptoms of faction and marks of party distinction', then they were dangerously destructive.[33]

Hume based his analysis of the social effects of religion in his *History* on two categories he had established in an essay 'Of Superstition and Enthusiasm' ten years earlier. But, for all his historical skills, the analysis was an unsubtle one. To isolate the two extremes of superstition and enthusiasm, Hume cut religion down the middle. Nothing was left between them. Superstition arose from men's weakness, fear and insecurity, it accounted for the early and medieval church and the post-Reformation episcopal churches. It made men tame and submissive, but was dangerous because it exaggerated the power of the clergy. Enthusiasm came from pride, success and confidence and gave rise to the Protestant reformers and the seventeenth-century sectaries. It was the more directly dangerous passion.[34] Hume showed remarkable fervour of conviction when he presented the arguments against the vernacular translation of the Bible. To place a complex and poetic book in the hands of the 'ignorant and giddy multitude' would lead to fanaticism. A thousand factions would arise and 'seduce silly women and ignorant mechanics into a belief of the most monstrous principles' which would undermine the authority and security of the magistrate.[35]

Hume supported, without undue optimism, the continuance of a balanced constitution and a limited monarchy. Religion, he believed, drove men to extremes; superstition led to despotism, enthusiasm to republicanism. It has recently been argued that Hume's philosophical attacks on both the concept of a social compact and the doctrine of passive obedience were designed to further his ideological aims to reduce conflict between Whig and Tory, Court and Country parties which could upset the careful balance of the constitution.[36] Clearly he saw precisely the same danger in religious commitment which (like a passion for philosophy) could accentuate the natural bias of the mind and push men further and further from the middle ground.[37] His desire to minimise religious passion led him to support

---

[33] Hume, *The History of England* . . . 8 vols. (London, 1822), vol. 1, pp. 19, 73, 296, 355; vol. 3, p. 291; vol. 4, p. 96; vol. 5, p. 13; vol. 6, pp. 21–2, 417; vol. 8, p. 131.

[34] Hume, *Essays and Treatises* . . . (1742), 2 vols. (Edinburgh, 1809), vol. 1, pp. 75–81.

[35] *History*, vol. 4, p. 122.

[36] D. Miller, *Philosophy and Ideology in Hume's Political Thought* (Oxford, 1981), pp. 163–84. Duncan Forbes, *Hume's Philosophical Politics* (Cambridge, 1975), also interprets his political philosophy as a response to the needs of his age and society, esp. pp. 91–101, 193–223.

[37] Hume, 'Enquiry Concerning Human Understanding' (1748), in Hume, *Enquiries Concerning Human Understanding and Concerning the Principles of Morals* (London, 1975), p. 40.

toleration and the Anglican establishment in England. Persecution fostered zeal, martyrs were the seed of the church; the way to destroy a faith was to ignore it. He favoured ecclesiastical establishments in inverse proportion to their spirituality. The characteristics of the Church of England which recommended it to him were precisely those which ecclesiastical historians have condemned. In combining superstition with Erastianism, it enjoyed the advantages of submission without the danger of an over-powerful, independent clergy. The value of the English Reformation lay not in its Protestant theology (with its dangerous enthusiastic overtones) but in the royal supremacy. What Hume sought, ideally, was not religion at all but an unspiritual, Erastian establishment, completely under the control of the civil magistrate.[38] In an imperfect world, the Church of England suited him fairly well.[39]

When the body of Christian political thought outlined in Chapter 2 is set in a philosophical context it appears essentially old-fashioned. Although there was a growing emphasis on rational argument, there was little discussion of the effect of new ideas of moral epistemology on political obligation. Jenyns's and Gibbon's radical views of Christianity as incompatible with government were largely ignored and most Christians continued to debate within the old Filmer–Locke spectrum. Hume's analysis was complete, and largely available, by the early 1760s. It found, however, few outright supporters in Britain in the thirty years before the outbreak of the French Revolution.[40] It was, essentially, too frontal an attack on religion to be widely acceptable.

In so far as Hume's views eventually triumphed, they did so by a less obvious and more insidious route. Hume is widely regarded as 'the founder of Utilitarianiam'.[41] Bentham, whose debt to Hume is undoubted, did not publish his *Introduction to the Principles of Morals and Legislation* until 1789. Like Hume's works, this too was written from an infidel standpoint, and many Christians attacked it. But there were utilitarians within the churches too. In his *Essay on the First Principles of Government* (1771) Joseph Priestley wrote,

To a mind not warped by theological and metaphysical subtleties, the Divine Being appears to be actuated by no other views than the noblest we can conceive, the

---

[38] Hume, *History*, vol. 4, pp. 91, 137, 369; vol. 5, pp. 88, 388; vol. 7, p. 40; vol. 8, p. 49; *Essays and Treatises*, vol. 1, pp. 523–40.

[39] At least, the Court Whig and Latitudinarian traditions did. He was less happy with the high-church and Evangelical strains, both of which emphasised the spiritual nature of religion.

[40] D. L. Le Mahieu, *The Mind of William Paley* (Lincoln, Nebraska, 1976), pp. 29–54, suggests some erudite and persuasive reasons for this, though Brown, *The Chatamites*, p. 134, is probably also right in suggesting simply that few, even of the highly educated, understood Hume.

[41] See, *inter alia*, John Plamenatz, *The English Utilitarians* (Oxford, 1966), pp. 22–44.

happiness of his creatures. Virtue and right conduct consist in those affections and actions which terminate in the public good; justice and veracity, for instance, having nothing intrinsically excellent in them, separate to their relation to the happiness of mankind; and the whole system of the right to power, property, and everything else in society, must be regulated by the same consideration: the decisive question, when any of these subjects are being examined, being, What is it that the good of the community requires?[42]

However, the most influential Christian apostle of utilitarianism was not the rational Dissenter, Joseph Priestley, but the Anglican Archdeacon of Carlisle, William Paley. To see how utilitarianism related to the Christian political theory outlined in Chapter 1 and set in its religious, political and philosophical contexts in the following three chapters, it is to Paley we must now turn.

---

[42] *Works*, vol. 22, p. 13. For the significant differences between Priestley's and Bentham's conceptions of utilitarianism see Margaret Canovan, 'The Un-Benthamite Utilitarianism of Joseph Priestley', *JHI*, 45 (1984), pp. 435–50.

5

Case study I: William Paley

In many ways William Paley was a highly conventional man, but it can be argued that his influence was far more radical, intellectually, than either he or his disciples were aware. The facts of his life were unremarkable enough. He was born in 1743, the son of a minor canon of Peterborough Cathedral and headmaster of Giggleswick Grammar School. He was educated at Christ's College, Cambridge, where he later became a fellow and taught metaphysics and morals. After a number of minor clerical appointments, he became Archdeacon of Carlisle in 1782 in succession to his friend John Law, the son of the bishop. In 1785 he became chancellor of the Diocese as well. Later he became a prebendary of St Paul's and a sub-dean of Lincoln, but he held on to his archdeaconry until his death in 1805. It was as an author that Paley was best known. The work his contemporaries most admired was his *Evidences of Christianity* (1794), but arguably his most significant book was his *Principles of Moral and Political Philosophy* published in 1785.[1]

Judgments of the significance of Paley depend very much on the position from which he is viewed and the context in which he is considered.[2] A

[1] This case study will concentrate on the *Principles of Moral and Political Philosophy* (1785), and will not discuss Paley's political views after 1789. These are examined in Parts II and III below, pp. 129–30, 136–7, and 180–2, where they are set in the context of the wider religious and political views of their day.

[2] Christie's picture of Paley as a conservative thinker (*Stress and Stability*, pp. 159–64) is as crisp and perspicacious as Paley's own writings. M. L. Clarke, *Paley: Evidences for the Man* (London, 1974) is a reliable biography and straightforward exposition of his arguments. Le Mahieu, *The Mind of William Paley*, provides a more critical analysis of his thought and demonstrates the unity of the *Principles*, *Evidences of Christianity* (1794) and *Natural Theology* (1802) as part of a coherent, 'rational-Christian' response to Hume. Patience Burne, 'The Moral Theory of Jeremy Bentham and William Paley' (unpublished M.A. dissertation, London University, 1948) contrasts secular and theological utilitarianism in a way not wholly unsympathetic to Paley. Canovan, 'Un-Benthamite Utilitarianism', considers the differences between the utilitarianism of an atheist and a rational-Christian, and many of her comments about Priestley apply equally to Paley. T. A. Horne, '"The Poor Have a Claim Founded in the Law of Nature": William Paley and the Rights of the Poor', *Journal of the History of Philosophy*, 23 (1985), 51–70, makes the same point (pp. 55–6), though he does also note that Paley was out of step with contemporary Anglican thought (p. 67). His main concern, however, is with Paley's social, not his political thought. T. P. Schofield, 'English Conservative Thought and

person who assumes that political theory should be a wholly secular pursuit will view him differently from one who believes it should have a theological content. Equally, Paley considered as one of the Utilitarians and compared to Bentham and Mill will appear very different from Paley considered as an Anglican cleric and compared to Horne and Watson. Most views of Paley have, in the past, come from writers who consider politics a secular business and have looked at Paley as a utilitarian thinker. In the context of a history of political thought which traces the 'progress' from theocentric to secular theories of the state and government (as does the intellectual version of the Whig Interpretation), he is seen as a conservative thinker, a limited man unable to let go of outmoded beliefs: 'Bentham is Paley *minus* a belief in hell-fire . . . Paley *plus* a profound faith in himself and an equally profound respect for realities.'[3] Only when Paley's utilitarian theory of political obligation, which denied God a structural role and left him only a cosmetic one, is compared to the ideas of obligation traditional amongst the Anglican clergy, can his true radicalism be seen.

The *Principles* were written in response to an immediate need for a student text. Paley was already lecturing on moral philosophy at Christ's and the book was based on these lectures. The graces of 19 and 20 March 1779 from the 1784 edition of the University Statutes showed that moral philosophy was being re-enforced in the BA disputations at that time.[4] Paley's book was adopted by students almost immediately on its publication. Gunning remembered reading Paley on Utility in 1787, and Le Grice's *Analysis* showed that tutors were using Paley as a text in 1794. On 18 January 1800 Wordsworth was told that the subjects for the BA examination would be Euclid I, Arithmetic, Vulgar and Decimal Fractions, Simple and Quadratic Equations, Locke and Paley.[5] The book was also widely read by students at Oxford and went through fifteen editions before Paley's death in 1805. Its critics notwithstanding, generation after generation of undergraduates read Paley, and his influence upon the moral and political thought of the English clergy was profound.

All of this might suggest that Paley was a very conventional thinker. Certainly he was seen as such by many, though not all, of his contemporaries, and present-day writers are able, quite properly, to cite his

Opinion in Response to the French Revolution 1789–1796' (unpublished Ph.D. dissertation, University of London, 1984), pp. 45–9, distinguishes between conservative and radical utilitarians and suggests significant differences between Paley and Priestley. Schofield discusses Paley in essentially secular terms, esp. pp. 17–25.

[3] Stephen, *History of English Thought*, vol. 2, p. 125. See also É. Halévy, *The Growth of Philosophic Radicalism* (1928; new edition, London, 1972), pp. 22–6, 80.

[4] I am indebted to Dr E. S. Leedham-Green, Assistant Keeper of the Archives, Cambridge University Library, for drawing these to my attention.

[5] Henry Gunning, *Reminiscences of . . . Cambridge . . .*, second edition (London, 1855), vol. 1, p. 74; B. R. Schneider, *Wordsworth's Cambridge Education* (Cambridge, 1959), p. 35.

work as part of the intellectual tradition upon which the conservative philosophy of Burke and others was founded.[6] However, it has also long been recognised that Paley went occasionally to the brink of radicalism, and then drew back. The most famous example is his metaphor of the flock of pigeons in which the mass slave and starve to maintain one in luxury.[7]

His friend, John Law, warned him the passage would bar him from a bishopric, but Paley insisted upon its standing. However, he proceeded to argue why, despite this, the principle of property was a sound one. Paley was indeed a social conservative, but one of the new breed not the old. His conservatism was not nostalgic or traditional, but founded in the political economy of men like Adam Smith. Nine years after Smith had put forward a labour theory of value in *The Wealth of Nations* (1776), Paley observed,

It is a mistake to suppose that the rich man maintains his servants, tradesmen, tenants, and labourers; the truth is, they maintain him. It is their industry which supplies his table, furnishes his wardrobe, builds his houses, adorns his equipage, provides his amusements. It is not his estate, but the labour employed upon it, that pays his rent. All that he does, is to distribute what others produce; which is the least part of the business.[8]

However, it was not these kinds of economic reflections (the radical import of which caused Paley to draw back) which made the work so significant. It was rather his central argument, his major theme, his Utilitarianism, for this lay at the heart of the secularisation of English Christian political theory and replaced a concept of a divinely revealed obligation with that of a humanly perceived one. Before arguing the case for the radical implication of this (in intellectual not political terms), it is necessary first to establish the argument of the *Principles* and the precise role of utility within it.

Paley's whole argument was constructed upon an epistemological base largely inherited from Locke.[9] He considered three possible sources of a moral rule for life – the law of honour, the law of the land, and the law of scripture – rejecting each as inadequate. He suggested that, while the scriptures laid down some general rules, they presupposed a knowledge of the principles of natural justice.[10] Rejecting the possibility of an innate moral sense as the source of this knowledge, he concluded that morality was socially learned.

[6] Christie, *Stress and Stability*, p. 159.
[7] 'Principles', *Works*, vol. 4, pp. 72–3.
[8] *Ibid.*, pp. 154–5.
[9] Paley, of course, rejected Locke's compact theory. See Dickinson, 'Debate on the Glorious Revolution', pp. 42–3. But Lockean sensationalist epistemology and the idea that the purpose of life is human happiness was central to the utilitarian ethic.
[10] 'Principles', *Works*, vol. 4, pp. 1–6.

But that explained only how men acquired a moral sense; it did not determine what that morality should be; it was neither a source of moral authority nor of moral obligation.[11] For both of these Paley turned to the principle of utility. He argued that those things were moral and virtuous which maximised human happiness, those immoral and vicious which minimised it. From this, he concluded, man was under a moral obligation to do those things which maximised happiness because that was the will of God. Only if men did those things which led to the greatest happiness of others could they ensure their own happiness in the world to come. So the eschatological dimension of the moral calculus used self-interest as a 'violent motive' which obliged a man to act in a way consistent with the greatest happiness of the greatest number of his fellow citizens.[12]

The first three-fifths of Paley's book concerned moral philosophy, the last two-fifths political philosophy. His political analysis was firmly based on his moral analysis, and the arguments on political authority and obligation mirrored those on moral authority and obligation. Political authority arose, for Paley, from the needs of utility. He contrasted the natural rights which existed in the absence of civil government (life, limbs, liberty, produce of labour) with the adventitious rights which obtained only where there was civil government. These included the king's rights over his subjects, the people's right to choose their magistrates, and the government's right to collect taxes, settle disputes and organise the inheritance of property. The authority on which these rights were based rested, Paley argued, on the fact that they were necessary to achieve the greatest happiness of the greatest number of the people. Paley's idea of divine benevolence led him to assert, without any clear evidence, that this was also the will of God. Therefore, political authority and political obligation rested upon the principle of utility. All things necessary for the greatest happiness were authorised and men were obliged to accept them.[13]

By equating the greatest happiness of the greatest number with the will of God and thus obscuring the real source of authority and obligation in his theory, Paley considered that God still had a crucial role to play in any utilitarian thesis of moral and political obligation. But the actual role was a complex one and depended upon Paley's concept of an obligation. It was traditional to draw a distinction between the determination of moral obligation and the effective enforcing of it. If one adopted that distinction in examining Paley's thesis (and Paley himself did not), then one could argue that God played no part in working out what, morally, man was obliged to

---

[11] *Ibid.*, pp. 13, 28.
[12] *Ibid.*, pp. 39–40, 339–40.
[13] *Ibid.*, pp. 59–60.

do. That was determined purely by the utilitarian calculus; 'whatever is expedient is right. It is the utility of any moral rule alone which constitutes the moral obligation of it.'[14] However, since the greatest happiness of the greatest number was equated with the will of God, once the human, secular calculus had determined what the correct moral course was, then God entered the argument as a means of enforcement, a sanction. If man failed to do that which the utilitarian calculus showed to be conducive to the greatest happiness of the greatest number, then he would be punished in Hell; only the pursuit of the general happiness gave him a passport to Heaven.

Paley drew a distinction between prudence and duty. When man came to reflect on what constituted his happiness, prudence made him consider the gains and losses in this world, while duty made him include gain and loss in the world to come as well. To ensure eternal felicity man must do the will of God, which had already been equated with the demands of utility. Thereby the individual calculus would not arrive at just an individual good, but at the good of the majority. When eschatological considerations were thrown into the calculus, selfishness disappeared. Only the awareness of eternal reward and punishment, Paley suggested, made the result of the calculation a moral obligation. He warned that any system of morality independent of a belief in eternal life had to find a new source of moral obligation.[15]

Nearly eighty years later, in 1863, John Stuart Mill addressed the same problem and proposed a very different solution, one based not on fear but on benevolence:

The happiness which forms the utilitarian standard of what is right in conduct, is not the agent's own happiness, but that of all concerned. As between his own happiness and that of others, utilitarianism requires him to be as strictly impartial as a disinterested and benevolent spectator. In the golden rule of Jesus of Nazareth, we read the complete spirit of the ethics of utility. To do as you would be done by, and to love your neighbour as yourself, constitute the ideal perfection of utilitarian morality.[16]

Paley would have agreed with this statement in so far as Mill equated the greatest happiness with the will of God as expressed in Christ's injunction. But he would have disputed that one could rely on human benevolence to enforce it. The bland, liberal optimism of Victorian atheism took a view of human nature which was a whole world away from the cynical realism of Paley's Christianity. The doctrine of original sin and human imperfection convinced him of the need to restrain man's selfishness; a religious faith in

[14] *Ibid.*, pp. 48–9.
[15] *Ibid.*, pp. 42–5.
[16] J. S. Mill, *Utilitarianism* (1863; Everyman edition, London, 1910, 1972), p. 16.

the Four Last Things (death, judgment, Heaven and Hell) provided for Paley the only effective restraint.

It appears on the surface that Paley's moral epistemology was secular, the enforcement of morality theological. This, however, was a distinction Paley refused to make. Rather, he insisted that moral obligation, like all other obligations, was merely an 'inducement of sufficient strength' coming from an exterior force.[17] Paley's refusal to accept that morality had any force separate from the power that enforced it was itself a product of his faith in utility and the supremacy of expediency. His contention that God was still necessary in utilitarian political theory depended upon this refusal, for in his theory God no longer revealed to man what was moral, He merely enforced the morality determined by the calculus. That was a function which Bentham regarded as not merely redundant but also a source of weakness. Since knowledge of Heaven and Hell was, in Bentham's view, epistemologically ill founded, it merely undermined a theory which could best stand on purely secular ground. Seen from this perspective, Paley has, quite correctly, been regarded as a backward-looking thinker who embraced progress only half-heartedly.

There is, however, another way of looking at Paley, which would have been more natural to most of his contemporaries. When he is considered in the context of Christian political theory in general and of Anglican political thought in particular, he can be seen as a highly influential and essentially radical figure. One of the many forms which the deist challenge to Christian thought took was the alleged superiority of natural religion to revealed religion. Enlightenment rationalism rejected wisdom allegedly revealed directly by God in favour of ideas which came through the medium of man's reason. The latitudinarian spirit in the Church of England, which was especially strong in the University of Cambridge, stressed the natural aspects of religion.[18] Richard Watson was a good example of a man who used arguments from natural religion whenever he could, but Watson's theory of political authority and obligation, for all his faith in popular sovereignty, was still founded on a firm theological base. At the other end of the

---

[17] 'Principles', *Works*, vol. 4, pp. 41–2.

[18] That spirit survives. It is not merely agnostics like Sir Leslie Stephen who have pictured Paley within this rationalist, secular version of the Whig Interpretation. Norman Sykes, doyen of the defenders of the Hanoverian Church, was sympathetic to the latitudinarian spirit which in some ways reflected his own style of churchmanship. Gerald Cragg describes Paley as 'perhaps the last great representative of the latitudinarian spirit' in *Reason and Authority in the Eighteenth Century* (Cambridge, 1964), p. 213. However, Owen Chadwick reminds us that the term latitudinarian was a wide-ranging one and we should beware of generalisation (*From Bossuet to Newman* (Cambridge, 1957), pp. 74–86). Le Mahieu, Paley's most intelligent recent defender, champions his 'rationalism' against the 'emotionalism' of his Evangelical critics. On the radicalism of Cambridge see Schneider, *Wordsworth's Cambridge Education*, esp. chap. 5, pp. 112–63.

spectrum, men like George Horne emphasised the divine nature of political society much more and their Hutchinsonian theology asserted the literal truth of divine revelation.

Although politically and socially conservative, intellectually and theologically Paley was at the extreme 'liberal' end of the Anglican spectrum.[19] The Latitudinarians no longer dominated the episcopal bench; a number of more conservative churchmen, such as Samuel Horsley and George Pretyman-Tomline, were appointed in the 1780s. The greater spirituality of the high-church Hackney Phalanx and the low-church Clapham Sect was directly hostile to the latitudinarian spirit. In political terms, both the high-churchmen and Evangelicals stressed the divine nature of political authority and obligation. From around 1782 the bishops increasingly preached the same message. When viewed in this context, Paley's Cambridge lectures in the early 1780s, and his *Principles*, published in 1785, both of which took so clearly a secular view of the source of authority and obligation and re-invigorated the fading latitudinarian spirit, can been seen as a radically secularising influence on Christian political theory.

Paley's attitude to this latitudinarian preference for rational, natural religion is sufficiently critical to the argument of this case study to warrant a reiteration of his position in the form of an extended quotation from a passage where he went on to consider whether rebellion could be justified:

The steps by which the argument proceeds are few and direct. – 'It is the will of God that the happiness of human life be promoted:' – this is the first step, and the foundation not only of this, but of every moral conclusion. 'Civil society conduces to that end;' – this is the second proposition. 'Civil societies cannot be upholden, unless, in each, the interest of the whole society be binding upon every part and member of it;' – this is the third step, and conducts us to the conclusion, namely, 'that so long as the established government cannot be resisted or changed without public inconveniency, it is the will of God (which *will* universally determines our duty) that the established government be obeyed,' – and no longer.

This principle being admitted, the justice of every particular case of resistance is reduced to a computation of the quantity of the danger and grievance on one side, and of the probability and expense of redressing it on the other.[20]

Again, the will of God was to be determined by the operation of the calculus.

In precisely the same way, when he discussed suicide Paley used the traditional argument that the state can derive power of life and death over

---

[19] On Paley's alleged unitarian bias see Schneider, *ibid.*, p. 121, Le Mahieu, *The Mind of William Paley*, p. 14, and G. A. Cole, 'Doctrine, Dissent and the Decline of Paley's Reputation', *ED*, 6 (1987), 19–30. His friend John Jebb became a Unitarian in 1775 and his pupil William Frend in 1787: see Frida Knight, *University Rebel: The Life of William Frend (1757–1841)* (London, 1971). On his practical conservatism see T. P. Schofield, 'English Conservative Thought', pp. 17–25.

[20] 'Principles', *Works*, vol. 4, p. 340.

its subjects only from God. Wesley and William Jones had both used this argument, taken from Filmer, to stress the divine nature of government. But Paley related it to utility; since such a power was clearly expedient, it was therefore presumed to be the will of God that it should be exercised and 'it is this presumption which constitutes the right'.[21]

At various points, Paley considered a number of problems to which he applied the same principle. The problems were those of property, civil liberty, punishment, a religious establishment, toleration and the confessional state.[22] In each case the argument was conducted in secular terms, according to the principle of utility as determined by human reason, and the conclusion reached was then asserted to be the will of God. Not only did he consider civil questions of punishment and liberty in secular, utilitarian terms, but also religious questions of toleration and establishments: only considerations of general utility should limit the powers of the magistrate, and there was nothing in the nature of religion that exempted it from his power if 'the safety or welfare of the community' required its control.[23] Although Paley's own views on toleration were extremely liberal, he was willing to follow his theory and restrict liberty if utility demanded it.

There was, however, one route which (if the logic of his argument had demanded he follow) he was not willing to tread. If man's eternal happiness depended upon the teaching of a particular sect (if, for example, *salus extra ecclesiam non est*), would not the calculus require the magistrate to adopt a confessional state and persecute heretics? Paley commented,

We confess that this consequence is inferred from the principles we have laid down concerning the foundation of civil authority, not without the resemblance of a regular deduction: we confess also that it is a conclusion which it behoves us to dispose of; because, if it really follows from our theory of government, the theory itself ought to be given up.[24]

In fact, Paley did dispose of it (somewhat unconvincingly) by the adoption of rule-utilitarianism rather than act-utilitarianism as his criterion, but if he had not been able to do so, why did he think his theory should have been abandoned? That suggestion implied it was unable to withstand some greater principle outside it. In view of his earlier comments, it seems unlikely that principle could have arisen from moral intuition; more likely it was pragmatic in nature. In insisting that the principle of utility was the will of God and that eternal happiness should be included in the calculus, Paley

---

[21] *Ibid.*, p. 264; Wesley, 'Origin of Power', *Works*, vol. 11, p. 52; Jones, *Fear of God*, p. 27.

[22] 'Principles', *Works*, vol. 4, pp. 60–83, 165, 354–417, 425–9, 449–77. The section on property showed how much Paley was a man of the age of improvement, capital enterprise, and development. On Paley's views on punishment see Burne, 'Moral Theory', pp. 133–42.

[23] 'Principles', *Works*, vol. 4, pp. 463–4.

[24] *Ibid.*, p. 466.

disguised (probably to himself as well as others) the secular nature of utilitarianism. But, if the religious accretions he superimposed on it had logically brought him to a conclusion which seemed to his pragmatic, secular judgment untenable, then he told us, he would have abandoned them.

The latitudinarian tradition attempted to come to terms with rationalist thinking by neglecting the supernatural revelations of Christianity and emphasising natural religion. No one did that more so than William Paley. When discussing the traditional texts of SS Peter and Paul on government he argued that no passage in the New Testament added anything to the conclusions reached on questions of politics and society by natural religion and natural law.[25] The latitudinarian spirit was, however, under assault from many quarters, from those who believed it was neglecting the spiritual essence of Christianity, its supernatural element. The Hutchinsonians stressed divine revelation not human reason as the source of authority. John Wesley challenged the secularising spirit just as vigorously and attacked the effete nature of much Anglican theology. The two most powerful revivalist movements within the Church of England, the Evangelicals in the late eighteenth and early nineteenth centuries and the Oxford Movement in the 1830s and 1840s, both stressed the supernatural elements of religion.

The Evangelicals were Paley's bitterest critics. Thomas Gisborne's *Principles of Moral Philosophy* (1789) was the most direct and forcefully argued of many Evangelical assaults on Paley. Gisborne saw morality as a categorical imperative imposed by God and revealed by Him to man, not as a human perception of what was expedient. The more central, establishment figure of George Croft, Bampton lecturer and friend of Lord Eldon, found much to criticise in Paley as well as in Gisborne, though the theory of utility worried him less than some of the minor arguments.[26] Croft underlined the widespread influence of Paley's *Principles*: they were to be found in every apartment. Despite the criticism by high-churchmen and Evangelicals alike, they remained in the Cambridge syllabus into the second half of the nineteenth century, though their influence declined in the 1830s.[27]

---

[25] *Works*, vol. p. 346.

[26] G. Croft, *A Short Commentary with Strictures, on Certain Parts of the Moral Writings of Dr Paley and Mr Gisborne* (Birmingham, 1797). On Gisborne's critique of Paley see T. P. Schofield, 'English Conservative Thought', pp. 73–7.

[27] The decline was, however, less extreme than J. Viner, *The Role of Providence in the Social Order* (Philadelphia, 1972), p. 74, suggests. A. M. C. Waterman, 'The Ideological Alliance of Political Economy and Christian Theology 1798–1833', *JEH*, 34 (1983), 231–44 (p. 232, note 2), says it remained a set text until 1857, though Richard Whately suggested it was still such when he attacked it in 1859, *Dr Paley's Works: A Lecture* (London, 1859). Le Mahieu reviews the major attacks, *The Mind of William Paley*, pp. 155–62. G. A. Cole, 'Doctrine, Dissent . . .', suggests

Paley not only revived and passed on the latitudinarian spirit to new generations of Anglican clergy, but also made acceptable the new, profoundly secular, concept of utilitarianism, which might well otherwise have been rejected as the godless product of infidel thought. In a long Christian tradition, when men invoked religious principles, they based these largely upon some avowedly objective source, usually revelation as enshrined in the teaching of the church or in the scriptures. Though different men interpreted scripture in different ways, they regarded the Word of God as something separate from and superior to human reason. What Paley did was to secularise religious argument. Whatever seemed to an individual to be fair, honest, reasonable and calculated to maximise human happiness (albeit in an eternal context) was presumed to be the divine will. But its determination depended upon subjective, human judgment, not the objective revelation of God.

The political thought of a large number of Anglican clergy in the early nineteenth century was based on Paley's *Principles of Moral and Political Philosophy* which they had studied at university and which gave them this rational, secular and human view of political society. When John Henry Newman, in his *Parochial and Plain Sermons* (1834–43) and elsewhere, reasserted the power of the supernatural and of Christian revelation as opposed to rational, human philosophy, it was the heirs of Paley who forced him from the Church of England. Their Erastianism, which Newman hated as much as Gisborne had done,[28] was born of Paley. No man made a greater contribution to the secularisation of political thought in Britain.

Paley's reputation declined somewhat earlier because of doubts about his theological orthodoxy.

[28] Nockles, 'Continuity and Change', pp. 1–30, points out that the old high-church men were as anti-Erastian as the Tractarians.

6

Secularisation and social theory

Secularisation

Christian political thought in the period from 1760 to 1789 largely followed
the ideological agenda set by the Restoration and Revolution Settlements in
the later seventeenth century. It was dominated by constitutional and
philosophical arguments relating to political authority, obligation and the
right of rebellion. In one sense the central tradition itself represented a
secularising tendency; the distinction between government in general as
the ordinance of God and the particular form of government as the
ordinance of man stressed that one area of political theory at least was left
for human, secular determination. Some thinkers, like Horne and Wesley,
limited this area as much as possible. Others, like Watson, Berington and
Robinson, stressed the human autonomy within it. But the degree of
secularisation within this latter tradition should not be exaggerated.[1] The
role of God in Locke's political philosophy has been demonstrated recently,[2]
and the political theory of his disciples in this period remained essentially
theocentric. As well as regarding the divine will as the ultimate source of
obligation, writers like Watson, Evans and Price based their concept of
popular sovereignty upon the God-given equality of man, and reformers
like Cartwright and Burgh based their radical arguments on the same
premise.

Secularisation came less from within the old Locke–Filmer spectrum and
more from the Enlightenment mode of thought. The atheist Enlightenment
was represented in Britain largely by Hume, Gibbon and Bentham, but their
effect was slight compared with that of Christian writers deeply influenced
by the new ways of thinking. Priestley's 'rational theology' led him to

---

[1] For a cautionary note on the degree of secularisation in political thought see Christie, *Stress
and Stability*, pp. 184–5. But see also his comments on the theology of the Church of England,
pp. 198–200.

[2] J. W. Yolton, *John Locke and the Way of Ideas* (Oxford, 1956); J. Dunn, *The Political Thought of
John Locke* (Cambridge, 1969).

propound arguments not far removed from those of deism. Paley played a
central role in transforming the old latitudinarian tradition into a new
utilitarian one. The other most important Anglican figure in this context
was Josiah Tucker, Dean of Gloucester from 1758 to 1799.[3] Tucker's main
interest was in economic matters relating to trade and commerce. Unlike
Paley, he was passionately, almost obsessively, hostile to Locke, whom he
regarded as too metaphysical, too doctrinaire and insufficiently cautious,
pragmatic and practical.[4] The theory of man, society and politics, which
Tucker developed over the years and summarised in his *Treatise Concerning
Civil Government* (1781), was essentially secular in its outlook and arguments. Like Priestley and Paley, he rejected the idea of there being absolute,
unchanging principles; for him all political principles were partial, relative,
changeable, practical and pragmatic.[5] Thereby, he excluded any centrally
important role for a God who is eternal and absolute. He did devote the final
chapter of his *Treatise* to a consideration of 'The Doctrine of Scripture
relating to the obedience due from Subjects to their Sovereign together with
the Grounds and Reasons for the Duty'. But these last eighteen pages of a
428-page book are more like a postscript, or an appendix, than the
culmination and denouement of its argument. Unlike William Jones, he
made no distinction between authority and power. His pragmatism led him
to argue that the possession of physical power constituted political authority
and required obedience.[6]

Social theory

One of the effects of the secularising process was to move religious
arguments away from the constitutional-philosophical agenda set in the
seventeenth century and to concentrate them much more on social theory –
the concepts of restraint and sanctions, of social hierarchy and of the need
for the poor to be content with their lot. There was, of course, nothing new
in such arguments. For centuries Christianity had taught the poor contentment and resignation, and religion had acted as a sanction and a restraint on

---

[3] George Shelton, *Dean Tucker and Eighteenth-Century Economic and Political Thought* (London,
1981) is a useful but not incisive biography. See also the review by Malcolm Jack, *ECS*, 18
(1984), 132–3.

[4] Tucker, *Four Letters to Shelburne*, pp. 109–10; *The Notions of Mr Locke*. Tucker's hostility was
accentuated by the American Revolution which he believed Locke's writings had
encouraged.

[5] pp. 97–8, 235–6.

[6] S. Rashid, '"He Startled … as if he saw a Spectre": Tucker's Proposals for American
Independence', *JHI*, 43 (1982), 439–60 (pp. 440–1, 460), argues that Tucker's Christianity
profoundly affected his political and economic thought. But, even if this was so, the
arguments he used were strictly secular.

behaviour. Doubtless such sermons were preached regularly thoughout this period, as in others. However, being directed at the illiterate poor, there was generally little incentive to publish them. Publication came in response to specific crises which led to an increase in the concern and interest of the educated classes and a desire to read such comforting compositions, and their appearance denotes the intensity of that concern.

The major crisis which changed the face of Christian political and social argument in England did not come until the 1790s. But that response was pre-figured in an increasing number of sermons between 1760 and 1790 which reflected the growing feeling of insecurity of the ruling classes. Disturbances such as the Wilkes demonstrations and the Gordon Riots, as well as the endemic food and harvest riots, resulted in a spate of publications on contentment and resignation. The arguments of the more radical reformers who were suspected of democratic sentiments led to the reinforcement of the theories concerning the divine nature of the social and economic hierarchy. The dispute and war with the American colonies led to some increase in such writings, but it was the period from the end of the war which saw the most marked growth. Just as the ideological tone of the episcopal Martyrdom Day sermons from 1782 became more conservative and authoritarian,[7] so the concern with the control of the poor occupied Christians more in the 1780s than in the preceding two decades.

The crisis of the early 1780s took many forms. The domestic political instability, the defeat in the American War and the imperial problems arising from unrest in Ireland and India, the problems of debt and taxation and the growing demand for parliamentary reform have already been considered.[8] In addition, the rapid rise in population, the impact of economic and social change in the countryside, the social dislocation which arose from urbanisation and from dramatic changes in the nature of employment led to an increase in pauperism and a degree of social instability which rightly caused alarm. The Gordon Riots in 1780 demonstrated the potential for violence of the urban mob. Although they did not spread into general insurrection, and other riots remained local and incidental, they filled propertied men with the fear of anarchy.

Compared to the panic of the winter of 1792–3, the heightened tension of the early 1780s may appear modest. But it was real enough and the clerical reaction to it wholly understandable. There was much concern with behaviour, morals and manners, and many were worried by the example set to the poor by the rich. This led, in June 1787, to George III's Proclamation against Vice and the subsequent foundation of the Proclama-

---

[7] See above, pp. 50–3.
[8] See above, p. 51.

tion Society, inspired by Wilberforce, to help enforce it.[9] In the Abbey Martyrdom Day sermons over half the references to the need for restraint in the period from 1760 to 1789 came after 1782. But, although the number of published arguments increased, those arguments did not change in kind. What is perhaps most significant of all is that those arguments were agreed by almost the entire field of Christian writers. Men who disagreed in their theology, ecclesiology, political theory and political practice were as one when discussing social theory. Any differences between them concerned the way in which the mechanism of restraint operated, not the necessity or the efficacy of that restraint. We shall, therefore, examine the nature of Christian teaching on the social and economic hierarchy, on poverty and the duty of contentment, on which there was virtually complete agreement, before going on to consider the effect of some theological and philosophical differences upon attitudes to the mechanism of restraint and the need for sanctions.

The social hierarchy
The concept of a divinely ordained hierarchy was accepted and preached by all of the Christians of the period who have been considered. The greater emphasis on this following the defeat in America is illustrated by the fact that both George Horne and William Jones chose to preach on it within five days of each other at Easter 1783. Horne insisted that the inequality of mankind was the result not of chance but of God's ordinance. The interdependence between rich and poor could be seen in both economic and spiritual terms. Economically, the rich could not live without the poor 'and they never support the poor but the poor have first supported them'. Spiritually, the poor made possible the divine duty of charity. Indeed, the real advantage the rich enjoyed over the poor arose from the fact that it is more blessed to give than to receive.[10]

Jones suggested that the social laws of God prescribed condescension, compassion and almsgiving for the rich, and contentment, industry and submission for the poor. Sarah Trimmer agreed that in apportioning different ranks, God provided for the good of the whole society.[11] On this

---

[9] Wilberforce, *Statement and Propositions from the Society for Giving Effect to His Majesty's Proclamation against Vice and Immorality* (London, 1970); Bristow, *Vice and Vigilance* (Dublin, 1977), pp. 38–9. The earliest ecclesiastical history of the period, J. Brewster, *A Secular Essay* (London, 1802), is obsessed with this question; see pp. 239–42, 291–7, 306–15. On the earlier movements see D. W. R. Bahlman, *The Moral Revolution of 1688* (New Haven, Connecticut, 1957). M. J. D. Roberts, 'The Society for the Suppression of Vice and its Early Critics 1802–12', *HJ*, 26 (1983), 159–76, brings out the essential differences between Victorian concepts and these earlier Evangelical ones. See also below, p. 130.

[10] Horne, 'Duty of Considering the Poor', *Works*, vol. 3, pp. 73–88 (pp. 75–80).

[11] Jones, 'Duty of Reviewing the Poor', *Works*, vol. 6, pp. 188–207 (pp. 188–95); S. Trimmer, *The Œconomy of Charity* (London, 1787), pp. 3, 11–12.

topic, far from being extreme, the high-church patriarchalists expressed the general view, not only of the Church of England, but of other groups as well. John Wesley confessed he was unable to understand why God gave some wealth, honour and power, and afflicted others with poverty – but as it was the will of providence, man must accept it.[12]

Those who argued that power rested in the people showed in their comments on hierarchy how far they were from any democratic or levelling tendencies. Richard Watson, in a sermon written in 1785 but not published until 1793, set out a range of arguments identical to those later used widely in the popular propaganda of 1792–3 to reconcile the lower orders to their lot. Joseph Berington argued in his *Essay on Depravity* (1788) that men in different situations in life had different duties, and the purpose of education was to teach subordination and discipline. Richard Price and Joseph Priestley were both prominent members of the bourgeoisie which sought to break the aristocratic hegemony, but neither of them had any taste for levelling.[13]

Nor did the new, secular-thinking conservatives, Josiah Tucker and William Paley. Tucker, in a Charity School sermon, suggested that the possibility of some social mobility should be held out as an incentive to the poor, but he agreed that the children of the poor should start from the lowest stages while the more genteel, refined and profitable trades should be reserved for the children of the wealthy and powerful. Paley also defended the necessity of the social hierarchy, although, predictably, he saw it decreed not by providence but by utility, and insisted that the distinction should be no greater than the principle required:

We recommend nothing adverse to subordinations which are established and necessary: but then it should be remembered, that subordination itself is an evil, being an evil to the subordinate, who are the majority, and therefore ought not to be carried a tittle beyond what the greater good, the peaceable government of the community, requires.

Again here, Paley was close to adopting a radical position and his view was untypical not only of his fellow clergy, but also of his fellow Christians.[14]

The poor

Attitudes to the poor and the duty of contentment also were widely shared.

[12] Wesley, Sermons 1771, *Works*, vol. 6, pp. 346–7.
[13] Watson, Dispensary Sermon, *Misc. T*, vol. 1, pp. 448–72; Berington, *An Essay on the Depravity of the Nation* (Birmingham, 1788), pp. 18, 23; Margaret Canovan, 'Paternalistic Liberalism: Joseph Priestley on Rank and Inequality', *ED*, 2 (1983), 22–37.
[14] Tucker, *A Sermon* . . . (London, 1766), p. 19; Paley, 'Principles', *Works*, vol. 4, pp. 283–4. See also T. A. Horne, 'Paley and Rights of Poor', pp. 51–70.

Great sympathy for the indigent was shown.[15] Watson, while observing that there must always be lower orders in every society, warned that the poor should not be looked down on as inferior beings purposely created to minister to the needs of their betters. Tucker warned against treating them as slaves and beasts of burden. They should be able to enjoy the fruits of their labour and have some hope of self-improvement. Horne stressed the dignity of the poor and urged the duty of charity.[16] Wesley, in contemplating the horrors of poverty, was comforted by the promise of resurrection.[17] Sympathy was tempered with an acceptance of the inevitability of poverty and a promise of recompense beyond the grave. William Jones reminded the poor that discontent was an act of rebellion against divine providence, and contentment was universally recommended.[18]

Bound up in their own bourgeois concerns, Price and Priestley gave little consideration to the poor. When Richard Price did turn his mind to the question in a sermon 'On Contentment' his views were wholly conventional. God had fixed a man's position in life and to be discontent with it was to question His providence. It was an act of disobedience and showed a failure to understand that, as God is a most *reason*able Being, whatever He decreed was for the best. This life must be considered in an eternal context and it was worth enduring discomforts on the journey to reach such a glorious destination as Heaven. The healthy, untroubled poor man might be much happier than the 'pampered voluptuary', ever open to temptation. However great man's sorrows, 'Death will soon end them, and amaze our souls with scenes now unknown'. This sermon, unpublished in Price's lifetime, could easily have come from the pen of Hannah More.[19]

Joseph Priestley devoted little more attention to the poor. In his protean and voluminous literary output, references to them are rare and largely incidental. In a *Sermon on the Slave Trade* (1788) he pointed out that the distinctions between men were temporary, being limited to this side of the grave; because they were the dispositions of providence they were for the benefit of all. In a collection of prayers he wrote for the use of Unitarian societies in 1783, the poor were almost entirely overlooked, but were included towards the end of a long and wide-ranging prayer for use on fasts. He asked that the poor should be industrious and frugal, and willingly

15 Practical action was, in this period, much greater than theoretical reflection. See G. F. A. Best, *Temporal Pillars* (Cambridge, 1964), pp. 137–45.

16 Watson, 'St Bride's Sermon' (1786), *SPO*, pp. 163–85 (pp. 170–1); Tucker, *Sermon* (1766), pp. 18–9; Horne, 'Duty of Considering the Poor', *Works*, vol. 3, pp. 80–1.

17 *Works*, vol. 4, p. 92. This comfort was not just one Wesley offered to others, but one he needed himself. In 1752 he had observed that his way of life 'is not pleasing to flesh and blood; and I would not do it, if I did not believe in another world' (Journal, *Works*, vol. 2, p. 252).

18 Jones, 'The Blessedness of Considering the Poor' (1786), *Works*, vol. 6, pp. 208–29 (p. 216).

19 Price, *Sermons on Various Subjects* (London, 1816), pp. 88–107.

submit to just laws and firm government; he ended by reminding them (and the Almighty) 'it is the study of all ranks and professions faithfully to discharge the proper duty of their place and station'.[20]

Restraint

All Christians agreed that religion was an important sanction and means of restraint on human will. On the question of how the mechanism of restraint operated, however, there were subtle and complex differences between them. To understand these it is necessary first to consider four theological and philosophical disagreements.[21] First, the Quinquarticular Controversy (over predestination, redemption, grace, justification and perseverance) divided the Calvinists from Arminians and Catholics. Despite Fletcher's polemics, the Calvinist position is more fairly described as solifidian than antinomian, but the emphasis placed on good works by Catholics, Arminian Anglicans and Methodists was certainly lacking in the insistence on justification by faith alone. A faith which stressed the importance of free-will and argued that redemption was not predetermined but depended, in part, on man's conduct on earth could, theoretically, be seen as more effective in restraining the passions. However, the role of perseverance in Calvinist theology must not be overlooked.

Secondly, the orthodox Christian doctrine of free-will conflicted with the necessarian ideas which Joseph Priestley inherited from David Hartley. These arose out of an essentially materialist theory of man and led Priestley to deny both the Thomist and the Traducian concepts of the soul. Priestley's critics, who included both Berington and Wesley, stressed the importance of free-will and man's moral responsibility for his conduct.[22]

Thirdly, there were differences about the fundamental nature of man which arose from the contrary doctrines of original sin and of progress and the perfectibility of mankind. While Berington maintained the Thomist position, it was the Augustinian formulation of the doctrine, strengthened by Protestant conceptions of the depravity of human nature, which informed most clerical thinking on the human passions. Price and Priestley, however, denied the doctrine of original sin, and therefore of the Atonement. Instead they joined French thinkers in expressing a faith in human progress and what Condorcet described as 'the doctrine of the indefinite

---

[20] Priestley, *Works*, vol. 15, p. 366; vol. 21, pp. 556–7. On the apparent contradictions in Priestley's social thought see M. Canovan, 'Paternalistic Liberalism'.

[21] These comments should be read in the light of the religious context outlined above in Chapter 2.

[22] Berington, *Letters on Materialism and Hartley's Theory of the Human Mind, Addressed to Dr Priestley* (London, 1776); Wesley, 'Thoughts on Necessity' (1774), *Works*, vol. 10, pp. 457–80.

perfectibility of the human race of which Turgot, Price and Priestley were the first and most brilliant apostles'.[23]

Fourthly, differences in theories of moral epistemology were important. Some considered that man had an innate moral sense based on rational intuition, others that morality was socially learned and that the church had an important role in teaching it.

The greatest stress was laid on the restraining role of religion by those who combined anti-Calvinist and anti-necessarian views with an acceptance of original sin and a belief in the need to teach morality. Some commented directly on the usefulness of religion to the state. George Horne often observed that many men said that religion was invented by priests and politicians to keep the poor in order, adding that it was good for that purpose at least. Wesley was aware, during the crisis of 1745, what immense service the preaching of submission and order could be to king and country. Watson, in 1783, stressed the importance of a resident clergy and argued that those who regarded priests as worthless were ignorant, not only of Christianity, but also of the science of government. Such a view could never be held, he argued, by anyone who understood the use of religion in enforcing morality, and so securing the communal good.[24] On this point, at least, the other bishops agreed with Watson. Christopher Wilson, one of the Younger Pitt's first appointments to the bench, spoke in 1785 of the importance of 'divine cement' in 'binding the restless ambition, or unbridled licentiousness of men, to the public welfare'. Robert Lowth, in 1767, had pointed out the ability of religion to 'control the inward and secret motions of the mind' and this awareness of the value of the Christian conscience acting as an interior policeman was very widespread.[25]

Religion, in this context, was seen not just as being useful, but as essential. Without it, 'the bond of human obligations will be as a thread of tow when it touches the fire'; to rely on secular philosophy to restrain the passions was like binding a tiger on a thread.[26] Richard Watson and Joseph Berington both expressed eloquently the widespread fear of the effect of Enlightenment irreligion which was growing in the 1770s. Philosophic self-interest, Berington insisted, would give free rein to individual selfishness and never lead to the public good. Watson argued that reason and natural religion were insufficient to civilise men, as was evidenced by the natives of Tahiti

---

[23] Condorcet, 'Esquisse d'un tableau historique des progrès de l'esprit humain', in *Condorcet: Selected Writings*, edited by K. M. Baker (Indianapolis, 1976), pp. 209–82 (pp. 232–3).

[24] Horne, 'Essays and Thoughts', *Works*, vol. 3, pp. 469–70; Wesley, 'Further Appeal to Men of Reason and Religion', *The Works*, edited by G. R. Cragg (Oxford, 1975), vol. 11, p. 315; Watson, 'Letter to the Archbishop of Canterbury' (1783), *SPO*, pp. 393–445 (pp. 413, 421).

[25] C. Wilson, *A Sermon . . .* (London, 1785), pp. 20–1; Lowth, *Sermon* (1767), p. 7; J. Cornwallis, *Sermon* (1782), p. 16; Horne, Assize Sermon (1773), *Works*, vol. 3, pp. 467–72.

[26] Wilson, *A Sermon*, p. 21; Horne, Assize Sermon (1773), *Works*, vol. 3, p. 470.

and New Zealand and by the American Indians. He also argued that the concept of natural law came from Christian writers, like Grotius and Puffendorf, not from pagan ones. He challenged Gibbon to find a better religion than Christianity for the coming generation, to animate their hopes, subdue their passions and make them better men.[27]

The need to restrain the passions was seen as critical. William Jones suggested that the truth of the doctrine of original sin could easily be confirmed by observation of man's natural depravity.[28] Bishop Egerton listed the passions in 1761 as 'pride, ambition, vanity, self-interest, hatred, envy'; George Horne's list in 1773 reflected the increase in public unrest and had a more political edge: 'anger, insolence, clamour, despondency, presumption, impetuosity'. Religious restraint of these 'turbulent passions' and 'unruly appetites of mankind' operated in two ways, through education and the teaching of morality, and by the threat of Hell and hope of Heaven.[29]

The concern over the need to restrain the poor, which increased markedly in the 1780s, in part reflected the growth of pauperism, the Gordon Riots, the problems of urbanisation and the growing radical questioning of the status quo. It was, in turn, reflected in the foundation of a number of societies to relieve and control the poor. It also saw a marked development in the provision of popular education in the form of Sunday and Charity Schools. Support for these was widespread.[30] None of the Christians examined above shared the view that the danger of teaching the poor to read was too great.[31] William Jones, perhaps in political terms the most reactionary of them all, recognised but discounted the danger in a charity school sermon in 1786. He argued that men should not destroy good opportunities in their attempt to avoid evil ones; schools would teach children their place in society and the religious duty of submission to providence. Sarah Trimmer noted the importance of Sunday schools in

[27] Berington, *Letters on Materialism*, p. 23; Watson, *Apology for Christianity*, pp. 208–16.

[28] Jones, 'Duty of Living Peacefully', *Works*, vol. 5, pp. 130–47 (p. 133).

[29] Egerton, *A Sermon* . . . (London, 1761), p. 12; Horne, Assize Sermon (1773), *Works*, vol. 3, pp. 466, 470; Pretyman-Tomline, *A Sermon* . . . (London, 1789), p. 16.

[30] On the range of attitudes, Harold Silver, *The Concept of Popular Education* (London, 1965), pp. 17–42; on episcopal views, R. A. Soloway, *Prelates and People: Ecclesiastical Social Thought in England, 1783–1852* (London, 1969), pp. 349–58; on Charity Schools, M. G. Jones, *The Charity Schools Movement* (London, 1964), pp. 73–96, 110–62; on the Sunday Schools the definitive study is T. W. Laqueur, *Religion and Respectability: Sunday Schools and Working Class Culture, 1780–1850* (New Haven, 1976); see especially his important analysis of the schools and social control, pp. 187–240, and his argument that the schools made an important contribution to radical culture; on religious education and industrial discipline, M. W. Flinn, 'Social Theory and the Industrial Revolution', in *Social Theory and Economic Change*, edited by Tom Burns and S. B. Saul (London, 1967), pp. 9–34; for a discussion of the issues on a local level, A. P. Wadsworth, 'The First Manchester Sunday Schools', *Bulletin of the John Rylands Library*, 33 (1951), 299–336.

[31] Laqueur, *Religion and Respectability*, pp. 125–7, also suggests such opposition was very limited.

controlling the poor, especially the children of servants, labourers and workmen. She produced entertaining tales, such as *The Servant's Friend* and *The Two Farmers*, for them to read, which are similar to those Hannah More wrote a decade later, though they lack her lightness of touch. Joseph Berington looked to religious education to remove the sources of discontent which threatened social stability and order, and praised the work of Robert Raikes of Gloucester. The Dean of Gloucester was equally enthusiastic, and the Archdeacon of Carlisle considered that to send an uneducated child out into the world injured the rest of mankind and was like turning out a mad dog or a wild beast into the streets.[32]

Sanctions

What made religious education so effective was the prospect it held out of a future life. This operated in two ways. First, it offered the poor the riches of immortality and so encouraged acceptance of temporary inequality and led to contentment. But it also carried the threat of judgment. Heaven was the reward for those who had successfully restrained their passions, Hell the eternal punishment for those who had failed.[33] Berington, in his *Letters on Materialism*, not only asserted the importance of free-will and man's responsibility to choose good not evil against Priestley's necessarianism, but also attacked Priestley's rejection of the doctrine of the soul. Although Priestley did believe in some form of eternal life, his materialism, Berington argued, weakened the Christian case. If men were to go on from Priestley's position to consider that death was the end of everything and meant total annihilation for both virtuous and vicious alike, then justice, goodness, vice and virtue were meaningless words in a world given over to chance, fate and confusion.[34]

Such eschatological concerns were, of course, absent in the Calvinist doctrine of redemption wherein judgment was predestined and did not, even in part, depend upon conduct. Accordingly the sermons of Robinson and Evans, like those of the Anglican Toplady, did not include such arguments. Although Joseph Priestley recognised that religion could be a great ally of the magistrate, he devoted little attention to the concept of restraint. His notion of human nature, as free of original sin and capable of perfection, gave him a view of the passions as being in little need of it. Price took an even more extreme line. His faith in an innate source of morality led

---

[32] Jones, 'Blessedness of Poor', *Works*, vol. 6, pp. 215–19; S. Trimmer, *Œconomy of Charity*, pp. 26–7, *The Two Farmers* (London, 1787), *The Servant's Friend*, second edition (London, 1787); Berington, *Essay on Depravity*, p. 22; Tucker, *Sermon* (1766), pp. 20–5; Paley, 'Principles', *Works*, vol. 4, p. 229.

[33] Soloway, *Prelates and Peoples*, p. 75, points out that the bishops were very restrained in the use of these arguments, but the same cannot always be said of parochial clergy, Dissenting ministers and some laymen.

[34] Berington, *Letters on Materialism*, p. 87.

him to lay less stress than Priestley on the need for moral education.[35]

However, amongst more orthodox Christians, restraint played a regular and important role. Both Tucker and Paley, whose theories of authority and obligation were largely secular, placed considerable emphasis on religious restraint. Indeed, it was only as an agent of restraint that Christianity played a really significant role in Paley's utilitarianism. In the Church of England more generally, the high-church patriarchalists, the latitudinarian contractarians and the bishops in the old Court Whig tradition all laid increasing stress upon it. Berington insisted that Catholics were especially well restrained as they were more carefully taught as children and more closely watched in later life.[36]

Recent assessments of the social and political effects of Methodism might lead one to expect a strong emphasis on restraint in Wesley's and Fletcher's writings, but there was in fact little explicit discussion of it. No arguments were advanced which were not shared by almost every other Christian writer. This is, of course, not to deny necessarily that Methodism had the effect attributed to it. The Arminian concentration upon good works as well as faith, and the attack upon predestination emphasised the importance of the Last Judgment, and the hope of salvation provided a powerful comfort to the poor. But any political effect was indirect and was less consciously referred to than by many in other denominations. The content of Methodist social teaching was very little different from that of the established church; more of the poor may have listened, but what was said was not peculiar.

Such elements of Christian social teaching were fairly constant over the centuries, but public awareness and discussion of their importance were increasing significantly in the 1770s and, especially, in the 1780s. This was in part a reaction to growing tension and unrest in society, to the failure in the American Struggle, the bourgeois challenge to the established power of the aristocracy, the growth of towns and the social dislocation which mobility involved, the growth of pauperism and Enlightenment ideas from France and the resurgence of the English radical tradition. However, despite this increased awareness of the importance of Christian social theory, such arguments continued to take second place until the 1790s. In the thirty years before 1789, Christian political thought continued to be dominated by discussion of the issues of authority, obligation and the right of rebellion, the lines of which had been clearly established during the Revolution Settlement in the late seventeenth century.

---

[35] Priestley, 'Considerations on the Difference of Opinions . . .' (1769), *Works*, vol. 21, p. 311; *Lectures on History*, pp. 349–50; 'Remarks on Blackstone', *Works*, vol. 22, p. 321; R. Price, *Evidence for a Future Period of Improvement* (London, 1787), pp. 42, 48; *Additional Observations*, pp. 30–2.

[36] *State and Behaviour*, p. 126.

Part II

Revolution, 1789–1804

7

The political and social context

The major themes

The political philosophy which dominated Britain for a century before the outbreak of the French Revolution consisted of two major elements, both of which drew upon religious arguments for their validation. The first gave spiritual justification to political authority, any authority, the powers-that-be; the second legitimised certain means of changing the form of government and explored the circumstances in which revolution was permissible. Only by maintaining a correct balance between these, so men believed, could they avoid either anarchy or despotism. Since it was widely agreed that the perfect balance was the British Constitution in largely its existing form, the educated members of the political nation could safely indulge in the luxury of abstract intellectual discussion of revolution without being regarded (except in moments of extreme political crisis) as subversive or a serious threat to the state.

The French Revolution – if not at once, at least after a few years – created quite a different intellectual climate by introducing on to the political stage a new character – *dēmos*. Abstract philosophical considerations somehow seemed inappropriate when faced with a violent mob; order, control and restraints rapidly acquired new value and urgency. The element in traditional theory which dealt with the varied forms of government disappeared from public debate most rapidly. The other element which looked at the religious origins of government and the spiritual basis of political obligation lasted rather longer and never completely disappeared from the scene, but that too declined relative to the great onrush of arguments stressing religious restraints and sanctions on social behaviour.

The arguments of Thomas Paine and other radical writers were also largely political, constitutional and philosophical in nature, and to an extent the established orders found their usual battlegrounds occupied by the radical forces.[1] Protestant Dissenters' and Catholics' claims to religious rights seemed a threat to the established church, just as the rights of man threatened the established governing classes in the state. The establishment certainly stood firm and argued its case on the traditional ground; there was no abandonment of this position as untenable. But it concentrated its major attack elsewhere, in a field which it had always occupied, but which now became the central arena.

While a few radical thinkers based their theory of human rights on religious foundations, most did not. In the 1790s, religious arguments were used mainly by the establishment to bolster up the traditional social order. It could easily be made to appear, both to radical and conservative, that the removal of religious faith was a prerequisite of social change.

The chronology of argument

The politico-religious arguments employed in Britain between 1789 and 1804 were closely related to the political and social events of the period and need to be set in a chronological context. The transition of emphasis from political to social theory can be clearly dated, though that transition was neither absolute nor universal. Both forms of argument were employed by both supporters and opponents of the French Revolution and, while the changes in the climate of predominant opinion towards France were very significant in the transition, the relationship was not a straightforward one. A number of outstanding works by Price, Priestley, Burke, Paine and others both stood out as landmarks in the intellectual process and provided focal points in the critical responses they evoked. There was also an extremely significant ground swell of sermons, pamphlets and so on from a wide spectrum of opinions, which itself evolved in attitude and arguments.

Reactions to the French Revolution

Many conservative thinkers had doubts about the desirability of the French Revolution well before the publication of Burke's *Reflections*. Bishops Porteus and Horsley and Mrs Hannah More all expressed reservations in their private writings, and William Jones of Nayland voiced them publicly from the pulpit of Canterbury Cathedral in September 1789. On 23 July 1789 Bishop Warren of Bangor led the House of Lords in turning down a proposal from the Commons to celebrate a day of thanksgiving for the French

---

[1] Thomas Cooper reviewed the major theories of the origin of government and political obligation in his 'Propositions Respecting the Foundations of Civil Government', read to the Literary and Philosophical Society of Manchester in 1787 and published by them in 1790; reprinted in Cooper, *A Reply to Mr Burke's Invective*, second edition (London, 1792).

Revolution.[2] But generally opinion was sympathetic towards the French for the first two or even three years of the Revolution and this was reflected in the balance of argument. Favourable views of events in France came from a fairly wide range of the denominational spectrum, from the Catholic Joseph Berington to the Unitarian Joseph Towers, and from the Baptist minister Robert Hall to Richard Watson, Bishop of Llandaff, though the latter did express a little caution as to what might ensue.[3]

The issues were debated, by both sides, predominantly in traditional, constitutional-philosophic terms, at least until the publication of Part Two of Paine's *Rights of Man* in February 1792. Richard Price's *Discourse on the Love of our Country*, delivered at the Old Jewry Meeting House on 4 November 1789, is best remembered for his welcome to the French Revolution and his reference to Simeon's *Nunc Dimittis*. But this was alluded to only in the peroration; the bulk of his discourse related to the 1688 Revolution and the discussion was on constitutional lines.[4] A few months later, Joseph Priestley in his *Familiar Letters to the Inhabitants of Birmingham* (1790) defended religious liberty and the rights of Dissenters against a church establishment in terms of the principles of political philosophy. Most of these writers' critics responded using the same form of argument.[5]

However, the most formidable of these responses, Burke's *Reflections*, went far beyond its immediate target both in the profundity of its thought and in the nature of its argument. It illustrated the complexity of the transition from political to social predominance as the book itself moved from one form of argument to another. Having examined the constitutional status of the 1688 Revolution and its essential differences from recent events in France, Burke rejected abstract philosophical approaches to political problems and concentrated upon the dire social consequences of the attack upon the French church. But Burke was in advance of his day in these sociological concerns as in many other considerations, and most of his critics challenged him on constitutional-philosophic grounds.

Thomas Paine's *Rights of Man* Part One (February 1791) set the tone for a

---

[2] LPL, MS 2103, f. 27 (Porteus Notebook, 1786–1800); LPL, MS 1767, ff. 202–3 (Horsley, Letters and Papers); More, Letter to Mrs Boscawen, in *Memoirs of the Life and Correspondence of Mrs Hannah More*, edited by W. Roberts, 3 vols. (London, 1835), vol. 2, p. 201; Jones, Sermon, 20 September 1789, *Works*, vol. 5, p. 284; LPL, MS 2103, f. 25.

[3] J. Berington, *The History of the Reign of Henry II* (Birmingham, 1790), Preface, p. iii (but compare F. Plowden, *The Case Stated* (London, 1791), p. 15); Joseph Towers, *Thoughts on the Commencement of a New Parliament* (London, 1790), p. 128; R. Hall, 'Christianity Consistent with a Love of Freedom' (1791), *Works*, vol. 3, pp. 21–2; R. Watson, *Charge . . . to the Clergy of the Diocese of Llandaff June 1791* (London, 1792), p. 4.

[4] R. Price, *A Discourse on the Love of our Country* (London, 1789), pp. 49, 27–8.

[5] W. Coxe, *A Letter to the Rev. Richard Price* (London, 1790), p. 13; R. Luke, *For the Defence of the Constitution in Church and State* (Exeter, 1790?); C. E. de Coetlogon, *God; and the King: . . .*, Accession Day sermon, St Paul's (London, 1790), pp. 6–18; Spencer Madan, *A Letter to Dr Priestley* (Birmingham, 1790).

host of other replies to Burke, many of which were more erudite, most less incisive and none more influential. George Rous, James Mackintosh, Thomas Christie, Brooke Boothby, Benjamin Bousfield and many others, like Paine, concentrated on constitutional issues and philosophical principles and argued in an abstract fashion on man's natural rights. The two replies to Burke which addressed themselves more directly to his social arguments, those from Mary Wollstonecraft and Capel Lofft, interestingly predated Paine, being printed in the last few weeks of 1790. Defenders of Burke and opponents of Paine *et al.*, like Samuel Cooper and Edward Tatham, employed the traditional Christian arguments in support of the established constitutional regime. The debate raged within the walls of Dissent as well. On 24 July 1791, in the context of the Birmingham Riots, John Clayton preached a sermon on *The Duty of Christians to Magistrates* forcefully asserting the traditional conservative arguments, only to bring a hornet's nest upon his head from fellow Dissenters, who urged the politico-philosophical principles of the religious and civil rights of man.[6] Between the publication of Parts One and Two of Paine's *Rights of Man*, the debate between supporters and opponents of the revolution in France was hotting up, the most notorious incident being the 'Church and King' mob riots in Birmingham against Priestley and his fellow Dissenters in July 1791.[7] But on the calmer, intellectual level, the argument remained predominantly political, constitutional and philosophical.

The twelve months which followed the publication of Part Two of *Rights of Man*, in February 1792, saw a significant change in both the political and intellectual climate in Britain. If one compares John Cartwright's *Letter to the Duke of Newcastle* of 1792 with his *Letter to a Friend at Boston* of 1793, one finds a broadly similar content but a profoundly different mood. In 1792 he thanked God and His divine providence for the French Revolution with great joy and enthusiasm, while a year later he maintained that position in a defensive and apologetic manner. The reasons for Cartwright's change of mood were largely patriotic ones occasioned by the outbreak of war between Britain and France in February 1793, but the general change of climate was more complex. During 1792, *Rights of Man* was widely distributed amongst the lower orders in Britain, despite a proclamation against

---

6 *A Consolatory Letter to the Rev. John Clayton from Fidelia* (London, 1791); *Remarks on a Sermon . . . by the Rev. John Clayton: in Three Letters to a Friend by a Protestant Dissenter* (London, 1791).

7 For contemporary accounts see A. Holt, *Joseph Priestley*, pp. 154–74; Bessie Belloc, *In a Walled Garden* (London, 1895), p. 50; and John Waddington, *Congregational History 1700–1800* (London, 1876), pp. 652–9. For recent assessments see R. B. Rose, 'The Priestley Riots of 1791', *PP*, 18 (1960), 68–88; E. Robinson, 'New Light on the Priestley Riots', *HJ*, 3 (1960), 73–5; J. Stevenson, *Popular Disturbances in England 1700–1870* (London, 1979), pp. 137–42. On loyalism and 'Church and King' riots in Manchester see J. Bohstedt, *Riots and Community Politics in England and Wales 1790–1810* (Cambridge, Massachusetts, 1983), pp. 100–25.

seditious writings being issued in May. Radical societies, which helped distribute copies, were established in many parts of the country and grew in number and members.

These developments disturbed the authorities all the more in the light of the way the revolution in France was evolving. In the autumn and winter of 1792–3 many Britons were shocked in turn by the September massacres, the abolition of the monarchy and the trial and execution of Louis XVI. Alarm was added to shock by the French military victories at Valmy in September and Jemappes in November and by the suggestion of the ensuing Edict of Fraternity that the revolution should be spread to other countries. In the three months which led up to the outbreak of war between France and Britain on 1 February 1793, the established orders in Britain had been devoting much of their energies to defeating the Jacobin enemy within. Their fear of serious trouble in Britain, if not realistic, was real. The Sheffield Constitutional Society, for one, congratulated the French Convention on its military victories, and many other societies established links with Paris. Rumours of a radical plot to seize London were readily believed in this atmosphere of fear, apprehension and dismay.[8]

Loyalist Associations were established all over the country to combat the radical societies, and John Reeves founded the Association for Preserving Liberty and Property against Republicans and Levellers. This society poured out a flood of propaganda pamphlets, some designed for an educated readership, others of a very popular nature, in the months of November and December 1792 and January 1793. There is a smell of panic behind these forcefully and urgently argued pieces. The popular pamphlets were eclectic in their reasoning. Any consideration which could help maintain public order was thrown into the pot. Religious arguments often appeared as a last, fine-meshed net to catch those who had eluded the looser weave of the secular arguments. William Jones appealed to the lower orders in the guise of John Bull and, as one would expect, traditional arguments of obligation flowed from his pen. While the pamphlets were also very much concerned with social unity and cohesion, these themes were largely explored in secular terms: the full force of religious restraint and sanctions was not urged on the poor until the Cheap Repository Tracts of 1795–8.[9]

---

[8] C. Emsley, 'The London "Insurrection" of December 1792: Fact, Fiction or Fantasy?', *JBS*, 17 (1978), 66–86; Austin Mitchell, 'The Association Movement of 1792–3', *HJ*, 4 (1961), 56–77; D. E. Ginter, 'The Loyalist Association Movement of 1792–93 and British Public Opinion', *HJ*, 9 (1966), 179–90; M. J. Quinlan, *Victorian Prelude: A History of English Manners 1700–1830* (1941, reprinted London, 1965), pp. 68–100.

[9] These pamphlets are more fully discussed in my 'British Counter-Revolutionary Popular Propaganda in the 1790s', in *Britain and Revolutionary France: Conflict, Subversion and Propaganda*, edited by Colin Jones (Exeter, 1983), pp. 53–69. See also E. C. Black, *The Association: British Extraparliamentary Political Organisation, 1769–93* (Cambridge, Massachusetts, 1963), pp. 233–74.

In the more intellectual works of 1792–3, the political, constitutional, philosophical arguments of authority and obligation were still set out, but they had increasingly to share the stage with sociological arguments of control, sanction and restraint. The episcopal attack on France was vigorous in March and April 1793; the national enemy was denounced as immoral, unprincipled and quite simply 'wicked'.[10] While many, like the Warden of St Mary's College, Winchester, G. I. Huntingford, stressed the vital role of religion as a restraint on man's behaviour, others reiterated traditional views of constitutional obligation, like the under-master of Eton College, W. Langford, in a sermon entitled *Obedience to the Established Laws and Respect to the Person of the Administrator Are the Joint Support of Civil Society.*[11]

By the end of 1793 the emphasis had switched from predominantly political, constitutional, philosophical arguments to predominantly social ones of control and social cohesion, of morality, individual belief and restraint. The former style of argument never disappeared; it remained a significant weapon in the arsenal, but from 1793 it was never again the paramount one. General opinion had at last reached the position Burke had occupied in the *Reflections* three years earlier and his social arguments were then more frequently repeated and challenged. William Godwin, in his *Enquiry Concerning Political Justice* (1793), vigorously attacked religious restraints and sanctions, but his work had little influence beyond his immediate circle.[12] The balance of the new establishment approach was well displayed in George Pretyman-Tomline's *Charge* to the clergy of the Lincoln Diocese in May and June 1794. This politically minded bishop urged his clergy to teach subordination and restraint as Christian virtues. After nine pages stressing the necessity of these religious principles in society, he reviewed in only six lines the religious basis of political obligation.[13] While Pretyman-Tomline delivered this charge, his old pupil Pitt acted firmly against the radicals, arresting their leaders and suspending habeas corpus.

But the challenge remained, and in 1795 there was still much to alarm the established orders. Hardy and Tooke had been acquitted of treason and Thelwall was active. A poor harvest resulted in food shortages in the autumn and winter of 1795–6, and in October the king's coach was attacked as he drove through Hyde Park. The government responded with two acts

---

[10] R. Lowth, *A Sermon Preached in Oxford Chapel on Sunday March 19, 1793* (London, 1793), pp. 6–7, 10; R. Beadon, *A Sermon Preached before the Lords . . . April 19, 1793* (London, 1793), p. 12.

[11] G. I. Huntingford, *A Sermon Preached before the Honourable House of Commons . . .* (London, 1793), pp. 9, 16–19; W. Langford, *Obedience to the Established Laws and Respect to the Person of the Administrator* (Eton, 1793).

[12] In June 1794, Bishop Porteus of London had barely heard of Godwin and had not read *Political Justice*. See LPL, MS 2103, f. 66. But Godwin acquired some following at Cambridge: see Schneider, *Wordsworth's Education*, pp. 116–17.

[13] (London, 1794), pp. 9–20.

against treasonable practices and seditious meetings; Hannah More began issuing the Cheap Repository Tracts; restraint was urged from pulpits and presses. More's *Tracts* were issued at the rate of about three a month from 1795 to 1798 and were designed to reaffirm the lower orders in the Christian faith and so turn them away from the temptations of revolution.[14] They did reflect the 'conspiracy theory' in 1797, but this led only to an intensification of their social arguments of Christian restraint and religious sanctions. More claimed, in 1799, that nearly two million had been sold for a halfpenny or a penny, not only by booksellers but also by hawkers and fairstall-holders. Many were given away, to children, employees, soldiers, sailors, paupers and prisoners. The tracts responded to the food crises of 1795–6 and to the fortunes of the war. 'The Loyal Sailor; or, No Mutineering' (1797) was the most direct response to a political incident; generally the tracts urged solidarity and hope.[15]

But the establishment did not have a monopoly on the use of religious arguments. The vigorous and immature Samuel Taylor Coleridge gave a series of lectures in Bristol in 1795 on politics and religion which stressed the revolutionary nature of Christ's message. The period from 1794 to 1796 saw an outpouring of millenarian interpretations of the French Revolution. These took both radical and conservative forms, but the radical ones predominated. Richard Brothers's writings passionately and sometimes incoherently denounced London as Sodom and predicted the destruction of the monarchy if the war with France were continued. An anonymous critic advised Pitt to prosecute Brothers as a Jacobin. But Brothers was not a serious revolutionary threat; he declared himself Prince of the Hebrews and called on George III to hand over his crown, power and authority, as God commanded. Others, like S. Whitchurch, combined their chiliastic fervour with a little more political realism.[16] Millenarian views were not of course limited to a lunatic fringe. Priestley combined them with his concepts of progress and perfectibility; J. Bicheno, the Dissenting minister and schoolmaster, discussed millenarian prophecies calmly and drew Newton and Warburton into his argument; nor was Bishop Horsley the only senior establishment cleric to debate the issues seriously.[17]

[14] The best general account of the tracts is in M. G. Jones, *Hannah More* (Cambridge, 1952), pp. 125–50.
[15] H. More, *Cheap Repository Shorter Tracts* (London, 1798), pp. 419–26, *Cheap Repository Shorter Tracts*, new edition (London, 1799), Introduction, p. iv. See below, pp. 130–1, 158–9.
[16] R. Brothers, *A Revealed Knowledge of the Prophecies and Times. Book the First . . .* (London, 1794); *A Revealed Knowledge of the Prophecies and Times . . . Book the Second . . .* (London, 1794), pp. 21–2, 26, 106; *A Word of Admonition to the Right Hon. William Pitt . . .* (London, 1795), pp. 12–13; S. Whitchurch, *Another Witness! . . .* (London, 1795), pp. 4–5, 12.
[17] J. Priestley, *A Sermon Preached at the Gravel Pit Meeting . . . April 19th, 1793* (London, 1793), p. 27; J. Bicheno, *A Word in Season . . . Fast Day, February 25, 1795* (London, 1795); *The*

The impact of war

The war between Britain and France in its various phases also provided a crucial context for the discussion of politico-religious issues. Not only was the morality of war and the compatibility of Christianity and patriotism discussed, but hope was also offered in times of defeat and, especially amidst the disasters of 1797, Britons were urged to stand firm and remain loyal. Many radicals felt a conflict between their political beliefs and their patriotism; the authorities were able to bracket both sedition and treason as 'pro-French'.[18] In the *Letters on a Regicide Peace*, Burke insisted that no peace should be made with France until the revolution there had been defeated and both church and state restored. In 1797, after the links between infidelity and revolution were (allegedly) established by Barruel and Robison and the conspiracy theory widely accepted, most conservative clerics took the same view and urged the continuation of the war until French atheism was extirpated.[19]

The peace of 1802 and the resumption of the war brought only minor and temporary variations to this argument. Indeed, the advent of Napoleon strengthened rather than weakened that resolve. The so-called 'Republican Bishop', Richard Watson, delivered a passionate anti-Enlightenment, anti-Revolution, anti-French Charge to the clergy of Llandaff in June 1798; so effective was it deemed that an extract was reprinted as a propaganda broadsheet.[20] Watson had, two years earlier, replied to Thomas Paine's *Age of Reason* which, in its outright deism and attack upon the truth of the Bible, had confirmed many in their suspicion that irreligion, sedition and support for the national enemy were synonymous.[21] The greater toleration of religion by the Directory, and Napoleon's reconciliation of church and state in the Concordat of April 1802 did little to pacify British religious thinkers;

     Probable Progress and Issue of the Commotions ... (London, 1797); for Horsley, see below Chapter 11. See also Fruchtman, 'The Apocalyptic Politics of Richard Price'; C. Garrett, 'Joseph Priestley, the Millennium and the French Revolution', *JHI*, 34 (1973), 51–66, and *Respectable Folly: Millenarians and the French Revolution in France and England* (Baltimore, 1975); J. F. C. Harrison, *The Second Coming: Popular Millenarianism, 1780–1850* (London, 1979); David Hempton, 'Evangelicalism and Eschatology', *JEH*, 31 (1980), 179–94.

[18] Deryck Lovegrove, 'English Evangelical Dissent and the European Conflict, 1789–1815', *SCH*, 20 (1983), 263–76, examines the views of radical Dissenters, and William Stafford, 'Religion and the Doctrine of Nationalism in England at the Time of the French Revolution and Napoleonic Wars', *SCH*, 18 (1982), 381–95, discusses general attitudes to patriotism and nationalism.

[19] A. de Barruel, *Memoirs of ... Jacobinism* (London, 1797); J. Robison, *Proofs of a Conspiracy ...* (London, 1797). See below, pp. 153–6.

[20] R. Watson, 'Charge' 1798, in *Misc. T*, vol. 1, pp. 126–50; *The Bishop of Llandaff's Thoughts on the French Invasion* ... (London, n.d. [1798?]). Watson's change of view was more apparent than real. See Brain, 'Richard Watson', pp. 234–55, 266–7.

[21] R. Watson, *An Apology for the Bible* ... (London, 1796). A. O. Aldridge, *Man of Reason: The Life of Thomas Paine* (London, 1960), stresses that Paine's deism was an attack on atheism as well

for most, France remained the home of blasphemy and sedition and was a dire warning of what Britain must avoid.

Denominational issues

The development of British politico-religious thought between 1789 and 1804 was, of course, dominated by the French Revolution and the fear of Jacobin activity in Britain, but these were not the whole context. For the first part of the period, at any rate, an amount of unfinished business continued. While the attack upon the Catholic church in France deeply affected English Catholics, they also had plenty to concern them at home. Negotiations with the government had been proceeding for a second Relief Bill which would at last free English Catholics from the penal laws. This was finally revised by the parliamentary draftsman on 25 March 1789 and became law on 10 June 1791. The intervening period saw divisions within the Catholic community and crises of conscience for individuals arising principally from the wording of the new oath Catholics were to be required to take. The dispute over this reflected crucially different interpretations of the fine lines to be drawn between the spiritual allegiance claimed by the papacy and the temporal allegiance claimed by the state. Some regarded the state's claim as invading the spiritual sphere, others believed the church's position involved temporal issues.

Reactions to the oath revealed and intensified two separate traditions in the English Catholic community. What might be called the *Garden of the Soul* tradition rested on the quietistic and pietistic attitudes of Richard Challoner and was led by most of the hierarchy of vicars apostolic; it was intensely loyal to the papacy and had no real political ambitions. By contrast there was the 'Enlightenment' tradition led by Joseph Berington and Charles Butler. This group dominated the Catholic Committee, which urged the Bill upon the government, and later formed the Cisalpine Club in April 1792. Its members had been profoundly influenced by the critical methodology of the Enlightenment and accepted a much higher degree of political secularisation than the Ultramontanes. They saw the line dividing politics and religion as fairly wide and clear, and were unwilling to be deprived of the opportunity to involve themselves in the political affairs of their nation by the restraints imposed by a reactionary papacy. They were, they claimed, Catholics, but not papists.

The oath as enshrined in the Second Relief Act (1791) was finally one

as on Christianity, and that Watson's reply was, in part, a capitulation. But he fails to link Watson's cautious view with his style of churchmanship and his attitude to biblical scholarship. F. K. Prochaska, 'Thomas Paine's *The Age of Reason* Revisited', *JHI*, 33 (1972), 561–76, suggests Paine's book was less influential than its critics feared. On Gilbert Wakefield's response to Paine and Watson see Prochaska, 'English State Trials in the 1790s: A Case Study', *JBS*, 13 (1973), 63–82.

acceptable to the conservatives and the vicars apostolic, but the Cisalpine Club continued to challenge the political, ecclesiastical and intellectual outlooks of the Ultramontane hierarchy. Catholic writers on political and church–state issues in the 1790s need to be understood in this context, none more so than the three Plowden brothers Charles, Francis and Robert. At a time in the mid 1790s when most Christian writers were concentrating on social arguments of restraint and sanction, the Plowdens in particular and English Catholics in general continued to debate the constitutional, philosophical and legal arguments. This was partly because, in the eyes of their contemporaries, Catholics still needed to prove their loyalty to the state, partly because of the issues involved in the Cisalpine–Ultramontane dispute, but also because the entire spiritual–constitutional dilemma which had faced English Catholics ever since the Protestant Reformation remained largely unresolved.[22] The Act of Union with Ireland in 1801, which brought thousands of Irish Catholics directly under the Westminster parliament, had little immediate impact upon Catholic political argument in Britain. Its significance lay in the future.

The common view that Catholics tended to despotism and extreme Protestants to republicanism may in part explain why relief acts were passed for English Catholics in 1791 and Irish ones in 1793, while the continuing attempts to repeal the Test and Corporation Acts for Protestant Dissenters failed.[23] In the late 1780s the movement for repeal appeared to be gathering strength and the Protestant Dissenting Deputies achieved a higher degree of unity and agreement on details than was usual. However, on 2 March 1790 Fox's motion for Repeal was defeated by 294 votes to 105, while a year earlier the rejection had been only by 124 votes to 104. The vigour of the Dissenters' campaign stimulated their opponents not their supporters, though it is far from clear that it was events in France which made the crucial difference. Certainly the arguments of the Dissenters for religious rights and of the French for political ones had much in common, not least a normative vocabulary. But the threat to the established church probably influenced Members of Parliament more than fear of revolution in March 1790. As the revolution developed, however, and especially after the events

---

[22] Bernard Ward, *The Dawn of the Catholic Revival in England 1781–1803*, 2 vols. (London, 1909) provides valuable detail but is excessively anti-Cisalpine. It needs to be read in conjunction with E. Duffy's dissertation 'Joseph Berington', and J. P. Chinnici, *The English Catholic Enlightenment* (Shepherdstown, 1980). For a strong attack on Berington's support for the French Revolution, see Charles Plowden, *Remarks on a Book Entitled Memoirs of Gregorio Panzani, Preceded by an Address to the Rev. Joseph Berington* (Liège, 1794), pp. 35–8.

[23] When Priestley invited Berington to attend the Birmingham 'Revolution Dinner' in July 1791, Berington (in a significant move from his pre-revolution attitude) replied, 'No Sir; we Catholics stand better with Government than you Dissenters, and we will not make common cause with you' (quoted from a contemporary letter in Belloc, *In a Walled Garden*, p. 50).

of 1792–3, the French and revolutionary factors were more substantial and repeal was not a serious possibility again until the 1820s.

Fox's motion of 11 May 1792, which was based on the Unitarian petition, stood even less chance of success. The formation of the Unitarian Society in 1791 gave a more formal existence to those who had long held Arian, Socinian and unitarian views, which technically placed them outside of the provisions of the Toleration Act. But the political stance of men like Joseph Priestley and the apparent similarity to French enlightened deists made them even more suspect than the orthodox Old Dissenters. The main result of Fox's bill was to elicit a speech from Burke which contained one of the finest and clearest expositions of his views on church–state relationships. However, these attempts by Dissenters and Unitarians to win greater civil liberties led them into the discussion of religious rights and so strengthened the constitutional, philosophical and legal area of debate, at least until the critical winter of 1792–3. Some also chose to stress their political loyalty to the king, though much of this took a purely conventional form.[24] Others, like the Norwich Baptist minister Mark Wilks and the Exeter Unitarian Thomas Kenrick, openly supported the French cause.[25]

The unfinished business which thus continued to occupy the denominations in the early years of the French Revolution led them into traditional constitutional and philosophical argument. As the revolution developed and these issues were allowed to fade from the foreground of public debate, so the denominational strife in England abated somewhat. 'Job Nott' declared, first in January 1793 and through to his eleventh edition in 1798, that he didn't care what the creed of a loyal man was:

> Dissenter, – Churchman, – Catholic,
> Whatever their persuasion,
> Good subjects are to me alike,
> Of all denominations.[26]

The welcome accorded to the French émigré clergy was warm and widespread; never had Catholic priests and bishops enjoyed such a reception in England since the reign of Mary Tudor. They were helped not only by traditional sympathisers like Burke, but also by Evangelicals such as Han-

---

[24] Burke, 'Speech', *Works*, vol. 6, pp. 113–26; B. L. Manning, *The Protestant Dissenting Deputies* (Cambridge, 1952); R. W. Davies, *Dissent in Politics 1780–1830* (London, 1971). See also LPL, MS 2103, ff. 26–7 on the 1790 application. On the question of toleration generally in the 1790s see Barlow, *Citizenship and Conscience*, pp. 272–94, and Henriques, *Religious Toleration*, pp. 61–7.

[25] M. Wilks, *The Origin and Stability of the French Revolution* (Norwich, 1791); C. B. Jewson, 'Norwich Baptists and the French Revolution', *Baptist Quarterly*, 24 (1972), 209–15; A. Brockett, *Nonconformity in Exeter, 1650–1875* (Manchester, 1962), pp. 142–5.

[26] J. Nott, *The Life and Adventures . . . .*, eleventh edition (Birmingham, 1798), p. 25.

nah More.[27] Burke asserted that the danger was not to a denomination, but to all religion. If church and constitution fell in England, he warned his son in February 1792, it would be replaced, not by Presbyterianism or Catholicism, but by an atheistic order.[28] If anyone doubted this, the conspiracy theory of 1797 generally disillusioned them. It would be going too far to speak of the denominations working together against the infidel threat in the later 1790s, but at least the denominational conflict cooled for a while as the enemy without was challenged. By 1804 the sectarian conflict was coming into the open again and passionate energy was being expended upon it, but the problems had been developing in the earlier quieter period.[29]

It was in the late 1790s that a great expansion in Methodism took place, and the more actively proselytising Dissenters, such as the Congregationalists and the Particular Baptists, also made many converts. Wesleyan numbers rose from 77,000 in 1796 to 87,000 in 1801 and 103,000 in 1806, and the establishment of the New Connexion in 1797 accounted for another 5,000 Methodist souls.[30] This Methodist schism gave rise to important discussions on the role of authority and liberalism in church government; Alexander Kilham's more radical views were rejected by Wesley's church, and the New Connexion adopted a stance which was liberal in its politics as well as its ecclesiology. The Church of England felt threatened, especially by the means the Methodists employed – notably that of itinerary. This was adopted by Baptists and Congregationalists as well as Methodists; indeed it was the Baptist Robert Hall who provided the most vigorous defence of 'village preaching' against Bishop Horsley's accusation of sedition, arguing the case for religion as a restraint and sanction.[31] But the major phase in that debate came after 1804. From 1794 to 1804 the surface was relatively free of denominational storms. Then, even more completely than in the early 1790s, events in France and the war dominated the context of politico-religious argument in England.

---

[27] D. Bellenger, 'The Émigré Clergy and the English Church, 1789–1815', *JEH*, 34 (1983), 392–410 (pp. 393–5).

[28] Burke, *Works*, vol. 6, pp. 69–70.

[29] The complex and diverse effects of the French Revolution upon the ecumenical activities of Anglican and Dissenting Evangelicals are fully analysed in R. H. Martin, *Evangelicals United: Ecumenical Stirrings in Pre-Victorian Britain 1795–1830* (London, 1983), esp. pp. 27–8. Also, see below, Chapter 13.

[30] Figures based on A. D. Gilbert, *Religion and Society in Industrial England . . . 1740–1914* (London, 1976), pp. 30–9.

[31] For Horsley see below, Chapter 12. R. Hall, 'Fragment on Village Preaching', 1801, 1802, *Works*, vol. 3, pp. 333–84.

8

Political theory and the rights of man

Political obligation

Of all the elements in the traditional political-constitutional-philosophical style of argument the theme of political obligation was most firmly fixed in scripture and theology. Hardly surprisingly, therefore, it was the issue most discussed in this sphere between 1789 and 1804, though that discussion was mostly focussed in the earlier part of that period. The nature of that obligation continued to be interpreted in a variety of ways.

The Church of England

The Dean of Canterbury, George Horne, delivered from the pulpit of his cathedral church, on 25 October 1789, a classic restatement of the establishment position. Citing the traditional texts from SS Peter and Paul, he asserted that the Bible made clear that 'the law of God enjoins obedience to every government settled according to the constitution of the country in which it subsists'. Horne proceeded to argue a case much closer to the balanced episcopal view than he had earlier in his career; though not yet in the Court Whig tradition, at least he was less obviously an unreconstituted patriarchalist. Men did have rights and need not submit unconditionally to government, but those rights were clearly expressed in the laws and constitution of the country.

Horne thus distanced himself from his friend William Jones of Nayland, who had delivered a passionately pro-royalist sermon from the same pulpit a month earlier. He had denounced the French roundly and asserted the divine preference was for royal government. So the paths of the high-church patriarchalists diverged. Horne's adoption of the more balanced and reasoned orthodox view led him eighteen months later to the Bishopric of Norwich. Jones's passionate royalism and love of controversy led him, under the pseudonym of John Bull, to produce a set of popular pamphlets in the winter of 1792–3 which stressed the religious obligation to obey kings. In practice the divergence was slighter than it appeared. In the *Charge* written for his primary visitation, Bishop Horne stressed the divine nature of government and the Christian's obligation to submit to it. Nor was Jones's vigorous line unpopular with the establishment; when the twelve volumes of his *Collected Works* appeared in 1801, sixteen bishops were among the subscribers with the Archbishop of Canterbury taking eight sets – a significantly greater degree of support than most such publications received.[1]

Political obligation remained an important theme of the annual episcopal Martyrdom Day sermon before the House of Lords, until these lapsed after 1795.[2] In January 1789, Bishop Pretyman-Tomline, in the context of an impeccable establishment sermon, had stressed the limits of obedience and the benefits of a liberal government in a balanced constitution. When Hannah More read Pretyman-Tomline's 1794 *Charge* to his diocesan clergy, she rejoiced that the moderation and balance of five years earlier remained. Some government supporters hated anarchy so much they seemed to recommend despotism; why, she asked, 'to prove that Scylla is a destructive rock, must it be implied that Charybdis is a safe shore?'

In fairness, the straits were difficult ones for the establishment to steer a clear course through. Both elements of the argument were dangerous in isolation. In times of political crisis there was, of course, a tendency to play down themes like the limits of obedience, the variety of forms of government acceptable to God, and the legitimate reasons for rebelling against an established form of government and replacing it with another. But to ignore these limits entirely and to interpret the apostolic injunctions to submission absolutely would be, in effect, to advocate passive obedience and non-resistance, which virtually everyone agreed were 'exploded theories' and quite unacceptable.

In practice, certain characteristics of the pre-1789 argument did disappear. First the references to English history went. Before 1790, argument after argument was related to 1688 or evoked the shades of Charles I and the Civil War. From 1790 such references were almost entirely absent from Anglican sermons. Burke, of course, took the bull by the horns and discussed 1688 at length, and other writers (especially Catholics such as Potts and the Plowden brothers) raised historical issues, but they were rarely heard from establishment pulpits. Almost as rare was direct discussion of the legitimacy of revolution; such a possibility was never denied, but it was

---

[1] Horne, 'Submission to Government . . . a Sermon', 25 October 1789, *Works*, vol. 3, pp. 384–97; Jones, 'Popular Commotions to Precede the End of the World . . . a Sermon', 25 October 1789, *Works*, vol. 5, pp. 274–95. Of the Bull tracts see, especially, *One Pennyworth of Truth from Thomas Bull to his Brother John* (London?, 1792); Horne, 'Intended Charge', *Works*, vol. 4, pp. 507–38; Jones, *Works*, vol. 1, Subscription List.

[2] There was no sermon in 1792 as parliament was not sitting on 30 January in that year. Bishop's Horsley's 1793 sermon is fully discussed below, pp. 164–5. There were sermons from 1807 to 1810, but none thereafter. Their lapsing was in accord with the general abandonment of historical arguments which drew attention to the English revolution.

embarrassing to debate at such an inopportune juncture. The argument concerning possible alternative *forms* of government was dominated by Dissenters, but even this discussion, at its height in 1790–1, fell away significantly after 1792. While these most obviously provocative, dangerous and negative elements of the theory could be abandoned, the balance had to be maintained to avoid imputations of passive obedience and despotism. Accordingly there was some discussion of the proper limits of obedience. It was made clear that it was neither absolute nor unconditional. But the question of what was to be done when governments exceeded those proper limits was rarely raised.

This was the balance which Hannah More admired and Pretyman-Tomline achieved both in 1789 and 1794. But to a certain extent the Church of England cut its homilies to suit its congregation. On the whole, the Abbey Martyrdom Day sermons retained the limited-obedience posture. In 1791 Bishop Cleaver of Chester restated in classic terms the traditional, balanced, pre-French Revolution view on obligation, though he combined it with a blistering attack on the French and on the concept of equality. In 1795, Spencer Madan, Bishop of Peterborough, no doubt sure that his noble congregation would not misunderstand his meaning, explicitly and at some length argued that St Paul enjoined submission only to those honest and lawful commands of the governor which did not harm 'the essential rights of mankind'. He balanced this liberalism with an extremely forceful statement of the obligation to respect government in general as the ordinance of God, and with a recognition of the crucial role of religion in establishing and enforcing that obligation.[3]

However, to a wider and potentially less reliable congregation than the House of Lords it was the obligation and not its limits on which establishment preaching concentrated in the 1790s. In 1792 Shute Barrington urged the clergy of his Durham diocese to remind their congregations that the duty to submit to government rested on obligations 'independent of all civil authority'. The year before, Dr Samuel Cooper, the curate of Great Yarmouth, had likewise stressed that the apostolic injunctions to submission arose from revelation not reason; the obligation was binding and human argument could not undo it.[4] Such views were urged repeatedly, particularly on special occasions such as fast day sermons, Assize sermons,

---

[3] Pretyman-Tomline, *Sermon*, 30 January 1789 (London, 1789), esp. pp. 9, 17; Hannah More, 'Letter to William Wilberforce 1794', in *Memoirs of the Life and Correspondence of Mrs Hannah More*, edited by W. Roberts, 3 vols., third edition (London, 1835), vol. 3, p. 402; W. Cleaver, *Sermon, Preached before the Lords . . . January 31, 1791* (Oxford, 1791), pp. 2–4, 11–12; Spencer Madan, *Sermon*, 30 January 1795 (London, 1795), pp. 4–10.

[4] Shute Barrington, *A Charge . . . to the Clergy of . . . Durham* (Bath, 1792), pp. 13, 16; S. Cooper, *The First Principles of Civil and Ecclesiastical Government Delineated* (Yarmouth, 1791), pp. 111–23, 149–53.

Militia sermons and Sunday school sermons.[5] On the whole, discussion of the limits of obedience was considered best left to works for a limited and educated readership, like Thomas Gisborne's two-volume treatise on *The Duties of Men*.[6] While the grounds of political obligation continued to be urged in more popular works throughout the period, their incidence was less frequent after 1795, except at moments of great crisis, such as the invasion scare of 1798.[7]

The other Christian churches

The balance between the injunctions to obedience and its proper limits was also important for the Dissenting communities to maintain. They were anxious to defend their religious rights and liberties, and were generally sympathetic to some degree of political reform – but that did not mean they were hostile to the concept of political obligation as such. First they were Christians and so could not ignore the Pauline and Petrine texts entirely, though their exegesis could blunt the impact considerably. Secondly, they did believe in government (although in the cases of Price and Priestley only in a very minimal form), and recognised that government without a concept of political obligation was impossible. Only an atheist and anarchist could ridicule unreservedly an obligation imposed on men by religious revelation. In 1793, William Godwin considered men 'miserable dupes' to accept a code which lacked wisdom and justice, just because it was alleged to come from God.[8] But, while Godwin could denounce the whole concept as a deception and fraud perpetrated by the 'hired ministers of falsehood and imposture', the Dissenting ministers had to find a more balanced position, while using a different fulcrum from that which produced the Anglican equilibrium.

On 15 August 1791, Bishop Porteus noted with delight that Rivingtons had republished extracts from a 1759 pamphlet of Richard Price in which he had praised the British constitution and enjoined loyalty. In fact, even in his *Love of Country* discourse in November 1789 Price acknowledged that 'a particular deference and homage' was due to the civil magistrates, and that no man could be truly wise or virtuous if he despised governments and spoke evil of his rulers. But, while he quoted the traditional texts of SS Peter and Paul, he made no further comments on them. Their citation was set in

---

[5] W. Gilbank, *The Duties of Man* (London, 1793) p. 10; W. Mavor, *Christian Politics* (Oxford, 1793), p. 11; R. Nares, *Principles of Government Deduced from Reason* (London, 1792), pp. x–xi, 6–9. On Mavor, who was also Mayor of Woodstock, see Diana McClatchey, *Oxfordshire Clergy 1777–1869* (Oxford, 1960), pp. 194–5, 202–3, 221–3.

[6] Vol. 1, pp. 77–100.

[7] R. B. Nickolls, *The Political as Well as the Moral Consequences Resulting . . . from Religious Education* (London, 1798); W. Cole, *Sermon Preached on the General Fast* (London, 1798); T. Ackland, *Religion and Loyalty Recommended* (London, 1798).

[8] W. Godwin, *Enquiry Concerning Political Justice* (1793; Harmondsworth, 1796), pp. 498–9.

the context of his assumption that governors were the servants of the people, and thereafter Price concentrated on the limits of such obligation to obedience.[9] Priestley's interpretation of the texts was more liberal still. Christ and the apostles, he asserted, never considered the question of civil government and had no opinion on it. Because they were unable to change the government they were under, they had recommended acceptance, but men who had the power to change government for the better were free to do so.[10]

Less extreme forms of these arguments were accepted by most of the Old Dissenters. Generally they saw no conflict between their desire for reform in church and state and their obligation to 'Honour the King'.[11] This was made very clear when one Dissenter, John Clayton, broke ranks and published the sermon he had preached in July 1791, in the wake of the Birmingham Riots, on *The Duty of Christians to Magistrates*. He was roundly condemned by his fellow Dissenters. The sermon was, indeed, provocative and extreme, and could well have come from the pen of William Jones. As a Congregationalist, Clayton attacked Priestley's 'rational Christianity' as abandoning the faith of the Reformation, and he suggested that this religious attitude was linked to social and political ones: the liberty Unitarians asserted in theology was mirrored in their opposition to government and dislike of social restraints; Christ and the apostles Peter and Paul were unequivocal that men were obliged to submit to the established government; Christians should lead a separate spiritual life, not involve themselves in political matters. 'Fidelia', in a bitter reply, accused him of preaching passive obedience and non-resistance and clearly regarded him as both traitor and spy. A more argued response sought to explain the biblical texts in their context and to defend Price and Priestley, but failed to conceal a deep bitterness at Clayton's betrayal.[12] In the early 1790s Protestant Dissenters were still openly arguing the case for reform.

John Wesley, a paragon of political loyalty, died in 1791; his followers continued to preach the religious basis of political obligation he had established as a key-note of Methodist ideology. The hostile attitude to their growth in the 1790s, which meant they were frequently denounced as subversives and Jacobins, made Methodists all the more anxious to assert

[9] LPL, MS 2103, f.45 (Porteus Notebook, 1786–1800); R. Price, *A Discourse on the Love of our Country* (London, 1789), pp. 20–8.

[10] Priestley, 'The Conduct to Be Observed by Dissenters . . .' (1789), *Works*, vol. 15, p. 396; 'A General History of the Christian Church' (1790), *Works*, vol. 8, p. 330.

[11] The general attitude was well expressed by the Baptist David Bogue in *Reasons for Seeking a Repeal of the Corporation and Test Acts* (London, 1790), p. 15.

[12] J. Clayton, *The Duty of Christians to Magistrates* (London, 1791), pp. v–vii, 17–23; Fidelia, *Consolatory Letter*, pp. 24–5; *Remarks on . . . Clayton*, pp. 11–18. Clayton's sermon was also probably the target of Robert Hall's *Christianity Consistent with a Love of Freedom* (London, 1791).

their political loyalty.[13] All that the 1794 Methodist Conference considered it necessary to observe on the current crisis in national affairs was to urge all to 'Honour the King', pray daily for their rulers and submit themselves 'to every ordinance of man for the Lord's sake'.[14] Two Methodists considered the issue of obligation more fully: Samuel Bradburn, in a thoughtful and well argued sermon on equality preached in Bristol in February 1794, and Benjamin Rhodes in his *Discourse on Civil Government* of 1796.

The sub-title of Rhodes's discourse made his position clear: 'The Duty of Subjects to their Sovereign, laid down, and enforced by the Scriptures, and the example of the Primitive Christians'. No Anglican thesis expounded the establishment position more clearly than this Methodist discourse. Government was ordained by God and governors appointed by Him; as long as they acted within the laws and constitution, submission to them must be absolute.[15] The general tone of Bradburn's sermon on *Equality* was more liberal, but its substantive position was precisely the same. Bradburn insisted that Romans 13.1 and I Peter 2.13–16 did not involve an absolute submission to arbitrary government. But he was thinking here of religious liberty not civil dissent, for

it is the privilege and duty of all Christians to obey Masters, Magistrates, Kings, or any Civil Governors, as freely and sincerely as would our Saviour himself, for these are all under his control and authority; and lawful obedience to them is, in reality, only obeying him.[16]

Catholics also needed to establish their loyalty and to distinguish between their spiritual and temporal obligations. This was, or course, only part of the much wider dilemma they faced of how to maintain loyalty to an exclusive faith in a hostile and pluralist society, while still involving themselves fully in the secular activities of life. On the limited question of political obligation, the Jesuit tradition of government arising from the consent of the people caused some embarrassment in the light of events in France and of threats and fears in England. In 1791 Charles Plowden attempted a mild defence of St Robert Bellarmine's doctrine, as providing a safer and more secure check on the behaviour of princes than violent, popular opposition. Bellarmine, he argued, should be looked upon not as an enemy of royalty but rather as a

---

[13] See J. Walsh, 'Methodism at the End of the Eighteenth Century', in *A History of the Methodist Church in Great Britain*, vol. 1, edited by R. Davies and G. Rupp (London, 1965), pp. 275–315 (pp. 302–8).

[14] *Minutes of the Methodist Conferences* . . ., vol. 1 (London, 1862), p. 312.

[15] B. Rhodes, *Discourse* . . . (Birmingham, 1796), pp. 7–8. The only point an Anglican probably would not have made (though he would not have denied it) was that governors and laws should be disobeyed (only) if they attempted to stop men doing their duty to God.

[16] S. Bradburn, *Equality. A Sermon* . . . (Bristol, 1794), pp. 22–4. Bradburn's rejection of his radical politics in 1795 was perhaps less abrupt than W. R. Ward implies, *Religion and Society in England 1790–1850* (London, 1972), p. 34.

friend of good government. A year later, Plowden's brother Francis argued that the *origin* of government made no difference to the obligation to obey: submission was a divine duty whether authority came directly from God or *via* the people.[17]

All the Christian denominations accepted a divinely imposed obligation to submit to government, but all adopted limitations of some sort upon an absolute subjection. The result was a doctrine which needed to be kept finely balanced. Whilst it could rally the faithful against atheists and anarchists, it was a less effective weapon against those, like Price and Priestley, who chose to challenge the degree of limitation which should be imposed upon it. It was also used, fundamentally, as an intellectual justification of government, rather than a psychological restraint, and it belonged in the tradition of abstract political philosophy.[18] It is significant that Burke never directly invoked it.[19] His view of 1688 was far more pragmatic and legalistic; he had little sympathy for the intellectual indulgence of non-jurors. While he would never have denied that Christians were so obliged, Burke preferred the concrete assurance of a prescriptive theory. To lay too much stress on an abstract principle, the limitations of which were essentially contestable, was, for Burke, to offer too many hostages to fortune in a world where the advocates of the rights of man had occupied theoretical and abstract positions.

The rights of man

'The Rights of Man' became a slogan in the 1790s and lost much of the precision necessary to theoretical argument. Different men meant different things by it, and it differed not only from Burke's legalistic concept of the established rights of Englishmen, but also from rights in the natural-law tradition. Various distinctions were made between natural rights, political rights, civil rights and religious rights, and there was disagreement on the precise relationship between these. The extent to which one regarded civil rights as God-given and inalienable depended in large part upon one's views

---

[17] Charles Plowden, *Observations on the Oath Proposed to the English Roman Catholics* (London, 1791), p. 34; Francis Plowden, *Jura Anglorum: The Rights of Englishmen* (London, 1792), pp. 195–6. Carl Cone, *The English Jacobins* (New York, 1968), pp. 92, 150, cites Francis Plowden in 1794 as alleging that it was Burke's *Reflections* which incited Paine, and that the 'neo-divine right pretensions of the loyal associations' were more dangerous than Paine's teaching, but he gives no reference for these citations.

[18] Hannah More's direct invocation of it in 'Village Politics', *Works*, vol. 2, pp. 372–3, is unusual. Generally it did not appear in this form in popular propaganda, but was, rather, reserved for the consciences of the educated, political nation.

[19] The nearest he came to it was when he argued that God willed the state as the means necessary to perfect man's virtue, *Reflections on the Revolution in France*, p. 196.

of the origin of government and the role of popular consent. When Price in his *Love of Country* discourse argued that the three sacred rights on which the 1688 revolution was founded were liberty of conscience, the right to resist power when it was abused, and the right to choose and cashier governors, he implied that rights were given by God to individuals not to society, and that even under government those individuals retained civil and religious rights which could and should be defended.[20]

Burke took an altogether more secular view of rights. The section of the *Reflections* in which he discussed these claims had few religious references, unlike other parts of that work. Abstract, inalienable, individual rights were incompatible with society and government. Social rights were specific and concrete. They were won, enshrined in law, and handed on from generation to generation. They were not God-given in any direct sense. Dr Samuel Cooper, supporting Burke and challenging Priestley, argued that, if all men had inalienable rights, then anarchy must ensue; men had a duty to obey even those laws which contravened virtue and religion until the extreme position of a breached compact had been reached. He asserted that natural rights, far from being God-given, arose from error and anarchy and, significantly, his argument to sustain this point was wholly secular.[21]

The replies to Burke which came in 1791 from Mackintosh and Paine took different positions on the religious and moral basis of rights.[22] Paine posed the greater political threat, Mackintosh the greater religious one. Paine's argument was weak intellectually, but powerful propaganda, as his critics recognised. Bishop Porteus noted that he wrote in 'a plain, familiar, forcible style very well calculated to captivate common readers', and Christopher Wyvill, described *Rights of Man* as being 'able and forcibly written, though with neither candour nor wisdom'.[23] Despite a basically secular approach, Paine was quite ready to throw in some religious arguments as additional support. The origin of the rights of man, he claimed, dated from the creation of Adam. God gave men equal rights, but governments subverted them and church establishments confirmed the loss: 'The key of St Peter and the key of the Treasury, became quartered on one another, and the wondering, cheated multitude worshipped the invention.'

---

[20] Price, *Love of Country*, pp. 34–5.

[21] Burke, *Reflections*, pp. 99–121; S. Cooper, *First Principles*, pp. 150–3.

[22] For a comparison of Mackintosh's and Paine's methods see J. T. Boulton, 'James Mackintosh: "*Vindiciae Gallicae*"', *Renaissance and Modern Studies*, 21 (1977), 106–18. See also his *The Language of Politics in the Age of Wilkes and Burke* (London, 1963), pp. 134–67.

[23] LPL, MS 2103, f.35; C. Wyvill, *A Defence of Dr Price and the Reformers of England* (London, 1792), p. 59. Wyvill was, however, considered sufficiently subversive to warrant the republication by Rivingtons of a sermon on *The Duty of Honouring the King* preached by his ancestor and namesake, Christopher Wyvill, Dean of Ripon, in 1685, to demonstrate the contrast.

In arguing that rights were given by God and taken away by the church, Part One of the *Rights of Man* was anti-clerical, but not atheistic.[24]

James Mackintosh's *Vindiciae Gallicae* was a more serious challenge to religion as a bulwark of government. He united a secular concept of rights to a secular concept of political morality and related both to utility. He accepted that, fundamentally, morality was determined by utility and that, in that sense, both natural and civil rights arose from expediency. However, once the 'moral edifice' had been raised, it concealed its utilitarian base from view so that (according to the best rule-utilitarian practice) rights became absolute. Thus absolute rights could arise from a secular, utilitarian origin; a secular morality could have the same power and force as a religious one.[25]

The variety of attitudes to civil rights within the English Catholic community reflected in part an awareness of the spiritual threat inherent in the concept. In 1790, Joseph Berington expressed the hope that the French Revolution would secure the rights of men, destroy despotism, and give millions their liberty, and Thomas Potts asserted that Catholicism was the champion, not the opponent of political liberty. It had been the religion of Englishmen under the ancient, free Saxon constitution, and later Magna Charta had been won from a despotic and irreligious king by Catholic barons. Moreover, far from seeking to destroy the French Revolution, many French Catholic clergy had supported it and their actions could be favourably compared with those of the Anglican clergy in 1688–9.[26]

However, in 1791–2, Francis Plowden adopted a more Burkean view. The doctrine of the rights of man was misconceived because it confused man in the speculative state of nature with man in the practical state of civil society. The rights applicable to the metaphysical state were inappropriate in the social one. Adam indeed had God-given rights, but he lived in a pre-social state. To transfer those rights to civil society would be to destroy political and civil liberty; no individual had rights equal to those of the community.[27] This difference of attitude is partly explained by the fact that, while Berington and Potts had both completed their theological education in a Europe increasingly influenced by enlightenment ideas, Francis Plowden's training was interrupted by the suppression of the Society of Jesus before he had taken orders. He had then undergone the very different socialisation process of Middle Temple.

Other critics of Paine insisted he had misinterpreted the meaning of the

[24] Paine, *Rights of Man* (1791–2; Harmondsworth, 1969), pp. 87–92, 106–9.
[25] Mackintosh, *Vindiciae Gallicae* (London, 1791), pp. 215–17.
[26] Berington, *Henry II*, Preface (Letter to C. J. Fox, 6 April 1790), p. iii; T. Potts, *An Inquiry into the Moral and Political Tendency of the Religion Called Roman Catholic* (London, 1790), pp. 132–3. Berington also noted the Catholic barons of Magna Charta, *Henry II*, p. 238; a point earlier made in the 1719 debate on the Occasional Conformity Bill, and in the Sacheverell trial.
[27] F. Plowden, *Case Stated*, pp. 7–8; *Jura Anglorum*, pp. 19–28, 160–2.

term 'rights of man'. Samuel Bradburn, the Methodist, regarded the phrase as having been abused; his list of rights included not only the rights to life, liberty and property and liberty of conscience, but also to civility and respect, to titles and dignities of office. Bishop Horne insisted that, if one accepted divine law, then the rights of men in society were 'the rights of duty, and virtue and religion'; no other rights could exist in a state of Christian civilisation. Robert Nares defined the rights of man as the right to serve God and imitate His wisdom and goodness.[28]

Some of the popular tracts of 1792–3 adopted a similar Christian and concrete view of rights. Jack Anvil, in Hannah More's *Village Politics* (1792), defined the 'true *Rights of Man*' as being the use of his limbs and his liberty (natural rights), of the laws (civil rights) and of his Bible (religious rights). William Jones, in one of the more seriously argued of the Bull family letters, accused Paine and Priestley of ascribing liberty to man in the abstract and giving him not the rights of a Christian, civilised, social being, but those of an animal. He contrasted natural (animal) rights with God-given rights, but did not define the latter, which appeared from the letter to have consisted only of rights over the animal creation and the right to respect property![29]

Equality

The various positions on the rights of man had been adopted by 1793 and discussion of the concept in general was more limited thereafter, although the exposition of the conspiracy theory in 1797 led to another minor eruption.[30] However, discussion of the specific right of equality remained lively throughout the period. This occupied a crucial place both in the political and the social genres of argument. Taken as a normative principle, the right to equality was a part of political theory, but the effect of putting equality into practice in society with its existing hierarchy and organisation constituted an important theme in social theory.

Paine insisted that equality had scriptural approval. The Mosaic account of the Creation, whether regarded as divine authority or mere history, was unequivocal on the equality of man, which, far from being a modern doctrine, was the oldest on record. In *The Age of Reason* (1794), Paine pronounced his disbelief in Christianity as a revealed religion, but asserted

---

[28] Bradburn, *Equality*, pp. 10–11; Horne, 'Intended Charge', 1791, *Works*, vol. 4, p. 530. This charge elicited an enthusiastic letter from Burke on 9 December 1791, *Corr.*, vol. 6, pp. 455–6; Nares, *Principles of Government*, pp. 20–1.

[29] More, 'Village Politics', 1792, *Works*, vol. 3, p. 377; [W. Jones], *A Letter to John Bull Esq.* (London, 1793), pp. 11–17.

[30] R. de Courcy, *Self-Defence Not Inconsistent with the Precepts of Religion* (Shrewsbury, 1798), p. 19; Watson, Charge 1798, in *Misc.T*, vol. 1, p. 136. See also Coleridge, 'Essays on his Times', 3 January 1800, *Works*, vol. 3, bk 1, p. 69.

that Christ, the man, preached excellent morality and the equality of man.[31] Coleridge, in his Bristol lectures on revealed religion in 1795, agreed that equality was a feature of Mosaic government, and Samuel Bradburn in his 1794 sermon conceded that the word was scriptural and so needed explanation.[32]

Indeed, the justification of inequality and of private property was one of the major aims of the popular propaganda tracts of 1792–3; the arguments they used were traditional and mostly secular; where religion was invoked it was usually in a social not a political context. The same was fundamentally true of the more erudite arguments of that winter.[33] When in January 1793 Samuel Hayes preached to a congregation of Association members in St Margaret's, Westminster, he presented all the usual secular arguments against equality. The only religious one he was able to add was that if God had intended men to be politically equal, he would have made them physically and mentally so. Others argued that equality was a spiritual quality and would obtain in the world to come; the society and government of this imperfect world required inequality, and therefore God willed it. It was asserted time and again that, because equality was a practical impossibility, God could not have intended it as a right.[34]

The concept of equality which men attacked was, however, largely a creature of their own invention which bore little resemblance to the arguments even of Paine, let alone of Price and Priestley. They were no levellers; certainly they did not want a mathematically equal distribution of property between all the people of England. It was religious liberty not economic equality which fired their passions. When Alexander Kilham advocated equality in the church government of Methodism he was labelled a 'leveller' and bracketed with Paine, although he disclaimed any economic or political intentions.[35] While Kilham's breakaway New Connexion was always more radical than the Wesleyan movement, the connexion between his ecclesiology and his politics was one of basic outlook and attitude, not one of theology. One could not simply extrapolate men's political and

---

[31] Paine, *Rights of Man*, pp. 88–9; *The Age of Reason* (Paris, 1794; reprinted New York and London, 1910), p. 27.

[32] Coleridge, 'Lectures on Revealed Religion', 1795, *Works*, vol. 1, pp. 124–35, 219–20; Bradburn, *Equality*, p. 6.

[33] See, for example, Richard Watson's 'Dispensing Sermon', *Misc. T*, vol. 1, pp. 448–9, and Mavor, *Christian Politics*.

[34] S. Hayes, *A Sermon . . .*, (London, 1793), pp. 9–13; E. Tatham, *Letters to . . . Burke* (Oxford, 1791), pp. 30–2; J. Scott, *Equality considered and Recommended* (London, [1794]); W. Buller, *A Sermon . . . March 9, 1796* (London, 1796), pp. 8–10; R. Prosser, *A Sermon . . . 24th July, 1797* (Newcastle-upon-Tyne, 1797), p. 11; T. Armitstead, *A Sermon . . . at the Spring Assize, 1798* (Chester, 1798), pp. 5–7.

[35] A Kilham, *The Methodist Monitor* (Leeds, [1796]), vol. 1, pp. 230–1.

economic views from their religious and ecclesiological ones.[36] It was the Wesleyan Methodist Samuel Bradburn who provided the most cogently argued case against equality, but his views, although subtle and eminently reasonable, were not new. His entire argument was designed to show that unrestricted religious liberty was entirely consistent with the staunchest support for king and constitution.[37]

Religious liberty and rights

Contrary to the beliefs and fears of the establishment, it was not political, or economic, but religious rights which dominated the thinking of the majority of English reformers at the time of the outbreak of the French Revolution. Few argued that the right to vote, or the right to an equal economic share was the direct and revealed will of God, but virtually every Protestant Dissenter, Methodist and Catholic (and even a few Anglicans) believed that religious liberty, the right to worship freely according to conscience, was God-given and should be enshrined in any just constitutional settlement.[38] Discussion of the issue in this period was conducted almost entirely within the political-constitutional-philosophical mould of normative argument, although there were a few people aware of the social advantages of toleration in terms of cohesion and control. For all the sobriquets assigned to Priestley, like 'Gunpowder Joe' or 'the Revolution Doctor', his main aim was not the reform of parliament, but the repeal of the Test and Corporation Acts. While Price pronounced his *Nunc Dimittis* in London, rejoicing in having seen the birth of the new order, Priestley was preaching in Birmingham on 'The Conduct to be Observed by Dissenters in Order to Procure the Repeal of the Test and Corporation Acts'.[39]

The claim that religious liberty was a fundamental right of mankind was widespread and by no means limited to Unitarians like Priestley. Sceptics, Old Dissenters, Catholics and Methodists all made the same point of principle. The poet, Sir Brooke Boothby, who defended Rousseau against Burke's attack, insisted that, as liberty of conscience was a spiritual, not a material thing, government had no *right* to take it away. Law should relate to men's actions, not their feelings or beliefs. Religion was the exclusive, private concern of the individual. The Protestant Dissenters Josiah Townsend and John Rippon accepted the duty to submit to the civil magistrate in

---

[36] Compare above, pp. 36–7.

[37] Bradburn, *Equality, passim*, but esp. p. iv.

[38] Though a number of Dissenters did concede that for many the issues of religious and civil rights were linked; see Hall, 'Apology for the Freedom of the Press', 1793, *Works*, vol. 3, p. 151; J. Priestley, *Letters to Burke*, second edition (Birmingham, 1791), p. 131. Compare above, pp. 37–9, 53–5.

[39] Price's sermon was preached on 4 November, Priestley's on 5 November 1789.

all temporal matters, but insisted, with great passion, that religion was a concern between man's conscience and God. Rippon's fellow Baptist, Robert Hall, considered man's right to worship God as he thought best an inalienable natural right which was pre-social and eternal and took precedence over any subsequent political obligation. In the Catholic community, Cisalpines and Ultramontanes were agreed on this issue. Thomas Potts argued that to deny the king ecclesiastical supremacy was in no way inconsistent with offering him full civil allegiance; he had a right to one, but not to the other. Francis Plowden agreed that men's right to a free relationship with God was paramount to all human power. The normative point was reinforced from a Methodist standpoint by Samuel Bradburn who insisted, quite unequivocally, that '... every man has an indefeasible, unalienable right to think and speak freely on all subjects purely religious'.[40]

The statement of the principle was clear, but what precisely did it involve? The Toleration Act had granted trinitarian Protestant Dissenters liberty of conscience in a strict sense, though Catholics and Unitarians were excluded. But the right to religious liberty was considered to involve more than mere freedom to worship according to conscience. It also had two serious civil implications. First it was argued that it was wrong to deprive men of civil privileges (rights in the Burkean sense) merely on account of their religion. Secondly, it was considered wrong to use state power and finance to maintain a religious establishment and state clergy, and to exclude ministers from it on account of their religious beliefs.

Liberty of worship

The right to legal freedom of worship was of real concern to Catholics and Unitarians. Despite the radical enthusiasms of some Cisalpines, Catholics were, on the whole, regarded as being supportive of established governments and the influence of those of the landed gentry and aristocracy who had kept the faith, such as the Stonors, Petres, Cliffords and Welds, reassured most of the political establishment of their essential loyalty. Fear of their 'allegiance to a foreign prince' seemed less dangerous in a Europe where the main threat to established order came from Jacobin France. In 1793 Burke compared fear of the much weakened Pius VI to the frog's fear of the poor old hare in Æsop's fable, and likened those who experienced it to nervous ladies who imagined they were teapots. However, Burke's argu-

---

[40] Sir B. Boothby, *A Letter to . . . Burke* (London, 1791), pp. 44–5; J. Townsend, *The Principles of Protestant Dissenters* (Bath, 1791), p. 14; J. Rippon, *The Baptist Annual Register* (London, 1793), Preface, p. i; Hall 'Love of Freedom', *Works*, vol. 3, p. 122, 'Fragment on Village Preaching', *Works*, vol. 3, p. 364; Potts, *An Inquiry*, p. 101; Francis Plowden, *Jura*, p. 82 (but compare R. Plowden, *A Letter to Francis Plowden* (London, [1794]), pp. 8ff); S Bradburn, *Methodism Set Forth and Defended* (Bristol, [1792]), p. 45.

ments were based on the need to recruit Catholics as a collateral aid to the state in restraining *dēmos*, especially in Ireland.[41]

In England the Second Relief Act of 1791 had been granted not because the establishment recognised any fundamental, inalienable right to religious liberty; expediency, not principle, was the order of the day. This Act in effect placed Catholics on the same legal footing as trinitarian Protestant Dissenters, but Unitarians were technically outside the law until 1812. Once again it was grounds of expediency, not normative principle, which led Burke to oppose their 1792 petition. Before the French Revolution, he had supported toleration for sects which had established a prescriptive right. But the Unitarians were new and, in his eyes, politically dysfunctional; they mingled 'a political system with their religious opinions' and threatened establishment in both church and state. In 1800, Bishop Randolph of Oxford suggested that Socinian theology, in its tendency 'subversive of the reverence due to Revelation', was as responsible as deism for the French Revolution and the war.[42] Religious freedom was a matter of expediency, not abstract right; in the case of heretics and subversives it was a danger to avoid.

Civil rights for Dissenters

The movement for Catholic emancipation and the struggle to repeal the Corporation and Test Acts, however, did not involve religious rights in this primary sense, but in the secondary one of being deprived of any civil rights on the grounds of religion. When expediency demanded the granting of Catholic emancipation in 1801 after the Act of Union with Ireland, it was refused not because the principle was rejected, but on the technicality of the Coronation Oath.[43] Neither Pitt in urging emancipation on the king, nor

---

[41] Lord Robert Petre, *Letter to the Right Reverend Doctor Horsley* (London, 1790), pp. 7–8, 18; Burke, *Corr.*, vol. 7, p. 350, vol. 9, pp. 133–4. On the role of the Catholic clergy in Ireland opposing popular disturbances see Maurice Bric, 'Priests, Parsons and Politics: The Rightboy Protest in County Cork, 1785–1788', *PP*, 100 (1983), 100–23, and Connolly, *Priests and People*, pp. 219–63; in 1800 a new section was inserted into the catechism to enjoin obedience to the state. On the desire of the papacy for good relations with the British government see M. Buschkuhl, *Great Britain and the Holy See, 1746–1870* (Dublin, 1982), pp. 37, 42–3. This attitude survived the Napoleonic Wars: see E. R. Norman, *The English Catholic Church in the Nineteenth Century* (Oxford, 1984), p. 56. But compare O. MacDonagh, 'The Politicization of the Irish Catholic Bishops 1800–1850', *HJ*, 18 (1975), 37–53, and J. H. Whyte, 'The Influence of the Catholic Clergy on Elections in Nineteenth Century Ireland', *EHR*, 75 (1960), 239–59.

[42] Burke, 'Speech on the Unitarian Petition', 1792, *Works*, vol. 6, pp. 31, 115–6; *Writings*, vol. 2, p. 388; J. Randolph, *A Sermon Preached before the Lords March 12, 1800* (Oxford, 1800), pp. 4–5.

[43] Even this involved an inconsistency for, as an anonymous pamphlet by Charles Butler pointed out, when Corsica was briefly in British hands in June 1794 the king had ratified its constitution, which declared Catholicism its national faith and approved the appointment of bishops 'concertanda colla Santa Sede', *The Case of Conscience Solved; or, Catholic Emancipation Proved to be Compatible with the Coronation Oath* (London, 1801), p. 22. See also, Elisa Carrillo, 'The Corsican Kingdom of George III', *JMH*, 34 (1962), 254–74 (p. 258).

Loughborough and Moore in opposing it, discussed the abstract principles involved in the alleged natural right of religious liberty. The king may have believed he was morally, indeed religiously, bound by his oath and the lord chancellor and archbishop might have stood on *legal* principle, but the main debate was on the disputed expediency of the measure.[44]

Most Protestant Dissenters did not claim that they should be eligible for public office because of any right they possessed as men *qua* men, merely that the special privileges won by men of their class, wealth and station should not be denied them purely because of their faith. In philosophical terms, the distinction was important and made their case far more limited and less radical than it might have been. Priestley blurred the distinction somewhat when he argued that all men of all denominations were 'all equally men, and Englishmen, and therefore equally entitled to all the natural and just rights of Englishmen'.[45]

But most Dissenters took clearly the more limited line. The Baptist David Bogue's *Reasons for the Repeal of the Test and Corporation Act* (1790) was characteristic. Like other members of the bourgeois Dissenting community, he argued for equality of opportunity for the enterprising and acquisitive; Protestant Dissenters were the most loyal of subjects and should be given access to all offices of honour and profit.[46] His views would have been subversive if England had been a closed aristocracy, but they were far from being democratic.

Dissenters frequently exploited the fears of Anglicans that the Test was a profanation of the Eucharist, and some Anglicans, like Christopher Wyvill, were sympathetic to repeal.[47] But many, such as Burke and Samuel Parr,

---

[44] Earl of Stanhope, *Life of . . . Pitt*, 4 vols., third edition (London, 1867), vol. 3, pp. 266–75 and Appendix, pp. xxiii–xxxiii; *The Later Correspondence of George III*, edited by A. Aspinall, 5 vols. (Cambridge, 1962–70), vol. 3, pp. 475–81. Neither lord chancellor nor archbishop put detailed arguments in writing before the king. When on 13 March 1805 Archbishop Moore, Eldon and Ellenborough spoke (to the king's approval) on the issue in the House of Lords, their main principled argument concerned the danger to the Act of Settlement if Catholics took an oath which made no reference to the *Protestant* monarchy. *Parl. Deb.*, vol. 4, first series, cols. 775–8, 783–5, 804–16; *Later Corr.*, vol. 4, p. 328. For a fuller discussion of the arguments on Catholic emancipation see below, pp. 232–44.

[45] Albert Goodwin, *The Friends of Liberty* (London, 1979), p. 78, claims they had 'recourse to neo-Lockean theories of natural rights', but the evidence he cites makes clear they were, in fact, arguing the more limited case. But Goodwin's general point about the implications of this argument is valid. G. M. Ditchfield surveys the events in 'The Parliamentary Struggle over the Repeal of the Test and Corporation Acts 1787–1790', *EHR*, 89 (1974), 551–77, and examines some of the episcopal speeches in the House of Lords in 'Dissent and Toleration: Lord Stanhope's Bill of 1789', *JEH*, 29 (1978), 51–73; *Letter to Burke*, pp. 53–4; Priestley, *The Conduct to be Observed by Dissenters* (Birmingham, [1789]), p. 14.

[46] D. Bogue, *Reasons for Repeal* (London, 1790), pp. 12–13.

[47] Priestley, 'Familiar Letters to . . . Birmingham', 1790, *Works*, vol. 19, p. 163; C. Lofft, *An History of the Corporation and Test Acts* (Bury, 1790), p. 9; Hall, 'Love of Freedom', *Works*, vol. 3, p. 49; Bicheno, *Word in Season*, p. 30; Wyvill, *Defence of Doctor Price*, pp. 55–6.

who had supported repeal in the past, opposed it in 1790. Burke had been annoyed by the Dissenters' desertion of the opposition in the 1784 election, and when Richard Bright sought his support for repeal in 1789 he had given a tetchy and conditional answer, but he refused outright in 1790 only after some Dissenters had shown by their support of the French Revolution that they were unwilling to deliver the political goods Burke required in payment for the granting of civil rights. He believed they wanted to destroy the constitution and that political power not religious liberty was their object. For most politicians, as for Burke, the issue was one of expediency, not of political principle.[48]

Establishment and tithes

Many Dissenters believed that the principle of religious rights required not only the repeal of the Test and Corporation Acts but also the disestablishment of the Church of England. Dissenters were excluded not only from civil offices, but also from all parish churches and their endowments. A condition of each incumbent's induction to his church was his subscription to the thirty-nine articles. Only men who accepted the state theology were to be entrusted with the official cure of souls which entitled them to receive tithes. The tithe system rankled Dissenters more that almost any other single issue; they saw it as a grave injustice and a serious infringement of their religious rights.[49] Dissenting ministers were unable to receive the tithes of their co-religionists; lay Dissenters were required to support financially a church of which their consciences disapproved. They were, moreover, required to serve as churchwardens and so on and meet the expense involved, or pay for substitutes.

Joseph Priestley dated the 'mischief' from the conversion of Constantine and suggested the country would be better off with no civil establishment of religion at all. He insisted that his argument that one man should not be compelled to pay for the religion of another was advanced not as a Dissenter, 'but on the principles of *political philosophy* in general'.[50] Thomas Potts dated the problem from the Protestant Reformation, when the church was subjected to the temporal power, canons became statutes, priests like justices of the peace, and 'religion was degraded into state policy'. Instead of the clergy defending the rights of the people, as he claimed they had in pre-Reformation times, they became agents of the state. By contrast, Francis

---

[48] S. Parr, 'Miscellaneous Remarks . . .', 1791, *The Works of Samuel Parr*, 8 vols. (London, 1828), vol. 3, pp. 214–15; Burke, *Corr.*, vol. 5, p. 470, vol. 6, pp. 82–3. Compare LPL, MS 2103, ff.26–7 (Porteus Notebook, February 1790).

[49] This impression is reinforced by W. R. Ward, 'The Tithe Question in England in the Early Nineteenth Century', *JEH*, 16 (1965), 67–81.

[50] Priestley, 'A General History of the Christian Church', 1790, *Works*, vol. 8, p. 276; 'Familiar Letters', *Works*, vol. 19, p. 182. See also Priestley, *Letters to Burke*, pp. 55–6.

Plowden was prepared to accept an establishment of the majority faith, but his brother Robert, a Jesuit priest, insisted that only the true faith should be thus enshrined.[51] Protestants also objected to establishments on religious principles, but this was, politically, dangerous ground to tread.

What to Catholics and Dissenters was an unjust establishment, was to Anglicans the sacred alliance of church and state, the cornerstone of the constitution. To attack the church establishment on grounds of religious liberty was to appeal to an abstract right against the very foundation of the British constitution. On this alliance, they insisted, rested not the self-interest of the Anglican clergy but the stability of the political regime. The Lord Mayor of London was assured by his chaplain in 1790 that religion was the 'principal cement' of society and only a national establishment could ensure it was secure. But the concept was under attack. In 1791 Benjamin Bousfield argued that to call the church the foundation of the constitution was 'impious' and tantamount to regarding religion as man-made and the scriptures as a 'pious fraud'.[52]

The dispute raged in the provincial press too. In the *Bath Chronicle*, the Rev. Robert Wells exchanged letters with 'Publicola' on the issue in the days after the 1791 Birmingham Riots. Wells implied that Christ had declared that the monarchy as well as the church was founded upon the rock and that the gates of Hell (or republicanism) could not prevail against it. Challenged as to the scriptural accuracy of this, he retorted: '. . . they are parts of one and the same fabric, the Constitution in Church and State. The Monarchy, the British Monarchy; the Church, the Established Church; . . . the Rock, the purity of the one and the excellency of the other . . .'.[53]

Here Wells was both repeating Burke's argument in the *Reflections*, and anticipating that of his speech against the Unitarians' petition in 1792. In the *Reflections* Burke described the church establishment as being not just convenient, but essential; Englishmen regarded it as the foundation of the constitution. In his 1792 speech, he went significantly beyond the common Warburtonian position, and argued that it was wrong to speak of an alliance between church and state, for an alliance was between distinct things like two sovereign states, while church and state were one and the same, 'different integral parts of the same whole'.[54]

The established clergy readily agreed that to attack the established church

---

[51] Potts, *An Inquiry*, pp. 104–5, 112–13; F. Plowden, *Jura*, pp. 84–8; [Robert Plowden], *Letter to Francis*, pp. 61–74, 102, 104–5.

[52] C. E. de Coetlogon, *The Test of Truth, Piety and Allegiance* (London, 1790), pp. 19–20; B. Bousfield, *Observations on . . . Burke's Pamphlet on the Subject of the French Revolution* (London, 1791), p. 41.

[53] R. Wells, *A Correspondence between the Rev. Robert Wells . . . and a Gentleman under the signature of Publicola* (Bristol, 1791), *passim*, and esp. p. 17.

[54] Burke, *Reflections*, pp. 197–8; 'Speech on Unitarian Petition', *Works*, vol. 6, p. 115.

was to attack the established regime in the state; the alliance must be maintained.[55] Thomas Paine's attack on the union of church and state merely confirmed their belief in its value, and when in the same year, 1791, a youthful Baptist minister called the alliance a compact between priest and magistrate, to betray the civil and religious liberties of mankind, then Dissent and republicanism seemed to many to be speaking with one voice. Richard Watson, who was rather equivocal in his support of the exclusive establishment of Anglicanism in 1791, had become almost whole-hearted by 1803.[56]

Conservative churchmen were prepared to continue arguing a political, constitutional and philosophical case for the alliance of church and state and for the religious base of political obligation. The two sermons Richard Ramsden preached to the University of Cambridge in January and November 1800 portrayed the magistrate as divinely appointed, and the brother and colleague of the priest.[57] But the traditional, theoretical ground was less comfortable than it had been. Their critics in church and state had occupied that ground by basing their claims upon the civil and religious rights of man. While religious arguments on the traditional grounds of political philosophy still dominated public debate in the period from 1790 to 1793, and never disappeared, from 1793 onwards churchmen were increasingly turning away from the discussion of political theory and the rights of man and moving to consider social theory and the nature of man.

[55] R. Thorp, *On Establishments in Religion* . . . Cambridge University Commencement Sermon, 1 July 1792 (Newcastle-upon-Tyne, 1798), p. 27; J. Plymley, *A Charge Given at the Visitation of the Archdeaconry of Salop* . . . *1794* (Shrewsbury, 1794), pp. 13–16; H. R. Courtenay, *A Charge Delivered to the Clergy of the Diocese of Bristol 1796* (Bristol, 1796), pp. 4–5; J. Buckner, *A Charge Delivered to the Clergy of the Diocese of Chichester* . . . *1798* (London, 1799), p. 13.

[56] Paine, *Rights of Man*, pp. 92, 109–10; Hall, 'Love of Freedom', *Works*, vol. 3, p. 24. Hall later regretted the tone of this piece, written when he was 27, and refused to agree to its republication; R. Watson, *A Charge Delivered to the Clergy of the Diocese of Llandaff June 1791* (London, 1792), p. 11; *Substance of a Speech Intended to Have Been Spoken in the House of Lords, 22 November, 1803* (London, 1803), p. 31.

[57] *The Alliance between the Church and the State* (Cambridge, 1800), p. 12, *The Origin and Ends of Government* (Cambridge, 1800), though pp. 15–18 reflect the changing climate.

9

Social theory and the nature of man

Although the arguments were not new, the French Revolution led the English increasingly to consider social theory and the religious base of their society. Religious arguments could be used both to validate the social order and to teach men in every class the duties necessary to maintain it. It could cement the unity of the community both in a local and in a national sense, and it could impose restraints and sanctions on unregenerate man and so order his social behaviour.

The social hierarchy

Edmund Burke was both the apostle and the prophet of social theory in this sense. Most in advance of his contemporaries was the centrality of the role of religion as a restraining and reconciling agent in society which he outlined in his *Reflections*. This concentration and emphasis was rarely found in other writers before 1793. Rather more of his contemporaries echoed his vision and defence of a divinely ordained social hierarchy which he produced in response to disputes in the Whig party in 1790–1 when he was anxious to establish that his interpretation, rather than that of Fox, was in the true Whig tradition. But this also did not become commonplace until 1793–4.[1]

Burke assumed that all except the Jacobins accepted that God gave men their station in society and that, being placed in that rank by divine not human will, they were intended to fulfil the role assigned them. He assumed that men consented to these social and civil obligations because they arose from the 'predisposed order of things'. That order involved a complex, social and economic hierarchy which should not be queried, for to doubt it would be to question God's wisdom. This divinely appointed set of social relationships and their concomitant and immanent obligations were so critical that

---

[1] The concept of a divinely imposed hierarchy was, of course, age-old. The tradition is discussed by G. Kitson Clark, *Churchmen and the Condition of England, 1832–1885* (London, 1973), pp. 5–11. Before 1793 it was usually silently assumed, afterwards more often explicitly articulated.

Burke defined a nation as being not just a physical locality but, to a great extent, 'the ancient order into which we are born'.

Nor could these obligations be cast off. Just as birth into a family gave man an obligation to his parents, so birth into a community involved social and political obligations which included the duties attached to his social station. Burke quoted some lines from Persius's *Third Satire*, which questioned how easy it was for man to turn from his appointed rank in the race of life and supported the view that only when we see where we have been placed in human affairs can we know what God has commanded us to be. The true Whig tradition, Burke implied, would use religion to defend aristocratic rights whilst the French Revolution undermined both.[2]

A few other men were also arguing this case in 1791, of whom the most notable was Edward Tatham, Rector of Lincoln College, Oxford. He explained that in creating society God had constructed a highly complex instrument; within it men had to be different and unequal to be of mutual assistance to each other and to supply the wants and necessities of life. Without the proper mixture of rich and poor, high and low, society would, quite simply, not work and God's will would be frustrated:

In the subordination and gradation of persons and rights, consists the very life and health of every well constituted state. In this political arrangement, made not by the wisdom or the will of man, but by the invisible hand of Providence, every man moves in that sphere of life, whether higher or lower, in which that Providence, not his own choice, has placed him at his birth.[3]

In 1791, these arguments were still overshadowed by constitutional ones, but by 1793–4 they dominated debate and were a constant theme from establishment pulpits.

Bishops, country parsons, city Evangelicals – the whole spectrum of Anglicans argued the religious case for social hierarchy consistently year after year, and particularly at times of political unrest, of threat and fear. Bishop Vernon of Carlisle argued in 1794 that, while the man-made inequalities in France were merely capricious, the God-given ones in Britain were ordered and established, subtle and complex. Bishop Watson of Llandaff regarded 1793 as the opportune time to publish a sermon on the social and economic interdependence of rich and poor that he had first preached in 1785, and in a newly added appendix he stressed his respect for

---

[2] Burke first alluded to the concept in a letter to Thomas Mercer in February 1790, *Corr.*, vol. 6, p. 95; he presented to the public his full argument in August 1791 in 'An Appeal from the New to the Old Whigs', *Works*, vol. 3, pp. 79–80.

[3] Tatham, *Letters to . . . Burke*, pp. 32, 40. It is interesting to speculate whether the phrase 'the invisible hand of Providence' alluded to Adam Smith's secular use of the term in *The Wealth of Nations*, Book IV, ch. 2 (Everyman Edition, n.d.), vol. 1, p. 400. Tatham's work in general suggests he was influenced by Smith's analysis.

peasants and mechanics. He was too aware of the importance of the 'natural or social chain' which connected all men together to be contemptuous of any link in it: peasants and mechanics were as useful to the state as anyone else providing they discharged the duties of their respective stations. William Mavor reminded his country parishioners in 1793 that it was God who had distributed the parts in the drama of life and the inequalities he had decreed 'constitute the harmony and perfection of the moral world'.[4]

Anglican Evangelicals combined their moral paternalism with a firm belief in the necessity and propriety of an unequal, divinely ordained, social hierarchy. The Rev. John Owen, in a 1794 Assize sermon, stressed that social union, essential for the protection and security of mankind, rested on inequality, power, property and rank. Wilberforce in 1797 argued that Christianity made inequality less galling to the poor and reminded them that their 'more lowly path' was a gift from God. Thomas Gisborne, in a sermon published in 1804, stressed that every man in society was required to labour (in a manner appropriate to his rank), both to glorify God and to ensure that the social machine operated properly.[5]

The religious case for social hierarchy was argued consistently, and especially at times of unrest, threat and fear,[6] by Anglicans of all complexions, Methodists, and even Unitarians as long as it rewarded the enterprising and upwardly mobile.[7] But, while other Christians thus justified inequality as the divine dispensation of providence, Archdeacon Paley, characteristically, took a more secular approach. In his *Reasons for Contentment Addressed to the Labouring Part of the British Public* (1793) he conceded that religion could 'smooth' inequalities, and reconcile the poor to sickness and distress, but argued that reason, without religion, should convince them of the utility of hierarchy:

in estimating the mere diversities of station and civil condition, I have not thought it necessary to introduce religion into the inquiry at all; because I contend that the man who murmurs and repines, when he has nothing to murmur and repine about, but

---

[4] E. V. Vernon, *A Sermon . . . January 30, 1794* (London, 1794), p. 15; R. Watson, *Misc. T*, vol. 1, pp. 450, 452–3, 487; Mavor, *Christian Politics*, pp. 6–8. See also, Gilbank, *Duties of Man*, p. 22; Pretyman-Tomline, *Charge*, 1794, pp. 8–9.

[5] J. Owen, *Subordination Considered on the Grounds of Reason and Religion* (Cambridge, 1794), pp. 3–12; W. Wilberforce, *A Practical View of the Prevailing Religious System* (London, 1797), p. 405; T. Gisborne, Sermon X, 'On Occupation', in *Sermons*, vol. 2, second edition (London, 1804), pp. 196–217. See also Gisborne, *Duties of Men*, vol. 1, pp. 120, 131, 167–8.

[6] For example in 1798–9: see W. Cole, *A Sermon*, pp. 7, 11; S. Crowther, *Sermon Preached before the Barking Association . . . 17 June, 1798* (London, 1798), pp. 9–10; Watson, 'Charge', 1798, *Misc. T*, vol. 1, pp. 132–5; W. Cleaver, *Charge Delivered by William, Lord Bishop of Chester* (Oxford, 1799), pp. 7–8.

[7] Bradburn, *Equality*, p. 31; J. Crowther, *Christian Order . . .* (Bristol, 1796), pp. 3–4; Priestley, *Letters to Burke*, pp. 89–90, although his views changed a little when in America: see 'A Comparison of the Institutions of Moses with those of the Hindoos and other Ancient Nations', *Works*, vol. 17, p. 204.

the mere want of independent property, is not only irreligious, but unreasonable in his complaint.

When he considered the issue in his *Natural Theology* (1802) his argument was a secular one; disparity of wealth and station was necessary to the efficient working of society, and inequalities could safely be left to chance.[8]

The popular pamphlets of 1792–3 generally followed Paley in relying on secular arguments to justify a social hierarchy (though *Village Politics* is an exception here). While religious arguments were set out as an additional safety-net, they did not dominate the pamphlets in the way they did the *Cheap Repository Tracts* of 1795–8.[9] In the latter, Hannah More did not expound theoretical arguments, but through her homely tales, created a picture of a just and caring hierarchical society based on and united by Christian principles. It was, of course, apparent to all that such an ideal society existed only in this fictional form, not in reality.

The irreligion of the rich was a source of major concern to moral writers who feared that it would both set the poor a bad example and provoke the wrath of God, who would send national disasters as a punishment. In 1802 the Proclamation Society of 1787 was transformed into the Society for the Suppression of Vice.[10] Those concerned with this problem ranged from Evangelicals like Hannah More and William Wilberforce to the Catholic lawyer, Francis Plowden, and from the 'Apostle of Liberty', Richard Price, to the aristocratic Bishop of Durham, Shute Barrington.[11]

The poor

Most Christian writers on social matters in this period took a distanced view of the poor based on a mixture of fear and compassion. Four reactions, all from the year 1795, illustrated well the range of attitudes: Coleridge and Cartwright employed arguments rarely expressed in print; Burke's and

[8] Paley, 'Reasons for Contentment', 1793, *Works*, vol. 3, p. 330; 'Natural Theology', 1802, *Works*, vol. 5, pp. 352–62.
[9] On the power and limitations of the *Cheap Repository Tracts* see Olivia Smith, *The Politics of Language 1791–1819* (Oxford, 1984), pp. 91–5. Also see above, p. 103.
[10] *Proposal for Establishing a Society for the Suppression of Vice* (London, n.d.); *Part the First of An Address to the Public from the Society for the Suppression of Vice* (London, 1803); *Address to the Public . . . Part the Second* (London, 1803). See above, pp. 85–6.
[11] H. More, 'An Estimate of the Religion of the Fashionable World', 1790, *Works*, vol. 11; Wilberforce, *Practical View*; F. Plowden, *Case Stated*, p. 15; Price, *Love of our Country*, p. 16; Barrington, 'A Sermon before the Lords', Fast Day 27 February 1799, in *Sermons*, p. 58. See also LPL, MS 2103, f.33. On the assumed connexion between vice and social disorder see M. J. D. Roberts, 'Society for the Suppression of Vice', pp. 164, 175; R. A. Soloway, 'Reform or Ruin: English Moral Thought during the First French Republic', *Review of Politics*, 25 (1963), 110–28 (esp. p. 115); and Bristow, *Vice and Vigilance: Purity Movements in Britain Since 1700* (Dublin, 1977), pp. 32–44.

Gisborne's themes were much more common. Coleridge, still in his radical phase, denounced property as unscriptural and poverty as 'the Death of public Freedom', which made men slaves and generated vice.[12] John Cartwright, the parliamentary reformer, was struck by the tender regard for the poor he found in the Gospels. He noted that Christ, 'the Great Reformer', chose his apostles from among the poor, and he compared Burke and Windham to the Pharisees and the shoemaker Hardy to the fishermen of Galilee. He argued that, just as the foundations of Christianity were laid among the poor, so must be those of parliamentary reform.[13]

Burke tempered his compassion with a truly pharisaical regard for 'the laws of commerce, which are the laws of nature, and consequently the laws of God'. He argued in his *Thoughts on Scarcity* that, while charity to the poor was an important duty for individual Christians, it was vital to resist the idea that either the government or the rich could give the poor the necessaries which providence withheld from them.[14] Thomas Gisborne drew the age-old distinction between Christ's poor and the Devil's. The virtuous and industrious should be encouraged and helped; the profligate and idle discountenanced and reformed.[15]

Burke's opinions were shared by a wide denominational spectrum of writers. Bishop Buckner considered the poor had sufficient opportunities for self-improvement, though Bishop Buller feared lest their poverty led them to be seduced into sedition. Joseph Priestley attacked the poor laws as encouraging idleness and profligacy rather than industry and initiative.[16] Gisborne's view reflected that of his fellow Evangelicals and, to a considerable extent, of the Methodists. Wilberforce stressed the primacy of salvation and Hannah More, both through her Mendip schools and her tracts, sought to turn the Devil's poor to Christ – a process which incidentally made them loyal and well-ordered citizens. True happiness could be found only in Heaven, and radical attempts to achieve it on earth ('founded on the mad pretence of loving the poor more than God loves them') would only lead them away from the path of eternal bliss.[17] For most, the poor were a separate element in society, either to be pitied and reformed for their own

---

[12] 'Lectures on Revealed Religion', *Works*, vol. 1, p. 126.

[13] *The Commonwealth in Danger* (London, 1795), Introduction, pp. lxxi–lxxviii.

[14] 'Thoughts on Scarcity', *Works*, vol. 5, pp. 92–100.

[15] *Duties of Men*, vol. 1, p. 120.

[16] J. Buckner, *A Sermon before the Lords November 29, 1798* (London, 1798), p. 15; W. Buller, *A Sermon . . . 1796* (London, 1796), p. 8; Priestley, *Letters to Burke*, p. 119, and *An Appeal to the Public*, second edition (Birmingham, 1792), pp. 76–87.

[17] Wilberforce, *Practical View*, pp. 405–6; More 'Strictures on Female Education', 1799, *Works*, vol. 5, p. 25. See also More's address to the poor of Shipham, Somerset, in the food crisis of 1801, in M. More, *The Mendip Annals* (London, 1859), pp. 242–5. See also [J. Bean], *A Charge Addressed to the Clergy of any Diocese* (London, 1792), p. 12.

eternal welfare, or to be feared and controlled for the good of society. Only the implementation of religious restraints and sanctions could achieve both aims.

Restraint

On 30 January 1789 Bishop Pretyman-Tomline reminded the House of Lords that Christianity was the religion best adapted to restrain men's passions and control their appetites.[18] He was not being prophetic; such comments were commonplace – all that was to change as a result of the French Revolution was their frequency, centrality and intensity.

Burke was the earliest writer to emphasise the new importance this argument was to assume. Much of his *Reflections* was devoted to an examination of the damage being done to the French state by the severance of its relationship with the church.[19] Those post-*Reflections* writings which constituted his anti-Jacobin crusade re-echoed with vibrant denunciations of deism and atheism. But among the passion, the assertions and the fury, Burke set out an argument; he explained why he believed religion was indispensable in maintaining social order, stability and a just state.

Burke believed that a state with no religion would fall either into anarchy or into despotism. Man was an imperfect creature who had fallen from grace; original sin was a reality. Something was necessary to restrain men's appetites; they must excise all 'the lust of selfish will', and that could never happen without religion. Christian theology traditionally opposed duty to will. Duties were imposed by God, will was a thing of the Devil. Only a society controlled by religious restraints was sufficiently stable to enjoy some degree of political liberty. Only religion could restrain by means of internalised obligations. In its absence, despotism was the only alternative to anarchy.[20]

Burke believed that political liberty depended upon the acceptance of religious restraints by the people because in a free state the people enjoyed a degree of power and all those who possessed power had to be made to feel they acted in trust and were accountable to God for their conduct. Such restraint, of course, operated not only on the governed, but on all sections of society, on electors, on landowners and on governors. Those who ruled

---

[18] *Sermon*, 1789, p. 16.

[19] See Burke, *Corr.*, vol. 6, p. 92.

[20] *Ibid.*, p. 270; Burke, *Reflections*, pp. 190, 192, 256; and *Works*, vol. 3, p. 79. On the profound philosophical gulf between Price and Burke, and Burke's support of Locke's epistemology against Price's concept of an innate moral sense, see Frederick Dreyer, 'The Genesis of Burke's *Reflections*', *JMH*, 50 (1978), 462–79, and Rodney Kilcup, 'Burke's Historicism', *JMH*, 49 (1977), 394–410 (pp. 395–7).

states must do so not according to their own arbitrary will, but under the law; divine obligation demanded it.[21]

Burke had already partially developed this argument before the French Revolution led him to refine it. In the Hastings case he had argued in 1788 that law and arbitrary power were opposites and that eternal laws of justice bound judges along with everyone else; 'man is born to be governed by law; and he that will substitute *will* in the place of it is an enemy to God'.[22] In 1791 he reflected on what happened if one removed God from political consideration. Not only did the people lack social restraint, but the power of rulers became limitless. There was no independent 'tribunal of conscience' to which people could turn. If rulers were not responsible to God who enforced the moral law, then there was no way of limiting 'the will of prevalent power'.[23] That sanction depended upon the ruler's faith, for the divine enforcement came in eternity.

Burke's *Reflections* was in advance of its time. However, a few other conservative writers, between 1790 and 1792, advanced similar and sometimes identical arguments.[24] Samuel Cooper argued that since religion restrained rulers as well as ruled there was less need of popular participation in government in a Christian state than in an atheist one. The Baptist minister, Lawrence Butterworth, suggested it was the obligation to restraint which reconciled the doctrines of providence and free-will. Shute Barrington in his 1792 *Charge* to the clergy of Durham argued that it was the 'primary sanctions' of religion, and the duties and obligations 'independent of all civil authority' which they imposed, which stood between society and chaos.[25]

The thesis also had its opponents between 1790 and 1793. Some argued from a unitarian, others from an atheist standpoint. Both James Mackintosh and Mary Wollstonecraft echoed Hume, though only Mackintosh acknowledged the debt. He recalled Hume's argument that religious passions tended to fanaticism and were far more destructive of public peace than conducive to order.[26] Wollstonecraft, who was then still in the unitarian camp, merely questioned whether religious restraints were an *effective*

---

[21] *Reflections*, pp. 190, 192, 195, 274. See T. P. Schofield, 'English Conservative Thought', pp. 133–7.

[22] Burke, *Works*, vol. 7, p. 101.

[23] *Works*, vol. 2, p, 543; vol. 3, p. 79.

[24] For example, *Observations on Doctor Price's Revolution Sermon* (London, 1790), pp. 4–5; H. More, 'An Estimate of the Religion of the Fashionable World' (1790), *Works*, vol. 11, p. 122; 'Remarks on the Speech of M. Dupont' (1792), *Works*, vol. 11, p. 220; [W. Jones], *A Small Whole-Length of Dr Priestley* (London, 1792), p. 10.

[25] S. Cooper, *First Principles*, p. 142; L. Butterworth, *Thoughts on Moral Government and Agency . . .* (Evesham, 1792), pp. 51, 53, 62; Barrington, *Charge*, 1792, pp. 16–17.

[26] Mackintosh, *Vindiciae Gallicae*, pp. 141–2; Hume, 'Of Superstition and Enthusiasm', *Essays and Treatises*, vol. 1, pp. 75–81. On Hume's position see above, pp. 69–71.

sanction, suggesting men would sooner give to charity on their deathbed than restrain their passions during life.[27]

In 1790 Joseph Priestley idealistically rejected the social need for religious restraints. While he agreed that a religion, especially Christianity, was *useful* in maintaining social order, he denied it was essential. Good laws and proper administration should be sufficient to keep men from injuring one another. The Birmingham Riots of the following year changed his tune; then he sang a lament on the inability of the established church to restrain the mob.[28]

The most important critique of the thesis, from an intellectual point of view, came in 1793 from William Godwin, though its immediate practical influence was limited. His whole argument was based on the assumption that Christian eschatological claims were false and the restraints and sanctions arising from them deceptions. He argued that any system based on deceit was fundamentally insecure, and that it would, in any case, influence only the sober and thoughtful, not the violent and ungovernable. Moreover, he claimed that the Greek, Roman and ancient Egyptian religions had involved no threat of eternal retribution and yet public order had been maintained. Christian fables might amuse the imagination, but could never replace reason and judgment as the fundamental principles of human conduct. Government should be open to scrutiny and rational enquiry. The governed should not take, on blind trust, the decisions of their rulers; but before men could freely participate in government, the deception of religious restraint must be removed.[29]

However, Godwin's utopian logic notwithstanding, the religious restraint argument came to dominate Christian political and social thought in 1793 and 1794. The same points were made time and again in episcopal and archidiaconal charges, in sermons on fast and thanksgiving days, in Assize and Militia sermons, in pamphlets and books.[30] The predominant position

---

[27] M. Wollstonecraft, *A Vindication of the Rights of Men* . . . (London, 1790), p. 78.

[28] Priestley, *Appeal to the Public*, pp. 76–7; 'Familiar Letters', *Works*, vol. 19, pp. 186–7. By 1798, in Newfoundland, Priestley was arguing 'when there is no sense of religion, no fear of God, or respect for a future state, there will be no good morals that can be depended upon. Laws may restrain the excesses of vice, but they cannot impart the principles of virtue' (article in *Aurora*, February 1798, reprinted in *Memoirs of Dr Joseph Priestley* (London, 1806), p. 446).

[29] Godwin, *Political Justice*, pp. 493–505. The development of Godwin's views on religion is usefully surveyed in D. Fleisher, *William Godwin: A Study in Liberalism* (London, 1951), pp. 136–45. For his influence on some Scottish religious thinkers, see Kirkland, 'Impact of French Revolution on Scottish Religious Life', pp. 42, 44–51.

[30] C. F. Sheridan, *An Essay upon the True Principles of Civil Liberty* (London, 1793), p. ix; A. Maclaine, *Religion, a Preservative against Barbarism and Anarchy* (London, 1793), pp. 16–17; Gilbank, *Duties of Man*, p. 10; Huntingford, *Sermon* . . . *1793*, pp. 16–19; Plymley, *Charge*, p. 15; Pretyman Tomline, *Charge*, 1794, p. 9; J. Owen, *Subordination Considered*, pp. 13–16, and *The Retrospect; or, Reflections on the State of Religion and Politics in France and Great Britain* (London, 1794), p. 27.

these established in 1793–4 was maintained consistently throughout the rest of the period, especially during critical phases of the war.[31] Essentially the argument had two main aspects. First, religion established what social behaviour should be; secondly, it provided powerful motives for individuals to comply with those standards.

The reluctance of conservatives to engage in abstract, philosophical theorising meant that there was little discussion of moral epistemology. Mary Wollstonecraft, from the standpoint of 'rational Christianity' she was adopting in 1790, insisted only moral laws deduced by her reason were valid for her.[32] Like William Godwin she based her morality on reason and utility.[33] The Baptist Lawrence Butterworth and the Anglican Samuel Cooper defended the epistemological role of revelation. Cooper insisted that reason could never establish a *fact*, and, although the moral law deduced in a system of natural religion was very similar to the Christian code, only divine revelation, when it came, gave us certain knowledge of what God willed our behaviour to be.[34]

But such arguments were rare in the 1790s. While virtually every Christian would have agreed with Cooper, most considered the time inopportune for such theoretical debate. They took the epistemological argument for granted and concentrated instead upon the social process. Religion was the source of morality, and morality influenced general opinions and attitudes, which were reflected in the manners of society, that is, in the social behaviour of man.

Morality and social order

Like many of his contemporaries, Burke was well aware of the social control function involved:

Manners are of more importance than laws. Upon them, in a great measure, the laws depend. The law touches us here and there, and now and then. Manners are what vex and soothe, corrupt or purify, exalt or debase, barbarize or refine us, by a constant, steady, uniform, insensible operation, like that of the air we breathe in. They give their whole form and colour to our lives.[35]

Non-Christians agreed with Burke thus far, but denied that religion

---

[31] For example, in 1798: Armitstead, *Sermon*, p. 6; J. Buckner, *Charge . . . to the Diocese of Chichester . . . 1798* (London, 1799), p. 12; J. W. Wickes, *Sermon . . . March 7, 1798* (London, 1798), pp. 7–8; F. Cornwall, *A Sermon . . . before the Lords March 7th, 1798* (London, 1798), pp. 11–12.
[32] Wollstonecraft, *Rights of Men*, p. 74.
[33] Godwin, *Political Justice*, pp. 98–101, 165–8.
[34] Butterworth, *Thoughts on Moral Government*, pp. 14, 42; S. Cooper, *First Principles*, pp. 73–4, 100–5, 111–18. See T. P. Schofield, 'English Conservative Thought', pp. 46–8.
[35] Burke, 'First Letter on a Regicide Peace', *Works*, vol. 5, p. 208.

should be the moral base of manners. Godwin conceded that opinion was 'the most potent agent' in political society. But he argued that, in the past, religion had taught false opinions, based on superstition and prejudice and that these had supported despotic governments which usurped individual rights. Mackintosh argued that a secular morality which informed conduct was more reliable and effective than a religious one. Paine, in the second part of *The Age of Reason*, agreed that the 'fragments of morality' were the bonds by which society was held together, and without which it could not exist, but he insisted that they were not peculiar to revealed religion but arose naturally from the human conscience as their operation in ancient Greece showed.[36]

But these views of Godwin, Mackintosh and Paine were exceptions. The vast majority of writers of the period agreed with Burke that the morality which informed manners must have a religious base. As an anonymous critic of Price in 1790 observed, just as government depended on opinion more than 'the terror of actual force', so religion supported some opinions in a way nothing else would. Although many may not have been as brutally frank as Burke was in talking of 'the preventive police of morality', they would not have dissented from the concept.[37]

The problem of religion and social control was pondered deeply in the mid 1790s by a number of Christian thinkers ranging from the utilitarian William Paley to his Evangelical critic Thomas Gisborne. In his *Inquiry into the Duties of Men* (1795) Gisborne examined the Christian basis of duty. Towards the end of this lengthy work he reflected that increasingly men did not regard themselves as being bound by Christian revelation. Some denounced religion as superstition; others, the 'rational Christians' and deists, regarded themselves as obliged to obey only those precepts of morality God allowed them to discover by reason; still others nominally accepted Christianity, but claimed a strict observation of its precepts was incompatible with their political and professional duties and was not required of them in the existing circumstances. Religion appeared to Gisborne to do little to control such men.[38]

Paley, towards the end of his *Evidences of Christianity* (1794), struck an equally reflective, but more optimistic, note. The influence of Christianity on social order was one which history, in its concentration on the public acts of famous men, concealed, for

---

[36] Godwin, *Political Justice*, pp. 579–81; Mackintosh, *Vindiciae Gallicae*, pp. 215–19, 329; Paine, *Age of Reason*, pp. 186–7.

[37] *Observations on Doctor Price's Revolution Sermon* p. 41; Burke, 'Letter to a Noble Lord' (1796), *Works*, vol. 5, p. 128. Nor was Burke as crude and cynical as this might imply; compare *Reflections*, p. 200.

[38] Vol. 2, pp. 518–20.

religion operates most upon those of whom history knows the least, upon fathers and mothers in their families, upon men servants and maid servants, upon the orderly tradesman, the quiet villager, the manufacturer at his loom, the husbandman in his field.

Although he believed that reason and utility were adequate intellectually to reconcile any thinking man to government, Paley also recognised that in practice religion played a valuable role among the poor.[39]

The state of the war, the invasion scares, the food crises and the conspiracy theory of revolution led to more and more stress being laid upon the importance of religion and morality in keeping order in the years from 1797. Religion and morality were the cement of civil society, the moral equivalent to gravity in the physical world: remove them and society would dissolve. The clergy must, therefore, instruct men in correct manners and teach them their duties if society and government were to avoid confusion.[40] But against this establishment chorus, a few anxious voices could be heard, notably those of William Wilberforce and Robert Hall.

In 1797 Wilberforce developed at length Gisborne's fear that the morality of most men was not Christian; their principles and opinions were generally opposite to the essence of the Gospels. The bulk of nominal Christians quite ignored the Holy Spirit, preferring to invent a religious system for themselves instead of taking it from the Word of God. This was almost as bad as having no religion at all, and yet religion was vital to society and to liberty. With religion to restrain it liberty was beneficial, but when religion was abandoned, liberty became 'infinitely mischievous' and needed to be extinguished.[41]

Another fear of Wilberforce's that Christianity was being reduced to a code of morality, 'a set of penal statutes', was shared by Robert Hall. In the past, Hall argued, the principal purpose of religion had been to worship God, social morality was subordinate to that and the good of society to both. But in recent years these priorities had been inverted. Now, he argued, virtue and religion were only used to procure the temporal, physical good of individuals or society.[42] The social role of religion as a means of control and restraint was indeed the dominant theme of those years, but, although Wilberforce and Hall's voices were not the only ones to express disquiet, most Christians accepted the change of emphasis as necessary and proper.

[39] *Works*, vol. 3, p. 417.
[40] E. Edwards, *The Things Which Belong unto our Peace* (Brecknock, 1797), pp. 3, 14–15; Buckner, *Charge . . . 1798*, p. 10; Cornwall, *Sermon 1798*, pp. 7–10; Watson, 'Sermon to the Society for the Suppression of Vice' (1804), *Misc. T*, vol. 1, pp. 520–3.
[41] Wilberforce, *Practical View*, pp. 12–13, 76–7, 113, 142–3.
[42] *Ibid.*, p. 180; Hall, 'Fast Day Sermon', 19 October 1803, *Works*, vol. 1, pp. 161–2.

Popular education

It was necessary not only to establish a moral code but also to teach it.[43] In 1792 Sarah Trimmer further developed the thoughts on Charity Schools she had advanced in 1787, and produced some 'improving' books for children.[44] Hannah More turned seriously to popular tract writing only in 1795; she devoted the early years of the French Revolution to founding schools in the Mendips.[45] The Somerset farmers to whom she turned for financial backing were often hostile; one said education would make the poor 'lazy and useless', another that religion was 'a very dangerous thing' which had caused mischief ever since the monks had come to Glastonbury. In 1789, at Wedmore, a farmer predicted a rebellion like those in France and Ireland if a school were opened. One farmer's wife, More reported, appeared to understand the doctrine of philosophical necessity as she argued that the lower classes were fated to be 'poor, ignorant and wicked', and no one could alter what was decreed.

Hannah More countered these attitudes with arguments based on expediency and control, telling the farmers the schools would stop theft from their land and lower the poor rates. In practice, the schools taught social subordination and political loyalty, and the 'Bishop in Petticoats' delivered an annual 'charge' which reflected clearly the schools' social and political values. She stressed the obligation to obey social superiors, endure hardship and maintain social unity and harmony; the interests of the poor were represented as being identical with those of the rich. In her private correspondence, More stressed her schools' strictness and limitations; 'They learn of weekdays such coarse works as may fit them for servants. I allow of no writing ... Principles, not opinions, are what I labour to give them.'[46]

Not all were convinced by these reassurances. The Rector of Lincoln College, Oxford, considered Sunday Schools pious but ill-judged. Their well-intentioned supporters were playing into the hands of English Jacobins and Dissenters, who encouraged the movement and were, he claimed, privately rejoicing to see the Church of England thus contributing to its own destruction. By teaching the poor to read, the schools were opening the door to sedition and political poison.[47]

---

[43] See above, Chapter 6, note 30.

[44] S. Trimmer, *Reflections upon the Education of Children* (London, 1792), and *Instructive Tales*, third edition (London, 1815). Compare Chapter 6, note 32, above.

[45] *Village Politics* (1792) was the exception. Schools were opened at Cheddar (1789); Shipham and Rowberrow (1790); Congresbury, Yatton and Axebridge (1791); Nailsea (1792); Blagdon (1795); and Wedmore (1798). For a brief account see Jones, *Hannah More*, pp. 151–71.

[46] *Memoirs*, vol. 2, pp. 207–9; M. More, *Mendip Annals*, pp. 6, 9, 14, 38, 88, 151–4, 212, 237–8, 242–5.

[47] Tatham, *Letters to ... Burke*, pp. 94–5.

But, however many backwoodsmen might have agreed with Tatham in the privacy of their studies, the majority of published sermons and pamphlets by churchmen took the opposite view. One would, of course, expect the preachers at the annual Charity Schools Service in St Paul's Cathedral to be sympathetic to the movement. Year after year they stressed the crucial role of the religious education of the poor in the maintenance of social control, the need to train children to subjection, moderation and control, and to teach them to behave well before their superiors, to preserve order and tranquillity, and maintain and promote public prosperity. Nothing, it was claimed, could do this better than the church catechism the schools taught.[48]

However, what was much more significant was the number of bishops who chose to recommend the establishment of Sunday Schools to their clergy. Bishop Porteus was an enthusiastic supporter, and a personal friend of Hannah More, but sentiments in favour of popular education were commonplace in episcopal charges.[49] Pitt's old tutor, Bishop Pretyman-Tomline, recommended Sunday Schools in 1794 as

the means best calculated for diffusing a general knowledge of the Scriptures among the inferior classes of society, and for instilling into their minds just notions of their religious duty. This is the most effectual method of preventing turbulence and discontent, and of securing a due obedience to the civil magistrate. A good Christian cannot be a bad citizen.[50]

These episcopal sentiments were expressed on a more popular level in 1793 by 'Job Nott', who praised Hannah More and urged the poor of Birmingham to send their children to the Sunday Schools.[51]

The most eloquent opponents of religious education for the poor were not, in fact, clerical reactionaries but infidel radicals. While the 'rational Christian' Priestley was at least lukewarm in his support, the deist Paine and atheist Godwin were hostile.[52] Godwin argued that religious education restrained the mind and taught errors which had been exploded long ago.

[48] Nickolls, *Political as Well as Moral Principles*, pp. 28–9, 31–8; G. I. Huntingford, *A Sermon . . . 1796* (London, 1796), pp. 3–5, 7–8, 26; J. Law, *A Sermon . . . 1797* (London, 1797), pp. 10–12, 15–17; J. Buckner, *A Sermon . . .* (London, 1800), pp. 2–3, 12–14.

[49] LPL, MS 2103, ff.33, 106–7; J. Butler, 'Charge to the Clergy of the Diocese of Hereford', 1789, *Select Sermons* (Hereford, 1801), p. 348; S. Barrington, 'Letter to the Diocese of Sarum', 16 October 1789, *Sermons*, pp. 109–10, and 'Charge to the Clergy of the Diocese of Durham', 1797, *ibid.*, pp. 232ff; R. Prosser, *Sermon . . . 1797* (Newcastle-upon-Tyne, 1797).

[50] Pretyman-Tomline, *Charge*, 1794, p. 18.

[51] 'Job Nott', *Life and Adventures*, Preface, pp. 1–2, and *Further Advice from Job Nott* (Birmingham, 1800), p. 7.

[52] Priestley, 'Familiar Letters', *Works*, vol. 19, p. 289, and *Appeal to the Public*, pp. 77–8; Paine, 'Worship and Church Bells', 1797, *Writings*, vol. 4, p. 257; Godwin, *Political Justice*, pp. 612–18. On *Political Justice*'s aim to demystify human relations see M. Schrivener, 'Godwin's Philosophy: A Revaluation', *JHI*, 39 (1978), 615–26 (p. 617).

He suggested the English universities were a century behind enlightened thought; instead of echoing Aristotle, Aquinas, Bellarmine and Coke, men should be critical, questioning, thinking for themselves. The Sunday schools, Godwin believed, were just as bad; 'the chief lessons that are taught, are a superstitious veneration for the Church of England, and to bow to every man in a handsome coat. All this is directly contrary to the true interests of mankind.'

Conscience and eschatology

Godwin's chief objection to Christianity was the psychological coercion of its eschatological claims. This was the crucial element in the social control process. Revelation had established the moral code, Sunday Schools could teach it, but only conscience and interior motives could enforce it effectively. In the context of rebellion and invasion scares, Bishop Buckner reminded the clergy of Chichester of its importance in his 1798 *Charge*. Civil laws and physical coercion were very limited in their operation; religion alone, by its hold on the consciences of men and promise of an hereafter, could keep men to a virtuous path.[53] He was reiterating a point made increasingly in the 1790s. Man must reflect on the brevity and proportional insignificance of earthly life in the context of eternity, and must ponder the Four Last Things. Such eschatological awareness had a dual role, restraining men from revolt and reconciling them to their lot; it both threatened punishment and promised bliss.[54]

Burke reflected this dual role well. In the *Reflections* he sarcastically expressed the hope that the writings of Voltaire and the *philosophes* on the future state of rewards and punishments were to be sent to the soldiers of the revolutionary army.[55] But he never used religion merely as a crude and cynical threat of retribution. That would indeed be 'a mere invention to keep the vulgar in obedience'.[56] He implied rather that religion fulfilled a profound psychological need; comforting men on their 'short but tedious journey through the world'.[57] Much of the bitterness of Burke's attack upon

---

[53] Buckner, *Charge*, 1798, p. 12.
[54] See, *inter alia*, *A Vindication of . . . Burke's Reflections* (London, 1791), p. 110; Watson, *Apology for the Bible*, p. 3; Edwards, *Things Which Belong*, p. iv; John Law, *Sermon . . . 1797*, pp. 16–17; Wickes, *Sermon*, pp. 7–8; W. Vincent, *A Sermon Preached before the . . . House of Commons June 1, 1802* (London, 1802), p. 10.
[55] *Reflections*, p. 335. Burke had, presumably, missed Voltaire's comment on the value of a belief in a god and a future life in keeping in order his servant, his lawyer, his tailor and even his wife; Voltaire, *Philosophical Dictionary*, pp. 251, 605.
[56] *Reflections*, p. 200.
[57] Burke, *Works*, vol. 6, p. 67. In reducing these views to the comment 'religion is a sort of opium for the people', Michael Freeman, *Edmund Burke and the Critique of Political Radicalism* (Oxford, 1980), pp. 65–6, 81, misses much of the complexity and ambiguity of Burke's beliefs. Burke's reference to the poor's 'consolation in the final proportions of eternal justice' in the

the Jacobins in the last years of his life rested upon his genuine anguish that they would take from men the comfort, consolation and hope of the Christian faith and replace them with nothing but 'a system which makes life without dignity, death without hope'.[58] The depth of feeling is understandable, for Burke wrote those lines only a few months after the death of his adored son, Richard. While he recognised religion and its prospect of eternity as a potent source of social control, he also saw it consoling men in times of sickness, pain, poverty and death, and argued that the hope of immortality dignified human nature.[59] Both of these sentiments were ones which all Christians, and indeed some others, could share. Priestley pointed out that, despite their other doctrinal heterodoxies, Unitarians did believe in the Resurrection, and even the deist Paine recognised some retribution in an after-life.[60]

The whole social argument reflected far fewer denominational differences than the constitutional ones had done. True, the Catholics were still preoccupied with constitutional issues and paid less attention to the social arguments than other Christians, but they did not ignore them completely. They stressed the importance of the doctrine of Purgatory, and the role of the confessional, and insisted that Catholic education was more efficacious than the Protestant.[61] But many people considered it was the Methodists who made the greatest practical contribution to teaching Christian social theory to the poor, although Bradburn was anxious to divorce morality from eschatology.[62] Nor should the importance of Hannah More's *Cheap Repository Tracts* be underestimated. They reduced eschatological paraenesis to a popular level and their social message was a powerful one.

Reflections, p. 372, which Freeman cites, is neither cold nor remote, but rich and real in intention.

[58] Burke, *Works*, vol. 5, p. 205.

[59] Burke, *Works*, vol. 6, p. 125.

[60] Priestley, 'Familiar Letters', *Works*, vol. 19, p. 193, and 'Letters to the Philosophers and Politicians of France on the Subject of Religion' (1793), *Works*, vol. 19, p. 124, though Bishop William Cleaver questioned this in his 1791 Abbey Martyrdom Day *Sermon*, p. 18.

[61] Potts, *Inquiry*, pp. 14–16, 23–4, 32–4, 46–7; F. Plowden, *Case Stated*, pp. 7, 32–3. On the effectiveness of Catholic education see John Marmion, 'The Beginnings of the Catholic Poor Schools in England', *Recusant History*, 17 (1984), 67–83, and J. Kitching, 'The Catholic Poor Schools 1800–1845', *Journal of Educational Administration and History*, 1 (1969), 1–8, and 2 (1969), 1–12.

[62] Bradburn, *Methodism Defended*, p. 47. The importance of the Methodist role was recognised at the time by, for example, Priestley, 'Familiar Letters', *Works*, vol. 19, p. 197, and *Appeal to the Public*, pp. 77–8; Coleridge, 'The Watchman', 1 March 1796, *Works*, vol. 2, p. 13. The twentieth-century debate is reviewed above, Chapter 1, note 30.

The nature of man

The lines between Christian and infidel, religion and irreligion are not easy ones to draw. Edmund Burke and Samuel Johnson both suggested that there was a kind of gradation from Catholics at the top who believed most, down through Anglicans and Methodists to Protestant Dissenters, who believed increasingly less, so to Unitarians, then deists and finally to atheists, who believed there was no God of any kind. One is faced more with an increasingly diluted stream than with clear-cut divisions. A distinction could be made between Unitarians, who acknowledged if not Christ's divinity at least His Resurrection, and deists, who did not. Or a line could be drawn between deists like Paine and Voltaire, who believed in a god of some sort and for whom a religious form of social control could have some meaning, and atheists, who did not.

But a good case can be made for making the fundamental division between the Protestant Dissenters and the Unitarians, for that is the point which marks a dramatic and crucial difference in views about the nature of man. Unitarians such as Price and Priestley, in common with most (though not all) deists and atheists, took an optimistic view of man and saw him as being capable of, and progressing towards, perfection in this life. Catholics, Anglicans, Methodists and Old Dissenters all saw man as an unregenerate, fallen creature who was, on earth, necessarily imperfect. Nothing influences a person's views about politics and society more than his beliefs and assumptions about the nature of man.

The belief that man was a necessarily imperfect creature led Christians to two political conclusions which seemed particularly pertinent in the 1790s. First they asserted that man's flawed nature made life in a state of nature exceedingly unpleasant; the threat of anarchy should be avoided at all costs. Secondly they argued that it was illogical to expect imperfect man to create a perfect system of government, and unfair to criticise king and constitution because they were not such.[63] The traditional Catholic doctrines of original sin and the Fall of man were widely accepted by Protestants. Anglican bishops referred to them, but it was Evangelicals and Methodists who stressed the doctrines most strongly. Samuel Bradburn insisted that original sin was the leading principle of Christianity; men were really equal only in their common corruption. Hannah More adopted the same position implicitly in the stories and rhymes of her tracts and explicitly in her serious works. Wilberforce complained that men underestimated human corruption; vice was constitutional and habitual, not accidental and temporary; man was radically and profoundly tainted with evil and this must be taken

---

[63] Hayes, *Sermon*, pp. 6–7; *Observations on Doctor Price's Sermon*, pp. 4–5, 7 (fn).

into account in establishing and in judging any system of government.[64]

Priestley, however, rejected the doctrine of original sin. Man, he believed, was a being capable of achieving perfection, and Priestley related this belief both to his doctrine of progress and to his millenarian views. The world was destined to improve wonderfully in knowledge, virtue and happiness and the changes would lead to an earthly paradise.[65] Paine also believed in the essential goodness of man; it was the existing form of society that was evil, and government which corrupted human nature.[66] But the infidel case was stated most clearly and eloquently by Mary Wollstonecraft in her *History of the French Revolution*.

By 1794 she had left the society of the Newington Green Unitarians, had lived in Paris, and was moving into the Godwin circle. 'We must', she insisted,

get entirely clear of all the notions drawn from the wild traditions of original sin: the eating of the apple, the theft of Prometheus, the opening of Pandora's box and other fables too tedious to enumerate, on which priests have erected their tremendous structures of imposition, to persuade us, that we are naturally inclined to evil.

Instead, man must allow the human heart to expand, to grow wiser and happier. It was only the repression of natural desires which made man vicious, deprived him of the dignity of character which rested on truth. Man must free himself of this belief in his evil nature and respect himself. She went on to expound a visionary humanism and belief in the progress of knowledge and understanding and argued that thus came perfection.[67]

To Christian eyes, however, the fruits of the French experiment appeared to confirm the theological doctrine, and human corruption, not perfection, appeared to be man's true nature.[68] It was, of course, against the French context both of Enlightenment and of Revolution that the Christian concept of the nature of man was most vigorously reasserted. The challenge was crucial, for not only did it question the nature and working of society, and therefore of government; it also queried the whole theology of man. By contrast, the earlier political concentration on constitutional validation by abstract philosophical argument seemed almost trivial. The switch to sociologically and psychologically orientated arguments reflected not only a political desire to defend an established government and form of society, but

---

[64] Barrington, 1797 Durham Charge, *Sermons*, pp. 207–9; Bradburn, *Methodism Defended*, pp. 6–7, 52–6, and *Equality*, pp. 7–8; More, 'Strictures', *Works*, vol. 5, p. 25; Wilberforce, *Practical View*, pp. 24–30.

[65] Priestley, *Sermon*, 19 April 1793, pp. 31–5.

[66] Paine, *Rights of Man*, p. 230.

[67] M. Wollstonecraft, *An Historical and Moral View of . . . the French Revolution* (London, 1794), vol. 1, pp. 17–20, 239.

[68] See, for example, More, 'Strictures', *Works*, vol. 5, p. 25; J. Hewlett, *The Christian Hero* (London, 1803), pp. 10–12.

also the spiritual need to defend an entire theology. To reject the doctrine of original sin would be to embark on a course which had profound political, social and moral consequences. Christians were defending not just the established political and social order, but also an intellectual and conceptual universe. The concept of the nature of man not only ordered man's vision of the world and the social relationships within it; it also defined, in its cosmic and eternal dimensions, the relationship of men with God.

10

Christianity, infidelity and government

Christianity and government

Conservative and radical Christians

The widespread assumption that Christianity was a natural prop to government rested upon an interpretation of the faith which did not go unchallenged or undefended. On the most superficial level, there was some discussion of whether or not it was proper to introduce politics into the pulpit. Most agreed in practice that, whilst it was improper for their political opponents to do so, their own views were so quintessentially truthful they were not out of place. Burke argued that politics should be kept out of the pulpit if the preacher were a man like Richard Price; such a 'confusion of duties' benefited neither liberty, government nor religion.[1] Like most establishment writers, he assumed that sermons defending the political and social status quo were acceptable, while those advocating change were not.[2]

Many radicals pointed out that political sermons from conservative clerics were traditional on Martyrdom Day and on fast days appointed by the king and ministers for political reasons; moreover, from 1793 the clergy had prayed for the success of the nation's fleets and armies against those of another political ideology.[3] In 1793 the Vicar of Wellsbourn, J. H. Williams, complained that the clergy had become mere instruments of the secular government. The church was no more than an 'engine of state' valued and rewarded for its social usefulness. Conscience made a clergyman defend government in general, but ambition led him to support the policies of an administration. Williams was objecting specifically to being required to defend the war in a fast day sermon, but he was also aware of the more

---

[1] Burke, *Reflections*, p. 156.
[2] Mavor, *Christian Politics*, pp. 13–15; J. Butler, *Brief Reflections upon . . . Burke* (Canterbury, [1790/1?]), p. 22; Clayton, *Duty of Christians*, pp. 37–8. See also T. Christie, *Letters on the Revolution of France* (London, 1791), pp 10–15.
[3] Bousfield, *Observations on . . . Burke's Pamphlet*, p. 10; Priestley, *Letters to Burke*, pp. 46–7; *Remarks on Clayton*, p. 17; Coleridge, 'Essay on Fasts', The Watchman, 9 March 1796, *Works*, vol. 2, pp. 52–3.

profound problem caused when the administration forced an established clergyman into 'the insidious dilemma' of either acting contrary to his religious convictions, or opening himself to the accusation of disloyalty.[4]

At the heart of this conflict were differing interpretations of the nature of Christianity and its relationship to the state. There were, in England, two major traditions. One was the establishment tradition, which saw Christianity as political only to the extent necessary for it to support government in general, the 1688 constitutional settlement, and the established social order. The other was the Dissenting tradition, which insisted that religion and politics were quite separate, to the extent that dissent from the established order in the church should not exclude men from playing a full role in the established order in the state.[5] A variation of the traditional Dissenting position was the Catholic argument that, since religion and politics were quite separate things, a spiritual allegiance to the pope in no sense conflicted with a temporal allegiance to the sovereign.[6]

A few, however, adopted more radical positions. In the 1790s there was a small group of thinkers, deists, Unitarians and Christians who argued that Christ and His earliest followers should be seen as radical opponents of the established social order of their day. On 14 July 1791, the Baptist Minister Mark Wilks opened his sermon with the words 'Jesus Christ was a Revolutionist'. He urged his congregation to carry on the work Christ had begun and assured them that the French Revolution was of God and would endure.[7] Paine regarded Christ as an amicable man who preached equality, a 'virtuous reformer and revolutionist', who was misunderstood and too little imitated.[8] Coleridge, in 1795, stressed Christ's insistence on strict equality. Inequality, he argued, arose from the institution of landed property and was exacerbated by the growth of manufactories and cities. These gave rise to hostile passions, disputes and wars, and were driving men away from simplicity, equality and God. The true Christian, Coleridge argued, was forbidden all property and could not enter into commerce; any possessions would activate his selfish passions. His point was not that men should own equal amounts of property, but that they should own none at all; goods should be held in common.[9] Such a concept of Christianity contrasted

---

[4] J. H. Williams, *Piety, Charity, and Loyalty* (Birmingham, 1793), pp. v–vii.

[5] For this dissenting tradition see, *inter alia*, Priestley, 'Familiar Letters', *Works*, vol. 19, p. 155, and 'Letters to . . . France', *Works*, vol. 21, p. 104; *Remarks on Clayton*, p. 7; J. Townsend, *The Principles of Protestant Dissenters* (Bath, 1791), p. 11; Hall, 'Love of Freedom', *Works*, vol. 3, pp. 9–10, 38–42.

[6] Potts, *Inquiry*, pp. 96–101.

[7] M. Wilks, *French Revolution*, pp. 5–7. On Wilks see C. B. Jewson, 'Norwich Baptists', and *The Jacobin City: A Portrait of Norwich in its Reaction to the French Revolution 1788–1802* (Glasgow, 1975), pp. 26–7, 63–4, 68–70, 138–41.

[8] Paine, *Age of Reason*, pp. 26–8.

[9] Coleridge, 'Lectures on Revealed Religion', 1795, Lecture Six, *Works*, vol. 1, pp. 215–29.

sharply not only with the established church's, but also with that of bourgeois Dissenters like Priestley (who complained of St Francis of Assisi that his mind was so wholly religious, he was 'unfit for business'!).[10] While adopting a less utopian view than a youthful visionary and poet like Coleridge, the practical parliamentary reformer and Unitarian, Major John Cartwright, still saw Christianity in uncompromisingly radical terms. He described Christ as 'the Great Reformer' and St Paul as 'a Jewish Jacobin of old', and stressed that the origins of Christianity were among the poor and oppressed.[11]

The apolitical argument

Another group of individuals adopted a different but equally radical standpoint. Unwilling to harness Christ either to the cause of reform or to the defence of the status quo, they argued that He was wholly apolitical and laid down no rules for, nor interfered in, civil government.[12] This view could lead men to two quite separate practical conclusions: either that Christianity was irrelevant to government and men were free to pursue their own secular political ends untrammelled by spiritual considerations; or that their faith demanded they abstain wholly from any involvement in political concerns and devote themselves entirely to spiritual things. The latter view was, of course, the age-old concept of the *vita contemplativa* of the man of the spirit as opposed to the active civic life of *zōon politikon*.[13]

A religion which discouraged its adherents from any civic involvement, which forbade them actively to engage in politics, which discountenanced the sentiment of patriotism and led men to pacifism could be seen as positively dysfunctional in political and social terms, and many churchmen sought to establish that Christianity was not such a faith. Conservatives and radicals interpreted Christian principles in ways which suited their political aims. George Horne suggested that Christian meekness was no more than a variety of passive obedience and non-resistance to government. Joseph Priestley, however, argued that meekness did not require men to give up their civil rights or prohibit them from struggling to retain them. Robert Hall insisted that Christianity did not take men out of the world, but merely preserved them from the pollutions within it.[14] Perhaps Burke expressed the

[10] Priestley, 'General History of the Christian Church', *Works*, vol. 9, p. 417.

[11] J. Cartwright, *Commonwealth in Danger*, pp. lxxi–lxxiii, lxxviii, and *The Constitutional Defence of England* (London, 1796), p. 45.

[12] Coxe, *Letter to . . . Price*, p. 13; G. Croft, *The Test Laws Defended* (Birmingham, 1790), p. 18; Potts, *Inquiry*, p. 96; Clayton, *Duty of Christians*, pp. 14–22, 40; Parr, Assize Sermon 1797, *Works*, vol. 5, p. 507. Compare the views of Robert Haldane and some Scottish Evangelicals in Kirkwood, pp. 102–10.

[13] See above, pp. 64–5.

[14] Horne, 'Submission to Government', *Works*, vol. 3, p. 390; Priestley, 'A General History of the Christian Church', *Works*, vol. 8, p. 329; Hall, 'Love of Freedom', *Works*, vol. 3, pp. 40–2.

establishment view best. He agreed that humility and meekness were indeed the greatest Christian virtues, but argued that they led, not as Machiavelli had suggested, to weakness and effeminacy, but to civilisation. Burke looked for security, acceptance and loyal obedience, and found political utility in the Christian virtue of meekness.[15]

Soame Jenyns's argument that Christian principles were incompatible with an active political life had first appeared in 1757, 1776 and 1782, but the publication of his *Collected Works* by Cadell in 1790 gave them wider circulation and led many to try to refute them. The most serious and significant response was that of William Wilberforce in 1797. Wilberforce agreed with Jenyns's estimate of the poverty of superficial religion, but argued that his conclusions were too extreme, crude and extravagant. While he conceded that religion was improperly used by politicians, who exploited the words of scripture while avoiding the spirit of the faith, Wilberforce was anxious to justify Christian involvement in politics. If providence placed him in public life, he insisted, the true Christian must fulfil the duties of that role. But he must retain his own spiritual life and adhere strictly to the code of moral behaviour; the path was a narrow one: he must be in the world but not of it. Society and government needed a Christian contribution, as St Paul recognised. Indeed, far from being politically dysfunctional, if all men lived in the spirit of Christ there would be no discord; civil life would work without obstruction or disorder. Wilberforce did not try to refute Jenyns by logical argument or profound theological reasoning, rather he sought to show how in practice it was possible to follow the teachings of Christ while involved in active political life.[16] Christianity was most hostile to the great evil of political life, selfishness:

Vigorous, operative benevolence is her master principle. Moderation in temporal pursuits and enjoyments, comparative indifference to the issue of worldly projects, diligence in the discharge of personal and civil duties, resignation to the will of God, and patience under all the dispensations of his Providence, are among her daily lessons.[17]

In practice there was nothing in Wilberforce's faith which prevented him frequently supporting Pitt's administration and, with some reservations, defending the war.[18]

[15] Burke, *Works*, vol. 2, p. 536, vol. 5, p. 125; *Corr*, vol. 2, p. 277. Compare Paley, 'Evidences', *Works*, vol. 2, pp. 229–31.

[16] Wilberforce, *Practical View*, pp. 13–16, 180–1, 189, 218–19, 274–5, 389–91, 393–5, 403–16.

[17] *Ibid.*, p. 404.

[18] This support was seen as an anomaly by (amongst others) J. Mills, *The Speech . . . Delivered at the British Forum* (London, 1819), p. 12, though, in fact, Wilberforce also urged peace on Pitt. V. Kiernan, 'Evangelicalism and the French Revolution', p. 48, suggests Wilberforce's book was, in part, a response to the naval mutinies.

The morality of war

In the context of the French war, Jenyns's suggestion that Christianity was inconsistent with patriotism was one many sought to refute. Richard Price had occupied something of the same ground as Jenyns in his *Love of Country* discourse in 1789, when he argued that Christians must work for universal benevolence, not national advantage, which was a species of selfishness. Men should combine a natural affection for their own land with an awareness that they were also citizens of the world.[19] But after the outbreak of war, and especially in its darkest days, patriotism was increasingly defended as a Christian duty. Thomas Gisborne sought to explain Christ's silence on the issue by considering the complex political situation in Palestine with its volatile mix of Roman, Greek and Jewish patriotisms posing dangers to society. Christ's whole doctrine and conduct was however, Gisborne argued, calculated to inspire patriotism in a united country like Britain.[20] Many fast-day sermons, especially in 1797 and 1798, such as that of Richard de Courcy to the North Staffordshire Yeomanry, insisted that patriotism should lead the Christian to fight for his country.[21]

Fast-day sermons were also used by the significant group of Christians who were actively opposed to the war.[22] Some took this stand because they approved of the political principles of the French (mostly in the early years), others on pacifist grounds. While J. Bicheno considered the war against the French Republic needless and impolitic, J. H. Williams denounced its blood-thirsty spirit.[23] Vicesimus Knox's anti-war views were largely (self)-suppressed and became known only a generation later.[24] This minority view had a sound intellectual base, and was well organised and vocal, not to say vociferous. But it was a minority of Christians, and an even smaller minority of trinitarian Christians.

Meanwhile, academics and bishops defended the justice of the war. In a Westminster Abbey fast-day sermon before the House of Lords on 28 February 1794, the Bishop of Norwich, Manners Sutton, restated the Christian 'just war' thesis and made the war against the French appear to be both an act of self-defence and a crusade against infidelity.[25] In the following

[19] Pp. 2–8.
[20] Gisborne, *Duties of Men*, vol. 1, pp. 111–16.
[21] Edwards, *Things Which Belong*, p. 4; W. Barrow, *Sermon . . . March 7, 1798* (London, 1798), pp. 6–10; S. Parr, 'Sermon' Fast Day 19 October 1803, *Works*, vol. 2, pp. 635–7; de Courcy, *Self-Defence*, pp. 24–30.
[22] J. E. Cookson, *The Friends of Peace: Anti-War Liberalism in England, 1793–1815* (Cambridge, 1982), pp. 4–15, 30–52, 118–21, 134–6, 190–6, 205–7, 238–54.
[23] J. H. Williams, *Piety, Charity and Loyalty*, p. vii; Bicheno, *Word in Season*, p. 2.
[24] Knox's position is fully discussed below, pp. 222–5.
[25] C. Manners-Sutton, *A Sermon* (London, 1794), pp. 7–11, 14–16. See also the specious casuistry of J. Wilde, *Preliminary Lecture to the Course of Lectures on the Institutions of Justinian* (Edinburgh 1794), pp. xlix–l, and the biblical exegesis of R. Watson, *Apology for the Bible*, p. 349.

year Coleridge noted bitterly that every bishop but one had voted for the continuance of the war:

They deemed the fate of their religion to be involved in the contest: – Not the Religion of Peace, my Brothers, not the Religion of the meek and lowly Jesus, which forbids to his disciples all alliance with the powers of this World – but the Religion of Mitres and Mysteries, the Religion of Pluralities and Persecution, the Eighteen-Thousand-Pound-a-Year Religion of Episcopacy.[26]

It was not only bishops who defended the war. In the crisis years a range of well-established clergy and laity including a Canon Residentiary of St Paul's, the Rector of St George's Bloomsbury, the schoolmaster and parish priest Dr Samuel Parr, and Mrs Hannah More, all defended the war and opposed peace on grounds broadly similar to those of Manners Sutton.[27]

De Courcy assured his congregation of Yeomanry in 1798 that it was 'erroneous and unmanly' to suppose the military life incompatible with the Christian one.[28] He asserted rather than demonstrated this, but the support for volunteer corps and armed associations suggests such assertions were widely accepted. Hannah More encouraged the men of Shipham in Somerset to volunteer as an expression of their loyalty and Christianity. Indeed, some Church of England clergy were so enthusiastic they even joined armed associations themselves and had to be reminded by their bishops of the nature of the priestly office. In April 1798 the Archbishop of Canterbury and the bishops agreed that clergy should be instructed not to accept commissions in the army, nor to be enrolled in any military corps, nor to be trained in the use of arms. In the case of invasion, they should use force only in the last resort.[29] In 1804 the Bishop of Bristol, George Pelham, repeated the message to his clergy: the gospel of peace and the Spirit and Word should be *their* only weapons; in the event of an invasion they should devote themselves to comforting the afflicted and inspiring others to defend their country. No reason should be given to anyone to criticise them, for in France it had been the profligate conduct of some of the clergy which led others to overthrow both church and state.[30]

---

[26] Coleridge, 1795 Lectures on Politics and Religion, *Works*, vol. 1, pp. 66–7.

[27] C. Moss, *A Sermon Preached before . . . the House of Commons* (London, 1798), pp. 20–2; T. Willis, *A Sermon Preached in the Foundling Hospital . . . 2 June 1798* (London, 1798), p. 15; More, 'Strictures', *Works*, vol.5, pp. 200–1; Parr, 1803 Fast Day Sermon, *Works*, vol. 2, pp. 633–7, 668.

[28] De Courcy, *Self-Defence*, pp. 24–5.

[29] Bodl., MS Eng. Misc., d 156/1, Letter from Bishop Horsley to the incumbent of Barming, Maidstone. For Horsley's own comment see below, p. 170. See also *Gentleman's Magazine*, May 1798, pp. 385–6; LPL, MS 2103, f.98; M. More, *Mendip Annals*, p. 242 (fn).

[30] G. Pelham, *A Charge . . . 1804* (Bristol, n.d.), pp. 8–10.

Infidelity

Burke and his supporters

The nature of Christianity and its relationship to government was seen most clearly when contrasted with French infidelity. At their crudest, and some of the arguments were crude, writers implied a sort of simultaneous equation; just as a=b and −a=−b, so religion equalled government and atheism equalled anarchy. Burke published his *Reflections* a year after the secularisation of church lands in France and four months after the Civil Constitution of the Clergy. He was convinced the revolutionaries saw these as only the first steps on a road to atheism and were determined utterly to abolish the Christian religion. Burke believed, however, that man was by nature a religious animal and that atheism was not only against his reason, but also his instincts. To reject Christianity and its restraints would be to destroy civilisation and fall into a state of anarchy.[31] Burke's early critics in 1790–1 suggested he was exaggerating the danger. Atheists were, they argued, rare animals, 'at least as uncommon as a Monster with two heads'; those like Hume and Gibbon had had little effect in England and Christianity was too well established to be overthrown.[32]

Burke's was not a lone voice, however. Hannah More considered that debates in the French Assembly in 1792 mixed anarchy and atheism and so disqualified man from the performance of his civil and social duties. An infidel was a bad member of society, but a Christian brought peace and good will to men.[33] However, this theme was taken up by the general chorus only after the outbreak of war with France in early 1793. Then, the echoes of Burke rang around the pulpits of England: irreligion and atheism removed moral restraints and opened the gates to the bloody spirit of anarchy and barbarism. If all sense of religious obligation were destroyed, government could rely only on compulsion. The French were fighting against religion and government and offered in its place only 'Materialism, Fatalism, Chance, Fortune'.[34] In 1794 William Jones republished his 1776 *Reflections on the Growth of Heathenism among Modern Christians*, and Bishop Pretyman-Tomline warned his clergy of the connexion between licentious opinions on

[31] *Reflections*, pp. 256, 186–8.
[32] G. Rous, *Thoughts on Government* (London, 1791), p. 13; *Temperate Comments upon Intemperate Reflections* (London, 1791), pp. 41–2; C. Lofft, *Remarks on . . . Burke* (London 1791), pp. 56–7. See also Godwin, *Political Justice*, p. 138, on man as a religious animal.
[33] More, 'Remarks on Dupont', *Works*, vol. 11, pp. 218–20, 229.
[34] Maclaine, *Religion, a Preservative*, pp. 16–17; Gilbank, *Duties of Man*, pp. 8, 10, 12; Hunting-ford, *Sermon . . . 1793*, p. 9. See also, Langford, *Obedience to the Established Laws*, pp. 6–7.

religion and on government. Deist works, by destroying the sense of religion in France, had led to the Revolution.[35]

In October 1793 Burke denounced the French Revolutionaries as atheists who had forced the people to abjure their faith in God and systematically turned them into savages. They excluded religion, the life-blood of the moral and political world, from their concept of the state. By 1795 he was urging that no peace should be made with Jacobin France, which had turned its back on the Christian world and based itself on regicide and atheism. He called it 'atheism by establishment', for the state denied God's existence as a moral governor, and adopted a system of manners to correspond to its infidel and immoral state. Burke inspired many church-men to argue, long after his death, that Christianity and monarchy must be restored in France before the true threat to Britain was over and peace could be concluded safely.[36]

By 1797 the theme was commonplace. Scepticism and infidelity were the 'engines of anarchy', irreligion dissolved restraints on men and led to the disintegration of society.[37] Richard Watson, who had given a guarded welcome to the Revolution in 1791, turned increasingly more bitter and hostile towards it. In 1795 he was already openly concerned with the attack on religion, and by 1796, when he responded to Paine's *Age of Reason*, he was forthright in his condemnation. In 1798, in *An Address to the People of Great Britain*, which urged a continuation of the war, he mounted one of the most detailed, powerful and passionately argued diatribes against irreligion and revolution written in these years. In 1802 his fears and his passions were still intense and made him retract some of his earlier liberal views on toleration and establishment. When religious views were subversive of the establish-ment in church and state, the magistrate had to restrain them. In 1803 he urged the continuation of the war to preserve Britain from atheism, despotism and anarchy.[38] None of the conservative bishops who had earlier criticised his liberal stance could have said more, or said it more convincingly.

---

[35] Jones, *Works*, vol.3, pp. 423, 445–6; Pretyman-Tomline, *Charge . . . 1794*, pp. 14–18.

[36] Burke, 'Remarks on the Policy of the Allies' (1793), *Works*, vol. 3, pp. 420, 427, 434; 'Regicide Peace Letter', *Works*, vol. 6, pp. 205, 206–8, 215–16, 236,245. Burke, however, was not without doubts. If the Revolution did triumph, perhaps it was indeed some mysterious instrument of God's providence. See Kilcup, 'Burke's Historicism', pp. 405–10.

[37] R. Prosser, *A Sermon Preached before the . . . House of Commons . . . February 13, 1801* (London, 1801), p. 13; Barrington, 1797 Charge, *Sermons*, p. 206. See also, *inter alia*, Edwards, *Things Which Belong*, pp. v–vi; A. Maclaine, *The Solemn Voice of Public Events* (Bath, [1797]); Law, *Sermon . . . 1797*, p. 17; S. Crowther, *Sermon*, pp. 9–10; Wickes, *Sermon*, pp. 7–8, 12; Randolph, *Sermon . . . 1800*, pp. 15–16.

[38] Watson, 1795 Charge, *Misc.T*, vol. 1, pp. 90, 101; *Apology for the Bible*, pp. 3–4; 'Address', *Misc.T*, vol. 1, pp. 185–92, 196; 1802 Charge, *Misc.T*, vol. 1, pp. 236–41, 252–3; *Substance of a Speech*, 1803, *passim*, esp. p. 3.

The conspiracy theory

The general intensification of hostility to French infidelity from 1797 onwards was partly because of the critical position reached in the war, but also because of the publication of two works alleging a conspiracy against religion and government in France: the English translation of the Abbé Barruel's *Memoirs of . . . Jacobinism* (1797) and John Robison's *Proofs of a Conspiracy against All the Religions and Governments of Europe* (1797), the latter single volume being published as the third of Barruel's four volumes was going to the press. Each author praised the other; their substance was similar in parts, but their style very different – Barruel's sweeping, emotional, passionate and rhetorical, Robison's controlled, logical, precise, almost dour. Barruel really alleged two connected conspiracies: first, one of *philosophes*, chiefly Voltaire, d'Alembert, Diderot and Frederick the Great; and secondly, one of freemasons and *illuminées*.[39] Robison concentrated on the latter, outlining the role of Dr Adam Weishart in founding the Order of Illuminati in 1775, and chronicling the order's later history in Germany.

In the following year, William Playfair published a long *History of Jacobinism* from the start of the Revolution to the death of Robespierre, but perhaps more influential were two brief, popular versions of the conspiracy theory. One, *New Lights on Jacobinism*, gave a forty-page abstract of Robison's work, stressing the more sensational stories of sexual depravity and suicide among the freemasons.[40] The other, *Jacobinism Displayed*, in a mere thirty pages, presented the case against Voltaire and the *philosophes* who, it alleged, believed religion had to be eliminated before monarchy could be destroyed.[41] Barruel asserted that the *philosophes'* attack on Christianity led directly and intentionally to the Jacobins' attack on the monarchy. Voltaire

had said to his first adepts, Let us crush the altar, and let not a single altar nor a single worshipper be left to the God of the Christians; and his school soon resounded with the cry of, *Let us crush the sceptre*, and let not a single throne, nor a single subject be left to the kings of the earth.[42]

There was, of course, nothing new in linking the irreligion of the *philosophes* with the political radicalism of the Revolution. Burke had done that in the *Reflections*. He accused the 'literary cabal' of planning the

---

[39] On the growth of the thesis in France, culminating in Barruel's work, see J. M. Roberts, 'The Origins of a Mythology: Freemasons, Protestants and the French Revolution', *BIHR*, 44 (1971), 78–97, and *The Mythology of the Secret Societies* (London, 1972), pp. 146–202, and (on Britain) pp. 206–10.

[40] W. Playfair, *The History of Jacobinism, its Crimes, Cruelties and Perfidies*, 2 vols. (London, 1798); *New Lights on Jacobinism* (Birmingham, 1798).

[41] Anti-Jacobin, *Jacobinism Displayed* (Birmingham, 1798), p. 23.

[42] Barruel, *Memoirs*, vol. 1, pp. 386–7.

destruction of Christianity and implied a conspiracy in 'a spirit of cabal, intrigue, and proselytism'. Burke's Christian critics, in the early 1790s, felt he made too much of the *philosophes'* irreligion; it was to be lamented but it was not dangerous and certainly not a conspiracy; it was, rather, the result of popish superstition which drove rational men to such unfortunate extremes.[43] James Mackintosh was more forthright and sweeping in dismissing the allegation: the *philosophes'* writings on metaphysics and theology ('remote and mysterious questions') were irrelevant – it was as political reasoners they should be judged in a political revolution. If Rousseau influenced the Revolution, Mackintosh argued, it was by his *Social Contract* not his *Letters from the Mountain*, if Voltaire made France more liberal it was by his defences of toleration not his *Philosophical Dictionary*; their atheism was a personal matter, it had nothing to do with the Revolution, which was neither promoted nor retarded by abstract theological discussion.[44]

Burke continued to make his point. Speaking of Louis XVI's downfall in his *Regicide Peace* letters he observed 'a silent revolution in the moral world preceded the political, and prepared it'.[45] But surprisingly, although his views on the disastrous social effects of removing religious sanctions and restraints were almost universally echoed by establishment writers, his thesis of a conspiracy by the *philosophes* to destroy religion and then government was largely neglected. There were rumours, of course, but these were discussed privately, rarely proclaimed from the pulpit.

Barruel's and Robison's work dramatically altered that situation almost overnight. Their thesis spread like wildfire and remained powerful and dominant for many years. Bishop Randolph of Oxford was exceptional among the establishment in being somewhat sceptical about it.[46] Dr Maclaine alluded to the role of the secret societies in a fast-day sermon on 8 March 1797 and Richard Prosser, in a visitation sermon in the summer of the same year, suggested that the 'enlightened' attacks on religion, morality and government were linked.[47] By 1798 the thesis already dominated addresses of almost every kind. De Courcy told the North Staffordshire Yeomanry that from Voltaire had come a monster which stalked the earth threatening every throne and every altar. This monster denied the immortality of the soul and the existence of God, and so asserted the rights of man as 'a licence to pillage and murder' and to make unprovoked attacks on all property.[48] Samuel Crowther told the members of the Barking

43 Burke, *Reflections*, pp. 211–14; Lofft, *Remarks on Burke* (1790), pp. 55–8; Towers, *Thoughts on . . . New Parliament*, pp. 110–14; *Temperate Comments*, pp. 41–2.
44 Mackintosh, *Vindiciae Gallicae*, pp. 139–40.
45 Burke, *Works*, vol. 6, p. 258.
46 Soloway, *Prelates and People*, p. 43.
47 Maclaine, *Solemn Voice*, pp. 10–11; Prosser, *Sermon . . . 1797*, pp. 8–11.
48 De Courcy, *Self-Defence*, p. 19.

Association that the French had sought to destroy religion prior to attacking government because they knew the gospel and the example of Christ enjoined peace, order and submission.[49] A provincial archdeacon, Robert Thorp, repeated the thesis, in his *Charge*, to any of the clergy of Northumberland who may have missed it. The arguments of Voltaire and Frederick the Great had come, he suggested, from English deists, like Hobbes, Collins, Tindal, Shaftesbury and Bolingbroke, but while England had only been faced with individual freethinkers, there had been in France a co-ordinated conspiracy, such as was now threatening England.[50]

Dean Nickolls of Middleham considered the climate now ripe to publish the Charity Schools sermon he had preached in 1795, in which he had alluded to such an atheistic conspiracy, and he specially mentioned Robison's and Barruel's works as creating the change in the climate of opinion.[51] Richard Watson made some scholarly references to the thesis in his 1798 *Charge* and some more forceful and popular ones in his *Address to the People of Great Britain* in the same year. Men who sought to subvert the government would, he warned the people, tell them

that there is nothing after death, no Heaven for the good, no Hell for the wicked, that there is no God, or none who regards your actions; and when you shall be convinced of this, they will think you properly prepared to perpetrate every crime which may be necessary for the furtherance of their own designs, for the gratification of their ambition, their avarice, or their revenge.[52]

In 1799 Robert Hall considered the question in a long sermon at the Baptist Meeting in Cambridge. He stressed the subversive social purpose behind atheism. Modern infidels, he claimed, sought to obliterate all ideas of God, of moral sanctions, or of an eternal life and so prepare the way for the total subversion of all social and religious institutions.[53] In 1802 Henry Majendie, Bishop of Chester, chose the occasion of a Westminster Abbey sermon before the House of Lords on the day of thanksgiving for the peace to review yet again the philosophical causes of the French Revolution.[54] It was a theme which did not die even after the final peace treaty, let alone this temporary one.

From 1802 to 1805. William van Mildert, then a London rector and later Bishop of Llandaff and then Durham, preached a series of Boyle Lectures on

---

[49] S. Crowther, *Sermon*, pp. 10–11.

[50] R. Thorp, *A Charge Delivered to the Clergy of the Archdeaconry of Northumberland in April 1798* (Newcastle-upon-Tyne, 1798), pp. 6–8.

[51] Nickolls, *Political as Well as Moral Consequences*, pp. iii, 28.

[52] Watson, 1798 Charge, *Misc. T*, vol. 1, p. 144; 'Address', *Misc. T*, vol. 2, pp. 186–8.

[53] Hall, 'Modern Infidelity Considered' (1799), *Works*, vol. 1, pp. 4–5.

[54] H. W. Majendie, *A Sermon Preached before the Lords . . . June 1, 1802* (London, 1802), pp. 12–14. The House of Commons that day heard a similar theme expounded: see W. Vincent, *Sermon*, pp. 9–12, 18–19, 23–6.

The Rise and Progress of Infidelity. He set the contemporary problem in a long historical context stretching back to the Garden of Eden. Having examined medieval and Renaissance heresy, he concentrated on three themes: English deism in the seventeenth century; the infidelity of the Enlightenment in France and England; and the apostasy of his own day. In contemporary England he denounced not only the obvious targets of Paine and Godwin, but also the Unitarians and Quakers. Even the Cisalpine Catholic Alexander Geddes did not escape censure for his critical translation of the Bible. But he insisted that the conspiracy as such was in France, not in England.[55]

The conspiracy theory was, of course, a species of social theory and reflected the fundamental shift away from constitutional and philosophical issues. Men believed it was because religion imposed social restraints and moral sanctions that it had to be destroyed before society and government could be subjected to revolutionary change. But the issue was more complex than that, for what the deism and atheism of some of the *philosophes* did was to posit a different theory of society, a different concept of the relationship of man with his fellows. This, in turn, was based on fundamentally different assumptions about the nature of man. It was the challenge of a new view of man and society that forced Christian writers to redefine and reaffirm their theological and social principles with precision and vigour.

Self-interest, benevolence and will

Burke led the way. His critique of the Revolution made clear his own social, moral and psychological theory. The great problem for the atheist politician was to find substitutes for those religious principles which had been used before to regulate human will and action. Burke was unimpressed by their attempts, largely because his basic concept of the nature of man was different from that of the *philosophes* and the revolutionaries. Instead of the humility which comes from a knowledge of fallen man's inherent sinfulness, they were filled with the inordinate vanity which arises from a belief in human perfectibility. The crucial concept of duty was replaced by a faith in self-interest; the *philosophes* believed, he argued, that an education based on a knowledge of their material wants would lead men to 'an enlightened self-interest' which would identify with the larger public interest.[56] Burke had no such faith in civic education. Indeed, long before the French Revolution,

---

[55] W. Van Mildert, *An Historical View of the Rise and Progress of Infidelity* (London, 1806), esp. vol. 1, pp. 405–14.
[56] Burke, *Works*, vol. 2, p. 536; *Reflections*, p. 256.

in a letter to Mrs Elizabeth Montague written in 1763, he had ridiculed as one of a series of foolish schemes the idea of promoting human happiness and national prosperity by the replacement of religion and virtue by self-interest. In 1794 the idea that religious restraints could be replaced by some vague humanity or benevolence seemed equally ridiculous to him. When men were guided only by their present feelings one could not depend on them.[57] The nature of man is such that he needs restraining principles imposed on him from without. If there were no God to impose them, then a despotic regime must.

These three themes, self-interest, benevolence and will, were widely discussed. Christians assumed that man's fallen nature was such that self-interest should be equated with selfishness. Benevolence was something which had to be required of man as a duty, a moral and religious obligation. Richard Price took this to an extreme few would follow when he equated national interest with selfishness and enjoined universal benevolence. But, in the more restricted personal sphere, almost all agreed that the passion of self-interest needed restraint.[58] Even Coleridge in his idealisic and radical phase of 1795 considered that only if men believed in life after death would 'self-interest be wedded to virtue'.[59] Mary Wollstonecraft, however, suggested that what she called 'enlightened self love' could lead men to a natural benevolence.[60] Joseph Priestley was led to occupy ground mid-way between the Christians and the infidels by his rejection of the doctrine of original sin, belief in the possibility of human perfection and acceptance of the resurrection of the dead.[61]

His position highlighted the very considerable difference of opinion within the infidel camp which contemporary critics largely ignored. Deists, like Voltaire or Paine, took a quite different position to that of atheists, such as Holbach or Godwin, on a matter like the need for (or possibility of) religious restraint. There were also two distinct traditions of thought in France on the question of progress which revealed different views of the nature of man. First, there was the caution, pessimism and disillusionment most readily associated with Voltaire, but also clearly discernible in many other *philosophes*, such as Montesquieu and Rousseau. Secondly, there was the faith in the limitless perfectibility of the human species found most notably in the thought of Turgot and Condorcet. Most conservative English churchmen, quite wrongly, attributed the views of the latter, especially on

[57] Burke, *Corr.*, vol. 1, p. 173, vol. 9, p. 387, vol. 6, p. 215.
[58] Price, *Love of Country*, pp. 5–11.
[59] Coleridge, 1795 Lectures on Revealed Religion, *Works*, vol. 1, p. 218.
[60] Wollstonecraft, *Rights of Men*, p. 75.
[61] Priestley, *Letters to Burke*, pp. 146–7, 150; *Sermon*, 19 April 1793, pp. 11, 17, 27, 32–5.

self-interest and benevolence, to the former group as well, ignoring the Voltairean leaven of pessimism and recognition of the reality of evil.[62]

Robert Hall was convinced the *philosophes* and revolutionaries over-estimated the power of man's reason and underestimated the force of his passions. By undermining marriage and the family, they destroyed the tender passions and expected benevolence to create in their place a passion-ate attachment to the general good. But this hope merely showed their ignorance of human nature. Reason would not give rise to new passions but would follow the primrose path of selfish pleasure.[63] J. W. Wickes described this as man following 'the dictates of his own capricious will' and argued that such a path would make him fierce, headstrong and unruly, so that not laws, government or social compact could restrain him.[64]

Back in 1790 George Horne had warned that self-will was taking the place of divine will and 'every man is become his own providence'; this would lead to sedition and confusion, and society could survive intact only if man's will were restrained.[65] The same point was still being made in 1804 by Bishop Huntingford of Gloucester: if self-will were allowed to disturb the social order, industry would be interrupted, trade neglected, property plundered and peace and security put at risk.[66] But it was the Bishop of Oxford, John Randolph, who in 1800 stressed the role of religion most forcefully. Government could control men by laws only if religion had first entered their hearts and eliminated the first desires of the will to act indulgently; this was the very foundation of government.[67]

The most telling, incisive and effective critique of the concepts of self-interest, universal benevolence and will came not in any episcopal sermon but in one of Hannah More's *Cheap Repository* tales. Her response to the conspiracy theory of 1797 was to write *The History of Mr Fantom*. Fantom was a disciple of Paine who considered himself emancipated from the restraints of religion, conscience and moral obligation. He read pamphlets and dreamed of plans for the improvement of mankind which were far too extravagant and impractical ever to be achieved. His addiction to speculat-ive, universal benevolence was not inspired by duty or charity, but by a desire for a great reputation, by vanity. To Fantom, More contrasted Mr Trueman, a simple, practical Christian who went around actively support-ing his neighbours and helping those in need, while Fantom refused to lend

[62] Voltaire, *Philosophical Dictionary*, pp. 251, 605; *Condorcet: Selected Writings*, edited by K. M. Baker (Indianapolis, 1976); *Turgot on Progress, Sociology and Economics*, edited by R. L. Meek (Cambridge, 1973); Maclaine, *Solemn Voice*, p. 11.
[63] Hall, 'Modern Infidelity', *Works*, vol. 1, pp. 53–7.
[64] Wickes, *Sermons*, pp. 7–8.
[65] Horne, 1790 Charge, *Works*, vol. 4, pp. 532–3.
[66] G. I. Huntingford, *A Sermon Preached before the Lords . . . May 25th, 1804* (London, 1804), p. 14.
[67] Randolph, *Sermon*, 1800, *passism*, but esp. pp. 7–8.

a hand or contribute a penny. Fantom's servant, William, was led into a life of crime after overhearing his master's table-talk that 'death was only an eternal sleep', and Hell and judgment 'an invention of the priests to keep the poor in order'. In his last confession before his execution, William reflected that, unlike the rich who do not experience want, the poor need religion to restrain them from crime. In the form of a simple tale, More presented a clear, theological, political and social argument. Jacobinism and impiety were inseparably connected because both were opposed to restraints.[68]

But not all Christians agreed with this version of Christianity. William Shaw, who renounced his native Presbyterianism to become an Anglican clergyman, attacked Hannah More under the pseudonym of the Rev Sir Archibald MacSarcasm, Bart. He compared her writings with her actions in the Blagdon School controversy and, writing of the Fantom story, argued that as her Christianity was not natural it could not be scriptural.[69] But most Christian writers agreed with More when she argued that the reason the revolutionaries believed restraint was unnecessary and that will and self-interest would lead to benevolence was that they misunderstood the nature of man and of society. In fact, man was a flawed being and from his sinful nature misery proceeded. It was pointless to accuse governments of defects which belonged to man. Men must seek to lead better lives, but must never expect perfection this side of the grave 'because God intended this world should be earth and not Heaven'. Though some may have been out of sympathy with Hannah More's Evangelicalism, they agreed with her that Christianity was the friend of government, and infidelity its enemy.

[68] H. More, 'The History of Mr Fantom' (1797), *Works*, vol. 3, pp. 1–42 (pp. 4, 12, 19–20, 33–4, 38–40). Thomas Davies, *Memoirs of the Life of David Garrick*, 2 vols. (London, 1780), vol. 2, pp. 59–60, tells of a Mr Mallet (*ob.* 1765), a follower of Bolingbroke, whose infidel talk at the dinner table corrupted his servant, who stole from his master, then confessed 'I had heard you talk so often of the impossibility of a future state, and that after death there was no reward for virtue or punishment for vice, that I was tempted to commit the robbery.' This story was repeated, with acknowledgment, by George Horne in *Sunday Schools Recommended in a Sermon . . . 18 December 1785* (Oxford, 1786), pp. 6–7. Hannah More was a friend of both Garrick and Horne and it is unclear from which of them she first learned the story.
[69] *The Life of Hannah More: With a Critical Review of her Writings* (London, 1802), pp. 56–62. For the Blagdon controversy see M. G. Jones, *Hannah More*, pp. 172–83.

11

Case study II: Samuel Horsley

Samuel Horsley was the son of a lecturer at St Martin-in-the-Fields and the grandson of a principal of Edinburgh University.[1] He was a student at Trinity Hall, Cambridge, and a tutor at Christ Church, Oxford. An enthusiastic Greek scholar, he took pleasure in discussing a range of authors, especially Thucydides, with his son.[2] He was a fellow of the Royal Society and a keen student of mathematics. From 1779 to 1785 he edited the works of Sir Isaac Newton, although it was later alleged that he overlooked, possibly destroyed, a 'cart-load' of papers on religious subjects which showed Newton to be unitarian in faith.[3] Horsley, a great trinitarian champion, probably regarded these as unfit for publication. He became Archdeacon of St Albans in 1781 and a prebendary of Gloucester in 1787. Horsley was an enthusiastic supporter of Pitt the Younger, to whom he owed his elevation to the episcopate in 1788 as Bishop of St David's. He spoke and voted for the government in the House of Lords and strongly supported Pitt's war effort and the need to finance it.[4] He enjoyed some modest preferment, becoming Bishop of Rochester in 1793 and of St Asaph in 1802. He combined a staunch conservatism in both social and political concepts, with a genuine Christian faith and concern for the well-being of the church. He was perceptive enough to be aware of the exigencies of the changing situation and to make the necessary adjustments in the general tenor of his argument. His position and ability was recognised by the opponents of the

---

[1] The careful but uncritical work of his great-grandson, Heneage Horsley Jebb, *A Great Bishop of One Hundred Years Ago: Being a Sketch of the Life of Samuel Horsley* (London, 1909), remains the only full-length biography.

[2] LPL, MS 1767, ff. 97–152, Letters from Horsely to his son.

[3] BL, Add. MS 29,300 M, f. 41, Letter from Horsley to Earl Buchan, 29 January 1786; BL, Add. MS 38,309, Liverpool papers, f. 47, Letter from Jenkinson to Horsley, March 1792; T. Thompson, *Annals of Philosophy* (London, 1813), vol. 2, p. 322; LPL, MS 1767, ff. 75–6, Letter from Dr Clement to Horsley's son (1815).

[4] LPL, MS 1767, ff. 19, 21, 128, 141, 143, 146.

established order who bothered to attack his views with some vigour and bitterness.[5]

The reason for examining Horsley's thought in more detail is quite different from that for studying Paley's. Paley was atypical of the prerevolutionary period; he played an important role in the development and secularisation of political thought. Horsley, by contrast, was characteristic of the intelligent, conservative, high-church Anglicans of his day.[6] The changes in emphasis in Christian political thought analysed in Chapters 7 to 10 were considerable. They have been represented so far as changes in the general climate of debate and, to some extent, the men who expressed the later sociologically centred views were different from those who earlier made the traditional political case. In Horsley's writings, however, we find this process of change in microcosm. His Martyrdom Day sermon of 1793 and his episcopal charge of 1796 could well be taken as paradigm statements of the constitutional and the social theories respectively. Horsley's thought shows clearly that the change was indeed one of emphasis, that the constitutional and social arguments were two parts of a coherent, integrated system of political thought, both informed by the same body of religious beliefs.

The synthesis of Horsley's thought

In February 1790, Bishop Horsley made a fair manuscript copy of an essay he had written recently, but never published, entitled 'Thoughts upon Civil Government, and its relation to Religion, but especially to the Christian Religion'.[7] This essay is important for two main reasons. First, it is evidence of immediate episcopal response to events in France. Written before the Revolution had given rise to widespread alarm in Britain, this was no calm and detached piece, but an early and hostile reaction to events in France and an anxious awareness of all the issues of resistance to authority they raised. Composed over nine months before Burke's *Reflections* was published, the general attitude and approach was similar. Nor was Horsley the only member of the bench to think thus. Writing in his private notebook in exactly the same month, February 1790, Bishop Porteus of London noted

---

[5] Horsley's 1793 Martyrdom Day sermon was attacked by R. Hall in a preface to his 'Freedom of the Press', *Works*, vol. 3, pp. 68–78; *Critical Review*, 7 (1793), 215–20, 473; *Analytical Review*, 15 (1793), 199–201. Coleridge's attack in 1795 concentrated more on Horsley's anti-Unitarian stance: see 'Lectures on Revealed Religion', Lecture 5, *Works*, vol. 1, pp. 209, 211, and 'The Plot Discovered', *Works*, vol. 1, pp. 285, 312 note 4.

[6] He was widely read; after his death, nearly two thousand items from his library sold for over £1,600. See MS annotations to the Bodleian Library copy of *A Catalogue of the Entire and Very Valuable Library of the Late Right Rev. Samuel Horsley . . .* (London, 1807).

[7] LPL, MS 1767, ff. 198–203.

the need to avoid the risk of any innovations in church or state at a time when the most powerful government in Europe had been overturned and a republic established in conditions of anarchy and confusion.[8]

Secondly, this essay is important because it demonstrates the synthesis and unity of Horsley's thought. It predates most of his printed sermons, charges and speeches in the House of Lords and shows the religious foundation from which his political and social arguments were derived. In the ensuing fifteen years, particular occasions drew forth from Horsley thoughts on the classical constitutional theory of both church and state, on social theory and the need for restraint and social control, on the moral issues involved in slavery and war, and on the conspiracy theory and the danger of subversion. These later expressions of views not only mirrored almost exactly the changes in emphasis of establishment thought in general, but they also arose from the principles earlier enunciated in this unpublished essay of 1790.

In the essay he recognised that any system of political thought needed both a social and a constitutional dimension, and saw that the two were inextricably entwined. Any stable constitutional and legal framework depended upon social order and restraint. Horsley suggested that the crucial problem for any legislator was to find 'a common measure of moral conduct universally applicable' which could provide a secure basis for the happiness and welfare of a community and all its members. The atheist denied that there was any common measure, and although the theist accepted that it was the divine will, he had no sure way of knowing what it was. Only Christianity, as a revealed religion, offered a solution.

Horsley shared the common distrust of the new Enlightenment faith in self-interest and benevolence. Any government based on human will was doomed to failure. Only divine will, revealed by God, provided a firm foundation for government. So Horsley moved to a Christological argument. The perfect union in the person of Christ of the eternal Word of God and of human nature brought the divine will into the human arena. The society Christ founded, the church, was ruled by Him and governed according to the divine will. Knowledge of that will, Horsley conceded, was still imperfect on earth, and divine government would be seen in all its perfection only in Heaven.[9] Man's main purpose on earth was to submit to a

---

[8] LPL, MS 2103, f. 27.
[9] Horsley related this point to his millenarian beliefs. Unlike Priestley, who linked his chiliasm to his view that human government could be improved to the point of perfection, Horsley believed that the imperfections of human government before the parousia must be suffered and accepted. While much millenarian thought was to take a radical turn in the mid 1790s, Horsley wedded it firmly to the conservative cause. See also his six manuscript letters to the author of *Anti-Christ in the French Convention*, LPL, MS 2809, pp. 111–84, 199–252, 255–352 (W. J. Palmer's transcript of Horsley's Papers, vol. 9).

discipline which would help prepare him for closer acquaintance with 'this one, only, perfect and just System of Government'. Man was guided in this by the scriptures which were authoritatively given, and by the Holy Spirit.

While thus insisting that the duty of political obligation was divinely imposed, Horsley did not deny that it was possible in certain extreme circumstances to change the form of government. If a ruler, one of God's vicegerents, abused his power, he could be judged in only two ways: either according to the established laws of his own state, or by God himself. But man must judge with charity and had no right to resist his superiors except in ways allowed by the constitution.

Thus Horsley combined his constitutional and social theory. The Christian subject, he insisted, should confine himself to his own proper sphere in society where,

incessantly occupied in regulating all his thoughts and Desires, and Appetites and affections, according to the Will of God, as declared in his written Word, he will thus be best prepared to fulfil any duties of wider extent, which his Family or Friends or Neighbours, may require from him, or which his Country may command. He makes no angry complaints of Power abused, nor hazards any Effects (better exerted within) to resist it;

but leaves God to punish and order 'the Moral Government of the World'.

Moving back to a political and constitutional point, and so demonstrating the integration and unity of his argument, Horsley next observed that in extreme circumstances a man might be swept up in events like those in England in 1688–9. But in such circumstances he must indeed be swept up and carried away by providence, not be acting under the impulse of his own will. The rise and fall of states and kingdoms must be the work of God not of man and must derive from a divine not a human initiative. It was quite wrong for men, of their own will, to throw off the sanctions and restraints of religion and attack in an unconstitutional way the abuses of their government, as he clearly considered the French were doing. Any violent or factious attack on an established government was considered by God as rebellion.

Finally in this essay, Horsley reiterated the connexion between political obligation and Christian sanctions and restraints. The infidel depended upon three (inadequate) sources: first, the power (as opposed to the authority) of their faction; secondly, the support of the people (which was essentially capricious and uncertain); and thirdly, a very Burkean concept, the established laws whose wisdom and usefulness had been confirmed over the years and whose long standing led to a general sense of obligation to obey them in the community. While the last was certainly the most considerable of all *human* sources of obligation, it depended too much on 'local and temporary opinion and prejudice'. It was only Christianity, Horsley insisted, that provided an eternal, enduring and certain sanction.

Constitutional thought

The constitution in the state

It was symptomatic of the change that was taking place in the emphasis of clerical political argument in the 1790s that Horsley made only one major statement of classical constitutional theory in that time – the 1793 Westminster Abbey Martyrdom Day sermon before the House of Lords.[10] It was for this sermon that Horsley was best known and is still most often cited by historians. Its unique place in his *opera* is usually ignored. It demonstrated how he selected from his whole body of political thought reflections suitable for a particular occasion, the audience for whom it was designed and the precise timing of its delivery.

It happened to be Horsley's turn to preach the Martyrdom Day sermon in Westminster Abbey before the House of Lords on 30 January 1793. This came at the end of three months of intensive pamphleteering in England and just nine days after the execution of Louis XVI in Paris; the crisis posed by Jacobinism was perceived by the English ruling class to be at its height. In this context of tension and deep-seated anxiety, Horsley preached a powerful and emotional sermon, which combined the traditional Anglican political theory of his predecessors with a forceful anti-revolutionary oratory. It was reported that the congregation rose to its feet at the start of his peroration and remained standing until the end; it was rumoured that Horsley owed both the Deanery of Westminster and his translation to Rochester to this performance.[11] It was no piece of cynical opportunism, however, but an expression of genuinely held views Horsley had formulated earlier. Given the traditions of the service, and the sense of crisis of the moment, nothing Horsley said in this sermon should surprise us, but he rose fully to the high drama of the occasion.

The stage reached in the transition of emphasis from political to social theory is well illustrated by the fact that Horsley opened the sermon by observing what folly it had been in years past to indulge in free dispute about such crucial matters as the origin of government, the authority of sovereigns, and the natural rights of man, but then proceeded to devote most of the rest of his sermon to an exposition of his views on those very issues of traditional political theory. The House of Lords doubtless seemed a safe audience for such an indulgence.

Horsley rightly understood that concepts of popular sovereignty, consent

[10] *A Sermon Preached before the Lords . . . January 30, 1793*, second edition (London, 1793).
[11] A. P. Stanley, *Historical Memorials of Westminster Abbey* (London, 1868), pp. 474–5.

and compact posed the crucial challenge to the traditional idea of a divinely imposed obligation to obey government. Accordingly, he first denied that a state of nature had ever existed, and then argued that, even if it had, obligation to obey government arose not from any compact supposedly entered into by our forefathers, but from our religious duty. St Paul in his advice to the Christians in Rome made no mention of consent, though the concept had been mooted earlier by Plato.

He agreed that in a limited monarchy there might be a *legal* contract between prince and people. In England this was summarised in the Coronation Oath, and set out more fully in Magna Charta, the Petition of Right, habeas corpus, the Bill of Rights and the Act of Settlement. This specified the form of government and could be changed, but it did not imply popular sovereignty or constitute the source of political obligation. The Act of Settlement was the sole foundation of the sovereign's title, but it was not the reason why his subjects were obliged to obey his government. That stemmed not from an act of parliament but from the will of God.

The constitution in the church
Horsley's subtlety of understanding and clarity of thought were manifest when he discussed the question of the church establishment. He also showed realism and flexibility. He believed passionately in the need for and the value of an established church, but also accepted that other Christian faiths should be tolerated. Membership of the political nation should be restricted to those of the established faith, but religious toleration should be taken to the extreme consistent with the security of the civil government. In vigorously opposing Stanhope's bill of June 1789, he stressed the separate jurisdictions of the conscience and the magistrate.[12] Conscience, supreme in her own realm, could not restrict the actions of the magistrate in his task of protecting society. Intent on defending the stability of government at this crucial time, Horsley insisted that this could be done only upon the correct theological base, and that, for him, meant the theology of Anglicanism.

In 1783 in a lengthy *Charge* he delivered as Archdeacon of St Albans, he roundly attacked Joseph Priestley and the whole Unitarian theology and concept of 'rational Christianity'.[13] In 1790 he turned his attention to the extremes of both Calvinist antinomians and their Methodist critics, who appeared to him to equate practical religion with morality. Practical Christianity, he insisted, could not be separated from faith, and faith depended on doctrine. It was wrong to assume that the vulgar were

---

[12] S. Horsley, Speech on Stanhope's Bill, *Speeches in Parliament* (Dundee, 1813), vol. 1, pp. 1–34 (p. 18).
[13] S. Horsley, *A Charge Delivered to the Clergy of the Archdeaconry of St Albans . . . 1783* (London, 1783).

incapable of understanding the dogma which made Christianity distinctive. It was not enough to teach that God created the world and human life and could punish men after death for crimes undetected during their human life, while neglecting the doctrines of the Trinity, the Incarnation, the Atonement, the Holy Spirit and the soul. Revealed religion was more than natural religion, Christianity more than deism, and practical religion more than morality; even the poor and uneducated could understand those beliefs which made Christianity separate and special.[14]

Horsley appeared to support the rights of Catholics more than those of Protestant Dissenters. This was partly a reflection of this doctrinal concern for, as a high-churchman, he shared many Catholic theological doctrines. He greeted the French émigré clergy with charity,[15] and in supporting the 1791 Catholic Relief Bill was instrumental in altering the words of the oath in a way which eased ultramontane consciences. He saw that Catholics were no longer a political threat; now they were 'led by the genuine principles of their religion to inoffensive conduct, to dutiful submission and cordial loyalty'. He considered the days of St Robert Bellarmine's advocacy of popular sovereignty were long since past.[16]

However, Horsley did not oversimplify the issue. He recognised that the pope's ecclesiastical jurisdiction in England (which was for Catholics a part of his spiritual authority they could not renounce) questioned the validity of Anglican orders, and therefore their role in the constitution. He showed his realism in refusing to let this theoretical problem sour practical relations. Providing Catholics were prepared to promise to defend the constitution in the church in practice, even if they could not subscribe to the theory on which it was based, he was prepared to grant them full religious toleration. But toleration was not political rights. Indeed, when Bishop van Mildert in 1825 spoke powerfully against Catholic emancipation in the House of Lords, he based his argument on part of Horsley's 1791 speech.[17] In its temporal dimension, the constitution in the church and in the state had to remain, in Horsley's view, strictly Anglican.

Social thought

Religion and social control
It was Horsley's 1796 episcopal *Charge* which set out most clearly his attitude to the role the clergy should play in enforcing social control. But these ideas

---

[14] S. Horsley, *Charges* (Dundee, 1813), pp. 5–19.
[15] See D. Bellenger, 'The Émigré Clergy', pp. 392–410.
[16] *Speeches*, pp. 38, 42–3. Compare Letter to Hippisley, 6 July 1805, LPL, MS 1767, ff. 15–16.
[17] W. Van Mildert, *Substance of a Speech Delivered in the House of Lords May 17, 1825*, third edition (London, 1827). See below, pp. 237–8.

can be clearly seen earlier in his insistence in 1790 on Christian ministers having orthodox theological doctrines rather than just a bland sense of morality. Morality might be useful to society in making men consider the rights of others, but was it enough? Did it

reach the secret meditations of the mind, and the silent desires of the heart? Does it impose restraint upon the sensuality of the imagination and the private prurience of appetite? Like the divine law, does it extend to every secret energy of the mind, the will and the appetite; and require the obedience of the inner no less than of the outer man?

An atheist may be as moral as a Christian, but he is not under the sanction imposed by a religious faith. Religion and morality must be separated, but the Methodists, in their attempt to popularise and vulgarise Christianity, introduced unscriptural language which confused the two. Thus Methodists undermined the social-control function of Christianity by the very means by which they tried to enforce it. The Calvinist antinomian and Methodist Arminian views of faith and works both, at their opposite ends of the spectrum, were theologically heretical and politically dangerous in that they separated faith from works, doctrine from practice, which in truth were inseparable.[18]

His belief that the vulgar could understand Christian doctrines and must be taught them led Horsley, like most of his episcopal colleagues, to support the Charity Schools. His sermon at the movement's annual meeting in St Paul's in June 1793 reiterated a Burkean theme. Religion and the restraint it imposed were essential to free government and so only a despotism which ruled the common people like animals could afford to neglect the education of its children. In a free constitution the greatest danger to the state and to society was when, by failing to educate them, the poor were overrun by barbarism and irreligion. Such a degradation would lead to either despotism or anarchy, whereas Christianity silently secured the orderly liberty provided for in the constitution. It did this, not by preaching popular sovereignty, nor by releasing subjects from their loyalty when they considered their sovereign at fault (what, he claimed, modern democracy called *'the sacred right of insurrection'*) but by teaching the individual to govern himself and so make himself fit for that degree of civil freedom consistent with the public safety.[19]

By 1796 Horsley had reflected fully on the threat to the church and to government posed by the principles of the French Revolutionaries, as he

---

[18] Horsley, *Charges*, pp. 28, 31–6, 40–3.
[19] Horsley, *A Sermon*, 6 June 1793 (London, 1793), pp. 22–6.

conceived them. He had seen the French church disendowed, disestablished and almost proscribed, and had watched various constitutional experiments in the state sink, as it seemed to him, in a sea of blood. He also perceived England infected by some of the same ideas; a threat which, after the first wave in 1792–3, still remained intense. In November 1795 he had warned the House of Lords that the seditious and blasphemous publications of the day, in undermining morals, religion and politics, would poison the minds of the lower orders and influence their actions.[20] So, in 1796 he delivered one of his most powerful, concerned, yet considered, statements on the role of the church in political society, in his *Charge* to the clergy on his Primary Visitation of his new diocese of Rochester.[21]

Having referred to the utility of religion to the state, and the hostility to religion in France and amongst the English Jacobins, Horsley went on to analyse the state of public opinion in England in 1796. There were, he suggested, three groups of people: the first and largest group were the genuine Christians; second, and fewer in numbers, were the 'Democratists', the avowed enemies of Christianity working to destroy both church and state; but there was also, he argued, a third group who rarely thought about religion, who were well disposed to the established faith in so far as it proved of political use to the stability of society, but who had no other regard for it. This third group would continue to support the established church as long as it fulfilled that social-control function; they considered tithes and endowments as a public payment earned by such a socially useful role. But should the church fail to persuade this group that it was essential to the political well-being of the community, then they might side with the enemies of the established church. This, Horsley warned, would lead to moves to confiscate ecclesiastical property and abolish clerical privileges. Relating this to the traditional subject-matter of an episcopal charge, the bishop implied that the church would be perceived to be politically dysfunctional if the pastors were negligent in their duty. He was not suggesting that clergy should avoid this by cynically preaching an abject political obedience alien to their true belief, just that they must be conscientious Christian ministers preaching the true faith, the plenitude of Anglican doctrines. That would achieve the desired result and so secure the necessary political support. Sloth alone could ruin the Church of England. If men lived admirable lives and were diligent in their duties they would win the affection of their flock and the friendship of the moralists. In practical terms the greatest danger to the influence of the clergy and the stability of the national church was non-residence, and this led Horsley into a detailed examination of the Curates

[20] Speech on the third reading of the Treason Bill, 30 November 1795, *Speeches*, pp. 168, 178–9.
[21] Horsley, *Charge* . . . (London, 1796), *passim*, but esp. pp. 2–4, 20–7.

Act. The bishop used theory only to lead him to the practical advice his flock needed.

Social morality in practice

The practical bent of Horsley's moral thought is well illustrated by his attitudes to the slave trade and to the French war. Common moral sense told him that the slave trade was contrary to the spirit of Christianity. Such an attitude could have serious implications for a social theory based on hierarchy and inequality. But Horsley made clear his attitude was based on humanitarian principles, not on concepts of justice or human rights. He insisted that the allegation that the anti-slavery movement was a branch of Jacobinism was nonsense. Abolitionists proceeded on 'no visionary notions of equality and imprescriptive rights of men', but strenuously upheld social gradations. However, while these assertions reflected his beliefs and those of most abolitionists, they made it difficult to defend abolition in a logically consistent way. Consequently, Horsley employed a battery of arguments of different types. In 1799 he argued the expedience case: the continuation of the trade would endanger civil society and lead to more trouble, like the recent rising in St Domingo. He countered the anti-abolitionist claim that only slavery would, in fact, bring the Africans out of a state of abject barbarism into civilisation, by urging that, if providence had decreed such barbarity for them, it was wrong for the slavers to interfere with the moral and political state so divinely ordained; at the same time he suggested that the state of African civilisation was much higher than the slave traders alleged. While conceding that slavery was not prohibited in the Bible, he argued that the slave trade was, citing St Paul's first epistle to Timothy where 'menstealers' are listed along with other sinners guilty of parricide, homicide and sodomy.

If this citation may be seen as somewhat specious, his explanation why slavery *per se* was not prohibited was more revealing. Slavery was certainly contrary to the nature of men in its perfection, but given the present depraved state of human nature, earthly societies were by definition imperfect. Christianity was designed as a universal faith for all ages, societies and forms of government and prohibited only what was 'universally omissible'. It was extremely cautious how it disturbed the peace of the world by sudden and violent changes in men's political and moral state. Rather than specific prohibitions, it laid down general principles and sought to eradicate moral evil by degrees, slowly and silently.[22] While Horsley's insistence that the abolitionist cause made no concession to the concept of

---

[22] Speech on a bill to regulate the slave trade, 5 July 1799, in *Speeches*, pp. 196–8, 232–4, 236, 246–9, 252–5, 257.

the rights of man resulted in this jumble of arguments, his support for the cause was steadfast.

Horsley's views on the morality of war were also highly practical. He was unwilling to follow Christian teaching along any theoretical path which seemed to him unrealistic. When he wrote to his parochial clergy in the Rochester diocese in May 1798 to tell them of the two recommendations reached by the meeting of bishops on the proper role of the clergy in loyalist militias,[23] he added some comments of his own. First, he considered the political morality of the situation:

Wars and Fightings unquestionably have their origin in the bad Passions of Men. Nevertheless, the World being as it is, it must needs be that Wars and Fightings, with other offences, come. War, therefore, in the general, is to be reckoned among the sinful practices of Mankind; but, in every individual instance, the guilt lies principally at the Aggressor's door . . . and it is little else than a Calumny upon the Christian Religion to pretend, as some have pretended, that Defensive War is either contrary to the general Spirit of the Morality of the Gospel, or forbidden by any particular precept, or discouraged by the example of the first Christians.[24]

Then he offered practical advice. The clergy should not take military commissions or train with the local militia, not because of any moral theory, nor because it would derogate from their character, but because they were likely to be inefficient as soldiers. Even in the case of invasion, they would be more use supervising the evacuation of women and children, the old and infirm, removing livestock and destroying buildings useful to the enemy. Only in the final extremity should they help with the fighting; then they might even 'level the Musquet or trail the Pike'.[25]

In his practical moral thought, Horsley followed the lead given by Burke in eschewing theory when judging practical institutions. Like Burke, he followed the path of pragmatism, moderation and caution. Even the dictates of the Christian gospel must be interpreted cautiously and not be taken to theoretical extremes.

The conspiracy theory

In his letter to his clergy on military service, Horsley coupled the danger of 'Foreign Invasion' with that of 'Domestic Treason'. As he grew older and the onset of senility made him far less active, he developed the fears he had aired a decade earlier about the Methodists. His charge to the Rochester clergy in

---

[23] See above, pp. 150–1.
[24] Bodl., MS Eng Misc., d 156/1, f. 178v. Horsley to the incumbent of Barming, Maidstone.
[25] *Ibid.*, f. 179v. His meaning was, however, far from calling on the clergy to be mobilised into an armed militia as E. R. Norman claims, *Church and Society in England, 1770–1970* (Oxford, 1976), p. 20. Norman cites Soloway, *Prelates and People*, p. 33, who in turn cites Jebb, *Great Bishop*, pp. 117–19.

1800 wove three strands into a highly charged politico-religious theme of an alarmist nature. He combined the Robison-Barruel conspiracy theory of the French Revolution with a millenarian interpretation of that event, and with a bitter attack upon Methodism as a tool of the Jacobins.

Horsley repeated the conspiracy theory *con brio* and added a few embellishments of his own based on his interest in mathematics in general and in Newton in particular. The *philosophes* of the French Enlightenment, he alleged, selected some of Newton's physics and 'slily mistook their meaning' and misused them to defend their concept of a wholly materialistic universe which had no need of any superior intelligence. Equally they misused the 'sage' Locke's metaphysics and sought to undermine Christianity. As for Condorcet's work on the doctrine of chances, this had a latent moral object,

to insinuate an opinion that there is no such thing as certainty, consequently no such thing as truth, – that verisimilitude or probability is the utmost to which we can attain, and that the only standard of verisimilitude is a majority of suffrages.

Such moral relativism was at the very heart of the changing perceptions of political and social morality in this age.

After equating the French Republic with the Beast of the Apocalypse, he considered the danger of the infection spreading. Developing the concept of a plot and linking this with suspicions he had harboured for the last twenty years (at least since the archidiaconal charge of 1783), he suggested that the philosophical assault on England had first taken place through the medium of the Unitarians on the assumption that the Socinian heresy had more chance of success than pure atheism. But that plot had failed and Priestley had fled to America. The line of attack on religion in Britian was, accordingly, changed. Now, instead of removing the mystery of religion and reducing it to philosophical speculation, their plan was to alienate men from the established clergy by suggesting they were worldly, indifferent to religion and neglectful of their charges.

The Methodists were being used as the new fifth column. Groups led by illiterate pastors opened schools which sought, by bribes of money, to woo children away from the excellent church schools which taught true religion and loyalty. Horsley believed the Methodist schools were under Jacobin influence and he did everything he could to destroy them. The opposition to Pitt's two acts, the sedition and treason legislation, made clear, he believed, that the real objects of those institutions were sedition and atheism, not religion. But he insisted he was not attacking Methodism *per se*. The Jacobins, he suggested, were making a tool of Methodism, just as the Illuminati of Bavaria had of Freemasonry, but the real Methodist was ignorant of the wicked enterprise.[26] By 1806 he considered the wound had

[26] Horsley, *The Charge . . .* (London, 1800), pp. 3–10, 12–14, 16, 18–27, 32–4.

been effectively cauterised, the Jacobin fire extinguished, and Methodists rescued from their delusion. Then they were again, as they had been in Wesley's lifetime, unquestionably faithful and loyal subjects.[27]

Conclusion

Samuel Horsley died on 4 October 1806 and was buried under the altar at St Mary's, Newington Butts. Later his remains were removed and the church demolished to make way for a railway. At first sight the symbolism seems apt. But in fact the decade of revolution did not see the replacement of an old established argument by a new one. Rather, Horsley's career shows clearly that the change in the character of Christian political thought in England between 1789 and 1804 was a change of emphasis from one aspect to another of a coherent theory. Horsley demonstrated the unity of that theory in 1790 and selected from it arguments suited to the time and occasion thereafter.

To what extent can the change of emphasis from political to social theory, the new preoccupation with social control rather than political obligation, be described in theoretical terms? Was it, in fact, a transition from a fundamentally deontological outlook to an end-directed one? Horsley and his ilk still, at heart, adopted a deontological stance. They believed that, if one could define man's duty and persuade all men to do it, then government and society would function properly. Religion was crucial both in defining and in enforcing that duty. The radical writers, however, tended to define the ends which men should work to achieve and then look to see what practical changes in government and society were necessary to bring about these goals. But it would be simplistic and misleading to suggest a clear dichotomy between an unambiguously deontological, traditional philosophy of political obligation and a clearly end-directed, radical vision. J. C. D. Clark has shown that in some ways 'radicals' continued to think in deontological terms, although the new element in their thought was greater than he allows. Moreover, the establishment position itself was somewhat ambiguous. The preoccupation with social theory, with order and control no longer occupied the heights of theoretical duty, but still sought to avoid the profound social change implicit in the adoption of an ends-based theory of human rights. It adopted essentially pragmatic grounds; its argument was that of expedience, of self-interest. It sought to maintain the status quo, to bolster up the traditional social structure, and looked for any social and psychological mechanism which would help achieve that end. Thus the establishment came to adopt a partially end-directed position themselves.

---

[27] Horsley, *The Charge . . .* (London, 1806), pp. 21–2.

While it is possible (and to some extent helpful) to describe the changes in these theoretical terms, it is also misleading to do so, for it was precisely this theoretical and philosophical outlook which the establishment abandoned. There is no evidence that any major conservative writer thought in these terms. They saw themselves reacting to an emergency; in the language of the day, being swept along by providence, not by their own will. The change was no conscious adoption of a new theoretical stance. It was an instinctive reaction, a natural defence reflex to the threat of revolution. The crucial question was, could such a stance survive the moment of danger? Would the post-revolutionary years see a return to the philosophy and theology of political obligation, or was the churches' preoccupation with social theory, with order and control, to be the new order of the day?

Part III

Post-Revolution, 1804–1832

12

Political and social theory

The change in emphasis from political obligation to social order survived the French Revolution and was reflected in Christian political theory in the first three decades of the nineteenth century. The major crises of the period for churchmen continued to stimulate the evolution of a Christian theory of society which would ensure social stability and unity; this was forged in the heated controversies over the development of popular education, the infidel challenge, the post-war distress and disturbances, the assault on the privileges of the established church and the challenge of reform in church and state.

Political theory

General trends

The episcopal sermons preached before the House of Lords in Westminster Abbey on Martyrdom Day were traditional occasions for an exposition of constitutional theory. However, these lapsed during the war and none were preached after that of 1795 until 1807, when they were revived at the request of George III. However, although annual sermons were preached from 1807 to 1810 the practice then lapsed again and was never revived. Of the four that were preached, those of Henry Bathurst in 1808 and William Mansel in 1810 were largely in the constitutional tradition of pre-war years. But Thomas Burgess's sermon in 1807 concentrated on the danger the French example posed to society and stressed the need for religious education, while Charles Moss in 1809 combined thoughts on the philosophic notion of political obligation with an awareness of the social role of religious restraints and sanctions.[1]

This relative neglect of the arguments traditional for over a century before 1789 is characteristic of the whole episcopal bench and of establishment

[1] T. Burgess, *A Sermon* (London, 1807), pp. 6, 8–10, 15, 17, 22–3; H. Bathurst, *A Sermon* (London, 1808), pp. 7, 10–16, 20–2; C. Moss, *A Sermon* (London, 1809), pp. 3–5, 6, 8, 10–13; W. L. Mansel, *A Sermon* (Cambridge, 1810), pp. 5–11, 14–15, 17–20.

Anglicans generally. They preferred in these years to address themselves to particular questions and concrete issues rather than to indulge in abstract theory. In his 1812 charge, which largely consisted of an attack on the alleged political claims of the Catholics, Bishop Pretyman-Tomline assumed constitutional principles but did not make them explicit. It was a London Catholic priest, J. C. Eustace, who, in responding to the charge, brought the latent theory of political obligation into the open. He argued that it arose from those aspects of religion shared by all Christians and was not distinctive of Anglican theology alone, and that it enjoined obedience to government in general, but did not specify a particular form.[2]

Generally speaking after 1804 the pre-revolutionary constitutional arguments were mainly voiced by those whose political loyalty was called into question. As during the 1790s, the Catholics were still preoccupied with such arguments and their emphasis on social restraint developed relatively late. The Methodists were also anxious to refute allegations of their seditious and disloyal intent. Year after year the Methodist Conference affirmed its loyalty, and in the Methodist Manual of 1810 Jonathan Crowther included a section on constitutional theory and political obligation in a statement of Methodist beliefs. The civil magistrates were ordained by God and should be obeyed; it was lawful for Christians to become magistrates and it was the duty of all the people 'to pray for their rulers, and all magistrates superior and subordinate, to honour their persons, to pay them tribute, and other dues, to obey their lawful commands and to be subject to their authority for conscience sake'.[3] John Wesley's attitude to government lived on in Adam Clarke, who almost prostrated himself in supplication before Lord Sidmouth in 1811 assuring him that every Methodist preacher proclaimed '"Fear God! Honour the King!" and *meddle not with them that are given to change.*' Clarke published a sermon, *The Rights of God and Caesar,* in 1821, and another on the *Origin and End of Civil Government* (dated March 1821) in 1822.[4] These two sermons were exactly like hundreds published by establishment Anglicans before 1789 but in this later period they are much rarer and their constitutional bias appears somewhat old-fashioned.

This is accentuated by the fact that they appeared in the wake of the disturbances of 1819 when the vast majority of Anglicans were preaching

[2] G. Pretyman-Tomline, *A Charge Delivered to the Clergy . . . of Lincoln* (London, 1812); J. C. Eustace, *Answer to the Charge . . .* (London, 1813), esp. p. 13.

[3] *Minutes of the Methodist Conference,* vol. 4 (1864), pp. 136–8, vol. 5 (1864), pp. 157–9, 174–6, 260, vol. 5 (1838), pp. 84–5; J. Crowther, *The Methodist Manual* (Halifax, 1810), p. 114. The Catholic position is discussed in a wider context below, pp. 232–8, and the Methodist one pp. 197–8.

[4] DRO, Sidmouth Papers, 152M Corr. 1811 OE, Letters from Clarke to Sidmouth, 14 May 1811, 15 May 1811; A. Clarke, *The Rights of God and Caesar* (London, 1821), and *The Origin and End of Civil Government* (London, 1822), esp. pp. 8–15.

on the themes of social control, sanctions and restraint. When Anglicans did repeat the traditional arguments of political obligation, as did Melville Horne, a curate in Salford, they set them in the larger context of the need for social order. Horne rehearsed the historical arguments and reasserted the importance of the 1689 settlement; he compared the parliamentary reformers to the critics of Charles I, but saved his real venom for the infidel conspiracy. So his constitutional argument became lost in his greater concern for order, sanctions and restraint.[5] While Clarke used the text 'Fear God! Honour the King!' as an intellectual injunction, Horne used it as a psychological sanction. But not all Methodists were as old-fashioned as Clarke. The most powerful and passionate Methodist sermon of the years of discontent, John Stephens's *Mutual Relations of Rich and Poor*, set the constitutional tradition firmly within the much larger context of social unity and interdependence, of restraint and order.[6]

To a certain extent, some evangelical Anglicans also felt a need to assert their loyalty in the face of common complaints that they were undermining the constitution in the church by associating with Dissenters and, for many, appearing indistinguishable from Methodists. Hannah More was bound, of course, to include a section on 'Saint Paul's respect for Constituted Authorities' in her *Essay on St Paul*,[7] but other Evangelicals went out of their way to make constitutional points. In November 1819 William Dealtry, who had replaced John Venn as Rector of Clapham in 1813, considered the time ripe to recall the scriptural account of man's duty to the magistrates. However, having quoted the traditional texts, rejected passive obedience, emphasised the duty to abide by the established laws and constitution in normal times while accepting that change is occasionally possible, Dealtry went on to examine the conspiracy theory, equate atheism and sedition and stress the need for restraint and sanctions, so moving into the social argument. Thus he came to a brief but paradigmatic statement of Christian social theory: 'It is Christianity which binds us together in common sympathy, under a sense of our common wants, as children of the same parent, and members of the same mystical body.'[8]

Other Evangelicals took a slightly more liberal view of the constitutional position (such as the future Whig bishop, William Otter, who stressed contract theory and St Paul's insistence on his rights as a Roman citizen),[9]

---

[5] M. Horne, *The Moral and Political Crisis of England* (London, 1820), pp. 4–21, 38. Horne provided, perhaps, the best 'independent' account of Peterloo which is sympathetic to the magistrates, pp. 16–19.

[6] J. Stephens, *The Mutual Relations, Claims and Duties of the Rich and the Poor* (Manchester, 1819), pp. v–vi, 13–14, 23, 30–2, 35, 37–8.

[7] H. More, *Works*, vol. 10, pp. 284–301.

[8] *The Dispositions and Conduct Required of Christians towards their Rulers* (London, 1819), p. 25.

[9] W. Otter, *Reasons for Continuing the Education of the Poor . . .* (Shrewsbury, 1820), pp. 23–6.

but there was widespread agreement on the social arguments. The fact that most Anglicans now omitted the preliminary constitutional argument does not, of course, mean that they rejected it, merely that the whole of their emphasis was placed on the social theory they considered so essential in the circumstances of the day. Nor should the Catholic, Methodist or Evangelical essays in constitutional theory mislead us; while relatively more frequent than Anglican ones, they too are only occasional and faint echoes of the pre-revolutionary strains, now that the major theme was social in nature.

Paley and Coleridge

Only in one area did the constitutional arguments make significant development in this period. The secularisation of political theory inherent in Paley's utilitarianism was, of course, part of the pre-revolutionary philosophical and theoretical argument. However, because it was couched in a way that concealed its real import, there was no major reaction to it during the Revolution years as there was against both infidel and Unitarian forms of secularisation. The publication of Paley's later works, especially his *Evidences of Christianity* (1794) and his *Reasons for Contentment* (1793), had reinforced the general view that he was a reliable authority.[10] But some writers were aware from the start of the revolutionary implications (in intellectual terms) of his *Moral and Political Philosophy*. The Evangelicals had serious reservations. Gisborne's critique of 1789 was echoed in the post-revolutionary period by More and Wilberforce. Bishop Richard Watson also had his doubts, and it was the infidel James Mackintosh who, despite one or two minor quibbles, broadly approved of the Archdeacon's theory of moral obligation which could stand independently of religion.[11]

Paley's major intellectual critic in this period was Samuel Taylor Coleridge. He criticised Paley in print seriously first in 1809 and returned to the theme in a more positive context in 1817. In 1818 he republished one of his 1809 pieces. By the time of these writings Coleridge's position had changed from that of the 1795 Bristol Lectures; he was now anti-French and had changed his Unitarianism for established Christianity, but his view was still far more unconventional, radical and passionate than, for example, the very orthodox stance Robert Southey had by then taken. The conventional platitudes of state religion did not constitute Christianity for Coleridge and he believed that nothing less than true Christianity was the heritage of the Anglican church. He regarded Paley's theory of political and moral obligation as no better than an infidel one; indeed he sandwiched him between

---

[10] But note G. F. A. Best's suggestion that in the latter work the Archdeacon's tongue may have been in his cheek, *Temporal Pillars*, p. 161.

[11] R. Watson, *Anecdotes*, pp. 9, 437; J. Mackintosh, *Dissertation on the Progress of Ethical Philosophy* (written 1828–9; published, Edinburgh, 1836), pp. 62–4, 273–9, 283–4.

British and French atheists, referring to 'Hume, Paley and Condillac, the parents or foster fathers of modern ethics'. Coleridge could see no difference between Paley's principle of utility and the *philosophes'* concept of benevolence, self-interest and will. Like Hartley and Godwin, Paley reduced virtue to selfish prudence and supported this with what Coleridge insisted on calling superstition because, in taking conscious selfishness as its central tenet, it had only a very distant connexion with Christianity, which was centred on man's love of God and his neighbour. As he expressed it succinctly in a letter, Paley taught '*obey* God, *Benefit* your neighbour; but *love* YOURSELVES above all'.[12]

This led Coleridge to set out his views 'On the Principles of Political Philosophy' – a rare activity in Britain in 1809. In these pieces Coleridge rejected as unchristian not only Paley's expediency, but also Enlightenment rationalism. Here at least he agreed with Burke – any system of government deemed equally applicable to any country must be erroneous. He considered in detail the theories of Rousseau and the Physiocrats, and, in rejecting both, drew heavily on German thinkers in general and Kant in particular. He also attacked those radical reformers who assumed that everything in the state was rotten, and that men had a solemn religious obligation to overthrow it. The demands of Christianity were more complex than that and should not be exploited in that way. Religious rights were inseparable from self-denial and self-restraint and could not be combined with the passions of self-will and love of power as they were by the reformers.[13] Between the first publication of this argument in 1809 and its re-appearance in 1818, Coleridge further developed his thoughts on the role of religion in political philosophy in *The Statesman's Manual* (1816), which was sub-titled 'The Bible the best guide to political skill and foresight', and a *Lay Sermon* (1817). These continued his two-pronged attack on abstract rationalism. The attack on expediency here was extended to embrace a critique of the commercial spirit: Christianity should limit avarice and the accumulation of capital. This critique, which is part of his response to the distress of the post-war years, was directed both against the Unitarians and their support of aggressive bourgeois enterprise, and against Paley. The danger of unrestrained enterprise was that it would lead men under the specious name of utility, to judge the worth of all things by their marketable value. Religion should provide the counterbalance to commerce and so ensure equilibrium, but Paley had reduced virtue to a form of prudence. While prudence had an earthly calculus, virtue for Paley had an

---

[12] *The Courier*, 22 December 1809, *Works*, vol. 3, bk 2, pp. 79–83; *The Friend*, 1818, *Works*, vol. 4, bk 1, p. 108; *Collected Letters* (Oxford, 1956), vol. 3, p. 153.
[13] *The Friend*, 1818, *Works*, vol. 4, bk 1, pp. 166–89, 314–20, 424–6, 446–7.

eschatological one and was dictated by calculation and fear – not by love of God or of our neighbour. Coleridge shuddered at the thought that this was the moral theology taught at Cambridge and cited in parliament and the law courts.

The true restraint of religion was, for Coleridge, a positive not a negative force, a force impelled by selfless love. But he saw this positive Christian love as a practical and concrete force too, and he rejected the rationalism of the French Enlightenment. France on the eve of the Revolution, Germany on the eve of the Reformation, and England on the eve of the Civil War, were all obsessed with abstract, speculative ideals. The errors of the French Revoluton came from the neglect of concrete maxims which, while found in Thucydides, Tacitus, Machiavelli, Bacon and Harrington, were initially all clearly established in the Bible.[14] Coleridge's rejection, on religious grounds, of utilitarian expediency, and of rationalist speculation, are easier to record than his positive alternative, which was never set out in direct terms. This alternative was founded on the simple maxims of the Bible as Coleridge interpreted them, but it was also enshrined in a highly complex, romantic concept of an organic society. For Coleridge too, political philosophy led to social theory.

Social theory

The exposition of a Christian theory of society overwhelmingly dominated the political writings of almost all religious thinkers in the post-revolutionary period. No one had a clearer view of what constituted the perfect Christian community than Hannah More. The fictional vision of the *Cheap Repository Tracts* was recommended in somewhat more theoretical terms in a number of works from 1805 to 1815. This vision of society was, of course, hierarchical, interdependent, caring and united. The rich showed concern for the poor, the lower orders respected their betters. Religion was not merely the cement of society, but Heaven provided the perfect pattern to be followed as far as human imperfection allowed. But that imperfection required restraints which only religion could provide and without which society could not survive. No group in society had economic interests which conflicted with those of any other group; the interest of each was the interest of all. When men 'do unto others as they would be done unto', society flourished; when men of any class neglected their religious duties,

---

[14] Coleridge, 'The Statesman's Manual', 1816, *Works*, vol. 6, pp. 16–17, and 'Lay Sermon', 1817, *Works*, vol. 6, pp. 185–7. On the influence of Harrington on Coleridge's thought in 1816–17 see J. D. Coates, 'Coleridge's Debt to Harrington: A Discussion of Zapolya', *JHI*, 38 (1977), 501–8.

society suffered.[15] She regretted, for example, the decline of household prayers:

It was a bond of political as well as moral union; it was the only occasion on which 'the rich and the poor met together'. There is something of a coalescing property in social worship. In acknowledging their common dependence on their common Master, this equality of half an hour would be likely to promote subordination through the rest of the day.[16]

Most of these features were common to a range of thinkers. The need for hierarchy was, of course, recognised almost universally. It was defended or assumed not only in the writings of establishment figures, like Thomas Calvert, Norrisian Professor of Divinity at Cambridge and royal preacher at Whitehall, or Thomas Whitaker, vicar of Whalley and justice of the peace for Lancashire and the West Riding of Yorkshire, but also by Evangelicals like Gisborne, Methodists like Stephens, and Baptists like Hall – not to mention by Coleridge.[17] Submission to the dictates of providence was widely seen as a religious duty, and hierarchy and subordination were both regarded as *sine qua non* for the existence of the social order. In his 1810 *Charge* the new Bishop of London, John Randolph, lamented that the pressure of the times had affected the temper and morals of the people, and the agitation of new opinions had weakened the spirit of subordination which united society. His fear was not of invasion but of internal agitation and disturbance. He urged his clergy to stand firm against this; a revival of religion would have valuable civil benefits as well.[18] In the following year, 1811, the Archdeacon of Rochester, John Law, urged his clergy into an even more directly political role. They should discourage the 'restless spirit of innovation' which led to insubordination, remind men that all human arrangements were unavoidably imperfect and that they were obliged to discountenance divisions in society and strive to advance peace and goodwill.[19]

But it was the economic distress and political discontent of post-war years

---

[15] H. More, 'Hints towards the Forming of the Character of a Young Princess', 1805, *Works*, vol. 6, pp. 73–5, 195–6; 'Coelebs in Search of a Wife', 1809, *Works*, vol. 7, pp. 19–20, 139, 185–7, 508–9; 'Practical Piety', 1811, *Works*, vol. 8, pp. 155–7, 174, 322–3; 'Christian Morals', 1812, *Works*, vol. 9, pp. 54, 68, 108–9, 113–17, 407–8; 'An Essay on St Paul', 1815, *Works*, vol. 10, pp. 1–6.

[16] More, 'Christian Morals', *Works*, vol. 9, p. 117.

[17] T. Calvert, *The Rich and the Poor Shown to be of God's Appointment* (Cambridge, 1820), pp. 3–13, 19–22; T. D. Whitaker, *The Substance of a Speech* . . . (Blackburn, 1817), pp. 2–8; Gisborne, *Sermons*, vol. 2, pp. 196–217; Stephens, *Mutual Relations*, pp. 8–20; Hall, Sermon 'On the Duty, Happiness and Honour of Maintaining the Course Prescribed to us by Providence', 26 May 1811, *Works*, vol. 6, pp. 83–6, and 'Advantages of Knowledge to the Lower Classes', 1810, *Works*, vol. 1, pp. 202–3; Coleridge, 'Statesman's Manual', *Works*, vol. 6, p. 7.

[18] J. Randolph, *Charge* (Oxford, 1810), pp. 6–7, 18.

[19] J. Law, *A Charge* (London, 1811), p. 15.

which elicited the most forceful statements of Christian social theory. Hannah More resurrected Mr Fantom, only to draw a lesson from his deathbed.[20] In 1817 Archdeacon Law reminded the Rochester clergy of their duty to help preserve the 'due order and subordination' necessary in all well-regulated governments.[21] Dr Whitaker recognised how bad the distress and want was in Lancashire and respected those who submitted to providence, but bitterly condemned the disaffection of others who presumptuously judged things they could not understand and censured their superiors whose motives they could not know. He defended the whole established order – tithe and church endowments, magistrates and the Corn Bill. The only reason the poor did not murmur against providence, he suggested, was because they had ceased to believe in it. Whitaker was speaking, as justice of the peace, to his fellow magistrates and clergy at Blackburn in February 1817 at a critical time of industrial, social and political unrest, when those he termed 'Jacobins' taught contempt for all that was venerable in society. His mood was not one of sadness, but of deep bitterness.[22]

His speech contrasted markedly with a sermon preached in the following month in London by the Evangelical Daniel Wilson, chaplain to Lord Galway. Whitaker, in the eye of battle, fell back on invective, but Wilson was detached, reflective and intellectually far more powerful in his argument. There was, he suggested, one simple remedy for all the evils in the world – a contented spirit. He analysed at length the links between contentment and godliness and then applied them to the situation in Britain in March 1817. This was an ideal situation for Christians to show, in genuinely testing circumstances, how real their submission to providence and to the established authorities was. Even so, their situation was far easier than that of the Christians under Nero, for they had a ₁aternal, Christian government which protected the rights of the poor as well as the rich, defended true religion and encouraged piety. Those wicked men who sought to exploit the distress and excite a spirit of discontent and sedition had to be resisted and care be taken to ensure that the real progress in education and religious and moral improvement which had been made was not lost.[23] Like most Evangelicals, Wilson had a vision of the Christian community as hierarchic, paternalist and humane. This vision of society was seriously threatened by the turbulence from below and he employed every intellectual and rhetorical skill he possessed to try to quell it.

---

[20] 'The Death of Mr Fantom, the Great Reformist' (1817), *Works*, vol. 3, pp. 45–74. See also 'The Delegate' (1817), *ibid.*, pp. 2–8.

[21] J. Law, *A Charge* (Rochester, 1817), pp. 7–8.

[22] Whitaker, *Substance of a Speech*, pp. 2–8.

[23] D. Wilson, *The Duty of Contentment* (London, 1817), pp. 3–27.

In the short run at least, things got worse rather than better in clerical eyes. Two and a half years later, John Kaye, Regius Professor of Divinity at Cambridge, lamented the continuing divisions and hostility in society, when the poor were taught to look at their superiors with suspicion and hatred.[24] Evangelicals continued to urge contentment and insisted that religion was 'the sovereign antidote to the poison of disaffection and infidelity' and alone could ensure social unity as the family of God.[25] Methodists argued that the word 'independence' was not in the Bible but came from the 'vocabulary of Satan'; its spirit led to the expulsion of the angels from Heaven and of man from Paradise and those who rebelled against the laws of the land also rejected the laws of God. Against this was placed the vision of a Christian community in which all parts of society were bound together by mutual duty, obligation and affection.[26]

That such a vision of society, although extremely widespread, was not universal amongst churchmen was made clear by Henry Bathurst, Archdeacon of Norwich, in a remarkable, long and public *Letter to Wilberforce* in 1818. Bathurst bitterly attacked Castlereagh and the government and argued that no one who applied Christian principles to politics (as Wilberforce claimed to do) could support their policies either at home or abroad. He argued that the government itself was undermining the 1688 settlement by introducing despotic government, for despotism was revolution as much as insurrection. He defended the radical critics of government and attacked the system of spies, and he reminded Wilberforce

that the world was made, and Government, like the world, for all equally to enjoy its blessing. The Almighty cannot sanction a monopoly of enjoyment to a few . . . Christianity, Sir, I am fully aware, does not meddle much with the interior arrangement of human government; but its analogies at least ought to be observed. Salvation is offered unto all. All souls are equally dear in the sight of God . . . Should not the justice and equity of human government correspond? Mr Burke may call a few classes of society the body politic; but I say, that the Genius of Christianity leads us to value Government in proportion as its blessings are co-extensive with every member of society.[27]

Not surprisingly, although Professor Kaye became a bishop in 1820, Henry Bathurst never followed his father on to the episcopal bench. Moreover, it was Kaye's, not Bathurst's, view which was typical of clerical opinion in the years of distress from 1816 to 1819.

[24] J. Kaye, *A Sermon . . . November 14, 1819* (London, 1819), p. 10.
[25] W. Dealtry, *Dispositions and Conduct*, 7 November 1819, pp. 23, 25, 27.
[26] Stephens, *Mutual Relations*, pp. 13, 20. On Methodist attitudes to public order in this period see D. N. Hempton, 'Thomas Allen and Methodist Politics, 1800–1840', *Hist.* 67 (1982), 13–31 (pp. 18–22).
[27] H. Bathurst, *Christianity and Present Politics* (London, 1818), pp. 3, 8, 33, 66–9, 72.

The informal role of the parochial clergy in maintaining social control in the villages continued, but the formal expression of it in the presence of parsons on the county Commission of the Peace grew considerably at the end of the eighteenth century. The number of clerical magistrates did not fall significantly until after 1832.[28] Perhaps the two most notorious were the Reverends W. R. Hay and C. W. Ethelston, who were magistrates involved in the 'Peterloo Massacre' of 1819. But the actions of repressive clerical magistrates in the East Anglian riots of 1816, at Spa Fields in 1816, and later in the Captain Swing riots of 1830–1 also caused much resentment and criticism.[29]

The years between 1819 and 1830 were relatively quieter. The passion and urgency had subsided somewhat by 1824 when James Law, Archdeacon of Richmond, calmly reminded his clergy of the restraining role of religion on which the social compact depended.[30] Four years earlier, however, his father, George Henry Law, in his episcopal charge to his diocese of Chester had been far less confident:

All respect and veneration for the establishments and customs of our forefathers are rapidly wearing away; those ties of attachment which formerly bound together the poor and rich are gradually dissolving; and, what is the most frightful and alarming symptom, the public are habituated to hear all religion derided, and to believe that God and a future judgment are mere political delusions, invented by the priesthood and adopted by the state.[31]

Law's diocese of Chester included, of course, industrial Lancashire – but men were having to reappraise the role of the church and the clergy in society more generally. Before considering this reappraisal, it is necessary to examine three themes in more detail: first, the roles of the established church and of the Dissenters in enforcing social controls through education and the pastoral ministry; secondly, the continuing infidel challenge to the social order; and thirdly, the arguments relating to Catholic emancipation and to reform in church and state.

---

[28] The best account of clerical magistrates is in Russell, *The Clerical Profession*, pp. 150–61. See also below, pp. 252–3.

[29] On clerical magistrates at Peterloo see Donald Read, *Peterloo: The 'Massacre' and its Background* (Manchester, 1958), pp. 75–7. For comments on a later radical squib on Rev. W. R. Hay as 'Rev. Robert Rednose' and on Rev. C. W. Ethelston as 'Rev. C. W. Wisdom' in *The Wiseacres* (1821), see Robert Walmsley, *Peterloo: The Case Reopened* (Manchester, 1969), pp. 372–5.

[30] J. T. Law, *The Origin, Progress, and Necessity, of an Established Church* (London, 1824), pp. 9–10.

[31] G. H. Law, *A Charge Delivered to the Clergy . . . of Chester* (London, 1820), pp. 32–3.

13

Establishment and social control

The need for social control and the ability and propriety of religion to enforce it were widely agreed. This control was exercised largely through religious education and the teaching function of the pastoral ministry. How far were these primarily functions of the established church and how far could all denominations share in their application? The relative unanimity and closing of ranks which was apparent in the late 1790s, especially in the light of the conspiracy theory, was already disappearing by 1804, although the major battles between Anglicans and Dissenters on this issue came between 1810 and 1813, and some co-operation survived even these.

Religion and education

The British and Foreign Bible Society was formed in 1804. There had been a number of societies of similar intent and earlier date,[1] but the 1804 society was unusual in that it was supported by both Anglicans and Dissenters.[2] Evangelicals such as Granville Sharp, Zacary Macaulay, William Wilberforce and Lord Teignmouth were closely involved. In 1808–9 a number of local auxiliary Bible Societies were formed as off-shoots of the parent body. Because of the trans-denominational nature of its support the Society issued only the Bible, with no explanatory notes and without an accompanying Prayer Book. Meanwhile, popular education developed on denominational lines. In 1797 the Anglican Andrew Bell published an account of his Madras system of education, and in 1803 the Quaker Joseph Lancaster advocated

---

[1] So.iety for Promoting Christian Knowledge (1698); Society for the Propagation of the Gospel in Foreign Parts (1701), Society in Scotland for Christian Knowledge (1709); Society for Proi 1oting Religious Knowledge among the Poor (1750); The Bible Society (for the Army and Navy) (1780); The Society for the Support and Encouragement of Sunday Schools (1785).

[2] On the ecumenical aspects see R. H. Martin, *Evangelicals United*, pp. 80–146. See also Harold Silver, *Popular Education*, pp. 42–52, and Raymond Cowherd, *The Politics of English Dissent* (New York, 1956), pp. 36–45.

the establishment of schools which taught an undenominational brand of Christianity which was, in practice, Dissenting. In 1811 the National Society was formed to set up Anglican schools based on Bell's system, and teaching the theology of the established church.

In a sermon for the Boys' Charity School in Lambeth in 1807, Dr Bell claimed his system of education checked vice, promoted good conduct and order, improved the morals of the poor and made them sober and subordinate, as was in their best interest. He observed that the great political, moral and religious advantages of popular education were now agreed by the best writers on political and moral economy.[3] This was no less than the truth; the bench of bishops spoke with almost a single voice on the issue and there were innumerable echoes from elsewhere.[4] When they spoke of the education of the children of the poor, they meant, of course, religious education. Hannah More spelt out the theory explicitly in her anti-machiavel; it was their gross vice and brutal ignorance

which leave the lower classes prey to factious innovators, and render them the blind tools of political incendiaries. When the youth of this class are carefully instructed in religion by their rightful teachers, those teachers have the fairest opportunities of instilling into them their duty to the state, as well as to the church; and they will find that the same lessons which form good Christians tend to make them good subjects. But without that moderate measure of sound and sober instruction, which should be judiciously adapted to their low demands, they will be likely neither to honour the King, reverence the clergy, nor obey the magistrate.[5]

Such commonplaces as these, together with innumerable references to religion as the cement of society, proliferated in the sermons, charges and clerical addresses of these years. They came from the whole spectrum of belief. They typified the attitude of Evangelicals, who were conservative in social and political matters. Just as their arguments relating to slavery were based less on a notion of the fundamental abstract rights which slaves possessed by virtue of their humanity and more on paternalist, humanitarian sensibility, so their educational views were humanitarian but also entirely compatible with the existence of a social hierarchy and the use of

---

[3] A. Bell, *Extract of a Sermon* . . . (London, 1807), pp. 19–20.
[4] See, *inter alia*, Watson, Sermon (1804), in *Misc. T*, vol. 1, p. 523, and Charge to the Clergy of Llandaff, *ibid*., pp. 201–2; T. Burgess, *Peculiar Privileges . . . A Charge . . . 1804* (Durham, 1805), p. 26; T. Dampier, *A Sermon Preached before the Lords . . . February 20th, 1805* (London, 1805), p. 13; S. Goodenough, *A Sermon Preached before the Lords . . . 8 February 1809* (London, 1809), p. 24; J. Buckner, *A Sermon Preached before the Lords . . . February 5, 1812* (London, 1812), pp. 14–15; D. Bogue, *The Nature and Importance of a Good Education* (London, 1808), pp. 2–3, 5–6; C. Daubeny, *A Sermon Preached in . . . St Paul's* (London, 1809), p. 8. The best account of episcopal attitudes is in Soloway, *Prelates and People*, pp. 349–89.
[5] More, 'Character of Princess', *Works*, vol. 6, p. 203.

religious education as social control. Wilberforce encouraged Hannah More to found schools, and supported most of the measures of Pitt's administration.

While Evangelicals were to disagree bitterly with other Anglicans on the question of denominational and non-denominational schools, in the basic belief in the value of religious education their commonplaces were precisely those of Bishops Majendie, Burgess and Bathurst. Henry Bathurst insisted that without the religious education of the poor the property and even the lives of the wealthy would be insecure and precarious possessions.[6] This was a view Catholics and Baptists shared with Anglicans. In a discourse at the annual meeting of the St Patrick Charity School and Asylum for Orphans in London in 1811, Charles Butler stressed the importance of the Catholic faith in teaching the poor duty, regularity and obedience; and, preaching for the benefit of a Baptist Sunday School in Leicester in 1810, Robert Hall insisted that teaching children their religious duty would enhance subordination and the tranquillity of the state, not endanger them.[7]

However, while the denominations agreed on the principle, there was plenty of disagreement over the practice. Just as evangelical Anglicans worked with Dissenters in the British and Foreign Bible Society, so also they supported Lancastrian schools in the years before the formation of the National Society. In both cases an undenominational brand of Christianity was purveyed to the poor. The question at issue was twofold: first, would this be an effective form of social control; and secondly, would such activity undermine the Church of England and so weaken the constitution? Beneath these questions lay more profound ones. Was obedience to the state and social order part of the common tradition of all Christian denominations, or did some systems of theology provide a stronger backing for it than others? Had the Dissenters wholly discarded the radical and subversive views which many believed they held before and during the early years of the French Revolution? Even more profoundly, they asked how essential was an established church to the well-being of the state.

In 1807 John Bowles, who had throughout the 1790s advanced exclusively secular arguments in favour of the conservative cause, wrote a public letter to Samuel Whitbread MP who had given unqualified support to the Lancastrian schools in a speech in the House of Commons. Bowles argued that the non-denominational religion taught was highly objection-

---

[6] H. Majendie, *A Charge Delivered to the Clergy . . . of Chester* (London, 1804), pp. 7–8, 13; T. Burgess, *Sermon*, 1807, pp. 22–3; H. Bathurst, *A Sermon . . . June 7th, 1810* (London, 1810), pp. 1–3, 7, 10, 12–14.

[7] C. Butler, *Miscellaneous Tracts* (printed not published, 1812), p. 56; Hall, 'Advantages of Knowledge', *Works*, vol. 1, pp. 202–3. On Catholic poor schools see the articles by Marmion and Kitching cited above, Chapter 9, note 61.

able from the religious, moral and political point of view. By excluding every doctrine over which there was disagreement (and if Unitarians were to be included that meant the doctrine of the Trinity) one was left with an anomalous, generalised system which no existing sect could call Christianity, and was in fact no more than deism. But effective social control was rooted in theology and doctrine – destroy the roots and the plant would die. Lancaster hoped that this religious education would produce the moral effects of Christianity, but that was to expect the effect without the cause, the fruit without the tree. Bowles argued that, if education were to be a national concern, then children should be educated in the faith of the national church, especially in the light of the alarming Methodist success in drawing the poor away from the established church to their own wild and fanatical beliefs.[8] In this powerfully argued letter, Bowles not only foreshadowed the dispute which was to rage in 1810–13 over the Schools Societies and the Bible Society, but he also anticipated Sidmouth's Bill of 1811 by suggesting that too many improper persons were being registered as Dissenting preachers under the Toleration Act. All these disputes of 1810–13 were based on the belief of many that social control could be safely entrusted only to the hands of the clergy of the established church.

The Bible Society, 1810–1812

On 12 February 1810, Christopher Wordsworth, domestic chaplain to the Archbishop of Canterbury, published his *Reasons for Declining to Become a Subscriber to the British and Foreign Bible Society*, bringing into the centre of debate issues which had worried some since the society's formation in 1804. As a member of the SPCK he regarded the new society as interfering and damaging. The Bible alone could easily be misunderstood by the ignorant, and needed to be accompanied by explanatory material to ensure that it was interpreted correctly. This was why the SPCK distributed (as well as Bibles) Common Prayer Books, Psalters, catechisms, books of devotion, tracts on the scriptures and on education, and a whole range of school books with suitable cautions against infidelity, popery, and fanaticism. While other Anglicans, like William Dealtry and William Ward, insisted that support for both the SPCK and the Bible Society was compatible, many shared Wordsworth's doubts.[9]

The dispute rumbled on until 1812 when the formation of the Cambridge

---

[8] J. Bowles, *A Letter Addressed to Samuel Whitbread, Esq. MP*, (London, 1807), pp. 1–2, 6–8, 10–14, 18, 22–3, 26, 30, 34–7.

[9] C. Wordsworth, *Reasons for Declining . . .* (London, 1810), pp. 9–10; W. Ward, *A Letter on . . . the British and Foreign Bible Society* (London, 1810), pp. 1–6; W. Dealtry, *A Letter Addressed to the Rev. Dr Wordsworth* (London, 1810), pp. 4, 6–7, 15.

auxiliary Bible Society caused a major eruption.[10] The auxiliary society was well supported: its patron was the chancellor of the University, the Duke of Gloucester; its vice-patrons included the lord lieutenant of Cambridgeshire and high steward of the University, Earl Hardwick, and the Dukes of Grafton and Bedford; its president was the Bishop of Bristol and master of Trinity, William Mansel; and its vice-presidents included, as well as Vicary Gibbs and Palmerston, the Bishop of Llandaff and regius professor of Divinity, Richard Watson.

It was, however, passionately opposed by the Lady Margaret professor of Divinity, Herbert Marsh. Marsh had preached the annual Charity Schools sermon in St Paul's the previous June (1811), and he had alluded to the issue of the Bible Society there, although his main concern had been to defend the National Society against the Lancastrian. When the formation of the auxiliary society at Cambridge was proposed, he presented an address to the University Senate in which he made clear some of the political issues which concerned him. He feared the constitutional equality between the denominations in the society lest the pre-eminence of the established church should be first forgotten and then lost. Because of its connexion with political dissension, religious dissent was an evil which should not be encouraged.

Marsh distributed this address widely, not only in the University, but also throughout the country. Later in the year, to stir up further the storm he had raised, he published a pamphlet which explained his political fears in greater detail. Every poor child from a Church of England family, he argued, should be given a Prayer Book, not as a correction to the Bible, but as a companion. Too many wild men expounded the gospel in their own way, and the poor should be given the proper (establishment) interpretation, which was contained in the collects, prayers and catechism of the *Book of Common Prayer*. He argued that, while of course the faith of the Church of England was founded on the Bible, it was not founded on the Bible as understood by – for example – Unitarians, but rather as interpreted in the liturgy and articles. It was, after all, to the liturgy and articles, as well as to the Bible, that clergy, undergraduates and school masters subscribed. The poor must, therefore, be *taught* the Bible by the established church if the constitution in church and state were to be defended. When ignorant men sought to understand the scriptures by themselves they could be led into sedition, as were the sectaries who opposed Charles I. For Marsh, of course, only the opponents of the establishment were political, never the establishment itself. He conceded that if Anglicans left the Bible Society, what had been

[10] The best general account of this is F. K. Brown, *Fathers of the Victorians: The Age of Wilberforce* (Cambridge, 1961), pp. 285–316, though Marsh's case was, perhaps, more understandable than Brown allows.

formed for the advancement of religion could, in solely Dissenting hands, become a 'political engine'. But he considered the risk of staying in was far too great if, to prevent political mischief, it meant undermining the established church.[11] The issue was, quite clearly in Marsh's eyes, precisely the same as that between Lancastrian and National Schools Societies: who commanded the instrument of social control – the church or its enemies?

Opposition to Marsh's views came not only from lay critics, like Nicholas Vansittart and Spencer Perceval, but also from some Anglican clergy, almost all of an evangelical persuasion. William Dealtry, who had opposed Wordsworth in 1810, published a series of letters vigorously criticising Marsh's *Inquiry*.[12] William Otter produced two separate letters in 1812. The first was restrained in argument: he explained how the campaign against the slave trade had shown how churchmen and Dissenters could work together, argued that such co-operation would lessen the evils of Dissent, and insisted that the Anglican clergy would go on teaching the poor as part of their pastoral ministry, not leave them with their Bibles to form their own creeds, or be misled by the first ignorant, itinerant preacher they met.

The second was more vigorous: Otter openly accused Marsh of implying that the Bible Society was political in intention rather than religious, seeking to wrest control of the poor away from the established church. He also implied that Marsh's motives were dictated by ambition and his stand designed to recommend him to the political establishment; Perceval's opposition might well, Otter suggested, have surprised Marsh.[13] Otter went on to link the Bible Society with the monitorial schools, arguing first that, as the school had created a reading public, it must be provided with safe reading, and secondly insisting that support for the Bible Society was perfectly consistent with opposition to the Lancastrian schools. The Dissenting schools were a challenge to the existence of Anglican ones, and the nature of the faith inculcated in childhood was crucial in forming character, whereas the distribution of Bibles to adults posed no political danger.[14]

The controversy ranged far and wide, and most were aware of its political dimension. Coleridge, who supported Marsh, linked it with the republican puritans of the seventeenth century.[15] A correspondent to *Jackson's Oxford Journal* was more prophetic. He argued that, while it was perfectly accept-

---

11 W. Farish (ed.), *A Report of the Formation of the Cambridge Auxiliary Bible Society* (Cambridge, 1812), p. 58; H. Marsh, *The National Religion the Foundation of National Education* (London, 1811), pp. 42–4, and *An Inquiry into the Consequences of Neglecting to Give the Prayer Book with the Bible* (Cambridge, 1812), pp. 4–5, 10–11, 13–15, 24–5, 48–51, 73–4.

12 W. Dealtry, *An Examination of Dr Marsh's 'Inquiry'* (London, 1812), pp. 49–51.

13 In the event it was Lord Liverpool who raised Marsh to episcopal rank in 1816; Otter had to wait for Lord Melbourne in 1836.

14 W. Otter, *A Vindication of Churchmen* (London, 1812), pp. 10–12, and *An Examination of Dr Marsh's Answer* (London, 1812), pp. 4–7, 9, 21, 30–1, 40–5.

15 Coleridge, The Courier, 11 January 1812, *Works*, vol. 3, bk 2, pp. 332–3.

able for real religion and political religion to subsist together, the distinction between them should be remembered and political interests should never be allowed to subsume true Christianity. The political and social value of an established church could be proved, but it was only that utility, not divine institution, which justified the establishment of the Church of England. He suggested that it was, in effect, just another sect, its establishment a political act. Religious duties, such as the distribution of Bibles, should not be influenced by political considerations, and Anglicans should continue to support the British and Foreign Bible Society.[16]

The Schools Societies, 1811–1812

As Otter's second Letter illustrated, this dispute was inevitably linked with that concerning the Schools Societies. Until the formation of the National Society 'for promoting the education of the poor in the principles of the Established Church', many Anglicans had supported the Royal Lancastrian Society. Sarah Trimmer had long campaigned against such support and others had warned of the political dangers.[17] Marsh refocussed the issue in June 1811 in his Charity Schools sermon at St Paul's. He argued that, whether men saw religion just as 'an engine of the State' or also as a means of salvation, in any case they had to admit the utility of its alliance with the state. Even if men were irreligious, their concern for the good of civil society should make them hesitate to patronise the Lancaster schools for these challenged the constitution of church and state. The liturgy of the Church of England was established by law, and the national system of education should be controlled by the national church. Dissenters could, of course, educate their own children in their own way – that was the privilege of a tolerated sect – but any general, public, national system must be in the hands of the established church.[18] Marsh was much more widely supported on this issue than on that of the Bible Society, although he considered the principle involved was precisely the same.[19]

When the Common Council of London decided to give money to the Lancaster schools and not to the Bell ones, and one Alderman argued that the Bell system was inconsistent with the spirit of toleration in the constitution, it was Samuel Taylor Coleridge who published in the *Courier* on All Fools Day 1812 a blistering piece of satire, entitled 'A Modest Proposal for

[16] Peter the Hermit, *Letters . . . in the Oxford and Cambridge Papers* (London, 1812), pp. 78–83, 89.
[17] See above, pp. 86, 138, and compare Bowles, *Letter to Whitbread*.
[18] Marsh, *National Religion*, pp. 2–9, 11, 13–15, 18–20, 38–44.
[19] See, *inter alia*, E. W. Grinfield, *The Crisis of Religion* (London, 1812), pp. 15–17, 19–21, 27–8; *The Origin, Nature, and Object, of the New System of Education* (London, 1812), p. 106; W. Otter, *Examination of Marsh*, pp. 30–1, 42–5; Pretyman-Tomline, *Charge*, 1812, p. 9; B. E. Sparke, *A Charge Delivered to the Clergy . . . of Ely* (London, 1813), pp. 8–9.

Abolishing the Church of England', based of course on Swift. Lancaster's secular curriculum was, he argued, just like the universal philanthropy of the French *philosophes*. When religion was taught as an extra, like dancing, any concept of an established church would be gone and faith would be no more than an optional study of liberal enquiry.[20]

While Coleridge subtly implied political danger, others bellowed it forth. William Firth argued that the Lancastrian project for non-conformist education was a seditious plot against church and state which would lead to political rebellion and atheism. Firth, a barrister and one-time attorney-general of Upper Canada, lacked any kind of judicial restraint. He claimed that, together with any concessions to the Catholics, the Lancaster schools threatened to bring down the Hanoverian dynasty, the Revolution Settlement and the British Empire. He assumed throughout that the schools would be Socinian in nature rather than trinitarian, but this was inaccurate.[21] As another critic of Lancaster pointed out, 'The Socinians have no poor; theirs is a religion which has never reached the lower classes and will never reach them.'[22] Despite the passion of Firth's rhetoric and the fantasy of his speculations, he had no substantial arguments to add to those of Marsh.

Marsh's most thoughtful critic was the utilitarian author of the pamphlet *Schools for All* (1812). He argued that there was a real political and social need for the education of the children of the poor, who would otherwise learn the idle and disorderly habits which made them bad members of society. But he had two main objections to the National Schools. First, he argued, they were bad for religious reasons. They made religion 'an engine of state' which could be twisted and used to the advantages of statesmen, thus making religion secondary to politics. This was, he claimed, practical irreligion. Secondly he argued National Schools were bad for political reasons. Government should be based on utility and its existence and continuance should depend upon its use to the community. A government which could rely on extraneous support, as from religious sanctions, could then afford to neglect the well-being of the people:

To teach governments, as is too frequently done, to look to religion for support is to encourage bad government as far as that support is depended upon. Religion is no further wanted to the support of any government than as far as that government is bad . . . To teach rulers how far they may depend upon religion for their support is merely to teach them how far they may neglect or betray their duty; how far the interests of the community at large may be sacrificed to the interests of their rulers.

---

[20] Coleridge, *Works*, vol. 3, bk 2, pp. 341–7.
[21] W. Firth, *A Letter to the . . . Bishop of Norwich* (London, 1813), pp. v–vi, 1–38, 90–110.
[22] *Origin . . . of Education*, p. 112.

This author repeatedly cited Paley's *Moral and Political Philosophy* in support of his utilitarian argument. He insisted that the National Schools sought to pervert religion to political ends, while the Lancastrian ones taught religion in a purer way.[23]

Lord Sidmouth's Bill, 1811

It was in the context of assaults like this on the traditional use of religion by the ruling classes that Lord Sidmouth sought to introduce a Bill to amend the Toleration Act.[24] Sidmouth raised the question in June 1809 and twelve months later announced his intention to introduce a Bill. This Bill, which was placed before parliament in May 1811, differed somewhat from Sidmouth's initial concerns and was related to the registration of Dissenting ministers. Sidmouth's correspondence after he raised the issue in 1809 showed a widespread fear amongst Anglicans of the Methodist advance, and the Bill came to be directed at the issue of itinerancy and the low educational level of many Methodist preachers. John Milne, writing from Manchester in August 1809, was astonished to see how many uneducated Methodist preachers there were 'disseminating dangerous principles inimical to the King and Constitution and destructive of the good order of society'. He suggested that they posed as great a danger to the state as the seventeenth-century sectaries who murdered the king, dissolved the civil constitution and abolished the ecclesiastical establishment. The fear and distrust of the Methodists which the Rev. John Skinner confided to his diary, were felt not only in Somerset but throughout the country. Sidmouth's correspondents were concerned with the political implications of much Dissenting preaching. While accepting religious toleration, an Oxfordshire correspondent in May 1810 argued that religious ideas which threatened the stability of society should be carefully watched by every patriotic statesman.[25]

Sidmouth's Bill proposed that in future, instead of licences as Dissenting ministers being handed out to all who applied for them, applicants should present to the licensing justices at Quarter Sessions testimonials of their abilities and characters from six substantial and reputable householders,

---

[23] *Schools for All, in Preference to Schools for Churchmen Only* (London, 1812), pp. 1–6, 16–21.

[24] See, R. W. Davis, *Dissent in Politics*, pp. 148–69; George Pellew, *The Life and Correspondence of the Right Hon. Henry Addington, First Viscount Sidmouth*, 3 vols. (London, 1847), vol. 3, pp. 38–70; Manning, *Dissenting Deputies*, pp. 130–43; M. Edwards, *After Wesley: A Study of the Social and Political Influence of Methodism in the Middle Period (1791–1849)* (London, 1935), pp. 75–82; W. R. Ward, *Religion and Society*, pp. 55–62.

[25] DRO, Sidmouth papers, 152M/C1809 OE, Dissenters Meetings; 152M/C1810 OE, Registration of Dissenting Ministers; J. Skinner, *Journal of a Somerset Rector, 1803–1834* (Oxford, 1971, 1984), pp. 40, 66, 68, 111.

and that the justices were to decide what constituted substance and repute. It was expected that Methodist itinerants would find this requirement difficult to meet. A Hammersmith correspondent wanted Sidmouth to go further and insist they had the support of the churchwardens too, complaining that local Methodist preachers in his area included a chimney sweep, a gardener, a tinman and a butcher. A magistrate from Nottingham suggested that many took out licences as Methodist preachers in order to evade the militia and parish-officer duties. There was widespread concern about the lack of formal education of many Methodist applicants, a problem, most agreed, which was not found with the Old Dissenters. The Methodists, magistrates reported, said they needed no education to preach as they were inspired by the Holy Ghost. The owner of a coal and iron works near Bewdley suggested that Methodists were as dangerous to society as Catholics, and said he believed they were a political society as well as a religious one but could not prove it. An 'old man' from Sheffield claimed to remember that, when Paine's *Rights of Man* was in fashion, Methodists in their hundreds with local preachers and class leaders spoke against king and government and ended by singing a hymn in praise of Paine to the tune of God Save the King.[26] A rector from Anglesey was among the most bitter opponents of the Methodists. In a number of letters to Sidmouth he accused Methodist preachers of giving a young woman a bastard, driving a young man mad and being dangerous to the public welfare.[27]

The curate of Norton-sub-Hamdon in Somerset was greatly saddened by the hostility to the Bill which, he suggested, was politically motivated. He told Sidmouth that everyone of correct theology and politics supported him; only Jesuitical arguments could support Jacobinal principles. But hostility there was. In May 1811, when the Bill was before parliament, Sidmouth received almost equal numbers of letters for and against his proposals. Methodists affirmed their loyalty and claimed they did much to enforce morality, order and control.[28] Others condemned the Bill as an infringement of religious liberty, one even suggesting that it was as hostile to the will of

---

[26] DRO, 152M/Corr. 1811 OE, Dissenting Ministers Bill, Letters to Sidmouth from Bryon, 16 May 1811, Nottingham Magistrate, 13 May 1811; J. Sparrow, 2 August 1811; Thomas Botfield, 22 May 1811; 'Old Man', 8 June 1811.

[27] DRO, 152M/Corr. 1808 OZ, Special Subject RCs and Nonconformity, Letter from Mr Owen; 152M/Corr. 1811 OE, Dissenting Ministers Bill, Letters from Mr Owen, 8 April and 30 April 1811. On the sexual promiscuity of Dissenters see Letter from Phil Meadows, 13 May 1811, on the Anabaptists.

[28] See especially the Letters from Clarke and Coke. On their role see S. Piggin, 'Halévy Revisited: The Origins of the Methodist Missionary Society: An Examination of Semmel's Thesis', *Journal of Imperial and Commonwealth History*, 9 (1980), 17–37 (pp. 18–19, 23–7). See also Hempton, Thomas Allen', pp. 14–18. On some of the political tensions within Methodism between leadership and grass-roots, see P. Stigant, 'Wesleyan Methodism and Working Class Radicalism in the North', *Northern History*, 6 (1971), 98–116, which ranges more widely than the title suggests.

God as Paine's *Rights of Man* and *Age of Reason* were to the interests of church and state.[29] One 'impartial observer' from Macclesfield suggested that Sidmouth was afraid that the Methodist message of 'Love your Neighbour' would discourage young men from joining the army.[30]

The government had no wish to stir up trouble at this time. Lord Liverpool reminded Sidmouth that the Dissenters as a body had brought forward no claim and engaged in no political controversy with the establishment for the last fifteen years. Perceval requested Sidmouth to withdraw the measure, but he refused. The Archbishop of Canterbury also opposed the Bill and it was defeated in the House of Lords. George Huntingford, Bishop of Gloucester, was disgusted at this; on reading Lord Stanhope's speech he likened him to Mirabeau and told Sidmouth that no French Jacobin was a more zealous advocate of anarchy and irreligion. Thomas Comber of Creech St Michael in Somerset was amazed at the attitude of Liverpool and Manners-Sutton and warned that the church would soon be completely subverted, and that the throne would fall with the altar as it did in France.[31] Liverpool's apparent lack of concern for establishment seemed complete to many, when, in 1812, toleration was extended to the Unitarians.

Although Coleridge considered that the defeat of the Bill showed the 'prudence and liberality' of the House of Lords, and that Sidmouth's proposals had outstripped the evil, he did nevertheless consider that there *was* an evil.[32] On the whole the debate surrounding the Bill brought out the most negative arguments of the church-in-danger school. Anglican self-interest was too apparent. But there was a sincere fear of Methodism and some theological grounds for thinking it subversive of society, despite the much vaunted loyalty of Wesley and Clarke and the repeated declarations of the Methodist Conference.[33]

In the summer of 1811 the rector of Camerton, Somerset, John Skinner, discussed the question of repentance with Green, a Methodist in his parish. Skinner was disturbed that the Methodists attended the dying and exhorted them to make a declaration that they had faith in Christ which was

---

[29] DRO, 152M/Corr. 1811 OE, Dissenting Ministers Bill, Letters from John White Middleton, 24 May 1811, and J. P. Jesemeny, 13 May 1811.

[30] *Strictures on the Expedience of the Addingtonian Extinguisher* (Macclesfield, 1811). See also his approval of Methodist teaching on a future state of retribution, p. 31.

[31] DRO, 152M/Corr. 1811 OE, Dissenting Ministers Bill, Letters from Lord Liverpool, 20 May 1811; Sidmouth to Perceval (copy), 20 May 1811, Bishop of Gloucester, 24 May 1811; T. Comber, 31 May 1811. See also Pellew, *Life and Correspondence of Henry Addington*, vol. 3, pp. 61–2.

[32] Coleridge, The Courier, 22 May 1811, *Works*, vol. 3, bk 2, pp. 158–9.

[33] *Remarks on the Failure of Lord Sidmouth's Bill* (London, 1811) shows that for some the concern remained. In the following summer Robert Nares reminded his Archdeaconry of Stafford of the Methodist danger in detail and at considerable length: R. Nares, *On the Influence of the Sectaries and the Stability of the Church* (London, 1813).

considered as 'a sufficient satisfaction for an ill spent life and as a sure passport to Heaven'. Skinner told Green that repentance was essential and that this, aided of course by divine grace, was a necessary human effort. A fortnight later he taxed an itinerant Methodist preacher on the question, pointing out how dangerous it would be if the ignorant were to believe that they must wait to feel conversion and that no efforts of their own were of any use until such a moment arrived. Clearly, if such a view prevailed religious sanctions might cease to operate until people arrived at their deathbed, and little morality would remain. The preacher agreed with Skinner, regretting such Calvinist tenets and clearly feeling he did not fully control the beliefs of the people.[34]

Bishop Randolph warned the clergy of London in his primary charge in 1810 that while deep questions, like sudden conversion and even antinomian views, could be discussed without danger on an intellectual level by speculative people, this was not the kind of gospel to be preached to the poor.[35] Most Methodists, however, understood this and few Christians preached social control and order more effectively. Even the Anglican fanatic William Firth approved of Methodist loyalty.[36] Whatever might have been the vagaries of some village preachers, mainstream Methodists were, as John Stephens declared them in 1819, 'a loyal people; and such they must remain, till they have a new code of Rules, a new Hymn-book, a new Bible, and till the last recollection and example of the Apostolic WESLEY shall be withdrawn from their faithless memory, and buried in the ashes of his mouldering bones'.[37]

Conclusion

The dispute over who should control the teaching of social order, in the schools, the homes and from the pulpits, was at the heart of the Establishment–Dissent debates of 1810–13. These debates continued to a lesser level in the ensuing years. The SPCK extended its efforts and many new diocesan and district committees were formed and were recommended in charges and sermons.[38] The National Society also extended its work and was likewise recommended strongly by the clerical establishment, especially after the disturbances of 1819, as a means of ensuring loyalty and social

[34] Skinner, *Journal*, pp. 40, 66, 68, 111.
[35] *Charge*, p. 13.
[36] W. Firth, *Remarks on the Recent State Trials* . . . (London, 1818), pp. vi–viii, x–xi.
[37] Stephens, *Mutual Relations*, pp. v–vi.
[38] G. H. Law, *Charge Delivered to the Clergy* . . . *of Chester* (Chester, 1814), pp. 9–14; C. Bird, *A Sermon Preached* . . . *July 4, 1816* (Wakefield, [1816]); B. E. Sparke, *a Charge Delivered to the Clergy* . . . *of Ely* (London, 1817), pp. 13–15; D. W. Garrow, *An Address of a Rector to his Parishioners* . . . (Barnet, 1826).

order.[39] William Firth continued to spew out vitriolic abuse against Dissenting education, and Coleridge, though in a more intellectual and philosophical context, still considered Lancaster's schools irredeemably pernicious.[40] But generally from 1813 the climate was more positive and the Anglican church sought to establish its role as the prime agent of social control less by assertion and more by activity. This meant that additional impetus was given to a movement which had already been growing. The need to build more churches in the populous cities had been apparent to perceptive churchmen for some time. Bishop Porteus of London had observed the need in the 1790s; Bishop Watson of Llandaff had made the point in a letter to Wilberforce in 1800 and in a sermon to the Society for the Suppression of Vice in 1804; Bishop Law was very aware of the need in his rapidly industrialising Diocese of Chester in 1820. Increasingly bishops urged support for the movement on their clergy.[41] Parliament was also aware of the need, and the Church Building Act of 1818 provided a million pounds to build churches; another half million was added in 1824. This was all part of the growing reform movement in the church of which Harrowby's Curates Act (1813) and the campaign against non-residence played an important part.

The movement had a dual purpose: to enforce social control effectively and so defend the constitution in the state; and to strengthen the Church of England against the Dissenting challenge and so defend the constitution in the church. Bishops continued to argue the need for an established church, but realised that if the argument were to continue to hold water that church had to be reformed.[42] Social control could be exercised only by a church with an effective pastoral ministry and system of education.[43] Unless the Church of England could be seen clearly to have both, its claim that it alone could successfully maintain social order would be seen to be hollow and the case for establishment seriously weakened.

---

[39] W. Barrow, *Pecuniary Contributions for the Diffusion of Religious Knowledge* (Nottingham, 1815), pp. 14–15; H. Ryder, *A Charge Addressed to the Clergy . . . of Gloucester* (Gloucester, 1816), pp. 28ff; G. H. Law, *Charge*, 1820, pp. 22–5; C. Henley, *Uniformity of Opinion in the Clergy* (London, 1822), pp. 11–13; W. Howley, *A Charge Delivered to the Clergy . . . of London* (London, 1826), pp. 19–21; S. Butler, *A Charge Delivered to . . . the Archdeaconry of Derby . . . 1825* (London, 1826), pp. 3–8, 12, 15.

[40] Firth, *State Trials*, pp. 145–6, 191–6, 223–4; Coleridge, 'Statesman's Manual', *Works*, vol. 6, p. 40.

[41] LPL, MS 2103, ff. 33–4, 48, Porteus Notebook, 1786–1800; Watson, *Anecdotes*, pp. 340–3 and, *Misc. T*, vol. 1, pp. 523–4; G. H. Law, *Charge*, 1820, p. 26; W. van Mildert, *Charge Delivered to the Clergy . . . of Llandaff* (Oxford, 1821), p. 8; C. Bethell, *Charge at the Primary Visitation . . . Gloucester* (Gloucester, 1825), p. 25; W. Howley, *Charge*, 1826, pp. 5, 14, 20.

[42] H. W. Majendie, *Charge*, 1804, pp. 8, 13; C. J. Blomfield, *A Remonstrance . . . to H. Brougham* (London, 1823), p. 21; J. T. Law, *Origins, Progress and Necessity*, pp. 24–5.

[43] Best, *Temporal Pillars*, pp. 152–65.

14

Blasphemy and sedition

In a speech in the Westminster election of 1818, the radical John Gale Jones recalled that a number of years earlier an institution had been founded under the auspices of several pious bishops, inclined to evangelical views, to distribute Bibles and spread religious education amongst the poor. Some of the aristocracy, especially Windham, '"foresaw the dangerous consequences, and anticipated, from the general dissemination of knowledge among the people, destruction to the church and state." (*Laughter and Applause*).' Windham, he noted, was taken little notice of, but now the establishment saw their error. '"We find that from reading religious books, the People begin to have a taste for politics and that when the Police officers have ransacked their habitations, instead of Bibles and Prayer Books, they have found under their pillow the *heretical* and *detestable* Works of Thomas Paine." (*Laughter and Applause*).'[1]

The laughter and applause which Gale Jones's irony evoked and which Richard Carlile reported in his publication of the speech, heralded a period when political radicalism and atheism stood together in the open. From 1819 to around 1822–3, the coalescence of infidelity and revolution, of blasphemy and sedition appeared to be established. A number of leading radicals not only openly confessed their irreligion, but argued that religious restraints must be thrown aside so that the people could enjoy political and individual liberty.

The clergy and conspiracy theory

The defenders of the established constitution in church and state devoted themselves more and more to social theory and reiterated the conservative sociology which had evolved in the years of the French Revolution. This was no new development; the links with the conspiracy theory of 1797 were clear and unbroken. Bishops had continued to point out the connexion in

---

[1] *Westminster Election: The Speeches of Mr Hunt and Mr Gale Jones on the Hustings . . . 25 June 1818* (London, 1818), pp. 14–15.

their charges and sermons.[2] In 1810 Bishop Randoph had warned the clergy of London that, although infidelity, studiously propagated, had declined, it had still unsettled men's minds and inclined them to 'a dangerous licentiousness of opinion'. This led to a lack of social cohesion and to discontent and, as the example of France showed, to that excessive liberty which led to extreme despotism. The relationship between infidelity and instability was reciprocal: revolution was both a cause and a result of errors in religious belief.[3] Randolph made these brief comments only after outlining the routine duties of the clergy, the traditional and commonplace thing to do in a primary charge.

In 1813 however, Bishop Sparke was so concerned about the political state of Europe that, in his primary charge to the clergy of Ely diocese, he launched into politics in his fourth sentence and went on to expound the conspiracy theory at length before turning to the traditional admonitions. He reminded his clergy that all Europe's present evils could be traced back to the false philosophy which had led men to scorn and ridicule Christianity, for this led to the dissolution of 'the sacred bonds of religious and moral obligation'. The Revolution had triumphed only with the aid of atheism. Although England had avoided revolution, there were those who sought to preach infidelity and to subvert the constitution. It was the duty of the clergy to inculcate 'the true principles of moral and civil obligation'.[4]

The defeat of Napoleon in 1814 caused other bishops soberly to reflect on what had started all the trouble. In his sermon at the thanksgiving service at St Paul's attended by the prince regent and both Houses of Parliament on 7 June 1814, Bishop Law of Chester again traced the French Revolution to the general decay of religious principle, and warned that minds insensible to loyalty or conscience were open to anarchy and violence. When the people were restrained neither by law nor religion, blood would flow.[5] That same summer, the new Bishop of London, William Howley, calmly laid down the doctrine in crystal clear terms to his clergy:

The French Revolution was not an accidental explosion, a burst of momentary passion or frenzy, but a deliberate and premeditated rebellion against authority human and divine: It was the struggle of desperate wickedness to shake off the salutary restraints imposed by Religion and Law on the worst passions of human nature ... The evil has derived an accession of extent and malignity from the systematic encouragement of licentiousness by a despotic government; from the destruction of churches; the neglect of public worship; and, above all, the abolition of

---

[2] For example, Majendie, *Charge*, 1804, pp. 13–14; J. Fisher, *A Sermon Preached before the Lords ... February 25, 1807* (London, 1807), pp. 7–8.

[3] Randolph, *Charge*, 1810, pp. 6–7, 9–12.

[4] Sparke, *Charge*, 1813, pp. 6–7.

[5] G. H. Law, *A Sermon Preached ... July 7, 1814* (London, 1814), p. 13.

the Sabbath, and the blasting influence of an unchristian education on the minds of youth.

But Howley considered that disbelief in England, worrying as it was, was quite different from French irreligion. Since its seventeenth-century origins, English infidelity had been discredited and, Howley considered, most deists were now concealed as Unitarians.[6] The second defeat of Napoleon and the ensuing peace led lesser clerics time and again to echo these episcopal thoughts.[7]

Coleridge followed a similar path, but gave it more philosophical substance. In 1809 he suggested the price of 'enlightenment' was too great if, to learn the folly of beliefs in ghosts, omens and dreams, men had also to abandon faith in providence, and the hope of a life after death. But in 1812 he conceded that the *philosophes'* dream of universal philanthropy was not an evil in itself, but argued that they began at the wrong end. Instead of seeking to make men less selfish by gradual means, they just destroyed the bonds of social unity and let the individual will run free. The single, paramount notion of universal benevolence they offered instead was too wide-ranging and too indistinct for men to be guided by it. So, social unity and cohesion were damaged by the assault on religious restraints and sanctions, and social confusion and anarchy ensued. *The Statesman's Manual* (1816) was designed to show how a stable society and good government must arise from the religion of the Bible and the duties it laid down.[8]

Jeremy Bentham

The post-war years in England saw, however, a resurgence of infidel activity. Views which before, if not exactly secret, had been kept private were now proclaimed openly. Jeremy Bentham's private papers show clearly his apostasy in the early 1770s.[9] But he was then circumspect in his published works. In his *Principles of Morals and Legislation* (1789) he largely followed the tradition of Hume and Gibbon and disguised his anti-Christian

---

[6] W. Howley, *A Charge Delivered to the Clergy of the Diocese of London . . . 1814* (London,1814), pp. 12–14.

[7] For example, C. Bird, *A Sermon Preached at Wakefield . . . at the Visitation of the Rev. Archdeacon Markham* (Wakefield, 1816), p. 19; H. I. Knapp, *The Origin and Termination of the Late Warfare . . .* (London, 1816), pp. 10–11, 17.

[8] Coleridge, The Friend (1809/1818), *Works*, vol. 4, p. 46; The Courier, 11 January 1812, *Works*, vol. 3, bk 2, pp. 329–30; 'Statesman's Manual', *Works*, vol. 6, pp. 3–49.

[9] UCL, Bentham Papers, Box 5, ff.9, 19, 27; Box 96, ff.263–310, 314–22. James Steintrager's early death has robbed us of the definitive work on Bentham's religion which almost certainly he would have written. His two brief articles remain indispensable: 'Morality and Belief: The Origin and Purpose of Bentham's Writings on Religion', *The Mill Newsletter*, 6 (1971), 3–15, and 'Language and Politics: Bentham on Religion', *The Bentham Newsletter*, 4 (1980), 4–20. See also Burne, 'Moral Theory', pp. 146–71.

comments as anti-clerical and anti-Catholic ones.[10] Even in the more open post-war years, Bentham remained cautious lest too much public anger at his irreligion deflected attention from his practical proposals for reform. But many of the views expressed in his private papers in 1772–4 were published between 1817 and 1832.[11]

The erroneous view that these anti-Christian pieces were mere occasional and accidental reactions to the Schools Societies controversy of 1811–12 has been demolished by James Steintrager, who rightly argued that a strong opposition to religion was built into the very fibre of Bentham's utilitarian system from the beginning in 1768 and that his opposition to religion was 'rooted in the inevitable collision between religion and utilitarian morality'.[12] Although Bentham has been relatively ignored by some recent writers on the development of British atheism, it could be argued that, in intellectual terms at least, he was a more significant figure than Carlile. His direct, detailed arguments were often trite, superficial and specious, but the fundamental assumptions of his utilitarian philosophy have done more than anything else to undermine the centrality of religion and to destroy it as a major intellectual force in modern society.

An essential change in political and social thinking in this period was the movement from a theological concept of political and social obligation to a utilitarian one. Many men gradually ceased to believe that they had a duty to submit to government and the social order because God willed it, and instead based their allegiance on their own human perception of the usefulness of that government and society. Paley argued from within the church, Bentham from outside it, but both pushed men down a secular road which replaced divinely imposed duty with selfish human calculation. Unlike Paley, Bentham could see that Christianity could not be harnessed to a utilitarian waggon without one or the other being destroyed.

Bentham's critique of religion on moral, social and political grounds

---

[10] Bentham's lengthy, anonymous preface to his translation of Voltaire's story *The White Bull* (London, 1774), was bitterly contemptuous of the scriptures; *An Introduction to the Principles of Morals and Legislation* (1789), edited by J. H. Burns and H. L. A. Hart (London, 1970, 1982), esp. pp. 17–21.

[11] *Church of Englandism and its Catechism Examined* (London, printed 1817, published 1818), appeared anonymously and predated the activities of Carlile, who later republished extracts from it as *Mother Church Relieved by Bleeding* (London, 1823). *Analysis of the Influence of Natural Religion* (London, 1822) was composed from Bentham's manuscripts by George Grote and published under the pseudonym Philip Beauchamp. *Not Paul But Jesus* (London, 1823) appeared under the name of Gamaliel Smith. The manuscripts on which these three major polemics were based are extant: BL, Add. MSS 29,806–29,809, and are prefaced by a letter to Grote, 806, ff.1–2, and include a suggested plan of the work dated 1819, ff.146–62. These bear out Burne's argument, 'Moral Theory', p. 149, that the views in the *Analysis* are all Bentham's; Grote may have paraphrased and possibly toned them down, but did not add to them.

[12] Steintrager, 'Morality and Belief', pp. 7, 11–12.

needs to be seen on a number of different levels. His 1817 *Church of Englandism . . .* was, on the surface, an attack upon the activities of the National Society.[13] Much of its argument and its passion came from Bentham's own experience of subscription to the thirty-nine articles while a student at Oxford, and from his reaction to the subscription controversy of the 1770s. But it is also an argument against a religious establishment and, more profoundly, an attack upon the social and political influence of religion as such. He argued that the aim of the National Society was the same as that of the discipline which demanded subscription to the articles – a 'humble docility' to the rulers of the Church of England and their subordinates and a 'prostration of the understanding and will' of those subscribing and being educated. He described Bishop Howley of London as 'Prostrator General of understanding and wills'.

As well as some passionate anti-clerical rhetoric, Bentham suggested that the Christian preoccupation with salvation was detrimental both to good government and utilitarian morality. Yet most 'thinking Englishmen', he went on to argue, were inspired by quite a different maxim of government, that the political and social purpose of religion was to secure, not the salvation of the soul, but the temporal well-being of mankind. The confessional state must give way to a welfare state. Religion merely crippled freedom of thought and divorced obedience from reason. By forcing the elite of graduates and teachers into subscription to the articles, one ensured that a church and state system which could not stand rational criticism was protected by the very men who should lead an intellectual assault upon it in the name of utility. He agreed that the Anglican catechism produced subjects who were abjectly subservient to the ruling few, but denied that such persons were good citizens.[14]

Bentham addressed the social rather than the political arguments which had predominated in clerical addresses since the French Revolution. Because he rejected the supra-empirical epistemological claims of religious revelation, he considered that religion contributed nothing to the happiness of mankind but merely bolstered up regimes which lacked true validity. Religion gave no new direction to mankind; it merely supported the ruler by the threat of unavoidable and eternal punishment. What religious men saw as their duty to God, Bentham regarded as detrimental to human happiness in this life. The religious sanctions and restraints which were so highly prized by churchmen were almost completely inefficient on any occasion when they could have added to the sum of happiness, and efficient only

---

[13] It was cited extensively by John Wade in 1820 in *The Black Book*, which claimed to be opposed not to Christianity but only to its corruptions, but was very heterodox; vol. 1, pp. 274, 276–8.

[14] *Church of Englandism* (London, printed 1817, published 1818), vol. 1, pp. xv, xix–xxviii, 7–8, 52–5, 61, 165, vol. 2, pp. 85–9, 148.

when they swelled the total of temporal misery. They did not prevent crimes, but added to the fear of death by the prospect of Hell.

Bentham argued that men's self-esteem and concern for what their neighbours thought of them constituted a much more powerful sanction than religion, and that, if people were properly educated, the sanction of popular opinion could be used to enforce the principle of utility. As it was, both governors and clergy had interests at variance with those of the community. The Aristocracy had the physical force to crush opposition, but

> to make this sure, they are obliged to maintain a strong purchase upon the public mind, and to chain it down to the level of submission – to plant within it feelings which may neutralize all hatred of slavery, and facilitate the business of spoliation. For this purpose the sacerdotal class are most precisely and most happily cut out. By their influence over the moral sentiments, they place implicit submission amongst the first of all human duties. They infuse the deepest reverence for temporal power, by considering the existing authorities as established and consecrated by the immaterial Autocrat above, and as identified with his divine majesty. The duty of mankind towards the earthly government becomes thus the same as duty to God – that is, an unvarying 'prostration of both the understanding and will'.[15]

Richard Carlile

Whatever the intellectual importance of Jeremy Bentham, it was Richard Carlile who led the practical struggle and fought in the front line. A tin-worker from Devonshire, Carlile set himself up as a publisher and bookseller in London and came, increasingly, to write his own copy. Both as author and publisher, he placed before the public the most passionate and urgent (if not always the most thoughtful) arguments against Christianity and in favour of political reform. For the established orders he typified the spirit of Paine, the continuance of Jacobinism, and the union of infidelity and revolution.

Much has been written of Carlile recently; his importance has been recognised, the events of his life and (to a slightly lesser extent) the nature of his thought have been widely explored.[16] His hostility to Christianity, and his commitment to radical political and social reform are clearly established. But the precise nature of the link between these two central aspects of his thought has not been analysed. Bentham's personal apostasy stemmed from his rejection of the epistemological base of Christianity, but his

[15] *Analysis*, pp. 3, 32–4, 38–9, 41, 53, 137–8.
[16] See, J. H. Wiener, *Radicalism and Free Thought in Nineteenth-Century Britain: The Life of Richard Carlile* (Westport, Connecticut, 1983); E. Royle, *Victorian Infidels: The Origins of the British Secularist Movement, 1791–1866* (Manchester, 1974), pp. 31–43, and *The Infidel Tradition from Paine to Bradlaugh* (London, 1975), pp. 16–37; E. Royle and J. Walvin, *English Radicals and Reformers* (Brighton, 1982), pp. 121–41.

practical hostility to it came from his conviction of its inutility. Had he believed it supported good government he would have tolerated it; it was only because he considered it positively dysfunctional in social and political terms that he attacked its influence. Carlile's attack upon religion, however, appears to have stemmed from a much more abstract and theoretical position: Christianity must be opposed because it was false. Carlile, of course, also believed religion to be politically and socially dysfunctional and he attacked it on these grounds, but these seemed to be, if not incidental, at least merely additional arguments. This distinction is a fine one and it may reflect simply the greater clarity, consistency and unity of Bentham's thought and the eclecticism, enthusiasm and energy of Carlile's, but Carlile gives the impression of a man who hated Christianity and desired to destroy it, while Bentham merely despised it as unhelpful and useless.[17]

Some specific pieces of Carlile may appear to contradict this overall impression, such as the introduction he wrote in Dorchester Gaol to the first collected and bound set of his weekly journal *The Republican*. While the overall impression stands, the passion with which Carlile and his supporters attacked the link between religion and the established social and political order must not be underestimated. To some extent the connexion was stressed in *The Republican* to justify the inclusion of theological articles (which were clearly close to Carlile's heart) to those of his readers who were preoccupied with political, not religious, issues.[18] Carlile published letters from a number of correspondents denouncing the political influence of religion; one, Thomas Cooke, considered 'a political judge and a political Parson two of the most dangerous characters that infest Society'.[19]

He also published a short series of 'Philosophical Essays on Government and Religion' by Julian Augustus St John.[20] St John argued that religion arose in the first place as a means of social control and as the handmaid of despotism, and insisted that it had to be destroyed before civil tyranny could be attacked, just as those undermining a castle had to clear away the earth and rubbish which concealed its foundations. Religion had always been 'a state engine', used to defraud the weak and ignorant.[21] Writing in this

---

[17] Carlile took delight in reporting trials of clergymen for sodomy, and often grossly exaggerated the nature of the evidence. See *The Republican*, vol. 8, July–December 1823, pp. 500–1, and for the case of Dr Cleeve, vicar of St George's Exeter, compare DRO, MS C2/73d, Exeter Quarter Sessions Minute Book, p. 158; *Trewman's Exeter Flying Post*, 16 October 1823; and *The Alfred*, 21 October 1823, p. 3. For other attempts to discredit clergy see Iain McCalman, 'Unrespectable Radicalism; Infidels and Pornography in Early Nineteenth-Century London', *PP*, 104 (1984), 74–110 (pp. 86, 91).

[18] Carlile conceded this point, *The Republican*, vol. 2, p. 298 (no. 9, 17 March 1820).

[19] *Republican*, vol. 1, pp. 88–99, Cooke, 10 October 1819; p. 74, J. A. Parry, 24 September 1819; p. 138, J. B. Smith, 22 October 1819.

[20] *Republican*, vol. 1, pp. 106–11, 156–60, 238–9.

[21] *Republican*, vol. 1, p. 111.

context it would have been easy for St John to slip into an attack upon the religious theory of political obligation, but instead he addressed himself firmly to the social argument then in the ascendant. He equated religion not with the cement of society, but with mud; society needed wisdom if it were to build a palace for men to live in.

Carlile showed as much hatred of Catholics as any Protestant and this was reflected in his interest in Hispanic affairs and his hatred of the Holy Alliance and Britain's co-operation with Catholic and despotic powers. He published a letter purported to have been sent by Metternich to the Austrian Ambassador in London which showed how Carlile agreed with, indeed gloried in, the accusations of his critics. The pseudo-letter recalled how rebellion had been preached in the British parliament during the American and French Revolutions and continued,

Had it not been for those precedents, fear of God and obedience to the King would have been the theme of all nations. But when men begin to canvass the adoration of their heavenly Creator, they will not long hesitate to assail the prerogatives of their earthly sovereigns. Rebellion is the twin brother of impiety: – Anarchy and atheism are their common offspring.[22]

The blasphemy trials

In 1819 Carlile had no wish to deny the connexions between those views his critics designated 'blasphemy and sedition'; but for the most part he expressed those views separately. It was his opponents who stressed the connexion, both from the pulpit and in the court of law. In 1817 Lord Sidmouth had sent a letter to the Lords Lieutenant of England and Wales expressing his concern over the circulation of blasphemous and seditious libels, and informing them that the law officers asserted that justices of the peace could demand bail of anyone accused of publishing or selling such pamphlets.[23] It was, in fact, Carlile's re-publication of Paine's *Age of Reason* in December 1818 which led to his first trial for blasphemous libel, and Carlile did not, at that time, go far beyond Paine's position in asserting the connexion between irreligion and revolution.[24] His opponents inferred a closer connexion than he stated, and both the Society for the Suppression of Vice and the government were involved in his prosecution. In January 1820 trials against other infidel republicans were instigated in Birmingham by the

---

[22] *Republican*, vol. 2, pp. 116–17, 11 February 1820.
[23] Lord Grey raised this question in a long speech in the House of Lords in which he examined the legal precedents and expressed concern for the continuing liberty of the press. Grey, *The Speech of the Earl Grey in the House of Lords, May 12, 1817, on Lord Sidmouth's Circular* (London, 1817).
[24] The chronology of the legal proceedings and the complexity of the various charges brought is set out clearly in Wiener, *Radicalism and Free Thought*, pp. 34–49.

Loyal Association for the Suppression of Sedition and Blasphemy. A number of provincial trials, mostly of booksellers, followed. In Janaury 1820 James Tucker was tried at Exeter Quarter Sessions for selling some of Carlile's publications which had been freely sold in London for the last two years.[25] The published version of Mr Justice Bayley's speech in passing sentence on Carlile in 1819 took as its motto Cobbett's observation on Paine: 'His religion is exactly of a piece with his politics; one inculcates the right of revolting against Government, and the other that of revolting against God.'[26] This was very apposite as Carlile's position in 1819 was indeed that of Paine, which was quite enough to ensure denunciation from a score of pulpits.

Clerical reactions
John Kaye, master of Christ's College and regius professor of Divinity at Cambridge, described the assault on Christianity as a deliberate attempt to subvert the foundations of society, and the high-church Archdeacon Pott of London, in the course of an assault on antinomianism, warned the clergy that infidelity flew its flag in shop windows, 'where the wretched scribblings of some unknown hireling is made subservient to the base purposes of paltry vendors'.[27] Bishop Law's 1820 *Charge* was rather more measured. He observed that almost everywhere, but especially the towns and manufacturing districts, had been deluged with cheap publications openly attacking religion, and warned that if the growth of infidelity were not checked every sense of moral obligation, reverence for authorities, and the very idea of God and eternity, would be obliterated from the people's minds.[28] The social consequences of that were obvious to all his clergy.

The Evangelical William Dealtry, preaching in the wake of Peterloo in early November 1819, was particularly horrified at the *open* nature of the infidelity and blasphemy, which he regarded as having a far more devastating effect on social harmony and order, than the secret dissidence of hypocrisy. He would have preferred a practical infidel who supported order to a speculative one who sought to destroy it. It was better for men to pretend to have principles they lacked than to remove religious restraint and set loose the passions of mankind.[29] The Methodist John Stephens,

---

[25] DRO, MSS C2/73d, Exeter Quarter Sessions Minute Book, pp. 11–12, C3/78, Exeter Recognizance Book, 2 March 1821; *Trewman's Exeter Flying Post*, 26 August 1819, p. 4, 30 September 1819, p. 4, 13 January 1820, p. 4; *Flindell's Western Luminary*, 31 August 1819, p. 2, 12 October 1819, p. 4, 18 January 1820, p. 2. *Republican*, vol. 1, pp. 26, 52–6, 93–4, vol. 2, pp. 47, 49. See also, Robert Newton, *Eighteenth Century Exeter* (Exeter, 1984), p. 133.
[26] Mr Justice Bayley, *Speech* . . . (London, 1819), title page.
[27] J. Kaye, *Sermon*, 1819, p. 10; J. H. Pott, *A Charge to the Clergy of Archdeaconry of London* . . . *1819* (London, 1819), p. 12.
[28] Pp. 18–19.
[29] Dealtry, *Dispositions of Christians*, pp. 20–1.

although he did not go this far, insisted that no man could be neutral when faced with a choice between demagogy, vanity and infidelity on the one side, and monarchy, social order and the traditional creed on the other.[30]

Carlile's presence with Hunt at Peterloo ensured that most establishment reflections on that incident included a denunciation of blasphemy as well as of sedition.[31] The curate of Salford, Melville Horne, in his sermon defending the magistrates' actions, observed that now sedition, blasphemy and revolt were publicly preached, and he specifically attacked Carlile's *Temple of Reason*. The reformers argued, he claimed, that Christianity was incompatible with 'the precious liberty of crime', and so must be abolished. He likened Manchester in 1819 to the crater of a volcano spreading fire and smoke over adjacent counties, specifying the Blanketeers and the Nottingham Rebellion; blasphemy, sedition and anarchy could be seen and heard on all sides.[32]

Such views were not confined to an extreme conservative minority, they were commonplace among the clergy. The evangelical and future Whig bishop, William Otter, noted that blasphemous pamphlets were widely circulated among the 'deluded multitudes' who made up the reform movement, and observed that their first step, which seemed to threaten the existence of the constitution itself, was to abandon their fear of God, and their allegiance to Christ. Otter, however, took a long view. He did not regard the union of disloyalty and irreligion as a new creation of the French Enlightenment and Revolution, but rather traced it back to the days of Isaiah.[33] But he would not have disagreed with the high-church William van Mildert, who became a bishop in the year of Peterloo, when he observed in his episcopal charge that, since the French Revolution, 'Infidelity and Disloyalty, Scepticism and Sedition, Blasphemy and Treason' had 'coalesced and cooperated'.[34]

Most clerical reactions to the political and social disturbances of 1819 and the accompanying infidel onslaught typified by the activity of Richard Carlile, were predictable and largely negative. Some of the most perceptive and thoughtful came from the master of Swansea Grammar School, the Rev. D. Anderson, in a sermon to the Deanery of Gower on 27 October 1819. In some ways his views were commonplace. He observed that the spirits of turbulence, rebellion, impiety and fanaticism threatened religion, liberty and individual social comforts. He noted that reformers and journal-

[30] J. Stephens, *Mutual Relations*, p.v.
[31] On Hunt's hostile attitude to Carlile's presence at Peterloo see Walmsley, *Peterloo*, pp. 312–13; on Carlile's escape, Read, *Peterloo*, p. 139 note 3.
[32] M. Horne, *Moral and Political Crisis*.
[33] W. Otter, *Education of the Poor*, p. 15.
[34] W. van Mildert, *Charge*, 1821, pp. 13–14.

ists readily listened to the infidel, and that heretical and schismatic catechisms were actively and openly disseminated.

But Anderson could look beyond these familiar laments and see the
fundamental changes in thought which brought about such a state of affairs.
The sceptics and infidels, he argued, rejected absolute values. Limiting
themselves to a narrowly empirical epistemological base, they could have
no faith in immutable and eternal truths. Instead they regarded all values,
truths and habits of thought as merely relative and derived from a specific
education. A different education would produce other values, other truths,
equally valid. Any concept of universal, absolute truth was denied them.
This, Anderson explained, was because they assumed, without evidence,
that there was only one kind of knowledge – scientific knowledge – and that
religious and moral truths must be proved in the same way as scientific
truths, thus demanding of them 'a kind and degree of evidence wholly
inconsistent with their nature'. This narrow concept of knowledge and
limited awareness of truth had serious social and political implications for it
led, Anderson implied, to a kind of moral anomie. Where truth was relative
and uncertain, social behaviour lacked direction and society was unstable.
When this anomie reached the lower orders, they disregarded their duties of
submission, obedience and respect. Anderson welcomed the prosecution
against Carlile and urged all friends of religion in the country to 'stem the
tide of sedition and impiety' and withstand the 'anti-Christian, anti-social
conspiracy' which endangered both religion and government.[35]

Radical reactions
Discussion of the Carlile blasphemy trial was not, of course, limited to
pulpits, and elsewhere very different views were expressed. When the
British Forum held a debate on the issue at the Crown and Anchor a large
majority supported Carlile. The most important pro-Carlile speeches there,
however, while vigorously anti-clerical, were not openly atheist in tone.
They asserted Carlile's right to freedom of speech and they condemned the
clergy as lapdogs of the state. Fleming, in the opening speech of the debate,
argued that church and state were two parts of a corrupt system and that
both Anglican and Methodist preachers supported the 'Borough-mongers'.
He suggested that 'their black-coated army of parsons and preachers is much
more effective and formidable than the red-coated army of soldiers'; the
clergy may have had the titles of magistrate and justice of the peace but in
fact they were vile spies. Fleming implied a symbiotic relationship between
church and state. Such a church, he argued, should be attacked, but he

---

[35] D. Anderson, *A Sermon* . . . (Swansea, 1819), pp. 1–6, 27–9. The limited view which
Anderson attacked is clearly illustrated in Carlile, *An Address to Men of Science* (London, 1821),
pp. 7–10.

stopped short of denying the fundamental beliefs of Christianity. He recognised the power of religion over men and described it as the 'blind side' of mankind where the mental eye or intellectual vision was most likely to blench or blink, and therefore he feared that a jury which might condone sedition would condemn blasphemy.[36]

A later speaker, J. Mills, went further, declaring he was brought up as a Christian and wished there was more Christianity. He defended Carlile's right to enquire into the conduct of government, but argued that Sidmouth, and even Wilberforce in supporting the war, had acted contrary to the dictates of Christ. Other speakers, like John Gale Jones, were less sympathetic to Christianity, even of a radical brand, but the general tenor of the debate was to defend Carlile's right to freedom of speech, while not compounding his blasphemy.[37]

The radical reformer Joseph Brayshaw actively sought to separate reform from irreligion, sedition from blasphemy. He insisted that Christianity was favourable to the principles of liberty and it was the government and clergy who were denying Christ's teaching by their actions. Their exploitative use of Christianity as a means to control society was the true blasphemy. In January 1822, Carlile published a letter from him in *The Republican* in which Brayshaw claimed that Christianity would lead him to a more radical reforming position than Carlile ever adopted.[38] This led Carlile vigorously to assert that reform and Christianity were wholly incompatible. A series of polemics culminated in this anathema:

Christianity is a human institution generated in fraud and fable, and embraced by the Government as an additional means of fleecing the people . . . that man is not half a reformer . . . that does not seek its annihilation as a state institution. I am a decided advocate for reforming the Parliament, and annihilating every vestige of Kingcraft, but I am so far convinced of the superior importance of annihilating every species of Priestcraft, that, if the matter were put to my choice, which of the two should be first got rid of, the corruptions of the State or of the Church, I should say the latter, as by far the worst of the two. Kingcraft would very soon become harmless if it had not the support of the Priests.[39]

But while this was an important theme for Carlile, his apostasy was always much more than a mere off-shoot of his political radicalism. In the

[36] Fleming, *The Opening Speech . . . at the Crown and Anchor* (London, 1819), pp. 4–9, 13–16.
[37] J. Mills, *Speech*, pp. 7, 12; J. G. Jones, *Substances of the Speeches . . . Delivered at the British Forum, March 11, 18 and 22, 1819* (London, 1819), pp. 4–7, 10, 12.
[38] J. Brayshaw, *Remarks on the Character and Conduct of the Men who Met under the Name of the British Parliament at the Latter End of the Year 1819* (Newcastle, n.d.), pp. 14, 16, 20, 23, 39–40; *Republican*, vol. 5, pp. 39–41, 11 January 1822. But Brayshaw's heterodoxy was made clear in another letter, vol. 6, pp. 113–28, 21 June 1822.
[39] *Republican*, vol. 6, p. 251, 19 July 1822; see also pp. 218–19, 233–4, 241–52. Carlile had made a similar point to R. W. Byerley of Leeds in a letter on 20 September 1821, published in Carlile, *To the Reformers of Great Britain* (London, 1821), p. 18.

later 1820s, he devoted himself more and more to his assault on Christianity and in 1827 published *The Gospel According to Richard Carlile* in which he managed to assert both that Christ was a fabulous creature akin to Prometheus and the Logos of Plato, and that He (or the spirit He represented) was a radical reformer. Social stability required justice and morality, not a religion based on falsehood in which the greed of the clergy was paramount. Public education should be based on secular morality for this was the paramount social principle.[40] He was later to claim that 'the only true political worshipper of Jesus Christ' he had discovered was Thomas Paine.[41]

It was at this time that Carlile became involved with the renegade clergyman and (in Hunt's phrase) 'Devil's Chaplain', Robert Taylor, and the two led each other into strange, heterodox byways. In May 1830 they opened the Rotunda in Blackfriars Road, London, as a centre of infidelity and revolution.[42] One of the plays Taylor wrote for performance there, *Swing: or Who Are the Incendiaries?*, illustrated well the blend of antiChristian deism and political and social revolution they preached. The play showed how judge and archbishop consciously and cynically manipulated religion as a form of social control and how a new breed of agricultural workers would not be taken in. John Swing's father stuck by Bible loyalty, but John led a successful revolt which resulted in the judge being hanged from a lamp-post and the archbishop renouncing his hypocrisy. Taylor's pulpit rhetoric led to his trial for blasphemy and his and Carlile's 'infidel mission' became more and more remote from the mainstream of reform.[43]

The coalescence of blasphemy and sedition in the post-war years was real enough. Robert Owen continued to preach his twelve primary laws of human nature, which denied Christianity and laid, he believed, a new foundation for the social order.[44] Shelley's poetry and prose combined his atheism and his political radicalism in a potent, if sometimes recondite form.[45] Some, like Carlile, were basically apostates *and* radicals; while the

---

[40] *The Gospel According to Richard Carlile* (London, 1827), pp. 3–6, 9–13, 23–5, 27–30.

[41] R. Carlile, *Jesus Christ the Only Radical Reformer* (Manchester, 1838), pp. 1–7.

[42] *Republican*, vol. 14, pp. 547–54, 10 November 1826. R. Taylor, *The Holy Liturgy* . . . (London, [1827?]), *The Trial of the Rev. Robert Taylor* (London, 1827), pp. 3–7, 11, 32, *Judgment* . . . *of King's Bench* (London, 1828), p. 16, and *The Devil's Pulpit* (London, 1831). Compare the deist liturgy and radical ideas of Detrosier; G. A. Williams, *Rowland Detrosier: A Working Class Infidel 1800–34*, Borthwick Papers, 28 (York, 1965), pp. 12–13, 24–32.

[43] R. Taylor, *Swing* . . . (London, 1831), pp. 7, 9–10, 12–14, 16, 24–6, 28, 33–4, 36–7, 44–7.

[44] Robert Owen, *Discourses on a New System of Society* (Louisville, 1825), p. 16, *Debate on the Evidences of Christianity* (Bethany, 1829), pp. 26–8, 122–6, and *The Addresses of Robert Owen* (London, 1830), pp. 33–4, 41–2.

[45] P. B. Shelley, 'Queen Mab: A Philosophical Poem with Notes' (1812–13), *The Complete Poetical Works of Percy Bysshe Shelley*, edited by Neville Rogers (Cambridge, 1972), vol. 1, pp. 231–342; 'The Necessity of Atheism', in *Shelley, Trelawney and Henley* . . ., edited by S. J. Looker (Worthing, 1950), pp. 132–45; 'Essay on Christianity' in *Shelley Memorials* . . ., edited by Lady Jane Shelley (London, 1859), pp. 278–9, 282–5, 287–9. See also M. Scrivener, *Radical*

two were connected, they could stand independently. For others, like Bentham, it was the link which was all important and it was the political inutility of religion which constituted the most powerful argument against it. Some insisted that Christianity was not only compatible with reform, but actually demanded it. But most churchmen saw more and more reason to denounce and resist both blasphemy and sedition.

Shelley: The Philosophical Anarchism and Utopian Thought of Percy Bysshe Shelley (Princeton, 1982), pp. 67–76, 79–83, 87–107.

15

Case study III: William Hone

The link between blasphemy and sedition was real and occasioned genuine alarm. But government over-reaction should not lead us to exaggerate the extent of the connexion. As well as numerous conservative infidels, many radicals were men of religious conviction, as the career of John Cartwright illustrated. The complexity of the link between blasphemy, faith and political radicalism is perhaps best illustrated by the case of the bookseller and publisher, William Hone.[1]

The case study of Paley concerned a man who significantly changed the development of Christian thought. That of Horsley examined a typical figure of the establishment and demonstrated the unity and synthesis of the body of ideas in which a change of emphasis took place. This study of William Hone does neither of these things; instead it is offered as a cautionary tale. The analysis of the role of religion in political thought in the post-revolutionary period presented above may suggest a greater degree of polarisation than was the case. Chapter 13 examined the conflict between the Anglican and Dissenting churches to be the major agent of social control, while Chapter 14 looked at the links between blasphemy and sedition. This may appear to confirm the contemporary assumption of links between religion and repression on the one side, and of infidelity and

---

[1] There is no definitive biography of Hone, only a compilation by the author of *The Good Old Times* and *Inns, Ales and Drinking Customs of Old England* – F. W. Hackwood, *William Hone: His Life and Times* (London, 1912). A number of Hone's later pamphlets are reproduced in facsimile in E. Rickword, *Radical Squibs and Loyal Ripostes* (Bath, 1971). Rickword's introduction, pp. 1–32, provides a brief biography of Hone, but quite neglects the Unitarian influence upon him and his later Evangelical conversion. For a summary of the trials see J. Ann Hone, *For the Cause of Truth: Radicalism in London, 1796–1821* (Oxford, 1982), pp. 332–6; for a comment on this book and her article on Hone see below, note 11. Olivia Smith, *The Politics of Language*, pp. 154–201, places Hone and the trials in a literary context but has little discussion of his religion. Her comments on the influence of the language of early Protestant dissent (especially *Pilgrim's Progress*) are interesting: pp. 188–96. John Wardroper, *Kings, Lords and Wicked Libellers: Satire and Protest 1760–1837* (London, 1973), pp. 197–200, makes errors of detail in the provenance of the satires, but his interpretation of Hone's motives is sound. 'The Late John Wilkes's Catechism' is reprinted in *British Pamphleteers*, vol. 2, *From the French Revolution to the Nineteen Thirties*, edited by R. Reynolds (London, 1951), pp. 63–7.

revolution on the other.[2] To a considerable extent those links did exist, but they should not be exaggerated. Because of his radical political views it was presumed at the time, and is still assumed by many historians, that William Hone was an infidel.[3] This case study will seek to show that Hone combined his radicalism with a Christian faith – albeit of an unitarian brand – and that, as a publisher, he used the views of an Anglican clergyman and a trinitarian Dissenter to advance his case. The study should warn us that the irreligious-radical equation should not be drawn too readily; the links between blasphemy, faith and political radicalism were highly complex.

Hone and Unitarianism

Hone's religious views

In 1817 Hone published a number of parodies: *The Political Litany, The Bullet Te Deum; with the Canticle of the Stone*, and *The Late John Wilkes's Catechism of a Ministerial Member*. He was indicted by the attorney general and tried for blasphemous and seditious libel, but was acquitted by juries in three separate trials. Richard Carlile at once re-published the parodies in question, and the link with infidelity appeared established. But, almost certainly, Hone did not intend to be blasphemous. Most of Hone's own comments on his early religious opinions were written after his Evangelical conversion in 1832. The sense of guilt which this induced led him to stress excessively the extent of his earlier 'ungodliness'.

Born in 1780, Hone entered his teenage when the Jacobin ideological assault on English minds reached a peak with the publication of the second part of Paine's *Rights of Man*, but it was not until his sixteenth year, he recorded, that he began to doubt. He was brought up in a traditional, Bible-dominated household where *Pilgrim's Progress* and Watts's hymns were highly honoured. He had an early experience of Catholic worship in the home of a friend, and also heard John Wesley preach and was impressed by him. More significantly, at the age of 15 he worked for a Unitarian and learned what Unitarianism was, talking and reading much about it. The light of his later Evangelical conversion dimmed the brightness of this experience in his memories, but Hone's published works testify to its lasting and profound influence upon him.

In the short run, however, it was thrust aside. When 16 to 17 years old, Hone adopted the new 'philosophy' of the French school, being persuaded

[2] This link was assumed by radicals as well as by the establishment. See R. Hendrix, 'Popular Humor and "The Black Dwarf"', *JBS*, 16 (1976), 108–28 (pp. 127–8). Some scholars continue to assume it: see Carl Woodring, *Politics in the Poetry of Coleridge* (Madison, Wisconsin, 1961), p. 30, and note 11 below.

[3] J. C. D. Clark, *English Society*, wrongly describes Hone as 'atheist', p. 431, and alleges that men like him used 'Deism' as 'a thinly disguised euphemism for militant atheism', p. 381.

by a friend that religion was a dream to be discarded as the intellect awoke and brought men from darkness to light. Thus freed, the intellect would lead to a state of virtue in which 'the rights of one would be the rights of all', governments would disappear, and every individual would be self-governed. He saw the Bible as a book of fables and religious institutions as means to enslave the ignorant.[4] These comments suggest that in 1796–7 Hone occupied a deist position, but ten years later he was firmly in the Unitarian camp.

In a letter to his brother in 1834, he declared, 'dark, cold, confusing Unitarianism was a stumbling block for years', but precisely when, or by what stages, he adopted that faith is unclear.[5] He described himself as a 'rational Christian'; like Priestley he accepted those teachings of the Bible and of Christianity which he considered did not conflict with reason, rejecting the doctrine of the Trinity and the divinity of Christ. The Bible was seen merely as a store of moral wisdom, not as a work of revelation or theology, and Hone cut out the parts he could accept and pasted them together in a new 'rational' version.[6] By 1817, when the parodies were published, Hone was no more an infidel than Joseph Priestley had been.

Political controversy

Hone's combination of radical politics and religious dissent was revealed in the spring of 1817 in an article in his short-lived journal, *The Reformists' Register*. At the end of April he responded to a sermon preached in early March by the Rev. Daniel Wilson. Wilson, who was then chaplain to Lord Galway and was later, in 1832, to become Bishop of Calcutta, had made his church a leading Evangelical centre. He chose, in the politically highly charged atmosphere of 1817 and indeed in the very week when habeas corpus was suspended, to preach on *The Duty of Contentment under Present Circumstances*. Wilson's sermon was powerful, accomplished and uncompromising, certain to anger Christian radicals. It reflected very clearly the change in emphasis of clerical thought. It included a brief passage in which the pre-revolutionary preoccupation with SS Peter and Paul's commands to fear God, honour the king and submit to rulers even when they are wicked were noted, but he laid little emphasis on these.

Rather, Wilson went on to consider the nature of man and of society, arguing that the foundations of law lay deep in the nature of man and that where there were minor faults in law and justice these arose not from government but from human weakness and providential appointment.

---

[4] BL, Add. MS 40,121. Hone Papers XIV, Autobiographical Notes ff. 6, 9, 11, 15, 18–19, 23, 45, 48–50, 52–8.
[5] BL, Add. MS 40,120, Part II, Hone Papers XIII, Part II, General Correspondence, f. 388.
[6] BL, Add. MS 40,121, Hone Papers XIV, ff. 56–7, 89.

Government could not make bad men good. Nor should government be blamed for a bad harvest or trade problems. Wilson warned that the distress of the poor had been exploited to stir up discontent and sedition. Pamphlets deceived men by using popular terms like petition, reform and retrenchment, but these were 'blasphemous as well as disloyal' and the Christian must reject them. The movement to teach the poor to read and make the Bible widely available would be seriously discredited if it were clear the poor were using their new ability to read seditious literature:

The advancement of education ... must continue, as it is now, to be strictly connected with the principles of religion and good order ... Humility and obedience to the laws, a regard to conscience, contentment with their lot, industry, piety must be imbibed together with those elements of knowledge, or those elements will lose their value.[7]

Wilson's sermon was a modern piece which reflected the developments in style and argument which had followed the French Revolution. However, if one were to read only Hone's riposte to it, one might believe it to be a very old-fashioned, pre-revolutionary, fear-God-honour-the-king sermon. At the outset of his first article on 'Political Priestcraft', Hone alleged that Wilson had misrepresented real Christianity as much as he had political liberty, but then, instead of exploring this crucial theme, both his articles concentrated entirely upon that very brief passage of the sermon in which Wilson re-asserted the political theory of obedience to governors.[8] Where Wilson was modern, challenging and provocative, Hone's reply was thoroughly old-fashioned and failed to provide a radical response to the critical new argument. His position was, in fact, characteristically Unitarian. He had little interest in the education of the poor, little desire to stir up discontent amongst the lower orders. His interest, like Priestley's had been, was bourgeois and intellectual; his concentration on political theory and abstract argument reflected the position of earlier 'rational Christians', not the new area of debate.

Three months later, George Frere Bates preached in St Paul's before the Lord Mayor and the judiciary at the start of the legal Trinity term. He too referred to 'the good old maxim of fearing God, honouring the King, and not meddling with those who are given to change', and (while his sermon was not the model of modernity that Wilson's was) this too was only a passing reference in a much more widely ranging sermon.[9] But Hone's reply again concentrated upon this brief theme. He implied that Bates had preached,

---

[7] D. Wilson, *Duty of Contentment*, pp. 19–27.

[8] W. Hone, *The Reformists' Register and Weekly Commentary*, 2 vols. (London, 1817), vol. 1, no. 14, pp. 417–37, no. 15, pp. 449–67.

[9] G. F. Bates, *A Sermon ...* (London, 1817), pp. 20–9.

and the Corporation of London had published, an old-fashioned 'passive obedience' sermon. Again, Hone's position was not that of a radical infidel, but of a somewhat backward-looking rational Dissenter.[10] However, what really infuriated Hone in Bates's sermon was an oblique, passing reference to Hone's parody of the Te Deum.

The 'Blasphemies'

To understand the relationship of Hone's religious and political views, it is important to establish whether or not he intended the parodies to be blasphemous.[11] This question requires a definition, in this context, of blasphemy. In *The Reformists' Register* of 26 July 1817, as part of his reply to Bates's sermon, Hone insisted he had no intention of bringing the services of the church into contempt. The parodies were nothing but political squibs, as, he suggested, everyone – Churchman or Dissenter – who read them without bigotry would immediately see.[12] In all of Hone's parodies (of the Te Deum, for which he was not prosecuted, and of the Litany, catechism and Athanasian Creed, for which he was), the substantive contents of the pieces were wholly political in their arguments and targets. All Hone did was to take a form of words, a structure of language, which was familiar as part of the liturgy of the established church and apply it to a secular purpose.

At the trial concerning the *Sinecurist Creed*, the attorney general repeated the view that 'Christianity was part of the law of England' and pointed out that the form of worship being mimicked had been laid down by Act of Parliament. While he conceded that it may not have been Hone's *object*, he insisted that the tendency was to encourage impiety and irreligion and to bring public worship into ridicule and contempt. If this happened, 'the great bond that linked man to man would be shaken'. The importance of religion in binding society together was clearly understood by the attorney general and by the judge, who noted that England was heading down the road which 'had so lately produced such melancholy results in France'.[13]

But was this blasphemy? From Hone's unitarian standpoint, clearly it was not. For Unitarians, it was the doctrines of the Incarnation and of the divinity of Christ that were blasphemous.[14] Moreover, Hone never parodied

[10] W. Hone, *Reformists' Register*, vol. 2, no. 1, pp. 2–25.
[11] J. Ann Hone raises this question both in her article 'William Hone (1780–1842), Publisher and Bookseller: An Approach to Early Nineteenth Century London Radicalism', *Historical Studies*, 16 (1974), 55–70, (pp. 65–7) and in her book *Cause of Truth*, pp. 332–3. In both she concentrates upon his politics, where her analysis is excellent. But she underestimates the influence of his Unitarian faith. He was certainly more than a 'nominal Christian', and although anti-clerical he was not an atheist.
[12] W. Hone, *Reformists' Register*, vol. 2, no. 1, p. 23.
[13] *The Third Trial of William Hone* (London, 1818), pp. 7–8, 43.
[14] BL, Add. MS 40,108, f. 30.

the Bible (as many had done before him) but only the liturgy of an established church from which 'rational Christians' dissented. The Litany, though not the catechism, stressed the doctrine of the Trinity, and it is significant that it was the Athanasian and not the Nicene or Apostles' Creed that Hone chose to parody, for this is the paradigm statement of trinitarian belief. One of Hone's correspondents in 1817 underlined the *Anglican* nature of the prosecution. The attorney general, he observed, failed to prosecute those who contravened spiritual injunctions; he 'watches over Sidmouth's and Castlereagh's religion, but the religion of the Bible he would leave . . . not so litanys and creeds, forms and establishments'.[15]

It is extremely doubtful whether the parodies can be considered as blasphemous even from an Anglican viewpoint; the main intention behind them was clearly a political one. But undoubtedly, from a unitarian position they were not. Unlike Carlile, Hone adopted a Christian stance at his trial, referring to Christ as 'Our Saviour' and accusing his persecutors of neglecting the true principles of Christianity.[16] There is no reason to doubt his sincerity. While in prison he received strongly supportive letters from Major Cartwright, the Unitarian and reformer, and from the Unitarian minister of the Gravel Pit meeting, Robert Aspland, who was clearly a close acquaintance.[17] The jury accepted Hone's argument that the parodies were political squibs and not profane libels and acquitted him, but the accusation had clearly stung Hone and he devoted much time and effort to collecting a large number and wide range of contemporary and historical parodies. He planned to publish a major collection of parodies of the scriptures and liturgy, with the account of his trial and acquittal as an appendix. This work never appeared, but the materials for it form the bulk of his papers in the British Library. A wide range of correspondents and supporters sent him material, and his own squibs, when seen in this context, seem minor and damp indeed. The collection reflects Hone's unitarian stance by its strong concentration on parodies of the doctrine of the Trinity.[18] Hone's case underlined that it was possible to be a Christian and a political radical, and the government's response to his political satires shows how closely they associated blasphemy and sedition.

[15] BL, Add. MS 40,120, f. 58.

[16] *Third Trial*, pp. 18–19.

[17] UCL, William Hone's Correspondents, f. 8, from Cartwright to Hone 26 May 1817; BL, Add. MS 40,120, f. 83. Later, the Rev. Neil Douglas, the Scottish Universalist and 'independent preacher', who had been tried for sedition and acquitted in Edinburgh in 1817, saw Hone as a fellow Christian and radical and sought his support. See letters from Douglas to Hone, 22 June 1818 and 3 May 1822, Bodl., MS Eng. Misc., c 32, ff. 4, 19. The best assessment of Douglas is in Kirkland, 'Impact of French Revolution', pp. 128–206.

[18] BL, Add. MS 40,108, ff. 13, 14, 122, 123, 124, 244, 311, 314; BL, Add. MS 40, 117, ff. 37, 53, 54, 62.

Hone as publisher

Although Hone did write occasional pieces himself (and the authorship of the parodies is not seriously in doubt), he is better described as a bookseller and publisher than as a writer. To understand his views on the connexion of religion and political thought one needs to examine what he published as well as what he wrote. In particular he chose to resurrect the works of two past authors, James Murray and Vicesimus Knox, which had made little impact when they were first published. This decision may have reflected the danger of prosecution he felt existed to living authors, but in fact both writers perfectly expressed his own views and values. Three factors explain this. First, as we have noted, Hone's approach to the question of religion and political power in his own writings had been somewhat old-fashioned. Secondly, Murray and, even more so, Knox were in many arguments in advance of their times and were addressing issues which in fact came to the forefront of discussion only after the outbreak of the French Revolution and war. Thirdly, many of the points made were of a fundamental nature equally relevant in either period.

James Murray (1732–1782)

Murray was a Scot, educated at the University of Edinburgh, who came via Alnwick to Newcastle-upon-Tyne. He was an independent-minded Presbyterian minister, who opposed both the American war and Saville's Bill to relieve the Catholics, but what most attracted Hone to his work was his combination of Christianity with radical politics. '*His* bible was not one of those which *open of themselves* at the 13th chapter of Paul's Epistle to the Romans', Hone commented, and printed an extract from Murray's *The Lawfulness of Self-Defence* (1780), examining this text, in *The Reformists' Register* in April 1817.[19] He planned to publish a volume of Murray's collected works in the same year, but his arrest and trial caused him to delay. When the volume appeared in 1819, as well as containing a biographical sketch of Murray, it included *Sermons to Asses* (1768), *Sermons to Doctors in Divinity* (1771), *New Sermons to Asses* (1773), *Lectures to Lords Spiritual* (1774), and *Sermons to Ministers of State* (1780). In one way, these works naturally reflect the political context in which they were written: Murray's hostility to John Wesley's high toryism, to the war against America and the move to improve the lot of the English Catholics; the Presbyterian dislike of bishops, and all the trappings of establishment, especially tithes. But equally significant is the fact that Hone chose to reprint them in the England of 1817–19, for he did this not as a detached commercial venture, but as a committed act of conviction publishing.

---

[19] W. Hone, *Reformists' Register*, vol. 1, no. 14, pp. 425–32.

Murray recognised that civil society needed the support of a state religion; without it government was impossible and law unenforceable. Only religion and law could operate as proper checks on the passions and appetites, but without religion men would find a thousand ways to evade the laws. However, Christianity was unsuited to the role of a state religion unless it was changed, corrupted, from the true religion of Christ. Politicians 'in almost every age, have meant no more by religion, than to make it an *engine of state policy*, or a *tool of secular interest*'.[20] No country could become a great flourishing nation by following the precepts of Christianity, any more than Christ could become a powerful temporal ruler by submitting himself to death. Self-denial and sacrifice was not the route to worldly glory, so Christianity had to be tampered with to suit the needs of civil government, and the Church of England was the result.[21] There was no basis in the New Testament for an alliance between church and state and this much vaunted union was really one between the richest men in the nation and a worldly self-seeking clergy – not the 'real' state nor the 'real' church.[22]

This led Murray to expound the usual Dissenters' arguments regarding the need to keep religion and politics separate in order to defend both religious and civil liberty, but his reflections on the nature of the operation of a state religion were less common and seemed to imply some prefigurement of the concept of false consciousness which Marx was to set out three quarters of a century later. Murray reflected in 1768, 'the first slavery that men are generally brought under is that of the mind . . . It requires the aid of *false teachers* to seduce mankind, before a state can *deprive them* of their *civil privileges*.' Three years later he carried the thought further:

Freedom and liberty, words of a mighty sound, have really no signification but under gospel-influence; – for people who are influenced by flattery, bribery or corruption of any kind, are not free. Those people are really as much forced, who are led by their passions and appetites, as those who are dragged with chains, and compelled by physical necessity. Politicians who know what handle to hold men by, can lead them at their pleasure and cause them to act contrary to all the principles of virtue and honesty.[23]

These thoughts were, as Hone recognised, even more relevant and perceptive in 1817–19 than they had been in 1771, for the whole of the post-revolutionary trend of clerical social theory had been to strengthen state Christianity as a sanction and restraint. Murray's point, and Hone did

---

[20] J. Murray, *Sermons to Asses* (London, 1768), pp. 115, 204, 122–13, and *New Sermons for Asses* (London, 1773), pp. 150.

[21] J. Murray, *Sermons to Doctors in Divinity* (1771) (Glasgow, 1798), pp. 41–2, 126–7.

[22] J. Murray, *Sermons to Asses*, pp. 30, 155, 191–2, 195 and *Lectures to Lords Spiritual* (London, 1774), pp. 48–9.

[23] *Sermons to Asses*, p. 154, and *Doctors in Divinity*, p. 118.

not dissent from it, was that only *true* Christianity could free men from this false consciousness of state religion, and that, such is the nature of man, that freedom would itself bring stability and security to society, 'prevent mobs and riots'.[24] Hone's re-publication of Murray was selective. Where he approved of only some of the sentiments in a piece, he did not reproduce it in full but merely quoted selections,[25] and this showed Hone was well aware it was Murray's attack on Anglican social theory that was most relevant in post-war England.

Vicesimus Knox

Hone's ability to use the works of earlier writers to argue his case is seen even more clearly in his selection of Vicesimus Knox's *Spirit of Despotism*. At first sight Knox was a much less obvious target for Hone's attention than Murray. While the Unitarian Hone might well be attracted by the Presbyterian Murray's anti-clericalism and anti-Erastianism, an outline of Knox's biography makes him appear a pillar of that establishment of which they were both so critical. Knox spent eight years at his father's college, St John's, Oxford, the last four as a fellow; he was ordained by Bishop Lowth in 1777 and composed a decorous, conventional and innocuous collection of *Essays Moral and Literary* (1778) which were very popular. In the same year he succeeded his father as headmaster of Tonbridge School, a post he held until 1812 when it passed to his son. He was a minor pluralist, a sound scholar and a firm Whig, who had some hopes of preferment when Fox came to power in 1806.

But Knox combined with this conventional career pattern a surprisingly radical stance. In August 1793, the same year as he published a fairly conventional call to the upper classes to reform and so justify themselves, he preached a powerful anti-war sermon in Brighton.[26] He stressed the brotherhood of all men and condemned all states which made use of religion to promote civil subordination. Christ's way was that of meekness, love and sacrifice, not that of offensive war.[27] A few days later, when he visited the theatre in Brighton, some soldiers staged a demonstration and caused Knox to leave.[28] Two years later he printed Erasmus's *Antipolemus* and added a preface which further revealed his anti-clerical and anti-Erastian strain: he denounced those who offered prayers for success in an offensive war and so rendered 'religion subservient to secular ambition'.

---

[24] *Ibid.*, pp. 118, 71.
[25] J. Murray, *The Lawfulness of Self-Defence* . . . (Glasgow, 1780), pp. 24–5, clearly did not suit Hone, who quoted only some of the earlier part in *Reformists' Register*, vol. 1, no. 14, pp. 425–32.
[26] 'Personal Nobility' (1793), *Works*, vol. 5, pp. 1–135.
[27] Knox, 'The Prospect of Perpetual and Universal Peace . . .', *Works*, vol. 6, pp. 363–9.
[28] V. Knox, *The Substance of a Sermon* . . . (London, 1793), pp. 9–12.

The disposition of malice and revenge which led to war was absolutely forbidden by the gospel.[29]

The Spirit of Despotism was the only one of Knox's works Hone chose to re-publish in full. This was written in early 1795 when Knox considered that the war against France was an offensive one directed against French liberty, and so against the best interests of mankind as a whole. By the end of the year, however, he saw the war in a new light, with the French as aggressors seeking military glory and the allies engaged in a defensive conflict, something he had never opposed. He decided, therefore, not to publish the work, which had been privately printed, and to destroy all the copies.[30]

A few copies of this edition, however, escaped destruction. Hone believed only three survived, though at least four copies still exist today in libraries in the United States of America.[31] One copy, possibly that now held by the Library Company of Philadelphia, found its way to America almost at once and was reprinted in Philadelphia in 1795.[32] Another copy was found by Hone in a London bookseller's, presumably around 1820, and he reprinted it anonymously in 1821. After the work was printed, Hone discovered the author's name, but withheld it until after Knox's death. Hone recorded that he met Knox to apologise for the unauthorised publication, and found his views on English liberty were still as he had expressed them in 1795.[33] When in 1822, immediately after Knox's funeral, Hone advertised the work under the author's name, he received a letter from Knox's son asking that this should be withdrawn, but he ignored the request.[34]

In republishing the work in 1821, Hone dedicated it to Castlereagh and suggested that Knox's comments on the alliance against France in 1795 applied even better to the activities of the Holy Alliance against the liberal movements in Europe in the 1820s. His excitement in discovering this work was evident and clearly he considered that it expressed his views perfectly.[35] Much of the work was concerned with condemning the war,[36] but other profound themes also dominated the book – the issue of equality, and the corruptions of the Christian church.

Knox did not make the conventional distinctions between social and

---

[29] Knox, Preface to Erasmus's *Antipolemus*, *Works*, vol. 5, pp. 417–22.
[30] Bibliographical Preface to Knox, *Works*, vol. 1, pp. vi–vii; Hone's Preface to his 1821 anonymous edition of *The Spirit of Despotism* (London, 1821); Hone's Advertisement to his 1822 named edition, pp. iii–vii; BL, Add. MS 40,120, ff. 168–9.
[31] One is at Philadelphia, one at Princeton, and two at Harvard. I am indebted for information on these to P. Lapansky, Library Company of Philadelphia, S. Ferguson, Princeton University Library, and R. E. Stoddard, The Houghton Library, Harvard University.
[32] By Lang and Ustick, for themselves and M. Carey, 1795.
[33] Hone's Advertisement to Knox's *Spirit . . . .*, pp. vi–vii.
[34] BL, Add. MS 40,120, f. 166, 15 September 1821.
[35] Hone's Preface to 1821 edition, p. 4.
[36] *Spirit of Despotism* (1821), p. 24.

spiritual equality. Equality was not confined to that at the moment of death and in the sight of God; Christ's teaching also implied equality on earth. Christ's message to the poor was one of freedom, independence and equality. Hone denounced as unjust the unnatural and unreasonable power of one human being over another in the existing order of society, and stressed the coincidence of Christianity and poverty. Christ and the primitive church followed the path of poverty. Since then, the church had been corrupted to suit it for social and political roles quite alien to those Christ envisaged. It was now dominated by the rich, powerful and well-connected. On the episcopal bench, men of merit like Watson, Porteus and Secker were expected to remain inferior to the well-born like North, Cornwallis and Keppel; how Christ and the poor fishermen would have been despised!

In the parish church those who did not bow at the name of Jesus did so to the lord-in-the-gallery. Many nominal Christians were as aristocratic as Herod and the high priests, their pride making them unable to accept Christ's teaching. The church had been seduced into a state of power and grandeur in which the poor had been forgotten. Those church leaders who set their faces against reform and improvement in the condition of life of the poor

would, if they had lived about one thousand and seven hundred and ninety five years ago, have joined with the *high priests* and rulers to crucify Jesus Christ. They would have prosecuted and persecuted him for sedition and high treason. They would have despised and rejected the friend of Lazarus; and taken the part of Dives, even in Hell.

The socially powerful, although indifferent to religion, were zealous for the church, which they saw as useful, not just in providing genteelly for their relations and dependants, but also as a means of repression 'in conjunction with military force, to press down the elastic spirit of the people'. The clergy should have condemned this, but promotion in the church came to those who preached against Christ's teaching. The alliance between church and state not only corrupted the church by using religion as a form of social control, it also implied a Christian benediction upon the policy of the state, while in fact it was a Machiavellian, not a Christian ethic which prevailed in court and cabinet.[37]

Clearly Knox's decision to withdraw and destroy his *Spirit of Despotism* in 1795 involved more than just a change in the character of the war. It is not difficult to see why Hone was attracted to it and saw it as extremely relevant to the issues of the early 1820s, the years of the Queen's Divorce and the Holy Alliance. He printed 15,000 copies which were sold at eighteen pence each, and so rescued it from oblivion, and considered that 'for this act alone

[37] *Spirit of Despotism* (1821), pp. 5, 10–13, 15, 17–19, 23–4, 32–3, 44–5, 47–8, 71–5, 81–7, 91–2.

... I have not lived in vain'.[38] Many of Knox's arguments were later developed by some of the Christian Chartists, and echoes can still be heard today. The theme of the radical message of Christ and the early church being corrupted and made subservient to the social and political interests of the rich and powerful is found in those parts of the works of Murray and Knox which he chose to republish and must certainly reflect Hone's own view. When he struggled to write pieces himself, his argument was laboured and out of date; only by selecting and re-presenting views of earlier writers who had been too advanced for their own day did Hone confront directly the central arguments of the social theory of the conservative clerics of his time.

Conclusion

Hone saw himself as a Christian as well as a radical, but such was the coincidence of atheism and sedition in men's minds that contemporaries assumed he was an infidel and blasphemer. His alarm and concern at this are well illustrated by his dealings with Samuel Butler, Archdeacon of Derby and headmaster of Shrewsbury School.

In 1820 Hone had published an *Apocryphal New Testament*, a collection in translation of the non-canonical writings concerning the life of Christ and the events surrounding it. The work was neither hostile, nor critical, though Hone's introduction did give the impression that the books of the New Testament had been selected somewhat arbitrarily in the fourth century from a much wider corpus, and that instead of being an inspired canon which stood alone and should be literally accepted, those works should be approached in a critical, scholarly and historical way. He also pointed out that the Apocryphal Gospels formed the basis of the narratives of many of the English Mystery Plays, a theme he followed up in 1823 in *Ancient Mysteries Described*.[39]

In his Charge to his Archdeaconry in 1822, Samuel Butler described the *Apocryphal New Testament* as unedifying, mischievous and malevolent.[40] Hone replied to this in *Aspersions Answered* (1824), vigorously denying it was intended as a profane or irreligious act and asserting that he sought to defend, not to undermine, public morality and the social good.[41] On 12 February 1824, Hone wrote to Butler a polite note telling him he had used his name in the pamphlet and enclosing a copy. Butler replied at once giving

---

[38] W. Hone, *Aspersions Answered* . . . (London, 1824).
[39] *The Apocryphal New Testament* (London, 1820), Introduction, pp. iv–vi, xi–vii; W. Hone, *Ancient Mysteries Described* (London, 1823), Preface, p. ii; BL, Add. MS 43,645, Thomas Sharpe, 'Dissertation on the Pageants or Dramatic Mysteries', ff. 376–7, Letter Hone to Sharpe, 17 November 1825.
[40] S. Butler, *The Genuine and Apocryphal Gospels Compared* (Shrewsbury, 1822), pp. 7, 11.
[41] Hone, *Aspersions Answered*, pp. 47, 59, 61.

conventional thanks, clearly not having read the pamphlet, and later in the year published a favourable notice of *Ancient Mysteries Described.* Hone, embarrassed lest Butler now read the attack on him in the pamphlet, wrote again in October apologising for and explaining the piece. This led to a long and generous reply from Butler in which, while he maintained his criticism of the *Apocryphal New Testament,* he expressed respect for Hone's integrity and honesty and accepted his assertion that he was a Christian, albeit of a different type, and recognised 'the high moral and intellectual tone which pervades your letter'.[42]

Hone, unused to such generosity, was enchanted and an unlikely correspondence ensued which was clearly a difficult one for the Archdeacon, and a lifeline to Hone, whose personal disasters multiplied at this time. As well as exchanging publications, Butler sent Hone news of the death of Dr Samuel Parr, and this elicited from Hone a long and circumstantial account of a visit he had paid to Parr, including a three-hour pre-breakfast discussion when Parr demanded Hone tell him 'honestly and truly' what his creed was, and Hone disclosed every secret of his heart.[43] What was revealed to Parr, Hone did not tell Butler and we can only infer his beliefs from his writings and publications, but there is no reason to believe that in 1824 Hone was not still a Unitarian.

In that year he publicly expressed the deep distress caused him by the imputation of irreligion which had been urged against him for the previous seven years. He was particularly upset at the suggestion that his brother Joseph's career as a barrister had been ruined because people assumed they shared the same political and religious views. Hone insisted not only that their political views were very different, but also that the accusations of irreligion against him were calumnies. He cited his publication of *The Spirit of Despotism,* at only eighteen pence a copy, as evidence of his desire 'to counteract the erroneous representations of religion, contained in various cheap political publications throughout the country'. For Hone, true Christianity had a radical message, and radical politics must be Christian in character. Christianity was

the Great Charter of mankind, defining all rights, prescribing all duties, prohibiting all wrong, proscribing all violence. Upon it everything that is beneficial in society is founded: without it, the advocates and supporters of public liberty can neither attain, nor maintain what they have.[44]

Hone's unitarian faith of 1824 failed to sustain him in the family and

---

[42] BL, Add. MS 34,585, Butler Correspondence III, ff. 318, 376–7, 378–80; BL, Add. MS 40,120, Hone Papers XIII, Part I, ff. 217–18.

[43] BL, Add. MS 34,586, Butler Correspondence, IV, ff. 1, 4–5. See also Warren Derry, *Dr Parr: A Portrait of the Whig Dr Johnson* (Oxford, 1966), pp. 327–8.

[44] *Aspersions Answered,* pp. 5–13, 65–7.

personal disasters which overtook him, and by the early 1830s his religious views had changed significantly.[45] In June 1831 he was critical of R. B. Beverley's *Letter to the Archbishop of York* (1831) whose anti-clericalism and anti-Erastianism might have attracted him a decade earlier.[46] He still supported the cause, but he suspected Beverley's motives. While Hone sought reform of the church for religious reasons, he thought Beverley's aims were merely political and essentially infidel.

Hone was by this time regularly attending worship at his local parish church, but on New Year's Day 1832 he moved into the camp of the trinitarian Dissenters, when he attended the Congregationalist chapel of Dr Thomas Binney and experienced an 'evangelical' conversion.[47] Binney had succeeded John Clayton at the Weigh House Chapel, but did not share his predecessor's conservative political views. He was famous for his attacks on the established church, and so Hone was able to retain many of his earlier views in his new faith, which he and his family embraced enthusiastically. But he adopted a much more humble, pietistic and inward-looking attitude to religion, a marked contrast from his Unitarian positivism.[48] A similar change can be discerned in his political stance. He became more detached and objective, although his substantive views remained radical. His attitude to the Reform Act was considerably more radical than that of the Whigs and, although many of his political friends forsook him, others still sought his views on such issues as municipal government reform and regarded him as a supporter of the radical cause.[49]

The case of William Hone illustrates well the complexity of the role which religion and religious arguments played in political and social thought in the post-war years. To the government, he was simply categorised as one of the blasphemy-and-sedition brigade. While establishment political argument had become more secular and the established church was concentrating more on a social role, much radical political thought had a religious inspiration. Within the radical cause, Christians and infidels worked together towards the same political end. The denominational brand of Christianity did affect the social and political stance to some extent, and the changes in Hone's faith were reflected in some changes in his political style, but in essence his political views remained fairly constant. Moreover, the use of the writings of a Presbyterian and an Anglican by a Unitarian

---

[45] BL, Add. MS 43,645, ff. 376–7; BL, Add. MS 40,120, Part II, ff. 312,35.
[46] R. M. Beverley, *A Letter to his Grace the Archbishop of York* . . . (Beverley, 1831), pp. 4–9, 17–22, 26, 36; BL, Add. MS 40,120, Part II, ff. 355–6, Hone to R. Childs, 13 June 1831.
[47] *Ibid.*, ff. 387–8, Hone to his brother, 22 April 1834.
[48] *Ibid.*, ff. 387–8, 389–90, 391–2, 395–6, 397–8, 442, 451, 460–1, 466.
[49] *Ibid.*, ff. 365–6, 370, 406. The reservations about the Reform Act which Hackwood notes, *William Hone*, p. 301, reflect Hone's later views, not those of 1832.

publisher showed that men from a wide religious spectrum could share the same radical views. Hone's career demonstrated clearly that blasphemy and sedition were not inevitable bedfellows, whatever the establishment in church and state believed.

16

Emancipation and reform

The Revolution of 1688–9 established in England a brand of political philosophy which dominated Christian political and social theory for a century. The French Revolution brought about a change of emphasis in English clerical argument, a movement from abstract political philosophy to practical social theory. The repeal of the Corporation and Test Acts in 1828, the passing of Catholic Emancipation in 1829 and the First Reform Act of 1832 constituted the most significant group of constitutional reforms since the Revolution Settlement. To what extent were these changes in the constitution of church and state, which had been resisted by the established powers for so long, influenced by that fundamental change of emphasis in Christian political thought, and how far were they simply a response to the exigencies of practical politics? Did they presage a movement back to further consideration of the philosophical and theological foundations of the constitution, or were they a reflection of the new concentration on the need for social stability? Were religious, normative arguments used to justify the policy stances which were adopted, and if so were they employed by reformers, conservatives or both, or did the desire to maintain social order and stability lead statesmen and churchmen to justify their positions on grounds of expediency? Did arguments of principle or of utility predominate?

The Emancipation and Reform movements, 1804–1828

Parliamentary reform to 1828

These constitutional adjustments did not spring like Pallas Athene fully armed from the head of Zeus; they were the subject of much debate and agitation in preceding years. Dissenters had argued for the repeal of the Corporation and Test Acts throughout the eighteenth century, although following the defeat of the resolution in the House of Commons in 1790 no further motion was proposed until 1828. The Act of Union between England and Ireland in 1801 made the issue of Catholic emancipation a far more pressing one than hitherto. The agitation for the reform of parliament had faded somewhat during the years of revolution and war, but the period of post-war distress and discontent saw a significant upsurge. The leader of the moderate wing of the movement in the earlier generation, Christopher Wyvill, was an Anglican parson, but he made no use of religious arguments. In the post-war years he strongly supported the movements for religious rights for both Dissenters and Catholics, and these arguments were based on a concept of natural rights, but his arguments for parliamentary reform remained detailed, practical and secular and never invoked any concept of God-given rights.[1]

The leader of the radical wing of the movement in the earlier generation, Major John Cartwright, was also a Christian. While Wyvill employed secular, pragmatic arguments for reform consistently throughout his career, before, during and after the French Revolution, the nature of Cartwright's arguments changed. Before the Revolution he indulged in expansive, abstract arguments in favour of the rights of man; after 1793 he largely abandoned these, passed up opportunities to argue that the right to vote was God-given and instead listed facts and figures and rehearsed the corruptions of the electoral system.[2] However, as a new breed of atheist parliamentary reformer emerged towards the end of the war, Cartwright began to re-emphasise the religious basis of his case. His arguments continued to be essentially pragmatic, and he never went back to the normative analysis of pre-revolutionary years, but he made a point of introducing Christian arguments which he had lately neglected.

This can first be seen in his reactions to the machine-breaking and rick-burnings of 1811. Cartwright denounced these as lawless, immoral and unwise; he conceded that God had given people the passion of resentment to rouse them to vindicate their rights, but urged them to campaign peacefully for reform. The consideration of religion led him to attempt to present a syllogism: since, first, God considered the humblest man competent to judge for himself the means of eternal salvation; and, secondly, good laws were the means of temporal salvation; therefore, the English constitution should involve the people in legislation.[3]

In the years of distress and discontent from 1816 to 1819, Cartwright was

---

[1] C. Wyvill, *A More Extended Discussion in Favour of Liberty of Conscience* (London, 1808), pp. 6, 15, *An Apology for the Petitioners for Liberty of Conscience* (London, 1810), pp. 6, 9–10, 19–24, 31–2, 36 and *Papers and Letters Chiefly Respecting the Reformation of Parliament* (Richmond, 1816), pp. 12, 17. For Wyvill generally in this period see J. R. Dinwiddy, *Christopher Wyvill and Reform 1790–1820*, Borthwick Papers 39 (York, 1971).

[2] J. Cartwright, *Reasons for Reformation* (London, 1809) and *The Comparison* (London, 1810).

[3] J. Cartwright, *Copy of a Letter . . . to a Burgess of Nottingham*, Broadsheet (Markham, 1811), *Copy of a Letter . . . to a Respectable Frame Work Knitter of Nottingham*, Broadsheet (Nottingham, 1811), and *Six Letters to the Marquis of Tavistock* (London, 1812), p. 23.

anxious to show that reform could have a Christian face. He countered some of the traditional, conservative religious arguments in a dialogue of 1817 between Sir Samuel Citiman, who argued that men should not interfere with God-given inequality, and John Hampton Freeman, who warned against an un-Christian pride, which made men forget they were brothers and equals by nature. Cartwright returned here to his favourite argument that Christianity had started among the poor, and risen to embrace whole nations. In 1819 he told the electors of Westminster that constitutional reform alone was strictly in accordance with the liberty God had given universally to man.[4]

While Cartwright was anxious that the conservatives should not have all the religious arguments on their side, he was also aware that now he lay with atheist bedfellows. He admired Jeremy Bentham as 'a profound reasoner' and recognised he was a useful ally, but some secret disquiet is suggested by the fact that he sent Bentham a copy of his anonymously published *Declaration of Principles* (1821).[5] In this work, Cartwright insisted that both patriotism and genuine Christianity were summed up in Christ's injunction to love God and our neighbour. To fulfil their duty to their neighbour, men were under a moral obligation to advocate parliamentary reform.[6]

Cartwright based his argument on rights, and made his rejection of utilitarianism clear in 1823 when he joined those other Christian thinkers who deplored the influence of Paley's *Moral and Political Philosophy* which, he claimed, directly tended to undermine the morality needed to revive religion and society. This led Cartwright to his fullest and clearest exposition of the relationship between political society and religion. He denounced those who pretended to attack blasphemy and sedition when their real target was Reform, and insisted that the 'Rights of Man and of Nature' were not granted by men but were the free gift of God to everyone. But, while he insisted that the constitution should be thus founded on religious principles, he rejected any concept of an alliance between church and state. True religion was too spiritual, divine and sacred to profane it in this way.[7]

Such religious arguments were, however, uncharacteristic of parliamentary reformers as a whole. Old Dissenters, like Capel Lofft, continued the

---

[4] J. Cartwright, *A Bill of Rights and Liberties* (London, 1817), pp. v, xiii and *Address to the Electors of Westminister* (London, 1819), p. 1. These religious arguments are neglected in N. C. Miller's otherwise sound 'John Cartwright and Radical Parliamentary Reform 1808–1819', *EHR*, 83 (1968), 705–28.

[5] A copy of this, now in the British Library, is inscribed '24 Nov 1821. From John Cartwright to Jeremy Bentham'. On Cartwright's respect for Bentham, see J. Cartwright, *Bill of Rights and Liberties*, and *A Defence, Delivered at Warwick . . . 1820* (London, 1831), p. 31.

[6] J. Cartwright, *Declaration of Principles* (London, [1821]), p. 2.

[7] J. Cartwright, *The English Constitution Produced and Illustrated* (London, 1823), pp. 50–5, 92, 96, 388–91.

stance of the earlier generation, but the main thrust of the new men was secular.[8] Henry Hunt's religious beliefs were similar to those of Cartwright, but he did not use religious arguments in his case for reform. The 1,700 pages of his memoirs included only half a dozen or so incidental references to religion, none being of any great consequence.[9] The argument of the infidel reformers, like Carlile, led many conservative Christians to invoke religion in their condemnations of parliamentary reform in a general way, but they advanced no specific theological arguments.[10] Occasionally reformers would take them to task for this, on Christian grounds.

The most powerful of these counterblasts was Joseph Brayshaw's *Remarks on the Character and Conduct of . . . Parliament* (1819), which vigorously attacked those Members of Parliament who had defended the Peterloo magistrates. Brayshaw insisted that Christianity was favourable to the principles of liberty and that it was the borough-mongers, who oppressed and plundered the poor, whom God would reject. The teaching of many ministers of the church on this theme was, he argued, at variance with the true spirit of Christianity; only an infidel would draw men away from the divine end of Reform.[11] A more comprehensive condemnation of corrupt clergymen came in John Wade's *Black Book* of 1820. In this he described Christ as 'the great Radical Reformer of Israel – waging fearless war with the bloated hypocrites, who, under the mask of religion and holiness, devoured in idleness the rewards of virtuous industry'. This work's bitter attack on the corruptions of the Anglican church, on tithes, bishops, pluralities, non-residence, and on Erastian establishment confirmed the fears of many that radical reform in the state would presage a reform of the church which would damage both vested interests and the alliance of church and state.[12] Most churchmen opposed reform, but advanced no religious arguments to support their opposition; a few reformers argued that the right to vote was God-given, but most adopted secular arguments.

Catholic emancipation to 1828

Was the argument any more religious in tone when the issue was the

---

[8] C. Lofft, *On the Revival of the Cause of Reform . . .* (London, 1809).

[9] H. Hunt, *Memoirs of . . .*, 3 vols. (London, 1820–2), vol. 1, pp. 51–2, 95–9, 189–92, 316–23, 388–9, 515, vol. 3, pp. 206–7. But compare Hunt, *To the Radical Reformers . . .*, 2 vols. (1 July 1820–14 October 1822), when, in the 11 March 1822 issue, pp. 14–16, he attacked Carlile's irreligion, adding, 'I abhor priestcraft as much as the great Reformer, Christ, did . . . I believe the great mass of the Reformers are religious, but I hope they are neither bigoted nor under the influence of priestcraft.' But most of the reformers, like Hunt, used secular arguments. Hunt's radical career is discussed, in properly secular terms, by J. C. Belchem, 'Henry Hunt and the Evolution of the Mass Platform', *EHR*, 93 (1978), 739–73.

[10] Whitaker, *Substance of a Speech*, pp. 3–8; Firth, *Remarks on State Trials*, p. 87; Otter, *Education of the Poor*, pp. 1–2.

[11] J. Brayshaw, *Remarks . . . 1819*, pp. 14, 16, 20, 39–40.

[12] *The Black Book; or Corruption Unmasked!*, 2 vols. (London, 1820), vol. 1, p. 274.

exclusion from public office of certain citizens because of their religious beliefs, or had discussion of the reform of the constitution in the church also been secularised? The issue of Catholic emancipation between 1804 and 1828 can be examined in two relatively distinct arenas: first, that of pragmatic politics; secondly, that of ideological and theological debate. The former has received, rightly, the lion's share of attention. George III's conviction that to agree to emancipation would be to deny his coronation oath led to the fall of Pitt's administration in January 1801 and of the Ministry of All the Talents in March 1807. In so far as the differences of view on the question by leading politicians were based on principle, it was on the legal principle of the Coronation Oath and the Act of Settlement, not the normative principle of the natural right of religious liberty.[13]

But essentially the disagreement was over different perceptions of what was expedient, both in England and Ireland. G. I. T. Machin asserts that 'the catholic emancipation question was essentially a part of the Irish problem', and Owen Chadwick observes that 'the bill passed . . . because the government expected civil war in Ireland if it refused to concede the Roman Catholic claims'.[14] Machin and Gash have set the issue firmly in the political context of the 1820s which, in fact, largely determined its outcome. This chapter will add nothing of real significance to their findings in this arena.

The great flood of controversial literature on both sides which poured out throughout this period has been relatively neglected, and with good cause. It is largely arid, uninspired, tedious and repetitious. The arguments advanced seem largely unconnected with the eventual decision to grant emancipation. But those arguments, limited as they were, need to be re-interpreted in the light of the thesis advanced above of a change of emphasis from political philosophy to social theory, both because they will illuminate that thesis, and because their rejection was made easier by that change in the predominant argument.

The intellectual battle-lines had been drawn up long before and, for the main Catholic and Protestant protagonists, changed little in this period. The disputes between John Lingard and Shute Barrington in 1806–8, between J. C. Eustace and George Pretyman-Tomline in 1812 and between William Cobbett, Robert Southey and Charles Butler in 1824–5 differed only superficially.[15] Despite the greater attention paid to the last of these because

[13] See above, pp. 122–3.
[14] G. I. T. Machin, *The Catholic Question in English Politics 1820–1830* (Oxford, 1964), p. 1; Owen Chadwick, *The Victorian Church*, vol. 1, second edition (London, 1970), p. 8.
[15] S. Barrington, *The Grounds on Which the Church of England Separated from the Church of Rome, Stated in a Charge . . . 1806* (London, 1807); J. Lingard, *Remarks on a Charge* (London, 1807). See also S. Barrington, *Vigilance . . .* (London, 1813); Chinnici, *English Catholic Enlightenment*, pp. 16–27; Pretyman-Tomline, *Charge* (1809, 1812), pp. 5–7 for the 1809 Charge, pp. 9–27 for the 1812 Charge; Eustace, *Answer to the Charge*; W. Cobbett, *A History of the Protestant*

of the public interest in 1825, the sensational and provocative style of debate and the national prominence of the protagonists, perhaps the Eustace–Tomline debate best reflected the typical exchanges.

In his 1809 *Charge*, which he published in 1812, Bishop Pretyman-Tomline insisted that Catholicism was a system not only of religion, but also of politics. He told the Catholics they were excluded from positions of power and trust because they held opinions incompatible with the safety of the constitution in church and state. They did this, he argued, by definition because Protestantism was an essential part of the British constitution, one of its fundamental laws. While Catholics could serve in the army and navy, where they had only to obey laws, they could not serve in parliament where laws were made, for there their hostility to the church establishment could be dangerous. The demands of church and state were so closely intertwined they could not be separated. The London Catholic priest, J. C. Eustace, who answered the bishop took a mildly liberal stance both in ecclesiology and politics. Catholics, he argued, considered that their religion, like the gospel on which it was founded, was adapted to all governments, especially those based on freedom and justice. Catholics were not seeking power as a body, but rights as individuals. They respected the pope but were not ruled by him:

We acknowledge in the Sovereign all the power over our persons, our properties, and all our temporal concerns, which the laws of the land give him; we swear *allegiance* to him exclusively, and we are willing to defend his constitutional prerogative at the expense of our fortunes and our lives.[16]

In an important article on the debate concerning Catholic emancipation in the 1820s, Geoffrey Best has argued that the strength of the Protestant case has been underestimated by historians. He challenges Halévy's view that the ideas of the Protestant die-hards were threadbare, and points out that the opponents of emancipation included Southey, Coleridge, Wordsworth, Sadler, Inglis, Newman, Keble and Blomfield. He suggests that many of them were lovers of toleration and religious liberty and genuinely feared that Roman ascendancy would threaten it. The Protestant theory of the constitution, he argues, insisted 'on the inseparableness of religious and secular concerns, in the mind and life of the individual as in politics and

---

'*Reformation*' (London, 1824); R. Southey, *The Book of the Church*, 2 vols. (London, 1824); C. Butler, *The Book of the Roman Catholic Church* (London, 1825). See also Sheridan Gilley, 'Nationality and Liberty, Protestant and Catholic: Robert Southey's Book of the Church', *SCH*, 18 (1982), 409–32; on Lingard's influence on Butler's reply, see Gilley, 'John Lingard and the Catholic Revival', *SCH*, 14 (1977), 313–27; on the 1825 debate in general, see G. I. T. Machin, 'The Catholic Emancipation Crisis of 1825', *EHR*, 306 (1963), 458–82.

16 Pretyman-Tomline, *Charge* (1809, 1812), pp. 11–17, 21–6; Eustace, *Answer to the Charge*, pp. 13–17, 29.

political theory', but the Acts of 1828 and 1829 went a long way to blow this theory out of the constitution.[17] This last and crucial point is surely correct, and Best's assertion of the good faith of the Protestant champions and their own genuine belief in their arguments cannot seriously be doubted. But in another sense Halévy *was* right in regarding these arguments as threadbare. When one considers them in the intellectual context of the movement of religious argument from the constitutional to the social sphere, they were outdated and largely irrelevant to the new spirit of debate which had developed since 1793.

In the 1790s the arguments for and against Catholic emancipation had remained somewhat old-fashioned, and had continued to look at the Catholic problem in terms of political theory, developing the social theme only slowly. The reason for this was clear. Catholicism met all the establishment requirements as far as social theory was concerned. It applied sanctions and restraints, and the theology of Purgatory and the practice of auricular confession made these even more effective than Anglican ones. Moreover, Catholic schools were probably more efficient in 'training-up children in the way that they should go' than those of any other denomination. Those who hated, feared and attacked Catholics found the social argument a useless weapon. However, as long as they could keep alive memories of Elizabethan Jesuits and of St Robert Bellarmine's doctrine of popular sovereignty, and continue to retail the falsehoods concerning the pope's supposed ability to depose monarchs and free Catholics from oaths made to heretics, then Catholicism could be made to appear to undermine the concept of political obligation. Some still believed the political argument was a useful stick to beat Catholics with, and Catholics still felt the need to protest their loyalty and deny the calumnies. Most of the shots fired in this battle between 1804 and 1828 repeated the old arguments, and, as the years passed, they had less and less relevance to the political and social situation in England or in Ireland which dominated ministerial thinking on the issue.[18]

In 1805 Richard Watson had already adopted a position which it took some of his co-religionists nearly a quarter of a century to reach. He agreed

---

[17] G. F. A. Best, 'The Protestant Constitution and its Supporters, 1800–1829', *TRHS*, fifth series, 8 (1958), 105–27 (pp. 107, 121). See also E. R. Norman, *English Catholic Church* (Oxford, 1984), pp. 29–68, esp. pp. 30–2.

[18] Characteristic of the anti-Catholic arguments in this period were: J. Fisher, *A Charge Delivered to the Clergy . . . of Exeter* (Exeter, 1805); G. Sharp, *Extract of a Letter on . . . Catholic Emancipation* (London, 1805); R. Churton, *The Reality of the Powder Plot Vindicated* (Oxford, 1806); T. Dampier, *A Charge Delivered to the Clergy . . . of Rochester* (London, 1807); S. Barrington, *A Charge to the Clergy . . . of Durham* (London, 1807); *Declaration and Protestation of the Roman Catholics of England* (London, 1812), a malicious reprint intended to embarrass; Barrington, *Vigilance*; Firth, *A Letter to the . . . Bishop of Norwich*; J. Ivimey, *The Supremacy of the Pope* (London, 1819); and M. Horne, *Moral and Political Crisis*. For Catholic defences see Lord Robert Petre, *Reflections on the Policy and Justice of . . . Emancipation* (London, 1804); J.

that there were circumstances in which a religious group should be excluded from political power, but insisted that the Catholics in England, and indeed in Ireland, in 1805, did not constitute such a threat. If there had still been a Catholic Stuart Pretender to the throne the case would have been different, but, as things were, he believed a few Catholic MPs and Peers would make little difference to the state, while the granting of Catholic emancipation would have considerable political and social advantages. Christopher Wyvill reiterated the theme and stressed the fact that emancipation would lead to political peace and social harmony. The stability of society would be enhanced, not threatened, by greater toleration and rights.[19]

On the whole, however, it was secular politicians rather than churchmen who advanced the social argument on empirical and pragmatic grounds. In 1819 Lord Grey, in an Emancipation debate, was looking at the question not from a theological point of view, but from that of public order when he suggested that the differences between Catholic and Protestant doctrines were slight.[20] Henry Phillpotts, then a parish clergyman in the Diocese of Durham, could answer him only in theological terms.[21] The socio-political case was, however, best expressed by George Canning in a speech on 21 April 1825 on the Catholic Relief Bill. First he defined the point at issue precisely: the matter was 'a practical political question' – was the creed of Catholics incompatible with their duties as good citizens? Having effectively confined his discussion strictly to the social argument, he advanced his case. He noted that Catholics emphasised the importance of human actions and asked,

... are those who lay so much stress on works, likely to be worse or better subjects than those who believe that good works are of no value, but that faith alone is all in all? I presume not to decide which is the more orthodox opinion; but for a good subject of the state, whose safety I am to provide for, I, for my part, would unquestionably prefer the man who insists on the necessity of good works as part of his religious creed, to him who considers himself controlled in all his actions by a preordained and inexorable necessity; and who, providing he believes implicitly, thinks himself irresponsible for his actions.[22]

Berington and J. Kirk, *The Faith of Catholics* (London, 1813); C. Butler, *An Address to the Protestants* (London, 1813); F. Plowden, *Human Subordination* (Paris, 1824).

[19] R. Watson, *A Charge Delivered to the Clergy . . . of Llandaff . . . June 1805* (London, 1808), pp. 10–12, 17–20, 22, 33, 35, 37, 40–1; C. Wyvill, *Extended Discussion, Apology for Liberty of Conscience, and Papers and Letters*. Such views from Anglicans were rare, but for an episcopal one see H. Bathurst, *A Charge Delivered to the Clergy . . . of Norwich* (Norwich, 1806), pp. 8–9, 11.

[20] *Parl. Deb.*, vol. 60, cols. 414–33.

[21] *A Letter to the Right Honourable Earl Grey* (Durham, 1819).

[22] *The Speeches of the Right Honourable George Canning*, 6 vols. (London, 1828), vol. 5, pp. 386–423 (pp. 394–5).

The major clerical responses to Canning were delayed and predictable. Charles Daubeny fell back on the theological differences which Canning had declined to discuss and, quoting Perceval, accused Canning of suggesting that one religion was as good as another and the Reformation merely a measure of political convenience.[23] Henry Phillpotts attacked Canning's argument on both theological and political grounds in 1827.[24] He repeated the old calumnies and the now outdated constitutional arguments; in the words of a critic, 'Clericus', he 'raked' together 'the polemical rubbish of former ages of bigotry and ignorance'.[25] But he also made some attempt to meet Canning's social argument. Catholics regarded the practice of auricular confession as a means of control and order, but Phillpotts alleged that, on a matter of security, a priest could absolve a man of a sin in which he himself had been an accomplice, including even murder, rebellion and treason.[26] The argument, of course, was not new, and had been repeated many times in the previous decade. In 1820, for example, Smith Hall sent to Lord Liverpool, whom he knew to favour Catholic emancipation, a copy of a broadsheet he had had printed of John Bull's *Thoughts on Catholic Emancipation*. This argued that '. . . the grand engine which destroys all morality, root and branch, amongst the lower orders; is the knowledge that they can get absolution, and finally escape the punishment of Hell, as they think, for every crime'.[27]

But this highly contentious point was the only real challenge which the defenders of the Protestant constitution had to the new social arguments. Predominantly they concentrated on the constitutional case, and no one put this better than William van Mildert in the House of Lords in 1825. In an attempt to re-establish the eighteenth-century doctrine of the alliance of church and state, which had been radically amended by Burke and by Coleridge, he returned to an argument of Samuel Horsley in the 1790s. He drew a distinction between the pope's Power of Order, the spiritual power to ordain priests, and his Power of Jurisdiction. The latter, which extended to the entire government of the ecclesiastical body, was, he argued, a spiritual power which could be exercised only by the state, or by the church and state in alliance. But his use of Horsley's argument is instructive. Van Mildert's case was based upon a pedantic and inflexible interpretation of this distinction; Horsley had argued that this theoretical problem should not be allowed to sour relations, and considered a Catholic promise to defend the constitution in the church as an adequate basis for religious toleration.

[23] Charles Daubeny, *A Letter to the Right Honourable George Canning* (London, 1827).
[24] H. Phillpotts, *A Short Letter to the Right Honourable George Canning*, fourth edition (London, 1827), and *A Letter to the Right Honourable George Canning on the Bill of 1825* (London, 1827).
[25] Clericus, *An Answer to Two Letters Addressed to . . . George Canning . . .* (London, 1828), p. 1.
[26] Phillpotts, *Letter to Canning*, pp. 143, 145–6.
[27] BL, Add. MS 38,283, ff. 307–10.

While Horsley insisted that the days of St Robert Bellarmine were long past and his argument no longer relevant, van Mildert quoted him at length, even providing the Latin text in a footnote to the published version of his speech.[28]

Geoffrey Best is, of course, right to insist that the Protestant arguments were sincerely advanced, and that many Protestants genuinely feared the effects of emancipation. But, intellectually, the arguments used were those of a past generation which paid little or no heed to the changed circumstances and parameters of debate. Canning, in restricting his discussion to the social area of argument, was reflecting the way in which religious arguments had predominantly been used in political thought since the French Revolution. The clerical, constitutional argument, if not quite threadbare, was at least outmoded.

The reform of the constitution in church and state, 1828–1832

Not the least of the virtues of Jonathan Clark's *English Society* is his insistence that the Repeal of the Test and Corporation Acts in 1828, the passing of Catholic Emancipation in 1829 and the First Reform Act of 1832 should be seen as a unity, and that within this process of reform the most significant change was not Reform but Emancipation. The argument advanced in this chapter strongly supports both contentions. The attempt to place that process in the context of the changes identified in earlier chapters, however, challenges some of Clark's assertions, and suggests some significant changes of emphasis within the general thesis he advances.

Much of the work done in the last thirty years on the reform of the constitution has over-emphasised its secular nature; 1831–2 has been divorced from 1828 and 1829, and Repeal and Emancipation, when they were noticed much at all, were seen as part of that Liberal Toryism which preceded the Whig reforms. An over-concentration on working-class agitators in Lancashire and Yorkshire has led to the 1832 Reform Act being explained almost exclusively in terms of industrialisation and class-consciousness which, while meaningful and relevant to the secular values of late-twentieth-century society, distorts its full contemporary context.

Religion lay near the heart of the old constitution, established in the later seventeenth century and reformed in these four years. The Corporation Act of 1661, not repealed until 1828, insisted that all mayors and officials in

---

[28] Van Mildert, *Substance of a Speech*, pp. 8–10, 12–16; Horsley, *Speeches*, pp. 48–52. It is, of course, true that in 1791 Horsley had opposed Catholic emancipation, but the logic of his arguments suggests that in the changed circumstances of 1825 he would have taken a more sympathetic view than Van Mildert. See above, p. 166.

municipal corporations had to receive the sacrament of Holy Communion according to the rites of the Church of England, take oaths of Allegiance, Supremacy and Non-Resistance, and declare the Solemn League and Covenant invalid. The Test Act of 1673, not repealed until 1828, required all holders of civil or military office or places of trust under the crown to take the oaths of Allegiance and Supremacy, and receive the sacrament according to the Anglican rites. The Test Act of 1678, not repealed until 1829, required all Members of Parliament to take an oath of Abjuration, denying the doctrine of transubstantiation, the invocation of the Blessed Virgin Mary, and the sacrifice of the mass. As well as being excluded from both houses of parliament, Catholics in England were also effectively disenfranchised, as they could be required to take the oath of Supremacy before casting their vote.

While these acts remained on the statute books, an annual indemnity act was regularly passed which allowed Protestant Dissenters to hold office, but it did so only by assuming that they had failed to take the Test for ignorance, absence or unavoidable accident. It did not allow them to refuse to take the Test on grounds of conscience and still hold office. Therefore, as Lord John Russell pointed out in 1828, '. . . many dissenters refused to obtain by a fraud on the statute, honours and emoluments which the law declared they should not be able to obtain in any other way'.[29]

The Corporation Act of 1661 and the Test Act of 1673 were repealed in 1828; in 1829 the Test Act of 1678 was repealed and the oaths of Abjuration, Allegiance and Supremacy replaced by a new oath acceptable to Catholics. By 13 April 1829, when the Catholic Bill received royal assent, the Anglican monopoly was broken, at least in legal terms. Protestant Dissenters and Catholics could vote freely, become MPs, hold local and national office with only a very few restrictions on their civil and religious rights. All Christians now enjoyed virtually all of the political privileges hitherto reserved for members of the established church. This was a huge step forward, much greater than that which was to follow in 1832; if anything shattered the old order, it was, as Clark has convincingly argued, Emancipation rather than Reform. The issues of principle, justice and civil rights involved in the Repeal of the Test and Corporation Acts and the passing of Catholic emancipation, and the admission of all Christians to the political nation, were far more significant and clear cut than those in the First Reform Act's complex and limited re-adjustments of the parliamentary franchise and redistribution of seats.

However, the arguments employed in parliament in the debates on Repeal, Emancipation and Reform were not, in general, either arguments of

---

[29] Quoted in B. Ward, *The Eve of Catholic Emancipation*, 3 vols. (London, 1911–12), vol. 3, p. 215.

basic principles and rights, or religious arguments. They were, rather, secular and pragmatic. To understand the significance of this for the reform process and for the longer-term development of political and social theory, it is necessary to look at the discussions of each issue in turn.

Repeal

Unlike Emancipation and Reform, there had been relatively little public debate concerning the Corporation and Test Acts between 1790 and 1828, when they were repealed 'almost casually'.[30] Some argued that this silence implied that there was no great need of change, though, as Lord Nugent suggested to the House of Commons, such an argument could encourage agitation and would be 'a dangerous lesson for a government to teach a people'. The regular granting of an annual indemnity from the Acts to Protestant Dissenters had undermined any establishment case to retain them and, while a number of devices and delaying tactics were put forward, no substantive arguments either of a religious or of a political or social nature were advanced against Repeal in parliament in 1828.[31]

The importance of religion in establishing the grounds of political obligation, and whether or not that role was an exclusively Anglican one, received no attention. Some insisted that the right to hold office regardless of religious opinion was a God-given, natural right but, this apart, the arguments were exclusively secular in nature. Palmerston asserted that in all the internal dangers to England in the last thirty years it was impossible 'to trace the workings of theological opinions'; rather, disorders had arisen from purely political causes and were entirely unconnected with religious differences.

Lord John Russell rejoiced in the secular tone of the debate; he no longer had to combat the theological distinctions or subtleties which had been raised in the past when the question really concerned civil duties. Many Anglicans were seriously worried by the profanation of the Sacrament of the Eucharist in turning it into a political test. Russell stressed the advantages of the separation of religion and politics; theological dispute embittered and aggravated political issues, and politics profaned religious ones. England had changed dramatically, Russell argued, from the days when the Corporation and the Test Acts had been passed. Now, the dispute for power was no longer between Catholic, Lutheran and Calvinist, but between the supporters of despotism, representative monarchy, and democracy.[32]

---

[30] Chadwick, *Victorian Church*, vol. 1, p. 3; see also Manning, *Dissenting Deputies*, pp. 217–53.
[31] *Parl. Deb.*, vol. 59, cols. 712, 741. On the issue of expediency versus principle see R. W. Davis, 'The Strategy of Dissent in the Repeal Campaign, 1820–28', *JMH*, 38 (1966), 374–93 (pp. 374–6).
[32] *Parl. Deb.*, vol. 59, cols. 778, 1185, 687–8, 1483, 678.

Generally the advocates of Repeal depended more on arguments of expediency than those of principle.[33] But this pragmatic stress was not enough for some of the opponents of Repeal who reprobated any normative argument at all. In the Commons, Sir R. H. Inglis attacked the suggestion that the Acts were restrictions on the rights of man: 'the question of power is one of pure, unmixed expediency: no man has an abstract right to it'.[34] In the Lords, van Mildert said he could have supported Repeal more easily if the Dissenters and their supporters had not based their claims on abstract rights he could not possibly accept. Lord Eldon was virtually alone among the opponents of the Bill in rejecting the arguments of expediency for those of principle, when he insisted 'that the Church of England was not an establishment erected for mere purposes of convenience, but was essentially and inseparably a part of the state'.[35] Generally, however, the arguments on both sides were not based on high principles of political philosophy and theology; they were, rather, practical, pragmatic and expedient, and were concerned more with the stability of society than with the abstract rights of man or the theoretical justification of political obligation.

Emancipation

The Repeal of the Test and Corporation Acts in the spring of 1828 led to an explosion of pamphlets on the question of Catholic emancipation throughout the remainder of that year and on into the next. The issue aroused violent passions, but essentially these were the passions of intolerance, hatred and irrational fear. What was needed, if the movement for emancipation were to be resisted successfully, was to articulate new refinements of the anti-Catholic argument which were relevant to the changed political and intellectual climate, but no one succeeded in doing this convincingly. Bishop Lloyd of Oxford had promised Peel in 1825 an article on the political implications of Catholic doctrines, but this was never produced.[36] Instead, the old calumnies, fears and lies were paraded time and again. The question, it was alleged, was a political, not a religious one; the bloody history of religious strife was rehearsed and the benefits of Catholic exclusion in 1688 remembered; Catholics were under the control of a

---

[33] *Parl. Deb.*, vol. 59, cols. 125, 679. This is not to suggest the Whigs themselves were without religious principles. See G. F. A. Best, 'The Whigs and the Church Establishment in the Age of Grey and Holland', *Hist.*, 45 (1960), 103–18. But a distinction must be drawn between their deeper motives, and the arguments they employed in public debate. See the comments of Alderman Thompson and of John Smith, *Parl. Deb.*, vol. 59, cols. 306, 699.

[34] *Parl. Deb.*, vol. 59, cols. 710–11.

[35] *Parl. Deb.*, vol. 59, cols. 1492, 1499–1500.

[36] See William Baker, *Beyond Port and Prejudice: Charles Lloyd of Oxford, 1784–1829* (Orono, Maine, 1981), p. 113.

foreign prince, the pope, and their divided allegiance made true loyalty impossible; Catholics' oaths could not be trusted and the practice of auricular confession gave the priesthood a powerful hold and destroyed any true confidence; Rome had not changed at all.[37]

Catholics and their Protestant supporters largely countered these traditional attacks with traditional defences. The separateness of temporal and spiritual spheres were re-asserted, as was Catholic loyalty and support for free government. Some stress was given to the new situation; Catholics were shown to be better citizens than infidels, and the need to unite the nation was emphasised.[38] The effect of emancipation on social stability, especially in Ireland, was much considered. H. G. Knight argued that only when distinctions were removed would the priesthood come on to 'our side' and so effect a real change in the character of the people.[39] The Catholic Earl of Shrewsbury asserted that Catholics were loyal and trustworthy citizens, and then quoted the social argument of Edward Blount to the British Catholic Association in July 1827:

... the Roman Catholic religion has taught the miserable victims of English cupidity to submit to injustice and oppression, and to seek consolidation in the hope of a better world; it has been their only solace, and has effected what was beyond the reach of human power – it has kept them loyal: and let the modern reformist pause before he attempts to rob the poor Irish peasant of these pastors and this religion, lest he remove the only barrier between Ireland and despair.[40]

The Bishop of Gloucester, Christopher Bethell, in a charge delivered to his clergy in June and July 1828 came closest to providing an argument which reflected the changed intellectual climate. He sought, by adopting the arguments of social theory, to hold back the waves of the incoming tide:

[37] Sir Roger Gresley, *A Letter to the . . . Earl of Shrewsbury* (London, 1828); *The Religion of England Considered Politically . . .* (London, 1828); *The Influence of Opinions in the Exercise of Political Power* (London, 1828); *The Catholic Questions Discussed and Decided* (London, 1828); Philopolites, *Thoughts on the Roman Catholic Question* (London, 1828); Zeta, *A Full View of the Catholic Question* (London, 1828); Duke of Newcastle, *A Letter to . . . Lord Kenyon* (London, 1828); T. Burgess, *The Bishop of Salisbury's Letters to the Duke of Wellington . . .* (London, 1829); R. Warner, *Catholic Emancipation . . .* (London, 1829); D. M. Perceval, *Quietus Optabilissimus . . .* (London, 1829); *A Brief Warning against . . . 'Catholic Emancipation'* (London, 1829); Devonshire Freeholder, *The Catholic Question* (London, [1829?]); G. Townsend, *Obedience to the Laws of the Church of Rome . . .* (London, 1829).

[38] *Address to the Clergy of England and Ireland* (London, 1828); *Address to the Electors of the United Kingdom* (London, 1828); T. M. M'Donnell, *Substance of Speeches . . . of the British Catholic Association* (Birmingham, 1828); *The Catholic Question in 1828 . . .* (London, 1828); Irish Catholic, *A Letter to . . . Robert Peel . . .* (London, 1828); E. Stanley, *A Few Words in Favour of our Roman Catholic Brethren*, third edition (London, 1829).

[39] H. G. Knight, *Foreign and Domestic View of the Catholic Question*, fourth edition (London, 1828), pp. 34, 36–8.

[40] J. Talbot, Earl of Shrewsbury, *Reasons for Not Taking the Test . . .* (London, 1828), Introduction, pp. lxxxii–lxxxiii, Appendix I, pp. iv–v.

... religious notions are the only effective security for the subjects' orderly and virtuous behaviour, and for the peace and prosperity of the commonwealth. But this provision cannot be made without the intervention of an Established Church, recognised by the Laws and supported by the Government ... Hence, while the Church remains faithful to its engagements, and performs its spiritual duties in a way fitted to promote public peace, morality, good order, regard for the laws, and obedience to the higher powers, it maintains its claim to protection and encouragement, and to that constitutional pre-eminence which entitles it to respect, and invests it with authority.[41]

Bethell was repeating here, in essence, Horsley's argument of 1796, but his assertion that only the Church of England could enjoin stability, order and restraint was now unconvincing. The social argument was inadequate to justify the exclusion of Catholics from parliament, only a convincing version of the political argument could do that.

None was forthcoming. In 1828 and 1829 the only religious arguments parliament heard were the old ones whose lurid depiction of the papacy had long since been discredited outside of the context of millenarian fantasy. In the debate in May 1828 following Sir Francis Burdett's motion, these arguments were still being used by ministers; the speech of the solicitor general in reply to Burdett was a powerful and bitter rendition of the traditional anti-papist arguments. But in March 1829 when Peel bowed to the pressure of opinion in the Commons and of events in Ireland, those arguments came only from the back-benches. Front-bench speakers were anxious to distance themselves from anything which could appear as an argument from abstract principles. Such principles, associated as they were with the Jacobins, could have far-reaching implications if once they were admitted. Indeed, in the 1828 debate Colonel Davies, in an anti-Emancipation speech, implied that the argument for the motion was old-fashioned in its dangerous dependence on the concept of natural rights, for, if abstract right gave a title to political power, why were women excluded? Others, including Huskisson in the Commons and Lansdowne in the Lords, agreed that the only justification for excluding Catholics was expediency.[42]

In 1829, the front-bench stressed the expediency argument for all it was worth. Peel insisted that the government's adoption of Emancipation was based solely on expediency, not at all on principle. He knew that a majority in the House of Commons was prepared to support Emancipation on higher grounds, but insisted he would 'abstain from all discussions on the natural or social rights of man. I shall enter into no disquisition upon the theories of government. My argument will turn upon a practical view of the present

---

[41] C. Bethell, *A Charge* ... (Gloucester, 1828), pp. 27–8, 32.
[42] *Parl. Deb.*, vol. 60, cols. 420–4, 607, 663, 1134.

condition of affairs.'[43] Later in the debate, Palmerston reiterated the argument for expediency and many MPs were influenced by it.[44] The debate in the Lords was dominated by arguments of expediency over those of principle to such an extent that both the supporters and opponents of the measure invoked them.[45]

No one can doubt the sincerity of the anti-papist rhetoric which poured from back-bench speakers. Jonathan Clark has shown clearly how Lord Eldon and his ilk felt, and how much rested on their case. But their arguments were ineffective for two reasons. First, they failed to recognise present political realities in England and in Ireland, and this separated them from their own front-bench speakers. Secondly, they were intellectually out of date. The fashion for constitutional abstractions had gone, and the allegations about Catholicism had been discredited. Clark suggests that the argument against Emancipation was lost, perhaps needlessly, by Peel's betrayal; that the old regime was as strong in 1828 as it had ever been. But when those arguments are set in the context of the developments in political and social theory since the 1790s, it can be seen that the Anglican case was already much weakened. Peel's action needs to be set in a wider intellectual and political environment than that inhabited by Lord Eldon and his friends. While Clark shows very clearly how great a break Peel's 'ratting' was from the traditional values of the ruling class, his focus is in danger of distorting the fuller intellectual climate in which Peel operated. Eldon's view of the world took insufficient account of the changes of the last forty years for us to regard it as an adequate and representative guide. Catholic emancipation was granted not because the religious arguments for it defeated the religious arguments against it, but because sufficient men of power were convinced by the secular arguments of political necessity and advantage. Social and moral restraint, to which Catholics could effectively contribute, was regarded as more important than the political legitimacy and obligation conferred by an exclusive established church.

Reform

As many had warned, this adjustment to the constitutional position of the church was soon followed by a change in the constitution of the state. The church was widely regarded as being anti-Reform, but the position was rather more complex than this, largely valid, conclusion would suggest. Many believed that the reform of parliament was only a prelude to reform in

---

[43] *Parl. Deb.*, vol. 61, cols. 729–30. The speech is summarised in Norman Gash, *Mr Secretary Peel: The Life of Sir Robert Peel to 1830* (London, 1961), pp. 570–5.
[44] *Parl. Deb.*, vol. 61, cols. 1243–5. See also G. I. T. Machin, 'The Duke of Wellington and Catholic Emancipation', *JEH*, 14 (1963), 190–208.
[45] *Parl. Deb.*, vol. 62, col. 264.

the church, and those who feared such reform, particularly most of the bishops, opposed parliamentary reform.[46]

In the debate on the second reading of the 1831 Bill, which was rejected by the House of Lords, only one of the bishops spoke, although their support had been invited by both the supporters and the opponents of the measure. The Earl of Falmouth reminded them of the role which the bishops had played in 1688 in resisting James II and his attempted innovations, but the episcopal bench did not respond. However, twenty-one bishops voted against the Bill; only the Bishops of Chichester and Norwich supported it, though Bishop Blomfield of London later claimed he would have voted in favour if he had been able to attend the House.[47]

The second reading of the 1832 Bill, however, found the bishops more vocal and more evenly divided; twelve bishops, including the Archbishop of York, voted for the Bill and fifteen, including the Archbishop of Canterbury, voted against it.[48] Episcopal sermons and charges of 1830–2 were, on the whole, reticent on the question of Reform. Many referred to the reforming spirit in general, and the danger of a harmful reform of the church in particular, but most avoided any specific reference to parliamentary reform.[49] Bishop Law of Bath and Wells did issue a Pastoral Letter on 9 November 1831 explaining the reason for his vote against the 1831 Bill; he supported reform in general but disliked the details of the Bill.[50] In 1832 he voted for Reform.

The most out-spoken clerical voice against Reform in 1831 came not from the episcopal bench but from the prebendary stalls of Wells. W. B. Whitehead applied the social argument to the question and warned that reform could lead to 'social subversion and lawless rule'. The reforming spirit sought to give more power to the lower orders who lacked religious principles and who were the enemies of God and established society. Such reform in the state would lead to the destruction of the church, for those elements saw in the influence of religion the greatest barrier to the 'anti-social disorder' they sought to introduce. The church would have to be subverted before such men could destroy the state.[51]

---

[46] For the general perception that Dissent was pro-Reform and the Church of England anti, see Michael Brock, *The Great Reform Act* (London, 1973), pp. 199, 246–8. See also, J. R. M. Butler, *The Passing of the Great Reform Bill* (1914; new edition, London, 1964), pp. 250–2.

[47] *Parl. Deb.*, third series, vol. 8, cols. 74, 339–43; vol. 11, col. 864.

[48] *Parl. Deb.*, vol. 12, cols. 453–9.

[49] R. Gray, *A Charge . . . to the Clergy . . . of Bristol* (London, 1831); W. van Mildert, *A Charge to the Clergy . . . of Durham* (Oxford, 1831); J. Kaye, *A Charge to the Clergy of . . . Lincoln* (London, 1831); H. Marsh, *A Charge to the Clergy . . . of Peterborough* (London, 1831); G. H. Law, *Charge*, 1831; W. Howley, *A Charge . . .* (London, 1832); J. B. Sumner, *A Charge to the Clergy of . . . Chester* (London, 1832); H. Ryder, *A Charge to the Clergy of . . . Lichfield* (London, 1831).

[50] G. H. Law, *A Pastoral Letter . . .* (Wells, 1831).

[51] W. B. Whitehead, *The Dangers of the Church . . .* (Bath, 1831), pp. 13–15.

But such arguments were surprisingly rare. Anti-Reform the church might have been, but in general its opposition was a silent one. When the bishops did speak in the Lords in April 1832, their arguments were almost exclusively secular. Van Mildert argued that such a change would be prejudicial to the moral and religious interests of the people, because it would lead to further innovation which would destroy the established church.[52] Expediency was only hinted at by the Bishop of Durham, but his episcopal colleagues openly embraced it. The Bishop of Lincoln temporised; London's support for the Bill rested on its expediency not its principle; Exeter's opposition was supported by political not religious arguments; Llandaff argued that Reform in England was necessary and for reasons of expediency urged support; Gloucester denied the self-interest of the church, but opposed the Bill, on political not theological grounds. While the Bishop of Rochester attacked those who supported the Bill on grounds of expediency, he advanced no principled, religious arguments against it.[53]

The contrast with the constitutional changes of 1689 is very striking. Many of the changes of the 'Glorious Revolution' were, of course, the result of expedience, just as much as those between 1828 and 1832, especially those forced by the premature flight of James II. But in 1689 it was considered important to clothe that expediency with the principled arguments of religion; by 1828–32 naked expediency was no longer considered shocking. In 1689 the support of the Church of England was considered essential to any successful constitutional settlement and therefore a religious justification of the changes was necessary. By 1828–32 the gap between church and state, between religious and secular, had widened significantly. The church had largely abandoned the exposition of a theologically based political philosophy and was devoting itself to social theory.

The influence of Paley and the Christian utilitarians ensured that secular arguments of expedience were then acceptable to many churchmen in the discussion of political questions, as the bishops' speeches in the House of Lords in April 1832 showed. The reforms of 1828–32 were seen in essentially constitutional not social terms, but the religious arguments of political principle and obligation which related to constitutional issues were becoming atrophied. The church, in fact, had nothing theological or philosophical to say about the changes which were being made. The new emphasis on social theory, on sanction, restraint, order and control, did not seem appropriate to the legal and constitutional terms of the discussion. The area of debate in which the church adopted a vital, vigorous, energetic stance had changed; the new emphasis was on the social role of the clergy, on pastoral and educational activity within the parish. Religion, of course,

[52] *Parl. Deb.*, third series, vol. 12, cols. 49–50.
[53] *Parl. Deb.*, third series, vol. 12, cols. 244, 267–71, 271–87, 287, 365, 403–8, 400.

remained a powerful influence on politicians and on the policies they followed, as Richard Brent has shown in his work on the Whigs in the 1830s, but theology no longer dominated the debate on constitutional theory.[54]

---

[54] R. Brent, *Liberal Anglican Politics: Whiggery, Religion and Reform 1830–1841* (Oxford, 1987).

Conclusion

The chronological boundaries of this book are largely arbitrary ones. It is not implied that there were seams in Clio's garment either in 1760 or in 1832. The changes that took place were significant, but gradual. The social arguments of the 1830s would have shocked no one in the 1760s, although the need to reiterate them so frequently, stridently and almost exclusively would have suggested a lack of confidence in the stability of society. The religious grounds of political obligation as advanced in 1760 would have been denied in the 1830s only by the most radical, although even to conservatives pragmatic or utilitarian arguments would have seemed safer than those based on abstract principles.

Yet something momentous had happened. Coleridge, in 1816, asserted that 'the *epoch-forming* Revolutions of the Christian world, the revolutions of religion, and with them the civil, social and domestic habits of the nations concerned, have coincided with the rise and fall of metaphysical systems'.[1] Somewhat less portentously, J. G. A. Pocock suggests that the history of political thought 'might be defined as a history of change in the employment of paradigms';[2] and, one might add, of change in the agenda of debate. Certainly, both the agenda and the paradigms most frequently used in 1832 were significantly different from those employed in 1760. Whether they can be regarded as belonging to a different metaphysical system is another question.

Changing paradigms and agenda

The agenda of debate established for abstract political discussion between about 1679 and 1719 defined a set of paradigms which continued to be employed until the 1790s. Then a new agenda arose and a new set of paradigms emerged which lasted well beyond 1832. The French Revolution was a crucial agent of change and its importance must not be under-

[1] 'Statesman's Manual', *Works*, vol. 6, pp. 14–15. See above, p. 1.
[2] *Politics, Language and Time*, p. 23.

estimated, but the new direction was, in fact, a dramatic intensification and acceleration of trends which had been prefigured in the 1780s. In a more profound sense too, both the development in political debate and the French Revolution itself were part of a change in 'the ascendancy of speculative principles, and the scheme or mode of thinking in vogue'.[3] The use made of religious arguments in political thought was near the centre of these changes, for between 1760 and 1832 both the agenda of abstract political debate and the paradigms employed underwent a crucial process of secularisation.

That process was a highly complex one. In England it was profoundly complicated by the fact that the establishment of the Church of England was regarded by many as an integral part of the constitution – the 'Constitution in Church and State'. While there was almost universal agreement amongst Christians that religious duty obliged them to obey the established constitution in the state, non-Anglicans did not consider that that obligation extended to the constitution in the church as well. To most Anglicans, the movements to change the constitution in the church by the repeal of the Test and Corporation Acts and the granting of Catholic emancipation seemed part of the secularisation process. However, as the Catholic distinction between the spiritual *source* of royal authority and the civil *nature* of that jurisdiction made clear, these changes were not, in themselves, necessarily secularising.[4] Secularisation concerned not the areas and issues covered by constitutional law, but the nature of the arguments used to sustain and enforce the settlement. To the extent that the church opposed reform in 1832, it did so essentially on secular grounds. By then any other kind of argument would have been ineffectual, as were the Protestant arguments in 1829, because of the change in agenda and paradigms which had taken place since 1760.

In 1760, the central issues of abstract political debate were those of the origins of government and society, of political obligation and the right of rebellion. There was a range of positions both within the Anglican church and outside it, but both the supporters of providential divine right and the advocates of contract theory and popular sovereignty employed arguments based on God-given rights, either of the monarchy or of the people.[5] At least in abstract terms, the concept of government and political society could still be regarded as theocentric, although the realities of the practice of politics made this position difficult to sustain. By 1832 most men saw politics as an autonomous secular activity. Political obligation rested, not on a divinely

---

[3] Coleridge, 'Statesman's Manual', *Works*, vol. 6, p. 14.
[4] See above, p. 26.
[5] It was for this reason that Josiah Tucker argued there was little difference between Jacobites and Republicans, *Treatise*, pp. 81–3.

imposed duty, but on a humanly perceived utility. The theoretical debate established by Locke and Filmer, which still divided Christians in the first three decades of George III's reign, was no longer actively discussed. Even as late as 1790, the 1689 settlement was regarded as a paradigm against which any constitutional adjustments were measured, but in 1828–32 the sacerdotal foundations of the Revolution Settlement were disturbed with no serious debate of the theological principles at issue.

Burke's proscription of abstract theoretical argument in the face of radical assertions of the rights of man was of crucial importance. It crystallised an existing trend into almost an adamantine principle, and essentially it excluded religious arguments from constitutional debate. Constitutional issues were no longer to be discussed in terms of the political authority which established legitimate political obligation. Both the rights of a people to rebel and change the form of the government, and the legitimate source of sovereignty were removed from the agenda of discussion.

Instead, the pragmatic and empirical dominated debate, and issues were to be determined by human reason and judgment with no need to dress up those decisions in the finery of theological legitimation. To that extent at least, Burkean prescription and Paleyite utility were fairly happy bed-fellows. The French Revolution gave rise not only to a fear of anarchy and disorder, but also to a fear of abstract argument. But that was itself only part of a more general movement away from the theoretical towards the empirical, in which human judgment of what was expedient was considered justification enough for a constitutional settlement. The concept of rights was largely abandoned; constitutional reforms came for reasons of political expediency, social reforms for utilitarian or humanitarian ones.

But religious arguments did not disappear from political thought. The age-old theme of religion as a form of restraint and a sanction on social behaviour now came to the fore. Burke placed a whole new emphasis on the concept of society, which he saw in organic terms. The idea that religion established morality which influenced manners and so sustained public order was an old one, as was the justification of the social hierarchy as providentially imposed. The concept of the interdependence of rich and poor played a role both in the development of capitalist economics and of Christian social theory. The Enlightenment concepts of benevolence and self-interest led Christian thinkers more and more to emphasise the theology of the human will, to the extent that one bishop defined the rule of government itself as 'the subdued Will of man'.[6] The church's role was to establish that subjugation which made effective government possible and the clergy had a crucial social function to perform. Increasing numbers of

---

[6] J. Randolph, *Sermon*, 1800, p. 8.

clergy left the desks on which they had written pamphlets on political philosophy and instead took their places on the magisterial bench. The new paradigms were reflected in the adoption of new policies. While the penal laws against Catholics and Unitarians and the Test and Corporation Acts were repealed, Curates Acts, Church Building Acts and Education Acts were passed.

The dual images of clerical schoolmaster and clerical magistrate were potent ones. They seemed to make the church more closely wedded to the established order than before, but the appearance of change was largely a misleading one. Despite rising tensions, growing constitutional debates and social unrest, from 1760 at least until 1782 and in some ways until 1793, society seemed to most clergy sufficiently stable to allow them to indulge safely in abstract political debate. However, as the challenge to the established order emerged, so the position which the clergy enjoyed in that establishment became clearer. *Philosophes* in France and radicals in England increasingly argued that Christianity had to be destroyed to clear the way for political change. The process of polarisation which followed, however regrettable, seems almost inevitable given the constitutional position of the established church. Blasphemy and sedition were seen as two sides of the same coin, and church and state appeared to many to be joined in a repressive alliance. The strand of radical Christians passing from the Coleridge of 1795, through Cartwright, Burgh and men like Mills, Brayshaw and Hone, on to the Christian Chartists and the Christian Socialists seemed a very thin one.

Most non-Anglican Christians also stressed the religious foundations of social order and vied with the established church to found schools to teach subordination. They continued to attack the tithe system, whereby public financial support for religion went entirely to the established church in a country in which religious pluralism was becoming more and more apparent. Slowly but inevitably the question of establishment was emerging as a real issue to be debated. Even some Anglicans questioned the advantages of establishment; Richard Whately considered its Erastian nature was incompatible with the spiritual constitution of the church, although he suggested that even a disestablished Church of England should continue to be the sole recipient of tithes.[7] But few Anglicans shared his doubts and it was no surprise that the church establishment survived the reform of the constitution in the church in 1828–9. However, the change in the role of religious arguments in political thought, away from political philosophy towards social theory, seriously weakened the case for establishment. When the religious arguments had been used to provide a theoretical and political

---

[7] *Letters on the Church by an Episcopalian* (London, 1826).

justification of the existing constitution in church and state, only Anglicans could employ them to the full. In 1832, however, religious arguments were being used mostly to stress hierarchy, order, restraint, sanctions and control, and these were themes in which Christians of all denominations could join. Indeed, some might claim to teach those doctrines more effectively than the established (and tithe-supported) clergy. The Education Act of 1833, passed by the Whig government, effectively recognised this by sharing the £20,000 it devoted to the education of the children of the poor between the National and the British and Foreign School Societies. Richard Brent has shown that 'practical religious toleration . . . was the chief cause of the liberal Anglican Whigs' in the 1830s and argues that 'the nineteenth century Liberal Party established a form of non-sectarian Christian polity following the repeal of the Test and Corporation Acts and Catholic Emancipation'.[8]

The changes which had taken place in the use of religious arguments in political thought meant that the perceived political and social functions of the church changed as well. But how well equipped was the Church of England to meet the new challenge and to fulfil the role it had assigned to itself?

The social function of the church

The need to relate the theoretical concerns of this book to clerical practice in the early nineteenth century has been largely obviated by Anthony Russell's admirable study of *The Clerical Profession*. In this he suggests that the period from about 1790 to the 1830s was a transitional one in a number of ways. Socially it was a time of change and dislocation both in the countryside and in the towns, which gave rise to a genuine fear of disorder, especially in the crisis years of 1795–6, 1800–1, 1810–13, and 1816–18. Accordingly, the clergy were required to play a more active role than hitherto by sitting on the magistrates' bench in greater numbers. At the same time the social status of the clergy was changing. They were becoming more wealthy and were more readily welcomed by the gentry as allies; indeed, they were fast becoming country gentlemen themselves. They were still fulfilling a variety of lay roles, as almoner, officer of law and order, medical adviser, schoolmaster and civil servant. Later, many of these functions were taken over by new professionals, the poor-law administrator, political agent, teacher, registrar, doctor, policeman and even sanitary engineer. At the same time the clergy were themselves professionalised, and came to concentrate more exclusively on their sacerdotal functions.

The days when the clergy could effectively carry out their traditional role

---

[8] Brent, *Liberal Anglican Politics*, pp. 299–300.

in the maintenance of order and control were numbered. The Church of England was based on landed wealth and organised on the basis of the rural parish. Not only was it ill equipped to meet the growing urban challenge organisationally, but Russell suggests that there was also an intellectual problem. Most of the ethical teaching of the Bible and the church, he points out, concerned personal relationships, and was more relevant in guiding men's behaviour in the face-to-face encounters of family life and the village community than in the impersonal role relationships of more advanced social systems. By the end of the eighteenth century, he argues, the traditional means by which the clergy communicated values and norms were seen to be inadequate. Having largely abandoned their political and constitutional role, the clergy were stressing their social function, and to fulfil it many turned to the magisterial bench. But that role soon proved counter-productive, and after 1830 the number of clerical magistrates fell. For all the emphasis on restraint, order and social control in the theoretical literature of the day, Russell's study must make us doubt how effectively those aspirations could be put into practice.[9]

If the clergy's social role were to disappear, as their political one had done, they would have to concentrate exclusively on their spiritual functions as ministers of the gospel, and some men were already drawing a distinction between the clergy's civil and their spiritual role. To a certain extent, Coleridge employed this distinction in his categorisation of the National Church and the Church of Christ. His work, *On the Constitution of the Church and State* (1829), can be seen as an attempt to re-establish the constitutional position of the church after religious argument had moved away from the constitutional and philosophical to the social sphere. He ignored the Warburtonian argument of an alliance, but suggested that a state (in the greater sense) should consist of the church and the state (in the lesser sense). The purpose of the National Church would be to provide a National Clerisy, an educated elite who could transmit values, standards and norms of behaviour. Their aim would be

to form and train up the people of the country to be obedient, free, useful, organisable subjects, citizens and patriots, living to the benefit of the state, and prepared to die for its defence. The proper *object* and end of the National Church is civilization with freedom, and the duty of its ministers . . . would be fulfilled in the communication of that degree and kind of knowledge to all, the possession of which is necessary for all in order to their Civility.[10]

The National Church and Clerisy were separate, in organisational terms, from the Church of Christ, which was a spiritual, not a temporal body, and

---

[9] Russell, *Clerical Profession*, pp. 32–41, 146–8, 149–67.
[10] Coleridge, 'On the Constitution of the Church and State', *Works*, vol. 10, p. 54.

which had no visible, earthly head. However, Coleridge expected the National Church to be Christian, and for theology to be an important element in its teaching. It should be supported by the tithes and endowments of the ages. He implied that these could be somewhat more widely shared than at present, but was insistent that they should not be extended to support the clergy of any church which accepted a foreign head, or enforced celibacy on its clergy. This, he argued, prevented them from becoming full members of the community by intermarriage with the gentry. Otherwise, he suggested that the National Church need not be exclusively Anglican, though it must be trinitarian. Thus he accepted that the social control and order function of the church was not something exclusive to Anglican theology. John Colmer's recent edition of the *Constitution* brings out very clearly its complex nature and relation to a wide variety of influences. To these a further point may be added: it was also a reaction to and a reflection of the fact that the church had moved from formally constitutional to more social arguments when considering the political value of religion and religious arguments.

Coleridge made clear his dislike of urbanisation and industrialisation, and his concept of the Clerisy is, in many ways, best suited to a rural church. But English society was rapidly changing and, if the church was to carry out the socio-political task it set itself and so justify itself in secular terms, drastic changes were necessary. There were, of course, men in the church well aware of the need for reform to meet the developing urban problems and to counter the advances made by the Protestant Dissenters and by the Catholics. However, despite the efforts of Bishop Blomfield and others, the necessary administrative reforms were in the event largely forced on the Church of England by secular politicians, most notably Sir Robert Peel. It would, of course, be wrong to depict the Whig reforms of the established church in the 1830s as designed merely to make the Church of England a more effective agent of social control. Many clergy and laymen alike saw that reform was necessary if the church were to fulfil its pastoral and sacramental responsibilites in the new cities. But the fact remains that the social role which the church had been stressing with increasing emphasis since 1793 could be played out only if new churches were built, new parishes and dioceses created, more clergy were resident, curates were paid a reasonable stipend, and, most fundamentally, the financial resources of the church were reorganised to meet the needs of a church in an industrial society.

Parliament's concern had been established in Curates Acts in 1795 and 1813 and in the Church Building Acts of 1818 and 1824, long before the setting up of the Ecclesiastical Commission in 1835; and Bishop Law's charges to the Diocese of Chester showed an awareness of the urban challenge over a decade before those of Bishop Blomfield of London. But many in the church resisted change, not only out of vested interest but also, in some cases, in reaction to the secular advances of parliament and out of a deep unease with the Erastian nature of the church.

Generally in the early Victorian period, the dominant image of the church was that of a reactionary body opposed to change. The spirit of the clerical magistrates lived on in men like the Rev. Francis Close, evangelical incumbent of St Mary's Cheltenham Spa from 1826 to 1856, who bitterly attacked the radicals and called for passive obedience.[11] Tithes remained a thorn in the flesh, and many of the demands of the Swing rioters were directed against them.[12] But there were radical Christians too, both rich and poor; the educated and clerical Christian Socialists of the late 1840s and early 1850s were preceded by working-class Christian Chartists, even in Cheltenham Spa.[13] The Chartists sought constitutional ends, but the new social emphasis of the church meant that most clergy looked away from the struggle for political power toward social policies. Some radical Christian sensibilities were shown over the Poor Law Amendment Act in 1834.[14] A much wider political spectrum of Christian thinkers supported Education Acts which provided state financial support for the Church and Dissenting Schools Societies. Also the movement for the reform of working conditions in the new factories had considerable support from those moved by specifically Christian principles.[15] Richard Brent's work on *Liberal Anglican Politics* in the 1830s shows a considerable Christian influence in the practical politics of reform, but little abstract, philosophical discussion of the political theology of an exclusive established church on questions of legitimacy and political obligation. Ian Bradley has shown the considerable effect of Evangelical thought on Victorian social attitudes, but makes fewer references to political attitudes and almost none to political theory.[16] It is significant that the major work on the political attitude of Anglican bishops in the first half of the nineteenth century concentrates on social policies and not constitutional and political philosophy.[17] The distaste for theory and preference for empirical thought affected all areas of society. The seventeenth-century concern with the science of the cosmos had been replaced by a preoccupation with practical engineering and invention; the discussion of

---

[11] Owen Ashton, 'Clerical Control and Radical Responses in Cheltenham Spa 1838–1848', *Midland History*, 8 (1983), 121–47.

[12] E. Hobsbawm and G. Rudé, *Captain Swing* (London, 1969; Harmondsworth, 1973), pp. 121–30.

[13] Eileen Yeo, 'Christianity in Chartist Struggle 1832–1842', *PP*, 91 (1981), 109–39; Ashton, 'Clerical Control'.

[14] Yeo, 'Christianity in Chartist Struggle', p. 111.

[15] J. C. Gill, *The Ten Hours Parson: Christian Social Action in the Eighteen Thirties* (London, 1959).

[16] I. Bradley, *The Call to Seriousness: The Evangelical Impact on the Victorians* (London, 1976).

[17] Soloway, *Prelates and People*.

constitutional theory by that of political and social practice; and much expansive theological speculation with detailed textual criticism and, later, the development both of muscular Christianity and of the social gospel.

'The Rise and Fall of Metaphysical Systems'

But was Coleridge right in thinking that all this amounted to a new metaphysical system, a different mode of thinking? In terms of the actual practice of political behaviour little may seem to have altered, but the theoretical justification of their actions which men saw fit to employ underwent a very radical change indeed in this period.

This book has examined the use of religious arguments in political thought and has defined the term 'religious argument' as 'an argument which consciously depended for its effectiveness on a belief in God and an acceptance of the authority of the scriptures or the church' as opposed to a secular argument 'which either did not make any reference to God at all, or did so only in a cosmetic way' when 'the structure of the argument remained intact whether or not one believed in His existence'.[18] The adoption of these definitions has meant that any movement from a dependence on revealed religion to one on natural religion, from a deontological to a utilitarian stance, has been characterised as secularisation.

In this period constitutional argument became increasingly secular. The empirical and pragmatic replaced the theoretical and speculative, and by 1832 the process of secularisation in constitutional thought was effectively complete. In that sphere the battle between the adherents of revealed religion and those of natural religion was over, and the constitutional changes of 1828–32 were justified on grounds of expediency. Paley's utilitarianism played a crucial role in this process and influenced many men's entire way of thinking and arguing on political and social questions. But Paley had many opponents and the supporters of revealed religion and a theocentric society had retreated from the constitutional battlefield only to fight the war elsewhere, on the more profound issues of the nature of man and human society.

The polarities are easy to establish, though most men lived uneasily between them. On one side was the belief that the purpose of life was to worship God and to prepare for death, the acceptance of the doctrine of original sin and the depravity of man and a stress on the need for good works and for faith in God's grace and Christ's atoning sacrifice. On the other side was a belief that the purpose of life was human happiness, as defined by Lockean sensational epistemology; for some, though not for all, this was

---

[18] See above, p. 7.

combined with a belief in the perfectibility of man, but even those who did not go that far considered that the pursuit of human happiness through utilitarian standards would result in an improved society, and they subscribed to the doctrine of progress. If the latter views were to become dominant society would inevitably become more secular, more materialistic and more dominated by human will.

These new secular attitudes led some churchmen away from the traditional belief in absolute values to a new statement of moral relativism. Priestley argued that different circumstances taught different men different moral principles. All were acceptable, none universal. Josiah Tucker regarded all political principles as partial, relative and changeable. Paley's utilitarianism gave a systematic form to this moral relativism and confirmed politics as an autonomous secular activity. This view had many opponents, but none expressed himself more perspicaciously than the Rev. D. Anderson, master of Swansea Grammar School, in 1819 when he denounced both the moral relativism and the narrow epistemological base on which it rested. Men were seeking of moral and religious truths 'a kind and degree of evidence wholly inconsistent with their natures'. The result, he implied, was moral anomie and social disorder. Ten years earlier, Coleridge had questioned whether the price of 'enlightenment' was too great, if, to discard the foolishness of beliefs in omens and ghosts, men also had to lose their faith in divine providence and eternal life.[19]

Another Christian poet, of more recent years, observed that

> Footfalls echo in the memory
> Down the passage which we did not take
> Towards the door we never opened
> Into the rose-garden.[20]

Normally it is unprofitable and delusory for the historian to consider what might have been. But there is also a danger of his being blinded by hindsight to the other possibilities and aspirations of an age. That danger is even greater when the path which was pursued is commonly regarded as the correct route to 'progress', the logical and proper development on which the fundamental presuppositions of his own culture and learning rest.

William van Mildert was one of the staunchest opponents both of Catholic emancipation and of the reform of parliament and disliked the reform of the church by the secular government. It would be easy to dismiss him as a bigoted and blinkered reactionary, although his personal generosity and good faith were never in question. But, while we may dissent from his conclusions, we should seek to understand his reasoning.

[19] Anderson, *Sermon*, p. 5; Coleridge, 'The Friend', *Works*, vol. 4, pp. 44–6.
[20] T. S. Eliot, 'Four Quartets', *Collected Poems 1909–1962* (London, 1963), p. 189.

When he wrote his 1831 charge to the clergy in his Diocese of Durham, at the height of the Reform Bill controversy, he saw dangers all around; 'Infidelity and Atheism on one side; Popery advancing in this direction, Socinianism in that; Dissent, Lukewarmness, Apathy, each with multitudes in its train.'[21] He stressed his support for a voluntary reform of the church, both concerning pluralities and non-residence, and re-endowment. But he bitterly opposed any Erastian and coercive reform by the state. As the 66-year-old bishop looked back on the progress of secularisation during his lifetime, and on the changing role of religious arguments in political and social thought, he reflected with sadness.

The main root of the evil lies in a want of sound, sober, and practical *religious* feeling, operating steadily throughout the community, and influencing the conduct in all the various departments of social life. The want of this is discernible in attempts to carry on the work of *popular education* without taking *Religion* for its basis; in the systematic and avowed separation of *civil* and *political* from *Christian* obligations; in the disposition to consider all truths, on whatever *sacred authority* they may rest, as matters of mere *human opinion*; and in a persuasion that the whole concern of human government, of legislation, and of social order, may be conducted as if there were no Moral Ruler of the Universe controlling the destinies of men or of nations; no other responsibilities than those which subsist between man and man, unamenable to any higher tribunal.[22]

[21] Van Mildert, *Charge*, 1831, pp. 15–16.
[22] *Ibid.*, pp. 43–4.

Bibliographical appendix

This study relates to literature in the four main areas of ecclesiastical, intellectual, political and social history.[1]

The classic works on the Church of England in the eighteenth century remain those of Norman Sykes which, rightly, did much to rehabilitate the Hanoverian church after the criticisms of earlier writers such as C. J. Abbey and J. H. Overton.[2] But Sykes's sympathy with the latitudinarian and Erastian strains in the church led him to concentrate, intellectually, upon men like Hoadley and Watson, and on Warburton's theory of the alliance of church and state. Like many ecclesiastical historians, his interests were more constitutional, ecclesiological and pastoral than metaphysical and theoretical. This is true even of a man of the breadth of vision and understanding of G. F. A. Best, who has provided the definitive account of church–state relations from the eighteenth to the twentieth century, and much else along the way.[3] Sykes paid only limited attention to the last decade of the century; unfortunately, the best study of the Church of England in the 1790s, by Nancy Murray, remains unpublished.[4] Murray also neglects theoretical arguments, but analyses the various parties in the church and the ideological and theological differences between them. She examines the high-church Hackney Phalanx, the orthodox bishops, the liberal Latitudinarians, and the Evangelicals. All these groups in the Church of England have had their historians, but the Evangelical movement has grabbed the lion's share of attention. A host of monographs, theses and articles examines the

---

[1] For convenience, full details of books are given even when they have appeared earlier in footnotes to the main text.

[2] *Church and State in England in the XVIIIth Century* (Cambridge, 1934); *From Sheldon to Secker: Aspects of English Church History, 1660–1768* (Cambridge, 1959).

[3] *Temporal Pillars: Queen Anne's Bounty, the Ecclesiastical Commissioners, and the Church of England* (Cambridge, 1964).

[4] N. U. Murray, 'The Influence of the French Revolution on the Church of England and its Rivals, 1789–1802' (unpublished D.Phil. dissertation, University of Oxford, 1975). The parties in the early nineteenth century are surveyed in Kenneth Thompson, *Bureaucracy and Church Reform* (Oxford, 1970), pp. 26–55.

evangelical phenomenon from almost every angle.[5] This concentration of attention is warranted by the movement's general importance, but not by its intellectual contribution to theoretical argument.

The Catholic community has been well served by its historians. While the older generation, men such as Edwin Burton and Bernard Ward, tended somewhat to the pietistic, their work was detailed and careful. More recent studies, like those of John Bossy, Eamon Duffy and Sheridan Gilley, represent the best of modern scholarship. But Catholic political and social theory has been neglected.[6] The same is largely true of Methodist thought, despite the great concentration of attention upon the political and social effects of the movement.[7] That debate, which has distorted the general study of Methodism, is now receding and coming to be placed in its proper perspective.[8] What Eamon Duffy has done for the study of Catholics, David Hempton is doing for the Methodists and J. E. Bradley for the Old Dissenters.[9] But Bradley concentrates upon the Dissenters' links with political parties and electoral politics; again the theoretical application of religious ideas to political and social issues is neglected. Studies of the Dissenting denominations, such as Olin Robinson's work on the Baptists, reflect the same preoccupations.[10] The political thought of both Dissenters and Catholics was much influenced by the campaigns for toleration and civil rights. Both the main studies of these, by Barlow and Henriques, deal to some extent with the underlying theory, but generally more attention has been paid to the parliamentary struggle, especially in the writings of G. M. Ditchfield and G. I. T. Machin.[11] The growth of unitarian thought, especially within English

[5] See, *inter alia*, V. Kiernan, 'Evangelicalism and the French Revolution', *PP*, 1 (1952), 44–56; E. M. Howse, *Saints in Politics: The 'Clapham Sect' and the Growth of Freedom* (London, 1953); F. K. Brown, *Fathers of the Victorians: The Age of Wilberforce* (Cambridge, 1961); Ian Bradley, 'The Politics of Godliness: Evangelicals in Parliament, 1784–1832' (unpublished D.Phil. dissertation, University of Oxford, 1974); Deryck Lovegrove, 'English Evangelical Dissent and the European Conflict 1789–1815', *SCH*, 20 (1983), 263–76; R. H. Martin, *Evangelicals United: Ecumenical Stirrings in Pre-Victorian Britain 1795–1830*, Studies in Evangelicalism, 4 (London, 1983); D. Rosman, *Evangelicals and Culture* (London, 1984).

[6] See the works of Burton, Ward, Bossy, Duffy and Gilley cited in the bibliography below. Eamon Duffy, 'Joseph Berington and the English Cisalpine Movement 1772–1803' (unpublished Ph.D. dissertation, University of Cambridge, 1973) includes some discussion of Berington's thought.

[7] See above, Chapter 1, notes 30 and 31.

[8] David Hempton, *Methodism and Politics in British Society, 1750–1850* (London, 1984).

[9] J. E. Bradley, 'Whigs and Nonconformists: Presbyterians, Congregationalists and Baptists in English Politics, 1718–1790' (unpublished Ph.D. dissertation, University of Southern California, 1978); 'Whigs and Nonconformists: "Slumbering Radicalism" in English Politics, 1739–89', *ECS*, 9 (1975), 1–27; 'Religion and Reform at the Polls: Nonconformity in Cambridge Politics, 1774–1784', *JBS*, 23 (1984), 55–78.

[10] O. C. Robison, 'Particular Baptists in England, 1760–1820' (unpublished D.Phil. dissertation, University of Oxford, 1967).

[11] R. B. Barlow, *Citizenship and Conscience: A Study in the Theory and Practice of Religious Toleration in England during the Eighteenth Century* (Philadelphia, 1962); U. R. Q. Henriques, *Religious Toleration in England, 1789–1833* (London, 1961). See the works by Ditchfield and Machin cited in the bibliography below. Although concerned with an earlier period, Mary Fulbrook, 'Legitimation Crises and the Early Modern State – the Politics of Religious Toleration', in

Presbyterianism, has been much discussed and a sound context established for the study of the Arian Richard Price, and the Socinian Joseph Priestley.[12] Their ideas have been studied in more theoretical terms, but have not been examined in the context of the thought of other Christian denominations as is attempted in this study.

Alan Gilbert's survey of all the Christian churches in this period takes a critical, non-denominational stance.[13] It is sociologically and statistically based, but largely neglects ideas. The same author's wide-ranging work on secularisation inevitably takes more notice of theory, but the sociological analysis in which the ideas are set becomes the dominant preoccupation of the book. Owen Chadwick's Gifford Lectures in 1973–4 were more philosophically centred, but they range over much of nineteenth-century European thought and pay relatively little attention to the area covered in this book.[14] The relation between secularisation and the growth of atheism is a complex one on which too little work has yet been done. Edward Royle has explored the connexion between atheist views and radical politics.[15] The idea that the destruction of Christianity was a pre-requisite of political and social change was perhaps less an intellectual conclusion, as Royle suggests, and more a response to the political stance of reactionary clergy. The atheist views Royle examines need to be considered alongside those of the minority of Christians who adopted radical positions themselves.

Intellectual histories of the period usually look upon religious views in a negative way. The classic work on English intellectual history in the eighteenth century remains that of Sir Leslie Stephen who, in the view of his biographer, brought an evangelical fervour to the spirit of agnosticism.[16] His work is a paradigm statement of the Whig view of the triumph of rationalism. This approach is reflected in most recent studies of eighteenth-century philosophy

---

Religion and Society in Early Modern Europe, 1500–1800, edited by Kaspar von Greyerz (London, 1984), pp. 146–56, has important insights into the problem in general.

[12] A. Lincoln, *Some Political and Social Ideas of English Dissent 1763–1800* (1938, reprinted New York, 1971), concentrates mostly on Unitarian thinkers, as does I. Kramnick, 'Religion and Radicalism: English Political Theory in the Age of Revolution', *PT*, 5 (1977), 505–34. Ian Sellers, 'Social and Political Ideas of Representative English Unitarians, 1795–1850' (unpublished B.Litt. dissertation, University of Oxford, 1956), surveys the periodical literature. On Price and Priestley see above, Chapter 1, note 53.

[13] *Religion and Society in Industrial England: Church, Chapel and Social Change, 1740–1914* (London, 1976).

[14] A. D. Gilbert, *The Making of Post-Christian Britain: A History of the Secularization of Modern Society* (London, 1980); Owen Chadwick, *The Secularization of the European Mind in the Nineteenth Century* (Cambridge, 1975).

[15] E. Royle, *Radical Politics 1790–1900: Religion and Unbelief* (London, 1971); *Victorian Infidels: The Origins of the British Secularist Movement 1791–1866* (Manchester, 1974).

[16] L. Stephen, *History of English Thought in the Eighteenth Century*, 2 vols. (1876; third edition 1902; reprinted New York, 1949); Noel Annan, *Leslie Stephen: His Thought and Character in Relation to his Time* (London, 1951).

and in surveys of the religious thought of the period.[17] Caroline Robbins's view of the Dissenting contribution to the Commonwealthman tradition can, to an extent, be seen as part of this attitude.[18].

The influence on the eighteenth century of an aspect of classical and Renaissance thought is demonstrated by J. G. A. Pocock's work on civic humanism.[19] The juxtaposition of pagan and Christian resulted in highly intricate views and attitudes which cannot be unravelled in any clear fashion. The impact of ideas from America and from Enlightenment France need to be studied much more extensively. Sheridan Gilley has briefly indicated something of the complexity and ambiguity of the reaction of English Christians to the Enlightenment.[20] Many major questions still need to be asked about that reaction.

By contrast, the effect of the French Revolution has received widespread attention. The literature on this up to the late 1970s is well surveyed by Albert Goodwin in the bibliography to his valuable study of the radical movement in England.[21] The conservative reaction has been summarised by Robert Dozier, and discussed in a critical and stimulating way by Ian Christie in the Ford Lectures for 1984.[22] Christie shows a rare perception and understanding in his analysis of the role of the churches in the maintenance of order and the contribution of Christians to the intellectual repulse of revolution. Dickinson's survey of the effect of the French Revolution on British thought remains unsurpassed;[23] his relative neglect of the religious arguments, however, has not hitherto been fully redressed.

---

[17] *A Guide to the British Moralists*, edited by D. H. Monroe (London, 1972). The early part of the process is surveyed, not entirely satisfactorily, in J. Redwood, *Reason, Ridicule and Religion: The Age of Enlightenment in England 1660–1750* (London, 1976). More judicious are Roland Stromberg, *Religious Liberalism in Eighteenth-Century England* (London, 1954); Gerald Cragg, *Reason and Authority in the Eighteenth Century* (Cambridge, 1964); Jacob Viner, *The Role of Providence in the Social Order: An Essay in Intellectual History*, The Jayne Lectures for 1966 (Philadelphia, 1972); A. Cobban, *Edmund Burke and the Revolt against the Eighteenth Century: A Study of the Political and Social Thinking of Burke, Wordsworth, Coleridge and Southey* (London, 1929).

[18] C. Robbins, *The Eighteenth-Century Commonwealthman* (Cambridge, Massachusetts, 1959), esp. pp. 221–70. On an empirical level, this now needs to be read in the light of Bradley's work.

[19] J. G. A. Pocock, *The Machiavellian Moment: Florentine Political Thought and the Atlantic Republican Tradition* (Princeton, 1975).

[20] Bernard Bailyn, *The Ideological Origins of the American Revolution* (Cambridge, Massachusetts, 1967); C. C. Bonwick, 'An English Audience for American Revolutionary Pamphlets', *HJ*, 19 (1976), 355–74. The influence of the Enlightenment is discussed in a number of studies of individual thinkers, but there is no adequate work of synthesis: see Sheridan Gilley, 'Christianity and Enlightenment: An Historical Survey', *History of European Ideas*, 1 (1981), 103–21.

[21] *The Friends of Liberty: The English Democratic Movement in the Age of the French Revolution* (London, 1979).

[22] R. R. Dozier, *For King, Constitution, and Country: The English Loyalists and the French Revolution* (Lexington, 1983); Ian R. Christie, *Stress and Stability in Late-Eighteenth-Century Britain: Reflections on the British Avoidance of Revolution* (Oxford, 1984).

[23] H. T. Dickinson, *Liberty and Property: Political Ideology in Eighteenth-Century Britain* (London, 1977), pp. 232–318.

A mass of studies of the working class and radical movements in England has appeared recently. Edward Thompson's *Making of the English Working Class* is possibly as important for the response it has evoked, both imitative and inimical, as for its own considerable contribution.[24] Even after twenty years though, the bad parts of that particular curate's egg still reek. Its insights into the growth of working-class consciousness are invaluable, but its assessment of the role of religious concepts in that growth is too hostile to be sensitive to subtlety. As well as the acknowledged contribution which Dissent made to the parliamentary reform movements, Christians participated in other radical causes as well. J. E. Cookson examines Christians hostile to the war against France,[25] but generally the religious element in radical agitation has received much less attention than the activities of repressive clerical magistrates.[26] Works on riot and disturbances suggest that religious intolerance played only a limited role; these studies are most useful in establishing the public-order context of many establishment sermons.[27]

The other crucial context in which the concerns of this work must be placed is that of the economic and social change which accompanied the rise in population and the processes of industrialisation and urbanisation. The general works on this are too extensive and well known to be reviewed here. Articles by C. M. Elliot and R. J. Morris demonstrate well the different attitudes taken to the churches' response by a traditional and a radical scholar.[28] The work of twentieth-century sociologists on the concepts of social control has informed many studies of social history.[29] The close connexion between religion, morality, manners and social order was recognised in the eighteenth century and a number of works examine the movements for moral reform, but do not discuss the links between the social theory involved in them and political thought in

---

[24] (London, 1963; revised edition, Harmondsworth, 1968). The critique of Thompson's comments on religion in R. Currie and R. M. Hartwell, 'The Making of the English Working Class?', *Economic History Review*, second series, 18 (1965), 633–43, is still largely valid, despite Hempton's qualifications, *Methodism and Politics*, p. 75. Thompson does avoid, however, the crude insensitivity of John Foster, *Class Struggle and the Industrial Revolution; Early Industrial Capitalism in Three English Towns* (London, 1974).

[25] *The Friends of Peace: Anti-War Liberalism in England, 1793–1815* (Cambridge, 1982).

[26] Edward Royle and James Walvin, *English Radicals and Reformers 1760–1848* (Brighton, 1982); J. A. Hone, *For the Cause of Truth: Radicalism in London, 1796–1821* (Oxford, 1982).

[27] J. Stevenson, *Popular Disturbances in England 1700–1870* (London, 1979); George Rudé, *Paris and London in the Eighteenth Century* (London, 1974), *Wilkes and Liberty: A Social Study of 1763 to 1774* (Oxford, 1962); J. Bohstedt, *Riots and Community Politics in England and Wales 1790–1810* (Cambridge, Massachusetts, 1983); E. Hobsbawm and G. Rudé, *Captain Swing* (London, 1969).

[28] C. M. Elliot, 'The Political Economy of English Dissent, 1780–1840', in *The Industrial Revolution*, edited by R. M. Hartwell (Oxford, 1970), pp. 144–66; R. J. Morris, 'Voluntary Societies and British Urban Elites 1780–1850', *HJ*, 26 (1983), 95–118.

[29] E. A. Ross, *Social Control: A Survey of the Foundations of Order* (New York, 1901); Ross, *Social Control and the Foundation of Sociology*, edited by E. F. Borgatta and H. J. Meyer (Boston, 1959); P. A. Landis, *Social Control: Social Organisation and Disorganisation in Process*, revised edition (Chicago, 1956).

general.[30] Schools for the education of the children of the poor played an important role in this process of social control, but Thomas Laqueur has shown that their relationship with the working-class community was much more complex than this. He argues that, in many ways, Sunday Schools served to develop not to subvert proletarian culture, and that religion made a positive contribution to the progress of working-class radicalism.[31]

Religious attitudes to society in this period have received more attention than most of the other concerns of this book. R. A. Soloway's work on episcopal social thought in England between 1783 and 1852 analyses the changes in attitude to a wide range of social issues.[32] He concentrates largely upon attitudes to social problems and social policies, but this necessarily involves some discussion of social theory as well. Harold Perkin's examination of English society from 1780 to 1880,[33] which appeared in the same year as Soloway's study, is more a work of social analysis. It includes an attempt to relate eighteenth- and nineteenth-century religious attitudes to Perkin's own model of a three-class society, but does not seek to understand the theories of society Christians held at the time.

W. R. Ward's *Religion and Society 1790–1850* demonstrates the invaluable insights which come from the proper combination of empathy and critical judgment. He examines the impact of the French Revolution on the churches and relates social, political and religious attitudes with considerable subtlety. His work concentrates largely upon the Methodists and the Old Dissenters, and needs to be supplemented by George Kitson Clark's comments on the social views of churchmen and by Anthony Russell's sociologically based study of the professionalisation of the Anglican clergy in the same period. Kitson Clark examines the effect of the French Revolution on the concept of the alliance of church and state in Britain and on Anglican perception of men's social duties. Like Ward, Russell is well aware of the potential of religion in the process of social control. He sees the social alliance of squire and parson, typified by the clerical magistrate, as a critical factor in alienating the working class from the established church, just as Ward claims Methodist attitudes to Peterloo 'for ever severed official Methodism from urban revivalism'.[34]

[30] M. J. Quinlan, *Victorian Prelude: A History of English Manners 1700–1830* (1941; reprinted London, 1965); E. J. Bristow, *Vice and Vigilance: Purity Movements in Britain since 1700* (Dublin, 1977); F. K. Brown, *Fathers of the Victorians*.

[31] T. W. Laqueur, *Religion and Respectability: Sunday Schools and Working Class Culture, 1780–1850* (New Haven, 1976). The contributions by Richard Johnson and Jennifer Hart to *Social Control in Nineteenth Century Britain*, edited by A. P. Donajgrodzki (London, 1977), while valuable in themselves, need to be looked at in the light of Laqueur's work.

[32] R. A. Soloway, *Prelates and People: Ecclesiastical Social Thought in England, 1783–1852* (London, 1969).

[33] *Origins of Modern English Society 1780–1880* (London, 1969), pp. 273–90, 347–64.

[34] W. R. Ward, *Religion and Society in England 1790–1850* (London, 1972), p. 93; G. Kitson Clark, *Churchmen and the Condition of England, 1832–1885: A Study in the Development of Social Ideas and Practice from the Old Regime to the Modern State* (London, 1973), pp. 24–55; A. J. Russell, *The Clerical Profession* (London, 1980).

Edward Norman's study of Anglican social teachings and attitudes from 1770 to 1970 is more problematic.[35] Its opening chapters consider many of the points discussed in this book and Norman's detailed comments on particular issues are often pertinent and valuable. But the pattern of development in Christian political and social ideas which can be clearly discerned between 1770 and 1830 does not emerge from his survey. Rather, a number of individually valid points are used to support his thesis that the social attitudes of the church derive from the surrounding intellectual and political culture and not from theological learning.[36] While this has some validity in relation to the period from 1770 to 1830, Norman sees it as a constant rather than a varying factor. It can be argued, however, that this period saw important developments in this process. Utilitarian ideas and the movement away from deontological thinking led some men, much more than they had before, to equate the will of God with those things which seemed to them to be just and right, while others strongly denounced this trend.

The degree of similarity between this book and Jonathan Clark's *English Society 1688–1832* should not be exaggerated. In *English Society* and in *Revolution and Rebellion*, Clark unfolds his Grand Design to re-interpret a great swathe of English history. In so wide-ranging and pioneering an undertaking, inevitably he sometimes paints in broad impressionistic strokes, and touches on issues only to leave them in an inchoate state. This book is, in part, a more detailed and concentrated study of one of Clark's themes, the role of theology in political theory, though it goes beyond his concentration on the ideology of the Establishment, the 'self-image of the state'. The evidence presented in this book does not provide a basis for a wide-ranging critique of Clark's whole thesis, such as that offered by Joanna Innes,[37] and it would be improper to attempt such here. What it does provide is the opportunity to refine, develop and contextualise one important strand of Clark's analysis, and to examine the implications of these processes for his broader argument.

In part, Clark's approach is historiographical. He distances himself from the 'orthodoxy' of the 1960s and outlines an alternative model of English society under the ancien regime, concentrating on those subjects which the 1960s had excluded from the agenda or relegated to a minor place – religion and politics, the monarchy, the church, and the social elite of aristocracy and gentry. Clark

---

[35] *Church and Society in England, 1770–1970* (Oxford, 1976), pp. 1–70.
[36] Compare the work done in the United States of America: Robert Bellah, 'Civil Religion in America', *Daedalus*, 96 (1967), 1–21; *American Civil Religion*, edited by R. E. Richey and D. G. Jones (New York, 1974), especially the essays by John Wilson, 'An Historian's approach to Civil Religion' pp. 115–38, and Herbert Richardson, 'Civil Religion in Theological Perspective', pp. 161–84; Cushing Strout, *The New Heavens and New Earth* (New York, 1974).
[37] Joanna Innes, 'Jonathan Clark, Social History and England's "Ancien Regime"', *PP*, 115 (May 1987), 165–200. Although Innes recognises that for Clark 'religion occupies the floodlit centre of the stage' (p. 165) her comments on his treatment of it add little illumination. For Clark's entertaining reply see, 'England's Ancien Regime', *PP*, 117 (November 1987), pp. 195–207.

demonstrates convincingly the very limited role which Lockean contractual thought played in eighteenth-century England, and he stresses throughout the great importance given to the concept of allegiance, and the binding nature of oaths sworn on the Bible. Men who had sworn an oath of allegiance to James II found it exceedingly difficult to accept William III as rightful monarch, and later, while accepting the Hanoverians as *de facto* kings, they continued to feel a duty of allegiance to the Stuart family. Jacobitism, Clark argues, was much more widespread, potent and long lived than often recognised. Allegiance was conceived in personal and in theological terms, and, when the natural duty of allegiance was re-enforced by a solemn oath, here was a powerful source of stability for a legitimate government. The values of ancien regime England were essentially religious values:

The salient fact for the social historian of eighteenth-century England is that Christian belief is initially almost universal ... a faith whose established Church taught obedience, humility and reverence to superiors with unanimity and consistency down the decades. A Christian faith and moral code was a common possession of all social strata: the realm of the communal ... was largely the realm of religion. Government, war, allegiance, law, capital punishment and the social hierarchy would be ultimately unintelligible to an historian of early-modern England who was unaware of the last three Articles of Religion of its established Church.[38]

This argument has much to commend it, and what has been established above about the religious basis of the concept of political obligation clearly supports it. However, what the present author has characterised as an equilibrium in the basic formula between the divinely imposed duty to obey government in general, and man's right to determine, and if necessary change, the form of that government, Clark sees as an equivocal fudge. Whether or not it should be regarded as such in intellectual terms (and, in truth, it does look like a characteristically Anglican 'compromise'), there was a real attempt to root it in the scriptural inconsistencies of the traditional Pauline and Petrine texts.[39] The vast majority of eighteenth-century men saw the two concepts as co-existing compatibly in some sort of creative tension, to the extent that the assertion of the formula incorporating both became a commonplace. The concept of allegiance, which Clark is correct to stress, must be seen within this context.

Because religion is only one of Clark's themes, or rather because it is subsidiary to his overriding desire to understand the ruling ideology in which one strand of religion, Establishment Protestantism, played a crucial role, it is seen from a somewhat distorting viewpoint. Established churchmen regarded Anglican attitudes as unique, and Clark does nothing to correct this impression. When their political and social views are placed in the context of the thought of other Christians, the unique element can be seen to be much more limited. Both

[38] *English Society*, p. 87.
[39] See above, p. 15.

the concepts of political obligation and social restraint were widely shared by Christians of all theological shades; the concept of a single established church, the Constitution in the Church, was the major unique element in Anglican theory and that was certainly a political, possibly an ecclesiological, but hardly a theological issue.

Indeed, Clark's use of the term 'theology' is a problematic one. He is fond of the phrase 'Political Theology', but he never defines precisely the theological element in Christian political ideology. Apart from a brief passage on unitarianism, the Atonement and clerical authority,[40] there is almost no serious discussion of theology as such. The assertions of the Thirty Seventh Article of Religion are repeatedly urged, but otherwise the dogmatic differences between Anglicans, Catholics and Dissenters are not debated. Clark's suggestion of a unique *theological* basis of Anglican political ideology needs to be considered in the light of the distinction made in Chapter 2 above between theology, ecclesiology and civil and religious rights.

This is important not only for our understanding of how unique the philosophy of the Church of England was, but also for our reading of Clark's view of 'radicalism' and dissent. This is particularly significant as it plays a crucial part in his Grand Design. The effective subversives, Clark argues, were not the class-conscious weavers seeking to reform the representative machinery, but those Dissenters intent on destroying the church establishment. In his response to Joanna Innes, Clark confirms, 'I had sought an account of the intellectual origins of "radical" ideas in other than nineteenth-century terms; finding a key in theology, I observed the considerable continuity of personnel between the different manifestations of reform in men who held heterodox theological opinions.'[41] But that is not to argue that those political views were rooted in theology, merely that they were coincident with certain theological views. If the adoption of those views led to a man's exclusion from all the privileges of establishment, then surely it is likely that the desire for reform in the Constitution of the Church arose out of a concern for civil and religious rights, rather than out of a theology. Indeed, this is why Emancipation was so important an issue.

Clark's neglect of Catholic thinkers is unfortunate, not because they were immensely influential, clearly they were not, but because they give the lie to some of his suggestions about the relationship of religion and politics. It may well be that some men were both religious 'heretics' and political 'subversives', but that does not establish a causal relationship (which Clark implies rather than demonstrates) between heresy and subversion. In terms of Christian doctrine no one could be more orthodox than the Catholics, and yet such were their political rights and their position in constitutional law that they sought to subvert the existing Constitution in the Church. Clark rightly stresses the great significance

---

[40] *English Society*, p. 281.
[41] 'England's Ancien Regime', pp. 204–5.

of Emancipation, without fully considering the political views of the religious community which was emancipated. He argues that 'Catholics made almost no contribution to radical ideology' and never refers to Berington and Geddes and mentions Bellarmine only in passing.[42] Moreover, on the continent, the same Catholic faith supported absolute monarchy. Fuller consideration of the Catholic position demonstrates quite clearly that there is no direct correlation between theology as such and politics.

Clark's thesis is consistent with, but not proved by, the major argument of this book that there was a change of emphasis from political obligation to social restraint around the 1790s, although it is not a theme he dwells on. His suggestion that 'in response to the French Revolution especially, assertions about monarchial *allegiance*, still forcefully raised by the American Revolution, gave way to a different emphasis derived from the same premises: what was now defended was monarchial *obedience*, social subordination'[43] is powerfully supported by the analysis offered above. He links this awareness of the social argument (which he does not choose to develop) with the question of radicalism. Consider the following passage from *English Society*: 'The agency of the state which confronted' people in their

everyday life was not Parliament, reaching out as a machinery of representative democracy: elections were infrequent, contests less frequent still, the franchise restricted, and access to MPs minimal for most electors. The ubiquitous agency of the State was the Church, quartering the land not into a few hundred constituencies but into ten thousand parishes, impinging on the daily concerns of the great majority, supporting its black-coated army of a clerical intelligentsia, bidding for a monopoly of education, piety and political acceptability. Consequently, the chief target for radical attack was not the representative machinery ... The radical critique was aimed mostly against what society saw as its fundamental political ideology: Trinitarian Christianity as interpreted by the Church of England. Consequently, the main impetus of attack was against the Church's established status, and against its official commitment to the key articles of its creed.[44]

This passage, which owes much to Burke's thoughts on the French *philosophes* and to later conspiracy theory in England, shows an acute recognition of the importance of religion in the maintenance of social order. The insertion of the adjective Trinitarian before Christianity, here and elsewhere, suggests a *theological* content. Certainly there were those unitarians, deists and atheists who sought to destroy the Christian religion along with the established form of government. But the relationship of theology and politics was contingent rather than causal. Moreover, as Clark argues so well elsewhere, these men were less significant in the process of change than those orthodox Christians who sought emancipation.

[42] *English Society*, pp. 282, 417.
[43] *Ibid.*, p. 234.
[44] *Ibid.*, pp. 277–8.

What destroyed the ancien regime in England, Clark argues, was 'not chiefly the widespread adoption of a democratic world view, but the advance of Dissent, Roman Catholicism and religious indifference'. Clark is right to insist that it was Emancipation, the defeat of the traditional Anglican arguments, the abandonment of the Protestant Constitution, and the effective destruction of the Union of Church and State in 1829, that 'provided the definition, and marked the dissolution of the ancien regime in England'.[45] But his suggestion that the ancien regime had weathered the storms of the 1790s and the post-war agitation of 1815–19, and was as stable in 1828 as it had ever been is true only in the most literal sense that the law had remained unchanged. If one considers that stability also depends upon the intellectual and political validity of the arguments which underpin a regime, then the changes of the 1790s had fatally undermined the case for an Anglican monopoly of state power. The transition from a political philosophy of obligation to a social theory of restraint in which all Christians shared, rendered the case for the Protestant Constitution intellectually invalid, and the situation in Ireland which arose from the Act of Union made Emancipation a necessity of practical politics. In his consideration of the Emancipation debates, Clark shows us, quite brilliantly, the view from Lord Eldon's window, but the Ultras were the heirs of a tradition whose time had passed several years before. The stress which Clark lays on Peel and Wellington's betrayal fails to take full-enough account of the change in emphasis of the 1790s and the secularisation and move away from deontology which was inherent in Paley's utilitarianism.

The arguments advanced in this book may require then some refinements and adjustments to that part of Clark's thesis which relates to religion and religious ideas. These in turn suggest some changes in his overall argument. But many crucial aspects of that Grand Design are neither confirmed nor refuted conclusively by the analysis offered here. There are still battles to be fought on secular fields. Clark sums up well the measure of the task which faces the historian when he points out that '. . . the problem is to explain real change without an unreal dynamic and an illusory teleology'.[46] He insists he does not have that privileged access to the past that some ideologies appear to provide. But nor is his work value free either, for if it were it would not be the product of a unique human being formed by nature, education and experience. We begin to understand the past rather as we come to see a figure on the stage when it is illuminated by lamps from many different angles, levels and directions. The same figure casts many different shadows. Some lights are brighter, but each one comes from a specific source. This present book makes no claim to be any more value free than others, but if the questions asked and the evidence understood by someone born and bred in Anglicanism and converted to Rome cast a slightly different light, then it may add a little to the general illumination.

---

[45] *Ibid.*, p. 354.
[46] 'England's Ancien Regime', p. 202, fn 25.

Bibliography

PRIMARY SOURCES

MANUSCRIPTS

Bodleian Library
Bodl., MS Eng. Misc., c 32
Bodl., MS Eng. Misc., d 156/1
Bodl., Montagu MS, d 13
Bodl., Montagu MS, d 21

British Library
BL, Add. MSS Eg. 2185–6
BL, Add. MS 22,130
BL, Add. MS 29,300
BL, Add. MSS 29,806–9
BL, Add. MS 33,542
BL, Add. MSS 34,585–6
BL, Add. MSS 36,458–9
BL, Add. MSS 37,949–50
BL, Add. MS 38,108
BL, Add. MS 38,283
BL, Add. MSS 38,301–2
BL, Add. MS 38,309
BL, Add. MSS 40,108–22
BL, Add. MS 41,694
BL, Add. MS 50,746
BL, Add. MS 50,788

Devon Record Office
City of Exeter Minute Book of Quarter Sessions 1819–29
City of Exeter Recognizance Book 1820 C3/78
Sidmouth Papers 152M Correspondence 1808–11

Lambeth Palace Library
LPL, MS 1767
LPL, MSS 2098–9
LPL, MS 2101
LPL, MSS 2103–5
LPL, MSS 2809–10

University College, London, D.S.M. Watson Library, Manuscript Room
Bentham Papers, Boxes 5 and 96
William Hone's Correspondents

PRINTED WORKS

An Account of the Society for Promoting Christian Knowledge (London, 1766)

Ackland, T., *Religion and Loyalty Recommended; and a Caution against Innovations* (London, 1798)

Address not yet signed, from the Bishops and Clergy of the Church of England to the Rev. Dr Priestley [1791]

An Address to the Clergy of England and Ireland on the Catholic Question by a Member of the Established Church (London, 1828)

An Address to the Electors of the United Kingdom, in Favour of the Catholic Claims by One of His Majesty's Justices of the Peace (London, 1828)

An Address to the Public from the Society for the Suppression of Vice (London, 1803)

The Age of Prophecy! or Further Testimony to the Mission of Richard Brothers, by a Convert (London, 1795)

The Alfred: West of England Journal and General Advertiser, 1820–31

Allott, R., *A Sermon Preached before the Honourable House of Commons . . . February 26th, 1806* (London, 1806)

The Analytical Review, 15 (January–May 1793)

Anderson, D., *A Sermon Preached at St Mary's Church, Swansea . . . October 27, 1819* (Swansea, [1819])

Andrewes, G., *A Sermon Preached before the Honourable House of Commons . . . 28th February 1810* (London, 1810)

Anti-Jacobin, *Jacobinism Displayed in a Address to the People of England* (Birmingham, 1798)

Antipas: A Solemn Appeal to the Right Reverend the Archbishops and Bishops . . . Concerning Blasphemy, Popery and Sorcery (London, 1821)

Anti-Romanus, *Look before You Leap; or, Caution Recommended in Deciding on the Claims of the Roman Catholics* (London, 1825)

An Appeal to the People of England, on the Subject of the French Revolution (London, 1794)

The Arminian Magazine, 1–10 (London, 1778–87)

Armitstead, T., *A Sermon Preached at the Cathedral Church in Chester . . . at the Spring Assize, 1798* (Chester, 1798)

Armstrong, A., and Sharp, A., *Very Familiar Letters Addressed to Mr John Nott* (Birmingham, 1790)

Association for Preserving Liberty and Property against Republicans and Levellers, *Association Papers* (London, 1793)

Atkinson, J., *Catholic Blinds for Protestant Eyes!* (London, 1829)

An Authentic Narrative of some Particular Occurrences Which have Lately Taken Place among a Denomination of Dissenters in the County of Devon (Plymouth, 1790)

Bagot, L., *A Serious Caution against the Dangerous Errors of the Anabaptists* (London, 1807)

A Sermon Preached before the Lords . . . January 30th 1783 (London, 1783)

Balguy, T., *A Charge Delivered to the Clergy of the Archdeaconry of Winchester, 1772* (London, 1772)

Barrington, S., *A Charge to the Clergy . . . of Durham at the Primary Visitation, 1792* (Bath, 1792)

A Charge to the Clergy of Durham . . . July 1801 (London, 1802)

A Charge to the Clergy of Durham . . . 1806 (London, 1807)

The Grounds on Which the Church of England Separated from the Church of Rome, Stated in a Charge . . . 1806 (London, 1807)

A Sermon Preached before the Lords . . . January 30 1772 (London, 1772)

Sermons, Charges and Tracts (London, 1811)

Vigilance . . . Recommended in Two Charges and a Letter to the Clergy of . . . Durham (London, 1813)

Barrow, W., *Pecuniary Contributions for the Diffusion of Religious Knowledge* (Nottingham, 1815)

A Sermon Preached in the Parish Church of St James, Westminster, March 7, 1798 (London, 1798)

Barruel, A. de, *Memoirs Illustrating the History of Jacobinism: A Translation* (London, 1797)

Bateman, T., *The Necessity and Advantage of Religious Principles in the Soldiery* (London, 1778)

Bates, G. F., *A Sermon Preached in the Cathedral Church of St Paul . . . the Eighth of June, 1817* (London, 1817)

Bathurst, Henry (Bishop of Norwich), *A Charge Delivered to the Clergy . . . of Norwich, at the Primary Visitation in 1806* (Norwich, 1806)

A Sermon Preached before the Honourable House of Commons . . . February 28, 1794 (London, 1794)

A Sermon Preached before the Lords . . . 30th January, 1808 (London, 1808)

A Sermon Preached in the Cathedral of St Paul . . . June 7, 1810 (London, 1810)

Bathurst, Henry (Archdeacon of Norwich), *Christianity and Present Politics* (London, 1818)

An Easter Offering for the Whigs (London, 1842)

Memoirs of the Late Dr Henry Bathurst, Lord Bishop of Norwich, 2 vols. (London, 1837)

[Bayley], *Speech of the Hon. Mr Justice Bayley in Passing Sentence on Richard Carlile* (London, 1819)

Beadon, R., *A Sermon Preached before the Lords . . . April 19, 1793* (London, 1793)

[Bean, J.], *A Charge Addressed to the Clergy of any Diocese in the Kingdom* (London, 1792)

Bell, A., *Extract of Sermon on the Education of the Poor . . . 28 June, 1807* (London, 1807)

[Benbow], *The Crimes of the Clergy, or the Pillars of Priest-Craft Shaken* (London, 1823)

Benson, C., *A Sermon Preached on Trinity Monday, May 26, 1826* (London, 1826)

Benson, J., *The Substance of a Sermon Preached on . . . the death of Mr Alexander Mather* (London, [1800])

Bentham, J., *Analysis of the Influence of Natural Religion on the Temporal Happiness of Mankind* (London, 1822)

The Church of England Catechism Examined, new edition (London, 1824)

Church of Englandism and its Catechism Examined (London, printed 1817, published 1818)

Deontology: or, The Science of Morality, 2 vols. (London, 1834)

An Introduction to the Principles of Morals and Legislation (1789), edited by J. H. Burns and H. L. A. Hart (London, 1970, 1982)

Mother Church Relieved by Bleeding (London, 1823)

Not Paul, But Jesus (London, 1823)

Remarks on a Charge . . . by the Lord Bishop of Lincoln . . 1794 (London, 1795)

[Bentham, J.], *The White Bull, An Oriental History from an Ancient Syrian Manuscript Communicated by Mr Voltaire* (London, 1774)

Berington, J., *An Address to the Protestant Dissenters Who Have Lately Petitioned for a Repeal of the Corporation and Test Acts* (Birmingham, 1787)

An Essay on the Depravity of the Nation (Birmingham, 1788)

The History of the Reign of Henry the Second and of Richard and John his Sons (Birmingham, 1790)

Letters on Materialism and Hartley's Theory of the Human Mind, Addressed to Dr Priestley (London, 1776)

The Memoirs of Gregorio Panzani . . . To Which are Added An Introduction and Supplement (Birmingham, 1793)

Reflections Addressed to the Rev. John Hawkins (Birmingham, 1785)

The Rights of Dissenters from the Established Church, in Relation, Principally, to English Catholics (Birmingham, 1789)

The State and Behaviour of English Catholics from the Reformation to the Year 1780 (London, 1780)

Berington, J., and J. Kirk, *The Faith of Catholics, Confirmed by Scripture and Attested by the Fathers of the Five First Centuries of the Church* (London, 1813)

Bethell, C., *A Charge Delivered at the Primary Visitation of the Diocese of Gloucester . . . 1825* (Gloucester, 1825)

A Charge Delivered at the Triennial Visitation of the Diocese of Gloucester . . . 1828 (Gloucester, 1828)

Beverley, R. M., *A Letter to his Grace the Archbishop of York on the Present Corrupt State of the Church of England* (Beverley, 1831)

Bicheno, J., *A Glance at the History of Christianity and of English Non-Conformity*, second edition (Newbury, 1798)

The Probable Progress and Issue of the Commotions Which Have Agitated Europe Since the French Revolution (London, 1797)

A Word in Season . . . Fast Day, February 25th, 1795 (London, 1795)

Bird, C., *A Sermon Preached at the Parish Church of Wakefield, July 4, 1816* (Wakefield, [1816])

A Sermon Preached at Wakefield, May 30, 1816 at the Visitation of the Rev. Archdeacon Markham (Wakefield, 1816)

Blakeway, J. B., *A Warning against Schism. A Sermon Preached . . on the 29th of May, 1799* (Shrewsbury, 1799)

Blomfield, C. J., *A Charge Delivered to the Clergy of the Archdeaconry of Colchester . . . May 1823* (London, 1823)

A Charge Delivered to the Clergy of the Diocese of Chester . . . 1825 (London, 1825)

A Charge Delivered to the Clergy of his Diocese . . . 1830 (London, 1830)

The Christian's Duty Towards Criminals: A Sermon Preached . . . June 22, 1828 (London, 1828)

The Importance of Learning to the Clergy: A Sermon Preached . . . July 1820 (Cambridge, 1820)

A Remonstrance Addressed to H. Brougham Esq. M.P. by One of the 'Working Clergy' (London, 1823)

The Responsibleness of Pastoral Office: A Sermon Preached . . . June 1, 1815 (London, 1815)

Bogue, D., *The Nature and Importance of a Good Education* (London, 1808)

On Universal Peace (London, 1819)

Reasons for Seeking a Repeal of the Corporation and Test Acts (London, 1790)

The Book of Common Prayer, and Administration of the Sacraments, and Other Rites and Ceremonies of the Church, According to the Use of the Church of England (Oxford, 1770)

[Boothby, B.], *A Letter to the Right Honourable Edmund Burke* (London, 1791)

Borradaile, W., *Idolatry the Prevailing Practice of the Church of Rome* (London, 1825)

Bousfield, B., *Observations on the Right Hon. Edmund Burke's Pamphlet on the Subject of the French Revolution* (London, 1791)

[Bowdler, J.], *Reform or Ruin: Take your Choice!*, second edition (1797)

Bowles, J., *The Dangers of Premature Peace* (London, 1795)

Dialogues on the Rights of Britons between a Farmer, a Sailor, and a Manufacturer (London, 1792)

A Letter Addressed to Samuel Whitbread, Esq. M.P. (London, 1807)

Objections to the Continuance of the War Examined and Refuted (London, 1793)

A Protest against T. Paine's 'Rights of Man' (London, 1792)

The Real Grounds of the Present War with France, second edition (London, 1793)

Reflections on the Political and Moral State of Society, at the Close of the Eighteenth Century (London, 1800)

Reflections Submitted to the Consideration of the Combined Powers (London, 1794)

The Retrospect (London, 1798)

Thoughts on the Origin and Formation of Political Constitutions (London, 1796)

Bradburn, S., *An Address to the People Called Methodists Concerning the Wickedness of Encouraging Slavery* (London, 1792)

Equality. A Sermon on 2 Cor. viii.14 (Bristol, [1794])

Methodism Set Forth and Defended (Bristol, [1792])

The Question, Are the Methodists Dissenters? Fairly Examined (Bristol, [1793])

Bradshaw, T., *The Slave Trade Inconsistent with Reason and Religion* (London, 1788)

Brayshaw, J., *An Appeal to the People of England, on the Necessity of Parliamentary Reform* (Newcastle-upon-Tyne, 1819)

Remarks on the Character and Conduct of the Men who Met under the Name of the British Parliament at the Latter End of the Year 1819 (Newcastle, n.d.)

Brewster, J., *A Secular Essay: Containing a Retrospective View of Events, Connected with the*

Ecclesiastical History of England during the Eighteenth Century (London, 1802)
A Brief Warning against the Measure Commonly Called 'Catholic Emancipation' (London, 1829)
Brothers, R., *A Letter from Mr Brothers to Miss Cott* (London, 1798)
    A Revealed Knowledge of the Prophecies and Times. Book the First (London, 1794)
    A Revealed Knowledge of the Prophecies and Times . . . Book the Second (London, 1794)
    Wonderful Prophecies, fourth edition (London, 1795)
    The Writings of Mr Richard Brothers, God's Anointed King, and Shiloh of the Hebrews (London, 1798)
Buckner, J., *A Charge Delivered to the Clergy of the Diocese of Chichester . . . 1798* (London, 1799)
    A Sermon Preached . . . before the Lords . . . November 29 1798 (London, 1798)
    A Sermon Preached before the Lords . . . February 5 1812 (London, 1812)
    A Sermon Preached in the Cathedral Church of St Paul . . . June 12 1800) (London, 1800)
John Bull's Constitutional Apple Pie, and the Vermin of Corruption, third edition (London, 1820)
Bull family letters, *see* under Jones, W.
Buller, W., *A Sermon Preached before the Lords . . . March 9 1796* (London, 1796)
Burgess, T., *The Bishop of Salisbury's Letters to the Duke of Wellington, on the Catholic Question* (London, 1829)
    Charity, the Bond of Peace and of all Virtues (Durham, 1803)
    A Letter to the Bishop of Norwich from the Bishop of Salisbury, second edition (Salisbury, 1830)
    Peculiar Privileges of the Christian Ministry Considered in A Charge Delivered to the Clergy of the Diocese of St David's . . . 1804 (Durham, 1805)
    A Sermon Preached before the Lords . . . January 30th, 1807 (London, 1807)
    A Short Catechism on the Duty of Conforming to the Established Church (London, 1806)
[Burgh, J.], *Political Disquisitions*, 3 vols. (London, 1774)
Burke, E., *The Correspondence of Edmund Burke*, 10 vols. (Cambridge, 1958–78)
    Reflections on the Revolution in France (1790) (Harmondsworth, 1968)
[Burke, E.], *Thoughts on the Cause of the Present Discontents*, second edition (London, 1770)
    The Works of the Right Honourable Edmund Burke, 6 vols. (London, 1877–83)
    The Writings and Speeches of Edmund Burke, vols. 2 and 5 (Oxford, 1981)
Butler, C., *An Address to the Protestants of Great Britain and Ireland*, second edition (London, 1813)
    The Book of the Roman Catholic Church (London, 1825)
    Historical Account of the Laws Respecting Roman Catholics (London, 1795)
    A Letter to a Nobleman on the Proposed Repeal of the Penal Laws (London, 1801)
    A Letter to a Roman Catholic Gentleman of Ireland, fourth edition (London, 1803)
    A Memoir of the Catholic Relief Bill Passed in 1829 (London, 1829)
    Miscellaneous Tracts (printed not published, 1812)
    A Short Reply to Doctor Phillpott's Answer (London, 1828)
[Butler, C.], *The Case of Conscience Solved; or Catholic Emancipation Proved to Be Compatible with the Coronation Oath* (London, 1801)
    A Letter to an Irish Catholic Gentleman (London, 1811)

Butler, John (Bishop of Hereford), *The Bishop of Hereford's Charge . . . at his Primary Visitation in June 1789* (Hereford, 1789)

Select Sermons (Hereford, 1801)

A Sermon Preached before the House of Lords . . . January 30, 1787 (London, 1787)

Butler, John, *Brief Reflections upon the Liberty of the British Subject; in an Address to the Right Honorable Edmund Burke . . .* (printed not published, Canterbury, [1790/1?])

Butler, S., *A Charge Delivered to the . . . Archdeaconry of Derby . . . 1825* (London, 1826)

A Charge Delivered to . . . the Archdeaconry of Derby . . . 1826 (London, 1826)

A Charge Delivered to . . . the Archdeaconry of Derby . . . 1827 (London, 1827)

The Genuine and Apocryphal Gospels Compared (Shrewsbury, 1822)

Butterworth, L., *Thoughts on Moral Government and Agency, and the Origin of Moral Evil* (Evesham, 1792)

Calvert, T., *The Rich and Poor Shown to be of God's Appointment* (Cambridge, 1820)

Cambridge, G. O., *A Sermon Preached in the Cathedral Church of St Paul . . . May 28, 1807* (London, 1807)

Campbell, G., *The Nature, Extent and Importance of the Duty of Allegiance* (Aberdeen, 1777)

Canning, G., *Corrected Report of the Speech . . . in the House of Commons on 30 April, 1822* (London, 1822)

The Speeches of the Right Honourable George Canning, 6 vols. (London, 1828)

Carey, W., *A Sermon Preached before the Honourable House of Commons . . . 8th February, 1809* (London, 1809)

Carlile, R., *An Address to Men of Science* (London, 1821)

The Gospel According to Richard Carlile (London, 1827)

A Letter to the Society for the Suppression of Vice (London, 1819)

A New View of Insanity (London, 1831)

A New Year's Address to the Reformers of Great Britain (London, 1821)

To the Reformers of Great Britain (London, 1821)

Carlile, R. (ed.), *The Republican*, 14 vols. (London, 1819–26)

[Carlile, R.], *A Copy of the Information Exhibited ex officio, January 23, 1819, . . . against Richard Carlile for Publishing Paine's Age of Reason* (London, 1819)

A Form of Prayer on Account of the Troubled State of Certain Parts of the United Kingdom (London, 1831)

Jesus Christ the Only Radical Reformer (Manchester, 1838)

Report of the Trial of Mrs Susannah Wright (London, 1822)

Vice versus Reason. A Copy of the Bill of Indictment . . . against Richard Carlile (London, 1819)

Cartwright, J., *Address to the Electors of Westminster* (London, 1819)

American Independence, the Interest and Glory of Great Britain (London, 1774)

An Appeal, Civil and Military on the Subject of the English Constitution (London, 1799)

A Bill of Rights and Liberties (London, 1817)

The Commonwealth in Danger (London, 1795)

The Comparison: In Which Mock Reform, Half Reform and Constitutional Reform Are Considered (London, 1810)

The Constitutional Defence of England, Internal and External (London, 1796)

Copy of Letter . . . to a Burgess of Nottingham, Broadsheet (Markham, 1811)

Copy of a Letter . . . to a Respectable Frame Work Knitter of Nottingham, Broadsheet (Nottingham, 1811)

A Defence, Delivered at Warwick . . . 1820 (London, 1831)

The English Constitution Produced and Illustrated (London, 1823)

The Legislative Rights of the Commonalty Vindicated (London, 1777)

A Letter to the Duke of Newcastle (London, 1792)

A Letter to the Earl of Abingdon (London, 1778)

A Letter . . . to a Friend at Boston, in the County of Lincoln (London, 1793)

A Letter to the High Sheriff of the County of Lincoln (London, 1795)

A Letter to Mr Lambton (London, 1820)

Major Cartwright's Letter to Sir Francis Burdett (London, 1818)

The People's Barrier against Undue Influence and Corruption (London, 1780)

Reasons for Reformation (London, 1809)

Six Letters to the Marquis of Tavistock (London, 1812)

The State of the Nation in a Series of Letters to . . . the Duke of Bedford (Harlow, 1805)

[Cartwright, J.], *Declaration of Principles Which are Deemed Incontrovertible* (London, [1821])

Take Your Choice! (London, 1776)

Cassan, S. H., *Considerations on the Danger of Any Legislative Alteration, Respecting the Corporation and Test Acts* (London, 1828)

Obedience to the Government a Religious Duty (London, 1819)

Catholic Emancipation Calmly Considered (London, 1825)

The Catholic Question Discussed and Decided (London, 1828)

The Catholic Question in 1828 by an Elector of the University of Oxford (London, 1828)

Christie, T., *Letters on the Revolution of France and on the New Constitution* (London, 1791)

Churton, R., *The Reality of the Powder Plot Vindicated* (Oxford, 1806)

Clarke, A., *The Origin and End of Civil Government* (London, 1822)

The Rights of God and Caesar (London, 1821)

Clarke, L., *A Sermon Preached in the Cathedral Church of Salisbury, August 8th 1826* (Salisbury, 1826)

Clayton, J., *The Duty of Christians to Magistrates* (London, [1791])

Cleaver, W., *Charge Delivered by William, Lord Bishop of Chester* (Oxford, 1799)

A Sermon Preached before the Lords . . . January 31, 1791 (Oxford, 1791)

Clericus, *An Answer to Two Letters Addressed to . . . George Canning by the Rev. Henry Phillpotts* (London, 1828)

Clinton, H. P., *A Letter to the Right Hon. Lord Kenyon* (London, 1828)

Cobbett, W., *An Address to the Clergy of Massachusetts* (Boston, 1815)

A History of the Protestant 'Reformation', in England and Ireland (London, 1824)

Cole, W., *A Sermon Preached on the General Fast, March 7 MDCCXCVIII* (London, 1798)

Coleridge, Samuel Taylor, *The Collected Letters of Samuel Taylor Coleridge* (Oxford, 1956)

The Collected Works of Samuel Taylor Coleridge (London and Princeton, 1976–)

A Collection of the Letters . . . Addressed to the Volunteers of Ireland on the Subject of a Parliamentary Reform (London, 1783)

Condorcet, Marquis de, *Condorcet: Selected Writings*, edited by K. M. Baker

(Indianapolis, 1976)

Constitutional Remarks Addressed to the People of Great Britain upon . . . the Late Trial of Richard Carlile (London, 1819)

A Controversial Letter of a New Kind to the Rev. Dr Price (London, 1790)

Cooper, S., *The First Principles of Civil and Ecclesiastical Government Delineated* (Yarmouth, 1791)

Cooper, T., *A Reply to Mr Burke's Invective against Mr Cooper and Mr Watt*, second edition (London, 1792)

Cooper, W., *A Charge Delivered to the Clergy at York, June 16th 1784* (London, 1785)

Copleston, E., *A Letter to the Right Hon. Robert Peel, MP, for the University of Oxford*, third edition (Oxford, 1819)

Report of the Society for Promoting Christian Knowledge and the Anniversary Sermon Preached in the Cathedral Church of St Paul (London, 1829)

A Second Letter to the Right Hon. Robert Peel MP (Oxford, 1819)

Corbett, J., *A Charge Given at the Visitation of the Archdeaconry of Salop . . . 1808* (Shrewsbury, 1808)

Cornwall, F., *A Sermon Preached . . . before the Lords . . . March 7th, 1798* (London, 1798)

Cornwallis, F., *A Sermon Preached in the Parish Church of Christ Church, London . . . April the 29th, 1762* (London, 1762)

Cornwallis, J., *A Sermon Preached before the Lords . . . January 30th, 1782* (London, 1782)

A Sermon Preached before the Lords . . . March 20, 1811 (London, 1811)

A Sermon Preached in the Cathedral . . . Canterbury . . . February 4, 1780 (Canterbury, [1780])

Courtenay, H. R., *A Charge Delivered to the Clergy of the Diocese of Bristol . . . 1796* (Bristol, 1796)

A Charge Delivered to the Clergy of the Diocese of Exeter . . . 1799 (Exeter, 1799)

A Sermon Preached at the Parish Church of Saint George, Hanover Square . . . 1st of June, 1802 (London, 1802)

A Sermon Preached before the Lords . . . February 25, 1795 (London, 1795)

Coxe, W., *A Letter to the Rev. Richard Price* (London, 1790)

The Craftsmen: A Sermon . . . Composed in the Style of the Late Daniel Burgess (Birmingham, 1791)

Crease, J., *Prophecies Fulfilling: or, The Dawn of the Perfect Day* (London, 1795)

A Critical Examination of the Bishop of Llandaff's . . . 'Anecdotes of his Life' (London, 1818)

The Critical Review or Annals of Literature Extended and Improved, 7 (London, 1793)

Croft, G., *Plans of Parliamentary Reform Proved to Be Visionary* (Birmingham, 1793)

A Sermon Preached before the University of Oxford, October 25, 1783 (Stafford, 1784)

A Short Commentary with Strictures on Certain Parts of the Moral Writings of Dr Paley and Mr Gisborne (Birmingham, 1797)

The Test Laws Defended (Birmingham, 1790)

Crowther, J., *Christian Order: or, Liberty without Anarchy* (Bristol, 1796)

The Methodist Manual: or, A Short History of the Wesleyan Methodists (Halifax, 1810)

Sermons (London, 1839)

Crowther, S., *A Sermon Preached before the Barking Association . . . 17 June, 1798* (London, 1798)

Dampier, T., *A Charge Delivered to the Clergy of the Diocese of Rochester . . . 1807* (London, 1807)

A Sermon Preached before the Honourable House of Commons . . . February 8, 1782 (London, 1782)

A Sermon Preached before the Lords . . . February 20th 1805 (London, 1805)

Daubeny, C., *A Guide to the Church, in Several Discourses* (London, 1798)

A Letter to the Right Honourable George Canning (London, 1827)

A Sermon Preached in the Cathedral Church of St Paul . . . June 1, 1809 (London, 1809)

Davies, T., *Memoirs of the Life of David Garrick Esq.*, 2 vols. (London, 1780)

Davis, G., *National Repentance the Only Means of Averting National Judgements* (London, 1758)

Davison, J., *A Sermon Preached in . . . Deptford . . . June 2, 1817* (Oxford, 1817)

Dealtry, W., *The Dispositions and Conduct Required of Christians towards their Rulers* (London, 1819)

An Examination of Dr Marsh's 'Inquiry' (London, 1812)

A Letter Addressed to the Rev. Dr Wordsworth (London, 1810)

Declaration and Protestation of the Roman Catholics of England (London, 1812)

de Coetlogon, C. E., *God and the King . . .*, Accession Day Sermon, St Paul's (London, 1790)

The Test of Truth, Piety and Allegiance (London, 1790)

de Courcy, R., *Self-Defence Not Inconsistent with the Precepts of Religion* (Shrewsbury, 1798)

[Defoe, D.], *Jure Divino: A Satyr* (London, 1706)

Depont, M., *Answer to the Reflections of the Right Hon. Edmund Burke* (Dublin, 1791)

Devonshire Freeholder, *The Catholic Question* (London, [1829?])

Diderot, D., *Thoughts on Religion* (London, 1819)

Douglas, J., *Select Works* (Salisbury, 1820)

A Sermon Preached before the Lords . . . January 30th, 1790 (London, 1790)

[Doyle, J.], *Letter of J. K. L. to his Grace Dr Magee, the Protestant Archbishop of Dublin* (Carlow, 1822)

The Duty of the King and Subject on the Principles of Civil Liberty (London, 1776)

Dyer, G., *Memoirs of the Life and Writings of Robert Robinson* (London, 1796)

Edwards, E., *The Things Which Belong unto our Peace* (Brecknock, 1797)

Egerton, J., *A Sermon Preached before the . . . Lords . . . January 30th, 1761* (London, 1761)

The Emancipation Bill Examined, by a Friend to Emancipation (Hereford, 1825)

Eustace, J. C., *Answer to the Charge Delivered by the Lord Bishop of Lincoln . . . 1812* (London, 1813)

Evans, C., *British Constitutional Liberty* (Bristol, [1775])

British Freedom Realized (Bristol, [1788])

A Letter to the Rev. Mr John Wesley (Bristol, 1775)

Experience Preferable to Theory. An Answer to Dr Price's Observations (London, 1776)

An Explanation of Some Passages in Dr Binke's Sermon . . . with Part of a Sermon Publish'd, Anno 1649, at the Hague. Intitled, The Martyrdom of King Charles: or His Conformity with Christ in His Sufferings (London, 1702)

Farish, W. (ed.), *A Report of the Formation of the Cambridge Auxiliary Bible Society* (Cambridge, 1812)

A Few Minutes Advice to the People of Great Britain on Republics (Bristol, 1792)

Fidelia, *A Consolatory Letter to the Rev. John Clayton* (London, 1791)

[Filmer, R.], *The Anarchy of a Limited or Mixed Monarchy* (1648)

Finch, R. P., *A Sermon Preached in the Church of St Michael, Cornhill . . . February 10, 1779* (London, 1779)

Firth, W., *A Letter to the Right Rev. Henry Bathurst D.D. Lord Bishop of Norwich* (London, 1813)

Remarks on the Recent State Trials, and the Rise and Progress of Disaffection in the Country (London, 1818)

Fisher, J., *A Charge Delivered to the Clergy of the Diocese of Exeter . . . 1804 & 1805* (Exeter, 1805)

A Sermon Preached before the Lords . . . February 25, 1807 (London, 1807)

[Flavel, J.], *Tidings from Rome; or, England's Alarm!* (London, 1828)

Flaxmer, S., *Satan Revealed; or The Dragon Overcome* (London, n.d.)

Fleming, *The Opening Speech and Reply of Mr Fleming at the British Forum, Held at the Crown and Anchor* (London, 1819)

Fletcher, John, *American Patriotism Farther Confronted with Reason, Scripture and the Constitution* (Shrewsbury, 1776)

The Bible and the Sword (London, 1776)

The Works of the Rev. John Fletcher, Late Vicar of Madely, 7 vols. (London, 1825)

Fletcher, John, *Thoughts on the Rights and Prerogatives of the Church and State* (London, 1823)

Flindell's Western Luminary, 1819

Fox, W. J., *The Duties of Christians towards Deists* (London, 1819)

Freethinker, *An Inquiry into the Pretentions of Richard Brothers in Answer to Nathaniel Brassey Halhed* (London, 1794)

Fuller, A., *The Calvinist and Socinian Systems Examined and Compared as to their Moral Tendency* (Market Harborough, 1793)

[Garrow, D. W.], *An Address of a Rector to his Parishioners on the Subject of a Bible Society Established in his Parish* (Barnet, 1826)

[Geddes, A.], *An Answer to the Bishop of Comana's Pastoral Letter by a Protesting Catholic* (London, 1790)

Letter to a Member of Parliament on the Case of the Protestant Dissenters (London, 1787)

A Letter to the RR the Archbishops and Bishops of England (London, 1790)

The Gentleman's Magazine, May 1798

George III, *The Later Correspondence of George III*, edited by A. Aspinall, 5 vols. (Cambridge, 1962–70)

Gibbon, E., *The English Essays of Edward Gibbon*, edited by P. B. Craddock (Oxford, 1972)

The History of the Decline and Fall of the Roman Empire, 6 vols. (1776–88), reprinted (London, Dent, n.d.)

[Gibson, M.], *A Pastoral Letter of Matthew Bishop of Comana and VA* (Newcastle-upon-Tyne, 1790)

Gilbank, W., *The Duties of Man* (London, 1793)

Gisborne, T., *An Enquiry into the Duties of Men in the Higher and Middle Classes of Society*, 2 vols., third edition (London, 1795), and sixth edition (London, 1811)

The Principles of Moral Philosophy Investigated (London, 1789), and a new edition (London, 1798)

Remarks on the Late Decision of the House of Commons Respecting the Abolition of the Slave Trade (London, 1792)

Sermons, 2 vols. (London, 1802 and 1804)

Glasse, S., *The Sinner Encouraged to Repentance* (London, 1794)

Godwin, W., *Enquiry Concerning Political Justice* (1793, Harmondsworth, 1976)

Uncollected Writings (1785–1822) (Gainesville, Florida, 1968)

Good, J. M., *Memoirs of the Life and Writings of the Reverend Alexander Geddes LLD* (London, 1803)

[Goodenough, S.], *A Sermon Preached before the Lords . . . 8 February, 1809* (London, 1809)

Goodricke, H., *Observations on Dr Price's Theory and Principles of Civil Liberty and Government* (York, 1776)

Gordon, J., *The Causes and Consequences of Evil Speaking against the Government* (Cambridge, 1771)

Gray, J., *Doctor Price's Notions of the Nature of Civil Liberty, Shewn to be Contradictory to Reason and Scripture* (London, 1777)

Gray, R., *A Charge to the Clergy of the Diocese of Bristol . . . 1831* (London, 1831)

Green, J., *A Sermon Preached before the Lords . . . January 31, 1763* (London, 1763)

Greene, J., *A Sermon Preached in the Cathedral Church at Norwich . . . June 19, 1764* (Norwich, 1764)

Gresley, R., *A Letter to the Right Honourable John, Earl of Shrewsbury* (London, 1828)

Grey, Earl, *The Speech of the Earl Grey in the House of Lords, May 12, 1817, on Lord Sidmouth's Circular* (London, 1817)

Grinfield, E. W., *The Crisis of Religion* (London, 1812)

Gunning, H., *Reminiscences of the University, Town and County of Cambridge from the year 1780*, 2 vols., second edition (London, 1855)

Haldane, R., *Address to the Public Concerning Political Opinions* (Edinburgh, 1800)

[Hales, W.], *The Scripture Doctrine of Political Government and Political Liberty* (Dublin, 1794)

A Survey of the Modern State of the Church of Rome (Dublin, 1788)

Haley, W. T., *The Curse and Cure of Ireland* (London, 1828)

Halhed, N. B., *A Calculation on the Commencement of the Millennium* (London, 1795)

The Whole of the Testimonies to the Authenticity of the Prophecies and Mission of Richard Brothers (London, 1795)

Hall, R., *Miscellaneous Works and Remains* (London, 1846)

The Works of Robert Hall, 6 vols. (London, 1832)

Hallifax, S., *A Sermon Preached before the Lords . . . February 8, 1782* (London, 1782)

A Sermon Preached before the Lords . . . January 30, 1788 (London, 1788)

Hamilton, J. E., *Reflections on the Revolution in France by the Honourable Edmund Burke, Considered* (London, 1791)

Hatchard, J., *National Mercies Demand National Thankfulness* (London, 1819)

Hayes, S., *A Sermon Preached in St Margaret's Church Westminster . . . January 27, 1793* (London, 1793)

Heathcote, G., *An Address to the Principal Farmers, Churchwardens and Overseers . . . on . . . Dr Bell's System of Instruction* (Winchester, 1817)

Henley, C., *Uniformity of Opinion in the Clergy, Essential to the Interests of the Established Church* (London, 1822)

Hewlett, J., *The Christian Hero* (London, 1803)

Hey, R., *Happiness and Rights* (York, 1792)

  Observations on the Nature of Civil Liberty (London, 1776)

Hildyard, W., *The Duty of Submission to Civil Governors Enforced* (London, 1819)

Hill, J., *A Charge Delivered to the Clergy of the Archdeaconry of Buckingham* (London, 1826)

Hinchcliffe, J., *A Sermon Preached before the Lords . . . January XXX, MDCCLXXIII* (London, 1773)

Hinton, J., *A Sermon on the Death of His Late Majesty, King George the Third* (Oxford, 1820)

Holloway, J., *A Letter to the Rev. Dr Price, containing a few Strictures upon his Sermons Lately Published* (London, 1789)

The Holy Alliance against the Freedom of Christendom (London, 1825)

Hone, W., *Ancient Mysteries Described* (London, 1823)

  Aspersions Answered (London, 1824)

  The Reformists' Register and Weekly Commentary, 2 vols. (London, 1817)

[Hone, W.], *The Apocryphal New Testament* (London, 1820)

  The Bullet Te Deum; with the Canticle of the Stone (London, 1817)

  The Divine Right of Kings to Govern Wrong (London, 1821)

  The Late John Wilkes's Catechism of a Ministerial Member (London, 1817)

  A Political Catechism (Bristol, [1816])

  The Political House that Jack Built (London, 1820)

  The Political Litany (London, 1817)

  The Sinecurist's Creed or Belief (London, [1817])

  The Third Trial of William Hone (London, 1818)

  The Three Trials of William Hone (London, 1818)

Horne, G., *Occasional Remarks: Addressed to Nathaniel Brassey Halhed, MP* (Oxford, 1795)

Horne, George (Bishop of Norwich) *A Sermon Preached before the Honourable House of Commons . . . February 4th, 1780* (Oxford, 1780)

  A Sermon Preached before the University of Oxford, at St Mary's . . . February 21, 1781 (Oxford, 1781)

  Sound Argument Dictated by Common Sense (Oxford, n.d.)

  Sunday Schools Recommended in a Sermon . . . 18 December, 1785 (Oxford, 1786)

  The Works of the Right Reverend George Horne . . ., 4 vols. (London, 1818)

Horne, M. *The Moral and Political Crisis of England* (London, 1820)

Horne Tooke, J., *A Letter to a Friend on the Reported Marriage of . . . the Prince of Wales*, third edition (London, 1787)

  Speech . . . at the Hustings . . . June 2, 1796 (1796)

  Speech . . . on the Hustings of Covent Garden . . . June 8 (n.d.)

The Speeches . . . during the Westminster Election 1796 (London, [1796])

To the Electors of Westminster June 6th, 1796 (n.d.)

The Trial (at large) of John Horne, Esq. (London, 1777)

Two Pair of Portraits Presented to All the Unbiassed Electors of Great Britain (London, 1788)

Warning to the Electors of Westminster (London, 1807)

Horsley, S., *A Charge Delivered to the Clergy of the Archdeaconry of St Albans . . . 1783* (London, 1783)

A Charge to the Clergy at the Primary Visitation . . . 1806 of the Late . . . Lord Bishop of St Asaph (London, 1806)

The Charge of Samuel, Lord Bishop of Rochester . . . 1796 (London, 1796)

The Charge of Samuel, Lord Bishop of Rochester . . . 1800 (London, 1800)

The Charges of Samuel Horsley (Dundee, 1813)

A Sermon Preached before the Lords . . . January 30, 1793, second edition (London, 1793)

A Sermon Preached in the Cathedral Church of St Paul . . . June 6th, 1793 . . . (London, 1793)

A Sermon Preached . . . in the Parish Church of St Mary-le-Bow . . . February 20, 1795 (London, 1795)

The Speeches in Parliament (Dundee, 1813)

[Horsley, S.], *A Catalogue of the Entire and Very Valuable Library of the Late Right Rev. Samuel Horsley* (London, 1807)

Horton, W., *Correspondence upon Some Points Connected with the Roman Catholic Question* (London, 1829)

Howley, W., *A Charge Delivered at his Primary Visitation . . . 1832 by William Lord Archbishop of Canterbury* (London, 1832)

A Charge Delivered to the Clergy of the Diocese of London . . . 1814 (London, 1814)

A Charge Delivered to the Clergy of the Diocese of London . . . 1822 (London, 1822)

A Charge Delivered to the Clergy of the Diocese of London . . . 1826 (London, 1826)

Hughes, H. A., *The Christian's Duty to his God, his King, and his Country* (Honiton, 1819)

Hull, E., *A Sermon on the Duty of Obedience to Civil Governors* (Liverpool, 1819)

Hume, D., *Dialogues Concerning Natural Religion* (1779, Indianapolis, 1980)

Enquiries Concerning Human Understanding and Concerning the Principles of Morals (1748, London, 1975)

Essays and Treatises on Several Subjects (1742), 2 vols. (Edinburgh, 1809)

Essays Moral, Political and Literary (Oxford, 1963)

The History of England from the Invasion of Julius Caesar to the Revolution in 1688, 8 vols., new edition (London, 1822)

A Treatise of Human Nature (London, Dent, n.d.)

Hunt, H., *Memoirs of Henry Hunt Esq.*, 3 vols. (London, 1820–2)

To the Radical Reformers, Male and Female of England, Ireland and Scotland, 2 vols. (1 July 1820–14 October 1822)

Hunter, H., *The Universal and Everlasting Dominion of God* (London, 1788)

Huntingford, G. I., *A Sermon Preached before the Honourable House of Commons . . . 1793* (London, 1793)

A Sermon Preached before the Lords . . . May 25th, 1804 (London, 1804)

A Sermon Preached in the Cathedral Church of St Paul . . . June 2, 1796 (London, 1796)

Hurd, R., *A Sermon Preached before the . . . Lords . . . January 30th, 1786* (London, 1786)

    The Works of Richard Hurd, DD, Lord Bishop of Winchester, 8 vols. (London, 1811)

The Influence of Opinions in the Exercise of Political Power (London, 1828)

Irish Catholic, *A Letter to the Rt. Hon. Robert Peel, MP* (London, 1828)

Irving, E., *A Letter to the King on the Repeal of the Test and Corporation Laws, as it Affects our Christian Monarchy* (London, 1828)

Ivimey, J., *The Roman Catholic Claims a Question Not of Religious Liberty, but of Political Expediency* (London, 1828)

    The Supremacy of the Pope Contrary to Scripture and Dangerous to the Safety of Protestant Governments (London, 1819)

Jackson, T., *The Lives of the Early Methodist Preachers*, vol. 3 (London, 1838)

[Jebb, A.], *Two Penny-Worth of Truth for a Penny* (London, 1793)

Jebb, J., *The Works: Theological, Medical, Political and Miscellaneous*, 3 vols. (London, 1787)

Jenkinson, J. B., *A Charge Delivered to the Clergy of the Diocese of St David's . . . MDCCCXXVIII* (London, 1828)

Jenyns, Soame, *The Works of Soame Jenyns Esq.*, 4 vols. (London, 1790)

Johnson, S., *Political Writings*, edited by D. J. Greene (New Haven, 1977)

Jones, J. G., *The Speech . . . Delivered at the British Forum Held at the Crown and Anchor* (London, 1819)

    Substances of the Speeches . . . Delivered at the British Forum, March 11, 18, and 22, 1819 (London, 1819)

Jones, W., *The Fear of God, and the Benefits of Civil Obedience, Two Sermons* (London, 1778)

    Memoirs of the Life, Studies and Writings of . . . George Horne (London, 1795)

    The Scholar Armed against the Errors of the Time (London, 1800)

    Sermons on Various Subjects and Occasions, 2 vols. (London, 1830)

    The Theological, Philosophical and Miscellaneous Works (London, 1801)

[Jones, W.], *A Letter to John Bull Esq., from his Second Cousin Thomas Bull* (London, 1793)

    More Reasons for Reform of Parliament: The Answer of John Bull to his Brother Thomas (London, 1793)

    More than a Pennyworth of Truth in a letter from John Bull to his Brother Thomas (n.d.)

    One Pennyworth More, or, A Second Letter from Thomas Bull to his Brother John (1792)

    A Small Whole-Length of Dr Priestley (London, 1792)

    One Pennyworth of Truth from Thomas Bull to his Brother John (London?, 1792)

Kaye, J., *A Charge to the Clergy of the Diocese of Lincoln . . . MDCCCXXXI* (London, 1831)

    A Sermon Preached in the Chapel of the Philanthropic Society . . . November 14, 1819 (London, 1819)

Keate, W., *A Free Examination of Dr Price's and Dr Priestley's Sermons* (London, 1790)

Keppel, F., *A Sermon Preached before the Lords . . . January 30, 1766* (London, 1766)

Kilham, A., *An Account of the Trial of Alexander Kilham, Methodist Preacher, before the General Conference* (Nottingham, [1796])

    The Hypocrite Detected and Exposed (Aberdeen, 1794)

    The Life of Mr Alexander Kilham, Methodist Preacher (Nottingham, 1799)

The Methodist Monitor (Leeds, [1796])

The Progress of Liberty, amongst the People Called Methodists (Alnwick, 1795)

A Short Account of the Trial . . . at a Special District Meeting . . . February 1796 (Alnwick, 1796)

The King and the Church Vindicated and Delivered (Dublin, 1833)

Kippis, A., *The Excellency of the Gospel, as Suited to the Poor* (London, 1777)

  Observations on the Coronation (London, 1761)

  Sermons on Practical Subjects (London, 1791)

  A Sermon Preached at the Chapel in Prince's Street, Westminster . . . February 28th, 1794 (London, 1794)

  A Sermon Preached at the Old Jewry on the Fourth of November, 1788 (London, 1788)

  A Sermon Preached at the Old Jewry on . . . 26th April, 1786 (London, 1786)

  A Vindication of the Protestant Dissenting Ministers (London, 1772)

Knapp, H. I., *The Origin and Termination of the Late Warfare with France Considered in a Sermon* (London, 1816)

Knight, H. G., *Foreign and Domestic View of the Catholic Question*, fourth edition (London, 1828)

[Knox, V.], *The Spirit of Despotism*, second edition (London, 1821)

Knox, V., *The Spirit of Despotism* (London, 1822)

  The Works of Vicesimus Knox, DD, 7 vols. (London, 1824)

[Knox, V.], *The Substance of a Sermon Preached in the Parish Church of Brighthelmstone* (London, 1793)

Lamb, R., *A Sermon Preached before the Lords . . . January 30, 1768* (London, 1768)

Langford, W., *Obedience to the Established Laws and Respect to the Person of the Administrator Are the Joint Support of Civil Society* (Eton, 1793)

Law, E., *The Grounds of a Particular Providence: A Sermon Preached before the Lords . . . January XXX, MDCCLXXI* (London, 1771)

Law, G. H., *A Charge Delivered to the Clergy of the Diocese of Bath and Wells . . . 1831* (Wells, [1831])

  A Charge Delivered to the Clergy of the Diocese of Chester . . . 1814 (Chester, 1814)

  A Charge Delivered to the Clergy of the Diocese of Chester . . . 1817 (Chester, 1817)

  A Charge Delivered to the Clergy of the Diocese of Chester . . . 1820 (London, 1820)

  On Education: A Sermon Preached in the Cathedral Church of Wells . . . October 9th, 1827 (London, 1827)

  A Pastoral Letter on the Present Aspect of the Times (Wells, 1831)

  A Sermon Preached at the Cathedral Church of Saint Paul . . . July 7, 1814 (London, 1814)

Law, James, *The Origin, Progress and Necessity, of an Established Church* (London, 1824)

Law, John (Archdeacon) *A Charge Delivered to the Clergy of the Diocese of Rochester in June 1811* (London, 1811)

  A Charge Delivered to the Clergy of the Diocese of Rochester in May 1817 (Rochester, 1817)

Law, John, (Bishop) *A Sermon Preached in the Cathedral Church of St Paul . . . June 1, 1797* (London, 1797)

The Legitimacy of Dissent Demonstrated and the Protestant Episcopal Church Proved Not to Be the Only Safe Means of Salvation (London, 1819)

A Letter to the Dissenting Ministers of Frome Occasioned by a Sermon . . . *by the Rev. Stephen Hyde Cassan* (Bath, 1819)

A Letter to the Rev. Dr Price, . . . *by a Lover of Peace and Good Government* (London, 1776)

A Letter to the Rev. Dr Price on his Observations . . . *by T. D.* (London, 1776)

A Letter to the Reverend Joseph Priestley . . . *Occasioned by his late Address to the Inhabitants of Birmingham* (Birmingham, 1791)

Liberty and Equality Treated of in a Short History Addressed by a Poor Man to his Equals (London, 1792)

Licentiousness Unmask'd; or, Liberty Explained (London, 1776?)

[Lingard, J.], *Remarks on Charge* (London, 1807)

Literary Magazine, The, vol. 2 (London, 1757)

Lofft, C., *Essay on the Effect of a Dissolution of Parliament on an Impeachment by the House of Commons* (Bury St Edmunds, 1791)

    An History of the Corporation and Test Acts (Bury, 1790)

    On the Revival of the Cause of Reform in the Representation of the Commons in Parliament (London, 1809)

    Remarks on the Letter of the Rt. Hon. Edmund Burke, Concerning the Revolution in France (London, 1790), and second edition with additional notes (London, 1791)

    A Vindication of the Short History of the Corporation and Test Acts (London, 1790)

Lowth, R. (Bishop of London), *A Sermon Preached before the Lords* . . . *January 30, 1767* (London, 1767)

Lowth, R. (Prebendary of St Paul's), *A Sermon Preached in Oxford Chapel* . . . *March 19, 1793* (London, 1793)

Lucas, W., *A Sermon Preached in the Parish Church of St Lawrence Jewry* . . . *on the Eighth of January 1792* (London, 1792)

Luke, R., *For the Defence of the Constitution in Church and State* (Exeter, [1790?])

Luxmore, J., *A Sermon Preached before the Lords* . . . *17 February, 1808* (London, 1808)

Lyttleton, C., *A Sermon Preached before the Lords* . . . *January 30, 1765* (London, 1765)

M'Donnell, T. M., *Substance of Speeches Delivered at the Open Meeting of the Committee of the British Catholic Association* . . . *January 22nd, 1828*, third edition (Birmingham, 1828)

Machiavelli, N., *The Discourses* (Harmondsworth, 1970)

Mackintosh, J., *Dissertation on the Progress of Ethical Philosophy* (Edinburgh, 1836)

    Vindiciae Gallicae (London, 1791)

Maclaine, A., *Religion, a Preservative against Barbarism and Anarchy* (London, 1793)

    The Solemn Voice of Public Events in a Discourse from Zephaniah (Bath, [1797])

Madan, S., *A Letter to Dr Priestley in Consequence of his 'Familiar Letters Addressed to the Inhabitants of . . . Birmingham'* (Birmingham, 1790)

    Letters to Joseph Priestley . . . *Occasioned by his Late Controversial Writings* (London, 1787)

    A Plain and Friendly Address to the Undergraduates of the University of Cambridge (London, 1786)

    A Sermon Preached before the Lords . . . *January the 30th, 1795* (London, 1795)

Majendie, H. W., *A Charge Delivered to the Clergy of the Diocese of Chester* . . . *1804* (London, 1804)

    A Sermon Preached before the Lords . . . *June 1, 1802* (London, 1802)

Manners-Sutton, C., *A Sermon Preached before the Lords* . . . *February 28th, 1794* (London, 1794)

Mansel, W. L., *A Sermon Preached before the Lords* . . . *January 30, 1810* (Cambridge, 1810)

[Mant, R.], *Puritanism Revived; or Methodism as Old as the Great Rebellion* (London, 1808)

Markham, W., *A Sermon Preached before the* . . . *Lords* . . . *January 31, 1774* (London, 1774)

Marsh, H. *A Charge Delivered to the Clergy of the Diocese of Peterborough in July MDCCCXXXI* (London, 1831)

An Inquiry into the Consequences of Neglecting to Give the Prayer Book with the Bible (Cambridge, 1812)

The National Religion the Foundation of National Education (London, 1811)

Martin, J., *Familiar Dialogues between Americus and Britannicus* (London, 1776)

Mason, W., *The Absolute and Indispensable Duty of Christians* (London, 1776)

Mavor, W., *Christian Politics* (Oxford, 1793)

Meadley, G. W., *Memoirs of William Paley* (Sunderland, 1809)

Minutes of the Methodist Conferences from the First Held in London by the Late Rev. John Wesley AM in the Year 1744, 10 vols., vols. 1–7 (1833–64)

Mill, J. S., *Utilitarianism* (1863; Everyman edition, London, 1910, 1972)

Mills, J., *The Speech* . . . *Delivered at the British Forum, Held at the Crown and Anchor* (London, 1819)

Milner, J., *The End of Religious Controversy in a Friendly Correspondence* (London, 1818)

A Serious Expostulation with the Rev. Joseph Berington (London, 1797)

Moore, J., *A Sermon Preached before the* . . . *Lords* . . . *January 30, 1777* (London, 1777)

A Sermon Preached before the Lords . . . February 21, 1781 (London, 1781)

More, H., *Memoirs of the Life and Correspondence of Mrs Hannah More*, edited by W. Roberts, 3 vols, third edition (London, 1835)

The Works of Hannah More, 11 vols (London, 1853)

[More, H.], *Cheap Repository Tracts; Entertaining, Moral and Religious* (London, 1798)

Cheap Repository Tracts for Sunday Reading (London, 1798)

Cheap Repository Shorter Tracts (London, 1798)

Cheap Repository Shorter Tracts, new edition (London, 1799)

More, M., *The Mendip Annals* . . . *Being the Journal of Martha More from the Year 1789 to 1801* (London, 1859)

Moss, Charles (Bishop of Bath and Wells), *A Sermon Preached before the* . . . *Lords* . . . *January 30, 1769* (London, 1769)

Moss, Charles (Bishop of Oxford), *A Sermon Preached before the Honourable House of Commons* . . . *March 7th, 1798* (London, 1798)

A Sermon Preached before the . . . Lords . . . January 30, 1809 (London, 1809)

Murray, J., *The Lawfulness of Self-Defence Explained and Vindicated* (Glasgow, 1780)

Lectures to Lords Spiritual (London, 1774)

New Sermons to Asses (London, 1773)

Sermons for the General Fast Day (London, 1781)

Sermons to Asses . . . (London, 1768)

Sermons to Asses, to Doctors in Divinity, to Lords Spiritual, and to Ministers of State (London, 1819)

Sermons to Doctors in Divinity (1771) (Glasgow, 1798)

Nares, R., *On the Influence of Sectaries and the Stability of the Church* (London, 1813)

Principles of Government Deduced from Reason, Supported by English Experience and Opposed to French Errors (London, 1792)

A Thanksgiving for Plenty and a Warning against Avarice (London, 1801)

New Lights on Jacobinism Abstracted from Professor Robison's History of Free Masonry (Birmingham, 1798)

Newcastle, Duke of, *A Letter to . . . Lord Kenyon* (London, 1828)

Newman, J. H., *Parochial and Plain Sermons*, new edition, 8 vols. (London, 1868)

Newton, T., *Of Moderation: A Sermon Preached before the Lords . . . January 30, 1764* (London, 1764)

Nickolls, R. B., *The Political as Well as the Moral Consequences Resulting . . . from Religious Education* (London, 1798)

North, B., *A Sermon Preached before the Lords . . . February 13, 1801* (London, 1801)

A Sermon Preached before the Lords . . . January 30, 1775 (London, 1775)

'Nott', 'Job', *Birmingham in Danger! Of Which Job Nott Gives Fair Warning* (Birmingham, [1799])

A Continuation of my Last Book, or a Back Front View of the Five Headed Monster (Birmingham, 1798)

A Front View of the Five Headed Monster (Birmingham, [1798])

Further Advice from Job Nott (Birmingham, 1800)

Further Authentic Proofs of French Perfidy and Cruelty (Birmingham, [1798?])

Job Nott's Humble Advice (1792), fifth edition (Birmingham, 1793)

The Life and Adventues of Job Nott, Bucklemaker of Birmingham (1793), eleventh edition (Birmingham, 1798)

The Lion Sleeps [Birmingham, 1803]

More Advice from Job Nott [Birmingham, 1795]

'Nott', 'John', *An Appeal to the Inhabitants of Birmingham: Designed as an Answer to Job Nott, Buckle Maker* ([Birmingham], 1792)

Very Familiar Letters, Addressed to Dr Priestley, in Answer to his Familiar Letters to the Inhabitants of Birmingham (Birmingham, 1790)

Nowell, T., *A Sermon Preached before the Honourable House of Commons . . . January XXX, 1772* (London, 1772)

Obedience the Best Charter, or, Law the Only Sanction of Liberty (London, 1776)

Observations on the Bill Now in Progress through Parliament in Support of the Spiritual Authority of the Church of Rome (Oxford, 1825)

Observations on Doctor Price's Revolution Sermon (London, 1790)

Ode addressed to the Rev. Dr Priestley (n.d.)

Oldershaw, J., *A Charge Delivered to the Clergy of the Archdeaconry of Norfolk in May 1828* (Norwich, [1828])

Olivers, T., *A Defence of Methodism: Delivered Extempore in Public Debate* (Leeds, 1818)

The Order for the Administration of the Loaves and Fishes . . . Commanded to Be Read at the Treasury the Day Preceding All Cabinet Dinners (London, 1817)

The Origin, Nature and Object of the New System of Education (London, 1812)

Otter, W., *An Examination of Dr Marsh's Answer to All the Arguments in Favour of the British and Foreign Bible Society* ([London], 1812)

Reasons for Continuing the Education of the Poor at the Present Crisis (Shrewsbury, 1820)

A Sermon upon the Influence of the Clergy in Improving the Condition of the Poor (Shrewsbury, 1818)

A Vindication of Churchmen Who Become Members of the British and Foreign Bible Society ([London], 1812)

Owen, J., *The History of the Origin and First Ten Years of the British and Foreign Bible Society*, 2 vols. (London, 1816)

The Retrospect; or, Reflections on the State of Religion and Politics in France and Great Britain (London, 1794)

Subordination Considered on the Grounds of Reason and Religion (Cambridge, 1794)

Owen, R., *The Addresses of Robert Owen* (London, 1830)

Debate on the Evidences of Christianity (Bethany, 1829)

Discourses on A New System of Society (Louisville, 1825)

An Explanation of the Cause of the Distress which Pervades the Civilized Parts of the World (London, 1823)

Paine, T., *The Age of Reason: Being an Investigation of True and Fabulous Theology* (Paris, 1794) (New York and London, 1910)

Common Sense (1776; Harmondsworth, 1976)

Rights of Man (1791–2, Harmondsworth, 1969)

The Writings of Thomas Paine, edited by M. D. Conway, 4 vols. (New York, 1894–6; New York, reprinted 1967)

Paley, W., *The Works of William Paley, with Additional Sermons*, 7 vols. (London, 1825)

The Parliamentary Debates from the Year 1803 to the Present Time (London, 1812–)

The Parliamentary History of England, from the Earliest Period to the Year 1803, 36 vols. (London, 1806–20)

Parr, S., *The Works of Samuel Parr*, 8 vols. (London, 1828)

Pawson, J., *Sermons on Various Subjects* (Leeds, 1809)

Pelham, G., *A Charge Delivered to the Clergy of the Diocese of Bristol . . . 1804* (Bristol, n.d.)

A Sermon Preached before the Lords . . . February 26, 1806 (London, 1806)

Perceval, D. M., *Quietus Optabilissimus; or The Nature and Necessity of Real Securities for the United Church* (London, 1829)

Peter the Hermit, *Letters that Have Lately Appeared in the Oxford and Cambridge Papers* (London, 1812)

Petre, Lord R., *Letter to the Right Reverend Doctor Horsley* (London, 1790)

Reflections on the Policy and Justice of an Immediate and General Emancipation of the Roman Catholics of Great Britain and Ireland (London, 1804)

Phillpotts, H., *A Letter to an English Layman on the Coronation Oath* (London, 1828)

A Letter to the Right Honourable Earl Grey (Durham, 1819)

A Letter to the Right Honourable George Canning on the Bill of 1825 (London, 1827)

A Short Letter to the Right Honourable George Canning, fourth edition (London, 1827)

Speech of the Bishop of Exeter in the House of Lords . . . 11th April, 1832, on the Second Reading of the Reform Bill (London, 1832)

Philopolites, *Thoughts on the Roman Catholic Question* (London, 1828)

Playfair, W., *The History of Jacobinism, its Crimes, Cruelties and Perfidies*, 2 vols. (London, 1798)

Plowden, C., *Observations on the Oath Proposed to the English Roman Catholics* (London, 1791)
   Remarks on a Book Entitled Memoirs of Gregorio Panzani, Preceded by an Address to the Rev. Joseph Berington (Liège, 1794)
   Remarks on Writings of the Rev. Joseph Berington (London, 1792)
Plowden, F., *The Case Stated* (London, 1791)
   Church and State: Being an Enquiry into the Origin, Nature and Extent of Ecclesiastical and Civil Authority (London, 1795)
   Human Subordination: Being an Elementary Disquisition concerning the Civil and Spiritual Power and Authority, to which the Creator Requires the Submission of every human being (Paris, 1824)
   Jura Anglorum: The Rights of Englishmen (London, 1792)
[Plowden, R.], *A Letter to Francis Plowden, Esq.* (London, [1794])
Plymley, J., *A Charge Given at the Visitation of the Archdeaconry of Salop . . . 1794* (Shrewsbury, 1794)
The Poor Man's Friend; or, A Farmer's Meditations on Religion and Morals (Hull, 1799)
Porteus, B., *A Sermon Preached before the Lords . . . January 30, 1778* (London, 1778)
   A Sermon Preached before the Lords . . . February 10, 1779 (London, 1779)
Pott, J. H., *A Charge to the Clergy of the Archdeaconry of London . . . May 13, 1819* (London, 1819)
   A General View of the Christian Dispensation in a Charge to the Clergy of the Archdeaconry of London . . . 1817 (London, 1817)
   The Scandals of Impiety and Unbelief and the Pleas Made for them by their Abettors, Considered (London, 1820)
   A Sermon Preached in the Cathedral Church of St Paul . . . June 5, 1794 (London, 1794)
Potter, F., *The Nature, Guilt and Consequences of Murmuring* (Oxford, [1763?])
[Potts, T.], *An Inquiry into the Moral and Political Tendency of the Religion Called Roman Catholic* (London, 1790)
Powys, T., *A Sermon Preached before the Honourable House of Commons . . . March 8th, 1797* (London, 1797)
Pretyman-Tomline, G., *A Charge Delivered to the Clergy of the Diocese of Lincoln . . . 1794* (London, 1794)
   A Charge Delivered to the Clergy of the Diocese of Lincoln . . . 1803 (London, 1803)
   A Charge Delivered to the Clergy of the Diocese of Lincoln . . . 1812 (London, [1812])
   A Sermon Preached at the Cathedral Church of St Paul . . . December 19th, 1797 (London, 1798)
   A Sermon Preached before the Honourable House of Commons . . . July 29, 1784 (London, 1784)
   A Sermon Preached before the Lords . . . January 30, 1789 (London, 1789)
Price, R., *Additional Observations on the Nature and Value of Civil Liberty*, second edition (London, 1778)
   Additions to Dr Price's Discourse on the Love of Our Country (n.d.)
   Britain's Happiness, and the Proper Improvement of it, Represented in a Sermon (London, 1759)
   A Discourse Addressed to a Congregation at Hackney, on February 21, 1781 (London, [1781])

A Discourse on the Love of our Country (London, 1789)

The Evidence for a Future Period of Improvement in the State of Mankind, with the Duty and Means of Promoting it (London, 1787)

Four Dissertations, third edition (London, 1772)

The General Introduction and Supplement to the Two Tracts on Civil Liberty (London, 1778)

Observations on the Importance of the American Revolution and the Means of Making it a Benefit to the World (London, 1784)

Observations on the Nature of Civil Liberty, the Principles of Government and the Policy of the War with America, third edition (London, 1776)

A Review of the Principal Questions in Morals, third edition (London, 1787)

A Sermon Delivered to a Congregation of Protestant Dissenters at Hackney, 10 February 1778 (London, 1779)

Sermons on the Christian Doctrine as Received by the Different Denominations of Christians, second edition (London, 1787)

Sermons on Various Subjects (London, 1816)

The Vanity, Misery and Infamy of Knowledge without Suitable Practice (London, 1770)

Price, R. and Priestley, J., *A Free Discussion of the Doctrines of Materialism and Philosophical Necessity* (London, 1778)

Priestley, J., *An Answer to Mr Paine's Age of Reason* (London, 1795)

An Appeal to the Public on the Subject of the Riots in Birmingham, second edition (Birmingham, 1792)

An Appeal to the Public on the Subject of the Riots in Birmingham, Part II (London, 1792)

The Conduct to be Observed by Dissenters in order to Procure the Repeal of the Corporation and Test Acts (Birmingham, [1789])

An Essay on the First Principles of Government and on the Nature of Political, Civil and Religious Liberty (London, 1771)

Essays on a Course of Liberal Education for Civil and Active Life (London, 1765)

Disquisitions Relating to Matter and Spirit (London, 1777)

Hartley's Theory of the Human Mind (London, 1775)

Lectures on History and General Policy (1761) (London, 1840)

Letters to a Philosophical Unbeliever, Part I, second edition (Birmingham, 1787)

Letters to a Philosophical Unbeliever, Part II (Birmingham, 1787)

Letters to the Right Honourable Edmund Burke, second edition (Birmingham, 1791)

A Letter to the Right Honourable William Pitt (London, 1787)

Memoirs of Dr Joseph Priestley to the year 1795 (London, 1806)

A Sermon on the Subject of the Slave Trade (Birmingham, 1788)

A Sermon Preached at the Gravel Pit Meeting . . . April 19th, 1793 (London, 1793)

A Sermon Preached before the Congregation of Protestant Dissenters . . . in Leeds, May 16, 1773 (London, 1773)

The Theological and Miscellaneous Works of Joseph Priestley, edited by J. T. Rutt, 25 vols. (Hackney, 1817–31)

The Use of Christianity, Especially in Difficult Times, second edition (London, 1794)

Principles of Order and Happiness under the British Constitution in a Dialogue between our Parish Clerk and the Squire (London, 1792)

Proby, C., *A Sermon Preached before the Honourable House of Commons . . . 30th January,*

1811 (London, 1811)

Prosser, R., *A Sermon Preached before the Honourable and Right Reverend Shute, Lord Bishop of Durham . . . 24th July, 1797* (Newcastle-upon-Tyne, 1797)

A Sermon Preached before the Honourable House of Commons . . . February 13, 1801 (London, 1801)

Quidam's Letters: Relative to the Church of Rome (London, 1825)

Radcliffe, E., *A Sermon Preached to a Congregation of Protestant Dissenters at Crutched-Friars Respecting Subscription* (London, 1772)

Ramsden, R., *The Alliance between the Church and the State* (Cambridge, 1800)

The Origin and Ends of Government (Cambridge, 1800)

Randolph, J., *A Charge Delivered to the Clergy of the Diocese of London . . . MDCCCX* (Oxford, 1810)

A Sermon Preached before the Lords . . . March 12, 1800 (Oxford, 1800)

[Reeves, J.], *Thoughts on the English Government* (London, 1795)

The Reformers' Catechism Intended for Reformers of all Classes (London, 1832)

Reid, W., *The Judgments of God in the Earth are Calls for Us to Learn Righteousness* (London, [1794])

The Religion of England Considered Politically with Reference to the Question of Roman Catholic Emancipation (London, 1828)

Remarks on Dr Price's Observations on the Nature of Civil Liberty (London, 1776)

Remarks on the Failure of Lord Sidmouth's Bill Relating to Protestant Dissenters (London, 1811)

Remarks on a Pamphlet Lately Published by Doctor Price, Intitled, Observations on the Nature of Civil Liberty (London, 1776)

Remarks on a Sermon Lately Published by the Rev. John Clayton (London, 1791)

Rennell, T., *Principles of French Republicanism Essentially Founded on Violence and Blood-Guiltiness* (London, 1793)

Rhodes, B., *A Discourse on Civil Government, and Religious Liberty* (Birmingham, 1796)

Rippon, J., *The Baptist Annual Register for 1790, 1791, 1792, and part of 1793* (London, 1793)

A Discourse on the Origin and Progress of the Society for Promoting Religious Knowledge among the Poor (London, [1804?])

Robinson, R., *Miscellaneous Works of Robert Robinson Late Pastor of the Baptist Church and Congregation of Protestant Dissenters at Cambridge*, 4 vols. (Harlow, 1807)

Posthumous Works of Robert Robinson (Harlow, 1812)

Sixteen Discourses on Several Texts of Scripture to Christian Assemblies in Villages near Cambridge (London, 1786)

Robison, J., *Proofs of a Conspiracy against All the Religions and Governments of Europe* (London, 1797)

Ross, J., *A Sermon Preached before the Lords . . . January 30, 1779* (London, 1779)

Rous, G., *Thoughts on Government: Occasioned by Mr Burke's Reflections*, fourth edition (London, 1791)

Rousseau, J. J., *The Social Contract* (Harmondsworth, 1968)

Ryder, H., *A Charge Addressed to the Clergy of the Diocese of Lichfield and Coventry . . . 1832* (London, 1832)

A Charge Delivered to the Clergy of the Diocese of Gloucester . . . 1816 (Gloucester, 1816)

Scholefield, R., *Love to Enemies Explained and Recommended* (London, 1791)

Schools for All, in Preference to Schools for Churchmen Only (London, 1812)

Scott, J., *Equality Considered and Recommended* (London, [1794])

Securities without Protection; or, Hints to Protestants (London, 1829)

Seddon, T., *A Sermon Preached at Hardwick . . . February, 1780* (Liverpool, 1780)

Sharp, G., *A Declaration of the People's Natural Right to a Share in the Legislature* (London, 1774)

    An Essay on Slavery, Proving from Scripture its Inconsistency with Humanity and Religion (Burlington, West Jersey, 1773; London, 1776)

    Extract of a Letter on the Proposed Catholic Emancipation (London, 1805)

    The Just Limitation of Slavery in the Laws of God Compared with the Unbounded Claims of the African Traders (London, 1776) and new edition with appendix (London, 1786)

    The Law of Liberty, or Royal Law, by which All Mankind Will Certainly Be Judged! (London, 1776)

    The Law of Passive Obedience or Christian Submission to Personal Injuries (London, 1776)

    The Law of Retribution (London, 1786)

    A Representation of the Injustice and Dangerous Tendency of Tolerating Slavery (London, 1769)

[Sharp, G.], *An Address to the People of England* (London, 1778)

    The Legal Means of Political Reformation Proposed in Two Small Tracts, seventh edition (London, 1780)

[Shaw, W.], *The Life of Hannah More: With a Critical Review of her Writings. By the Rev. Sir Archibald Mac Sarcasm, Bart.* (London, 1802)

Shelley, P. B., *The Complete Poetical Works*, edited by N. Rogers (Cambridge, 1972)

Shelley Memorials . . . to Which is Added an Essay on Christianity by Percy Bysshe Shelley, edited by Lady Jane Shelley (London, 1859)

Sheridan, C. F. *An Essay upon the True Principles of Civil Liberty, and of Free Government* (London, 1793)

Sherwin, W. T., *Memoirs of the Life of Thomas Paine* (London, 1819)

Shipley, J., *A Sermon Preached before the . . . Lords . . . January 30th, 1770* (London, 1770)

Sikes, T., *Dialogues between a Minister of the Church and his Parishioners, Concerning the Christian's Liberty of Choosing his Teacher* (London, 1802)

Skinner, J., *Journal of a Somerset Rector 1803–1834* (Oxford, 1971, 1984)

Smallweed, E., *A Sermon Preached before the Lords . . . July 30, 1784* (Oxford, 1784)

Smith, A., *The Wealth of Nations* (Everyman edition, n.d.)

Society for Constitutional Information, *Tracts Published and Distributed Gratis* (London, 1783)

Southey, R., *The Book of the Church*, 2 vols. (London, 1824)

Sparke, B. E., *A Charge Delivered to the Clergy of the Diocese of Ely . . . 1813* (London, 1813)

    A Charge Delivered to the Clergy of the Diocese of Ely . . . MDCCCXVII (London, 1817)

    A Sermon Preached before the Lords . . . 28 February, 1810 (London, 1810)

SPCK, *Religious Tracts Dispersed by the Society*, 12 vols., vol. 3 (London, 1807)

Squire, S., *A Sermon Preached before the Lords . . . January 30, 1762* (London, 1762)

Stanley, A. P., *Historical Memorials of Westminster Abbey* (London, 1868)

Stanley, E., *A Few Words in Favour of our Roman Catholic Brethren*, third edition (London, 1829)

Stanley, J., *The Increase, Influence and Stability of Unestablished Religion, No Cause of Alarm to the Established Christian* (Wednesbury, 1813)

Statement and Propositions from the Society for Giving Effect to His Majesty's Proclamation against Vice and Immorality (London, 1790)

Stephens, J., *The Mutual Relations, Claims, and Duties of the Rich and the Poor* (Manchester, 1819)

Stevens, R., *A Sermon Preached in Deptford . . . 6 June, 1814* (London, 1814)

Stevens, W., *Memoirs of William Stevens Esq.* (London, 1812)

[Stevens, W.], *A Discourse on the English Constitution* (London, 1776)

  The Revolution Vindicated and Constitutional Liberty Asserted (Cambridge, 1777)

  Strictures on a Sermon, Entitled The Principles of the Revolution vindicated, second edition (Cambridge, 1777)

Stewart, J., *The Total Refutation and Political Overthrow of Doctor Price* (London, 1776)

Stinton, G., *A Sermon Preached before the Honourable House of Commons . . . February 10, 1779* (London, 1779)

Strictures on the Expedience of the Addingtonian Extinguisher (Macclesfield, 1811)

Sumner, C. R., *A Charge Delivered to the Clergy of the Diocese of Llandaff in September, 1827* (London, 1827)

Sumner, J. B., *A Charge Delivered to the Clergy of the Diocese of Chester . . . MDCCCXXXII* (London, 1832)

Talbot, J., Earl of Shrewsbury, *Reasons for Not Taking the Test; For Not Conforming to the Established Church* (London, 1828)

Tatham, E., *Letters to the Right Honourable Edmund Burke on Politics* (Oxford, 1791)

Taylor, R., *The Holy Liturgy or Divine Service on the Principles of Pure Deism* (London, [1827?])

  Swing, or Who are the Incendiaries? (London, 1831)

[Taylor, R.], *The Devil's Pulpit*, 4 March 1831–25 March 1831 (London, 1831)

  The Judgment of the Court of King's Bench, upon the Rev. Robert Taylor (London, [1828])

  The Trial of the Rev. Robert Taylor . . . upon a Charge of Blasphemy (London, 1827)

Taylor, T., *The Hypocrite, or Self Deceiver, Tried and Cast* (Macclesfield, 1793)

  The Reconciler, or, An Humble Attempt to Sketch the Doctrine and Discipline of the Church of Christ (Liverpool, 1806)

  Redeeming Grace Displayed to the Chief of Sinners (Leeds, 1785)

  Ten Sermons on the Millennium (Hull, 1789)

Temperate Comments upon Intemperate Reflections: or, A Review of Mr Burke's Letter (London, 1791)

Theory Contradicted by Fact: or The Asserted Change in the Principles of Roman Catholics Refuted (London, 1827)

Thompson, Thomas, *The African Trade for Negro Slaves, Shewn to Be Consistent with Principles of Humanity and with the Laws of Revealed Religion* (Canterbury, n.d.)

Thompson, T., *Annals of Philosophy*, vol. 2, July–December 1813 (London, 1813)

Thorp, R., *A Charge Delivered to the Clergy of the Archdeaconry of Northumberland in April 1798* (Newcastle-upon-Tyne, 1798)

    On Establishments in Religion and Religious Liberty, Cambridge University Commencement Sermon, 1 July 1792 (Newcastle-upon-Tyne, 1798)

Three Dialogues Concerning Liberty (London, 1776)

Three Letters to Dr Price, Containing Remarks on his Observations on the Nature of Civil Liberty (London, 1776)

Three Letters to the Rev. Dr Price Containing Remarks upon his Fast-Sermon (by a cobbler) (London, 1779)

Thurlow, T., *A Sermon Preached before the . . . Lords . . . January 31st, 1780* (London, 1780)

To the Great and Learned among Christians, the Humble Petition of a Number of Poor, Loyal, Unlearned Christians (London, 1793)

Toplady, A., *The Works of Augustus Toplady A.B., Late Vicar of Broad Hembury, Devon*, 6 vols. (London, 1794)

The Total Eclipse: A Grand Politico-Astronomical Phenomenon which Occurred in the Year 1820 (London, n.d.)

Towers, John, *A Friendly Dialogue between Theophilus and Philadelphus* (London, 1776)

Towers, Joseph, *An Oration Delivered at the London Tavern . . . November, 1788* (London, 1788)

    Remarks on the Conduct, Principles and Publications of the Association at the Crown and Anchor . . . for Preserving Liberty and Property against Republicans and Levellers (London, 1793)

    Thoughts on the Commencement of a New Parliament (London, 1790)

    A Vindication of the Political Principles of Mr Locke (London, 1782)

Townsend, G., *Obedience to the Laws of the Church of Rome Incompatible with the Power of Legislating for Protestants* (London, 1829)

Townsend, J., *The Principles of Protestant Dissenters* (Bath, 1791)

Trewman's Exeter Flying Post, 1819–30

Trimmer, S., *Instructive Tales*, third edition (London, 1815)

    The OEconomy of Charity; or, An Address to Ladies Concerning Sunday Schools (London, 1787)

    Reflections upon the Education of Children in Charity Schools (London, 1792)

    The Servant's Friend: An Exemplary Tale, second edition (London, 1787)

    The Two Farmers: An Exemplary Tale (London, 1787)

Tucker, J., *An Apology for the Present Church of England*, second edition (Gloucester, 1772)

    Four Letters on Important National Subjects Addressed to . . . the Earl of Shelburne (Gloucester, 1783)

    Four Tracts on Political and Commercial Subjects, third edition (Gloucester, 1776)

    Hospitals and Infirmaries, Considered as Schools of Christian Education for the Adult Poor (London, 1746)

    An Humble Address and Earnest Appeal (Gloucester, 1775)

    Letter to Edmund Burke Esq. (Gloucester, 1775)

    Letters to the Rev. Dr Kippis Occasioned by his Treatise Entitled 'A Vindication of the Protestant Dissenting Ministers' (Gloucester, 1773)

The Notions of Mr Locke and his Followers (privately printed, Gloucester, n.d. [1778])

Reflections on the Expediency of a Law for the Naturalization of Foreign Protestants (London, 1751)

Reflections on the Present Matters in Dispute between Great Britain and Ireland (London, 1785)

Religious Intolerance No Part of the General Plan Either of the Mosaic, or the Christian Dispensation (Gloucester, 1774)

The Respective Pleas and Arguments of the Mother Country and of the Colonies Distinctly Set Forth (Gloucester, 1775)

A Sermon Preached in the Parish Church of Christ Church, London . . . May the 7th, 1766 (London, 1766)

A Treatise Concerning Civil Government (London, 1781)

Turgot, A. R. J., *Turgot on Progress, Sociology and Economics*, edited by R. L. Meek (Cambridge, 1973)

Turner, D., *An Exhortation to Peace, Loyalty and the Support of Government* (Henley, [1793?])

Two Letters Addressed to the Author of the 'Book of the Roman Catholic Church' (London, 1825)

Van Mildert, W., *A Charge Delivered to the Clergy of the Diocese of Durham MDCCCXXXI* (Oxford, 1831)

A Charge Delivered to the Clergy of the Diocese of Llandaff . . . 1821 (Oxford, 1821)

An Historical View of the Rise and Progress of Infidelity, with a Refutation of its Principles and Reasonings (London, 1806)

Sermons on Several Occasions and Charges (Oxford, 1838)

Substance of a Speech Delivered in the House of Lords . . . May 17, 1825 (London, 1827)

Vernon, E. V., *A Sermon Preached before the Lords . . . January 30, 1794* (London, 1794)

[Vice Society], *An Address to the Public from the Society for the Suppression of Vice . . . Part the Second* (London, 1803)

Occasional Report of the Society for the Suppression of Vice No. V (London, 1810)

Part of the First, of an Address to the Public from the Society for the Suppression of Vice (London, 1803)

Proposal for Establishing a Society for the Suppression of Vice and the Encouragement of Religion and Virtue (n.d.)

Vincent, W., *A Sermon Preached before the Honourable House of Commons . . . June 1, 1802* (London, 1802)

A Vindication of the Right Honourable Edmund Burke's Reflections on the Revolution in France (London, 1791)

The Voice of God: Being Serious Thoughts on the Present Alarming Crisis (London, 1775)

Voltaire, *Philosophical Dictionary* (New York, 1962)

Wade, J., *The Black Book; or Corruption Unmasked!*, 2 vols. (London, 1820)

Wait, W., *The Last Days of a Person Who Had Been One of Thomas Paine's Disciples* (Bristol, [1802])

War with France the Only Security of Britain at the Present Momentous Crisis (London, 1794)

Warburton, W., *The Alliance between Church and State* (London, 1736)

[Ward, W.], *A Letter on the Subject of the British and Foreign Bible Society* (London, 1810)

Warner, R., *Catholic Emancipation Incompatible with the Safety of the Established Religion, Liberty, Laws and Protestant Succession of the British Empire* (London, 1829)

Warren, J., *The Duties of the Parochial Clergy of the Church of England Considered in a Charge . . . 1784* (London, 1785)

  A Sermon Preached before the Lords . . . February 4, 1780 (London, 1780)

  A Sermon Preached before the Lords . . . January 30th, 1781 (London, 1781)

Watson, R., *An Address to Young Persons after Confirmation* (Edinburgh, 1817)

  Anecdotes of the Life of Richard Watson . . . Written by Himself (London, 1817)

  An Apology for the Bible, in a Series of Letters Addressed to Thomas Paine (London, 1796)

  An Apology for Christianity in a Series of Letters Addressed to Edward Gibbon (Cambridge, 1776)

  The Bishop of Llandaff's Thoughts on the French Invasion Originally Addressed to the Clergy of his Diocese (London, n.d. [1798?])

  A Charge Delivered to the Clergy of the Diocese of Llandaff June 1791 (London, 1792)

  A Charge Delivered to the Clergy of the Diocese of Landaff [sic] *in June 1805* (London, 1808)

  Miscellaneous Tracts on Religious, Political and Agricultural Subjects, 2 vols. (London, 1815)

  A Sermon Preached before the Lords . . . January 30, 1784 (London, 1784)

  A Sermon Preached in the Chapel of the London Hospital, April 8th, 1802 (London, 1802)

  Sermons on Public Occasions, and Tracts on Religious Subjects (Cambridge, 1788)

  The Substance of a Speech Intended to Have Been Spoken in the House of Lords, November 22nd, 1803 (London, 1803)

[Watson, R.], *A Letter to the Members of the Honourable House of Commons*, second edition (London, 1772)

Wedderburn, J. W., *A Letter to Henry Brougham Esq., MP, on the subject of Catholic Emancipation* (London, 1825)

Wells, R., *A Correspondence between the Rev. Robert Wells MA . . . and a Gentleman under the signature of Publicola* (Bristol, 1791)

Wesley, John, *The Works of John Wesley*, vol. 11, edited by G. R. Cragg (Oxford, 1975)

  The Works of the Rev. John Wesley, AM, sometime Fellow of Lincoln College, Oxford, third edition, 14 vols. (London, 1829–31)

Westminster Election: A Correct Report of the Proceedings of the Meeting Held at the Crown and Anchor . . . June 1, 1818 (London, 1818)

Westminster Election: The Speeches of Mr Hunt and Mr Gale Jones on the Hustings . . . 25 June, 1818 (London, 1818)

Whately, R., *Dr Paley's Works: A Lecture* (London, 1859)

[Whately, R.], *Letters on the Church by an Episcopalian* (London, 1826)

Whitaker, T. D., *The Substance of a Speech Delivered at a General Meeting of the Magistrates, Clergy, Gentry . . . of Blackburn . . . February 10, AD 1817* (Blackburn, 1817)

Whitchurch, S., *Another Witness! or Further Testimony in Favor* [sic] *of Richard Brothers* (London, 1795)

Whitehead, W. B., *The Dangers of the Church, as Connected with the Prevalence of an Excessive Spirit of Reform* (Bath, 1831)

Wickes, J. W., *A Sermon Preached at the Parish Church of St Michael, Queen-Hithe . . . March 7, 1798* (London, 1798)

Wilberforce, W., *The Correspondence of William Wilberforce*, edited by R. I. and S. Wilberforce, 2 vols. (London, 1840)

A Letter on the Abolition of the Slave Trade Addressed to the Freeholders . . . of Yorkshire (London, 1807)

The Life of William Wilberforce, edited by R. I. and S. Wilberforce, 5 vols. (London, 1838)

A Practical View of the Prevailing Religious System of Professed Christians in the Higher and Middle Classes in this Country Contrasted with Real Christianity (London, 1797)

Statement and Propositions from the Society for Giving Effect to His Majesty's Proclamation against Vice and Immorality (London, 1790)

Wilde, J., *Preliminary Lecture to the Course of Lectures on the Institutions of Justinian* (Edinburgh, 1794)

Wilkes, J., *et al.*, *The Controversial Letters of John Wilkes Esq., the Rev. John Horne, and their Principal Adherents* (London, 1771)

Wilks, M., *The Origin and Stability of the French Revolution* (Norwich, 1791)

Williams, J. H., *Piety, Charity, and Loyalty, Recommended in a Sermon* (Birmingham, 1793)

Willis, T., *A Sermon Preached in the Foundling Hospital, June 2nd, 1798* (London, 1798)

Wilson, C., *A Sermon Preached before the Lords . . . January 31, 1785* (London, 1785)

Wilson, D., *The Duty of Contentment under Present Circumstances* (London, 1817)

Wollstonecraft, M., *An Historical and Moral View of the Origin and Progress of the French Revolution* (London, 1794)

[Wollstonecraft, M.], *A Vindication of the Rights of Men in a Letter to the Right Honourable Edmund Burke* (London, 1790)

[Wood, T.], *Essays on Civil Government and Subjection and Obedience to the Higher Powers* (Wigan, 1796)

A Word of Admonition to the Right Hon. William Pitt . . . occasioned by the Prophecies of Brothers (London, 1795)

Wordsworth, C., *Reasons for Declining to Become a Subscriber to the British and Foreign Bible Society* (London, 1810)

Wyvill, C., *An Apology for the Petitioners for Liberty of Conscience* (London, 1810)

The Correspondence of the Rev. C. Wyvill with the Right Honourable William Pitt, second edition (Newcastle, 1796)

A Defence of Dr Price and the Reformers of England (London, 1792)

A Letter to John Cartwright Esq., second edition (York, 1801)

A More Extended Discussion in Favour of Liberty of Conscience (London, 1808)

Papers and Letters Chiefly Respecting the Reformation of Parliament (Richmond, 1816)

Political Papers, chiefly respecting the Attempt . . . to effect a Reformation of the Parliament of Great Britain, 6 vols. (York, 1794–1802)

Thoughts on our Articles of Religion with Respect to their Supposed Utility to the State, third edition (London, 1773)

Wyvill, C. (Dean of Ripon), *The Duty of Honouring the King, and the Obligations We Have Thereto* (1685; republished, York, 1793)

Yorke, J., *A Sermon Preached before the Lords . . . January 30, 1776* (London, 1776)

Zeta, *A Full View of the Catholic Question* (London, 1828)

SECONDARY SOURCES

UNPUBLISHED DISSERTATIONS

Bradley, Ian, 'The Politics of Godliness: Evangelicals in Parliament, 1784–1832' (D.Phil., University of Oxford, 1974)

Bradley, J. E., 'Whigs and Nonconformists: Presbyterians, Congregationalists and Baptists in English Politics, 1718–1790' (Ph.D., University of Southern California, 1978)

Brain, T. J., 'Some Aspects of the Life and Work of Richard Watson, Bishop of Llandaff, 1737 to 1816' (Ph.D., University of Wales, 1982)

Burne, Patience, 'The Moral Theory of Jeremy Bentham and William Paley' (MA, University of London, 1948)

Duffy, Eamon, 'Joseph Berington and the English Cisalpine Movement 1772–1803' (Ph.D., University of Cambridge, 1973)

Hole, R., 'Joseph Priestley and the Enlightenment' (MA, University of Manchester, 1978)

Kirkland, W. M., 'The Impact of the French Revolution on Scottish Religious Life and Thought with Special Reference to Thomas Chalmers, Robert Haldane and Neil Douglas' (Ph.D., University of Edinburgh, 1951)

McCabe, Joseph, 'The Attitude of Edmund Burke towards Christianity and the Churches' (Ph.D., University of Edinburgh, 1951)

Murray, N. U., 'The Influence of the French Revolution on the Church of England and its Rivals, 1789–1802' (D.Phil., University of Oxford, 1975)

Nockles, P. B., 'Continuity and Change in Anglican High Churchmanship in Britain, 1792–1850' (D.Phil., University of Oxford, 1982)

Robison, O. C., 'Particular Baptists in England, 1760–1820' (D.Phil., University of Oxford, 1967)

Schofield, T. P., 'English Conservative Thought and Opinion in Response to the French Revolution, 1789–1796' (Ph.D., University of London, 1984)

Sellers, Ian, 'Social and Political Ideas of Representative English Unitarians, 1795–1850' (B.Litt., University of Oxford, 1956)

Sterling, K., 'The Education of the Anglican Clergy, 1830–1914' (Ph.D., University of Leicester, 1982)

PUBLISHED BOOKS AND ARTICLES

Aldred, Guy A., *Richard Carlile, Agitator: His Life and Times* (Glasgow, 1941)

Aldridge, A. O., *Man of Reason: The Life of Thomas Paine* (London, 1960)

Allen, Peter, 'S. T. Coleridge's *Church and State* and the Idea of an Intellectual Establishment', *JHI*, 46 (1985), 89–106

Annan, Noel, *Leslie Stephen: His Thought and Character in Relation to his Time* (London, 1951)

Ansty, Roger, 'A Re-interpretation of the Abolition of the British Slave Trade, 1806–1807', *EHR*, 87 (1972), 304–32

Áquist, L., *The Moral Philosophy of Richard Price* (Uppsala, 1960)

Ashcraft, R., and M. M. Goldsmith, 'Locke, Revolution Principles, and the Formation of his Ideology', *HJ*, 26 (1983) 773–800

Aspinall, A., *Politics and the Press* (London, 1949)

Ayer, A. J., *Hume* (Oxford, 1980)

Bahlman, D. W. R., *The Moral Revolution of 1688* (New Haven, Connecticut, 1957)

Bailyn, Bernard, *The Ideological Origins of the American Revolution* (Cambridge, Massachusetts, 1967)

Baker, W. J., *Beyond Port and Prejudice: Charles Lloyd of Oxford, 1784–1829* (Orono, Maine, 1981)

Barlow, R. B., *Citizenship and Conscience: A Study in the Theory and Practice of Religious Toleration in England during the Eighteenth Century* (Philadelphia, 1962)

Bartel, Roland, 'The Story of Public Fast Days in England', *Anglican Theological Review*, 37 (1955), 190–200

Baxter, John, 'The Great Yorkshire Revival 1792–6: A Study of Mass Revival amongst the Methodists', in *A Sociological Yearbook of Religion in Britain*, 7 (1974), 46–76

Belchem, J. C., 'Henry Hunt and the Evolution of the Mass Platform', *EHR*, 93 (1978), 739–73

Bellah, Robert, 'Civil Religion in America', *Daedalus*, 96 (1967), 1–21

Bellenger, D., 'The Émigré Clergy and the English Church, 1789–1815', *JEH*, 34 (1983), 392–410

Belloc, Bessie, *In a Walled Garden* (London, 1895)

Bennett, G. V., 'Conflict in the Church', in *Britain after the Glorious Revolution, 1689–1714*, edited by Geoffrey Holmes (London, 1969)

   The Tory Crisis in Church and State 1688–1730: The Career of Francis Atterbury, Bishop of Rochester (Oxford, 1975)

Bennett, G. V., and J. D. Walsh (eds.), *Essays in Modern English Church History in Memory of Norman Sykes* (Oxford, 1966)

Berens, John F., '"A God of Order and Not of Confusion": The American Loyalists and Divine Providence, 1774–1783', *Historical Magazine of the Protestant Episcopal Church*, 47 (1978), 211–19

Best, G. F. A., 'The Protestant Constitution and its Supporters, 1800–1829', *TRHS*, fifth series, 8 (1958), 105–27

   Temporal Pillars: Queen Anne's Bounty, the Ecclesiastical Commissioners, and the Church of England (Cambridge, 1964)

   'The Whigs and the Church Establishment in the Age of Grey and Holland', *Hist.*, 45 (1960), 103–18

Black, E. C., *The Association: British Extraparliamentary Political Organisation, 1769–93* (Cambridge, Massachusetts, 1963)

Bohstedt, J., *Riots and Community Politics in England and Wales 1790–1810* (Cambridge, Massachusetts, 1983)

Bolam, C., J. Goring, H. Short and R. Thomas, *The English Presbyterians from Elizabethan Puritanism to Modern Unitarianism* (London, 1968)

Bolt, C. and S. Drescher (eds.), *Anti-Slavery, Religion, and Reform: Essays in Memory of Roger Ansty* (Folkestone, 1980)

Bonwick, C. C., 'An English Audience for American Revolutionary Pamphlets', *HJ*, 19 (1976), 355–74

Bosher, Robert, *The Making of the Restoration Settlement* (London, 1951)

Boss, R. I., 'The Development of Social Religion: A Contradiction of French Free

Thought', *JHI*, 34 (1973), 577–89

Bossy, John, *The English Catholic Community, 1570–1850* (London, 1975)

Boulton, J. T., *Arbitrary Power: An Eighteenth Century Obsession* (Nottingham, 1966)
    'James Mackintosh: "*Vindiciae Gallicae*"', *Renaissance and Modern Studies*, 21 (1977), 106–18
    The Language of Politics in the Age of Wilkes and Burke (London, 1963)

Bradley, I., *The Call to Seriousness: The Evangelical Impact on the Victorians* (London, 1976)

Bradley, J. E., 'Religion and Reform at the Polls: Nonconformity in Cambridge Politics, 1774–1784', *JBS*, 23 (1984), 55–78
    'Whigs and Nonconformists: "Slumbering Radicalism" in English Politics, 1739–1789', *ECS*, 9 (1975), 1–27

Brain, T., 'Richard Watson and the Debate on Toleration in the Late Eighteenth Century', *PPN*, 2 (1978), 4–26

Brent, R., *Liberal Anglican Politics: Whiggery, Religion and Reform 1830–1841* (Oxford, 1987)

Brewer, John, *Party Ideology and Popular Politics at the Accession of George III* (Cambridge, 1976)

Bric, M. J., 'Priests, Parsons and Politics: The Rightboy Protest in County Cork, 1785–1788', *PP*, 100 (1983), 100–23

Bridenbaugh, C., *Mitre and Sceptre: Transatlantic Faiths, Ideas, Personalities and Politics, 1689–1773* (Oxford, 1962)

Bristow, E. J., *Vice and Vigilance: Purity Movements in Britain since 1700* (Dublin, 1977)

Brock, Michael, *The Great Reform Act* (London, 1973)

Brockett, A., *Nonconformity in Exeter, 1650–1875* (Manchester, 1962)

Brose, Olive J., *Church and Parliament: The Reshaping of the Church of England, 1828–1860* (London, 1959)

Brown, F. K., *Fathers of the Victorians: The Age of Wilberforce* (Cambridge, 1961)

Brown, Peter, *The Chathamites: A Study in the Relationship between Personalities and Ideas in the Second Half of the Eighteenth Century* (London, 1967)

Brown, Philip Anthony, *The French Revolution in English History* (London, 1918)

Browning, Reed, 'The Origin of Burke's Ideas Revisited', *ECS*, 18 (1984), 57–71
    Political and Constitutional Ideas of the Court Whigs (Baton Rouge, 1982)

Burns, J. H., 'Bentham and the French Revolution', *TRHS*, fifth series, 16 (1966), 95–114

Burton, E., *The Life and Times of Bishop Challoner*, 2 vols. (London, 1909)

Buschkuhl, M., *Great Britain and the Holy See, 1746–1870* (Dublin, 1982)

Butler, J. R. M., *The Passing of the Great Reform Bill* (1914; new edition, London, 1964)

Butterfield, H., *George III and the Historians*, revised edition (New York, 1957)
    'George III and the Namier School', *Encounter*, 43 (April 1957), 70–6

Cameron, David, *The Social Thought of Rousseau and Burke: A Comparative Study* (London, 1973)

Canavan, F., *The Political Reason of Edmund Burke* (Durham, North Carolina, 1960)

Canovan, M., 'Paternalistic Liberalism: Joseph Priestley on Rank and Inequality', *ED*, 2 (1983), 23–37
    'The Un-Benthamite Utilitarianism of Joseph Priestley', *JHI*, 45 (1984), 435–50

Carrillo, E. A., 'The Corsican Kingdom of George III', *JMH*, 34 (1962), 254–74

Chadwick, Owen, *From Bossuet to Newman* (Cambridge, 1957)

   The Secularization of the European Mind in the Nineteenth Century (Cambridge, 1975)

   The Victorian Church, vol. 1 (second edition) and vol. 2 (London, 1970)

   Victorian Miniature (London, 1960)

Chaloner, W. H., 'Dr Joseph Priestley, John Wilkinson, and the French Revolution, 1789–1802', *TRHS*, fifth series, 8 (1958), 21–40

Chapin, C. F., *The Religious Thought of Samuel Johnson* (Ann Arbor, 1968)

Chapman, G. W., *Edmund Burke: The Practical Imagination* (Cambridge, Mass., 1967)

Childe-Pemberton, W., *The Earl Bishop: The Life of Frederick Hervey, Bishop of Derry, Earl of Bristol*, 2 vols. (London, 1924)

Chinnici, J. P., *The English Catholic Enlightenment: John Lingard and the Cisalpine Movement, 1780 to 1850* (Shepherdstown, 1980)

Christian, W., 'The Moral Economics of Tom Paine', *JHI*, 34 (1973), 367–80

Christie, I. R., *Stress and Stability in Late-Eighteenth-Century Britain: Reflections on the British Avoidance of Revolution* (Oxford, 1984)

   Wilkes, Wyvill and Reform: The Parliamentary Reform Movement in British Politics 1760–1785 (London, 1962)

   'The Yorkshire Association, 1780–4: A Study in Political Organisation', *HJ*, 3 (1960), 144–61

Clark, D. M., *British Opinion and the American Revolution* (1930, 1958, reissued New York, 1966)

Clark, G. Kitson, *Churchmen and the Condition of England, 1832–1885: A Study in the Development of Social Ideas and Practice from the Old Regime to the Modern State* (London, 1973)

Clark, J. C. D., 'England's Ancien Regime', *PP*, 117 (November 1987), 195–207

   English Society 1688–1832: Ideology, Social Structure and Political Practice during the Ancien Regime (Cambridge, 1985)

   Revolution and Rebellion: State and Society in England in the Seventeenth and Eighteenth Centuries (Cambridge, 1986)

Clarke, M. L., *Paley: Evidences for the Man* (London, 1974)

Clarke, W. K. L., *A History of the SPCK* (London, 1959)

Coates, J. D., 'Coleridge's Debt to Harrington: A Discussion of *Zapolya*', *JHI*, 37 (1977), 501–8

Cobban, A., *Edmund Burke and the Revolt against the Eighteenth Century: A Study of the Political and Social Thinking of Burke, Wordsworth, Coleridge and Southey* (London, 1929)

Cohen, L. H., 'The American Revolution and the Natural Law Theory', *JHI*, 39 (1978), 491–502

Cole, G. A., 'Doctrine, Dissent and the Decline of Paley's Reputation', *ED*, 6 (1987), 19–30

Coleman, W., 'Providence, Capitalism, and Environmental Degradation: English Apologetics in an Era of Economic Revolution', *JHI*, 37 (1976), 27–44

Colley, Linda, 'The Apotheosis of George III: Loyalty, Royalty and the British Nation', *PP*, 102 (1984), 94–129

Cone, Carl B., *Burke and the Nature of Politics*, 2 vols. (Lexington, 1957, 1964)

The English Jacobins (New York, 1968)

'Richard Price and the Constitution of the United States', *AHR*, 53 (1948), 726–47

Torchbearer of Freedom: The Influence of Richard Price on Eighteenth Century Thought (Lexington, 1952)

Connolly, S. J., *Priests and People in Pre-Famine Ireland, 1780–1845* (Dublin, 1982)

Cookson, J. E., *The Friends of Peace: Anti-War Liberalism in England, 1793–1815* (Cambridge, 1982)

Cowherd, R. G., *The Politics of English Dissent* (New York, 1956)

Cragg, G. R., 'The Churchman', in *Man versus Society in Eighteenth-Century Britain: Six Points of View*, edited by James L. Clifford (Cambridge, 1968), pp. 54–69

From Puritanism to the Age of Reason: A Study of Changes in Religious Thought within the Church of England, 1660–1700 (Cambridge, 1966)

Reason and Authority in the Eighteenth Century (Cambridge, 1964)

Crane, R., 'Anglican Apologetics and the Idea of Progress', *Modern Philology*, 31 (1934), 273–306, 349–82

Currie, R., *Methodism Divided: A Study in the Sociology of Ecumenicalism* (London, 1968)

Currie, R., A. Gilbert, and L. Horsley, *Churches and Churchgoers: Patterns of Church Growth in the British Isles since 1700* (Oxford, 1977)

Currie, R., and R. M. Hartwell, 'The Making of the English Working Class?', *Economic History Review*, second series, 18 (1965), 633–43

Daly, J., *Sir Robert Filmer and English Political Thought* (Toronto, 1979)

Davies, D. B., *The Problem of Slavery in the Age of Revolution, 1770–1823* (London, 1975)

Davies, R., A. R. George and G. Rupp, *A History of the Methodist Church in Great Britain*, vol. 2 (London, 1978)

Davis, R. W., *Dissent in Politics 1780–1830: The Political Life of William Smith MP* (London, 1971)

'The Strategy of Dissent in the Repeal Campaign, 1820–28', *JMH*, 38 (1966), 374–93

'The Tories, the Whigs and Catholic Emancipation, 1827–1829', *EHR*, 97 (1982), 89–98

Derry, Warren, *Dr Parr: A Portrait of the Whig Dr Johnson* (Oxford, 1966)

Dickinson, H. T., 'Benjamin Hoadley, 1676–1761: Unorthodox Bishop', *History Today*, 25 (1975), 348–55

'The Eighteenth Century Debate on the Glorious Revolution', *Hist.*, 61 (1976), 28–45

'The Eighteenth Century Debate on the Sovereignty of Parliament', *TRHS*, fifth series, 26 (1976), 189–210

Liberty and Property: Political Ideology in Eighteenth-Century Britain (London, 1977)

Dinwiddy, J. R., *Christopher Wyvill and Reform, 1790–1820*, Borthwick Papers 39 (York, 1971)

'Sir Francis Burdett and Burdettite Radicalism', *Hist.*, 65 (1980), 17–31

Ditchfield, G. M., 'Debates on the Test and Corporation Acts 1787–90: the Evidence of the Division Lists', *BIHR*, 50 (1977), 69–81

'Dissent and Toleration: Lord Stanhope's Bill of 1789', *JEH*, 29 (1978), 51–73

'The Parliamentary Struggle over the Repeal of the Test and Corporation Acts 1787–1790', *EHR*, 89 (1974), 551–77

Donajgrodzki, A. P. (ed.), *Social Control in Nineteenth Century Britain* (London, 1977)

Donovan, R. K., 'The Military Origins of the Roman Catholic Relief Programme of 1778', *HJ*, 28 (1985), 79–102

Dozier, R. R., *For King, Constitution and Country: The English Loyalists and the French Revolution* (Lexington, 1983)

Dreyer, F., 'Faith and Experience in the Thought of John Wesley', *AHR*, 88 (1983), 12–30

  'The Genesis of Burke's *Reflections*', *JMH*, 50 (1978), 462–79

Drummond, A. L., and J. Bulloch, *The Scottish Church, 1688–1843* (Edinburgh, 1973)

Duffy, Eamon, 'Doctor Douglas and Mister Berington – an eighteenth-century retraction', *Downside Review*, 88 (1970), 246–69

  'Ecclesiastical Democracy Detected', *Recusant History*, 10 (1970), 193–209, 309–31

Duffy, Eamon (ed.), *Challoner and his Church: A Catholic Bishop in Georgian England* (London, 1981)

Dunn, J., *The Political Thought of John Locke: An Historical Account of the Argument of the 'Two Treatises on Government'* (Cambridge, 1969)

Dybikowski, J., 'David Williams and the Eighteenth Century Distinction between Civil and Political Liberty', *ED*, 3 (1984), 15–35

Eccleshall, R., 'Richard Hooker and the Peculiarities of the English: The Reception of the *Ecclesiastical Polity* in the Seventeenth and Eighteenth Centuries', *History of Political Thought*, 2 (1981), 63–117

Edie, C. A., 'Succession and Monarchy: The Controversy of 1679–81', *AHR*, 70 (1964–5), 350–70

Edwards, Maldwyn, *After Wesley: A Study of the Social and Political Influence of Methodism in the Middle Period (1791–1849)* (London, 1935)

  John Wesley and the Eighteenth Century: A Study of his Social and Political Influence (London, 1933, revised edition, 1955)

Elliot, C. M. 'The Political Economy of English Dissent, 1780–1840', in *The Industrial Revolution*, edited by R. M. Hartwell (Oxford, 1970)

Emsley, C., 'The London "Insurrection" of December 1792: Fact, Fiction or Fantasy?', *JBS*, 17 (1978), 66–86

d'Entrèves, A. P., *Natural Law*, second edition (London, 1970)

Evans, E. J., 'Some Reasons for the Growth of English Rural Anti-Clericalism c. 1750–1830', *PP*, 66 (1975), 84–109

Every, G., *The High-Church Party, 1688–1718* (London, 1956)

Faulkner, H. U., *Chartism and the Churches: A Study in Democracy* (reprinted London, 1970)

Fennessy, R. R., *Burke, Paine and the Rights of Man: A Difference of Political Opinion* (The Hague, 1963)

Ferguson, J. P., *An Eighteenth Century Heretic: Dr Samuel Clarke* (Kineton, 1976)

Figgis, J. N., *Churches in the Modern State* (London, 1913)

  The Theory of the Divine Right of Kings (Cambridge, 1896)

Fitzpatrick, M., 'Joseph Priestley and the Cause of Universal Toleration', *PPN*, 1 (1977), 3–30

Fleisher, D., *William Godwin: A Study in Liberalism* (London, 1951)

Flinn, M. W., 'Social Theory and the Industrial Revolution', in *Social Theory and*

Economic Change, edited by Tom Burns and S. B. Saul (London, 1967), pp. 9–34

Forbes, D., *Hume's Philosophical Politics* (Cambridge, 1975)

Foster, J., *Class Struggle and the Industrial Revolution: Early Industrial Capitalism in Three English Towns* (London, 1974)

Freeman, M., *Edmund Burke and the Critique of Political Radicalism* (Oxford, 1980)

Fruchtman, Jack, 'The Apocalyptic Politics of Richard Price and Joseph Priestley: A Study in Late Eighteenth Century English Republican Millenarianism', *Transactions of the American Philosophical Society*, 73, part 4 (1983), 1–125

Garrett, C., 'Joseph Priestley, the Millennium, and the French Revolution', *JHI*, 34 (1973), 51–66

Respectable Folly: Millenarians and the French Revolution in France and England (Baltimore, 1975)

Gascoigne, J., 'Anglican Latitudinarianism and Political Radicalism in the late Eighteenth Century', *Hist.*, 71 (1986), 22–38

Gash, Norman, *Mr Secretary Peel: The Life of Sir Robert Peel to 1830* (London, 1961)

Gibbs, F. W., *Joseph Priestley, Adventurer in Science and Champion of Truth* (London, 1965)

Gilbert, A. D., *The Making of Post-Christian Britain: A History of the Secularization of Modern Society* (London, 1980)

Religion and Society in Industrial England: Church, Chapel and Social Change, 1740–1914 (London, 1976)

Gill, J. C., *The Ten Hours Parson: Christian Social Action in the Eighteen Thirties* (London, 1959)

Gillam, J. G., *The Crucible: The Story of Joseph Priestley LLD, FRS* (London, 1954)

Gilley, Sheridan, 'Christianity and Enlightenment: An Historical Survey', *History of European Ideas*, 1 (1981), 103–21

'John Lingard and the Catholic Revival', *SCH*, 14 (1977), 313–27

'Nationality and Liberty, Protestant and Catholic: Robert Southey's Book of the Church', *SCH*, 18 (1982), 409–32

Ginter, D. E., 'The Loyalist Association Movement of 1792–93 and British Public Opinion', *HJ*, 9 (1966), 179–90

Goldsmith, M. M., 'Public Virtue and Private Vice: Bernard Mandeville and English Political Ideologies in the Early Eighteenth Century', *ECS*, 9 (1976), 477–510

Goodwin, Albert, *The Friends of Liberty: The English Democratic Movement in the Age of the French Revolution* (London, 1979)

Gossman, L., *The Empire Unpossess'd: An Essay on Gibbon's 'Decline and Fall'* (Cambridge, 1981)

Greaves, R. W., *On the Religious Climate of Hanoverian England* (London, 1963)

Green, D. J., *The Politics of Samuel Johnson* (New Haven, 1960)

von Greyerz, Kaspar (ed.), *Religion and Society in Early Modern Europe, 1500–1800* (London, 1984)

Griffiths, O. M., *Religion and Learning: A Study in English Presbyterian Thought from the Bartholomew Ejections (1662) to the Foundation of the Unitarian Movement* (Cambridge, 1935)

Gunn, J. A. W., *Beyond Liberty and Property: The Process of Self-Recognition in Eighteenth-Century Political Thought* (Kingston and Montreal, 1983)

Factions No More: Attitudes to Party in Government and Opposition in Eighteenth Century England (London, 1972)

Gurr, T. R., 'Burke and the Modern Theory of Revolution: A Reply to Freeman', *PT*, 6 (1978), 299–311

Haakonssen, K., *The Science of a Legislator: The Natural Jurisprudence of David Hume and Adam Smith* (Cambridge, 1981)

Hackwood, F. W., *William Hone: His Life and Times* (London, 1912)

Halévy, É., *The Birth of Methodism in England* (1906), translated and edited by B. Semmel (Chicago, 1971)

The Growth of Philosophic Radicalism (1928, reprinted London, 1972)

A History of the English People in 1815 (London, 1924)

Hammond, J. L., and B., *The Town Labourer 1760–1832* (London, 1917)

Hampsher-Monk, I., 'Civic Humanism and Parliamentary Reform: The Case of the Society of the Friends of the People', *JBS*, 18 (1979), 70–89

Harris, R. W., *Political Ideas, 1760–1792* (London, 1963)

Harrison, J. F. C., *The Second Coming: Popular Millenarianism, 1780–1850* (London, 1979)

'"The Steam Engine of the New Moral World": Owenism and Education, 1817–1829', *JBS*, 6 (1967), 76–98

Hart, J., 'Religion and Social Control in the Mid-Nineteenth Century', in *Social Control in Nineteenth Century Britain*, edited by A. P. Donajgrodzki (London, 1977)

Harvey, A. D., *Britain in the Early Nineteenth Century* (Batsford, 1978)

Harvey, R., 'The Problem of Socio-Political Obligation for the Church of England in the 17th Century', *CH*, 49 (1971), 156–69

Hatch, R. B., 'Joseph Priestley: An Addition to Hartley's *Observations*', *JHI*, 36 (1975), 548–50

Hawkins, L. M., *Allegiance in Church and State: The Problem of the Non Jurors in the English Revolution* (London, 1928)

Hay, C. H., *James Burgh, Spokesman for Reform in Hanoverian England* (Washington DC, 1979)

'The Making of a Radical: The Case of James Burgh', *JBS*, 18 (1979), 90–117

Hempton, D., 'Evangelicalism and Eschatology', *JEH*, 31 (1980), 179–94

Methodism and Politics in British Society, 1750–1850 (London, 1984)

'Thomas Allen and Methodist Politics, 1800–1840', *Hist.*, 67 (1982), 13–31

Hendrix, R., 'Popular Humor and "The Black Dwarf"', *JBS*, 16 (1976), 108–28

Hennell, Michael, *John Venn and the Clapham Sect* (London, 1958)

Henriques, U. R. Q., *Religious Toleration in England, 1787–1833* (London, 1961)

Henry, Maureen, *The Intoxication of Power: An Analysis of Civil Religion in Relation to Ideology* (Dordrecht, 1979)

Hill, C., *Intellectual Origins of the English Revolution* (Oxford, 1965)

Hill, Sir Francis, 'Squire and Parson in Early Victorian Lincolnshire', *Hist.*, 58 (1973), 337–49

Hobsbawm, E., 'Methodism and the Threat of Revolution', *History Today* (February 1957), 115–24

Hobsbawm, E., and G. Rudé, *Captain Swing* (London, 1969: Harmondsworth, 1973)

Hole, R. 'British Counter-Revolutionary Popular Propaganda in the 1790s', in Colin

Jones (ed.), *Britain and Revolutionary France: Conflict, Subversion and Propaganda* (Exeter, 1983)

Holmes, D. L., 'The Episcopal Church and the American Revolution', *Historical Magazine of the Protestant Episcopal Church*, 47 (1978), 261–91

Holmes, Geoffrey, *The Trial of Doctor Sacheverell* (London, 1973)

Holt, A. D., *A Life of Joseph Priestley* (London, 1931)

Holt, R. V., *The Unitarian Contribution to Social Progress in England*, second edition (London, 1952)

Hone, J. A., *For the Cause of Truth: Radicalism in London, 1796–1821* (Oxford, 1982)
  'William Hone (1780–1841), Publisher and Bookseller: An Approach to Early Nineteenth Century London Radicalism', *Historical Studies*, 16 (1974), 55–70

Hopkins, M. A., *Hannah More and her Circle* (New York, 1947)

Horne, T. A., 'Envy and Commercial Society: Mandeville and Smith on "Private Vices, Public Benefits"', *PT*, 9 (1981), 551–69
  'Politics in a Corrupt Society: William Arnall's Defense of Robert Walpole', *JHI*, 41 (1980), 601–14
  '"The Poor Have a Claim Founded in the Law of Nature": William Paley and the Rights of the Poor', *Journal of the History of Philosophy*, 23 (1985), 51–70
  The Social Thought of Bernard Mandeville: Virtue and Commerce in Early Eighteenth Century England (London, 1978)

Howse, E. A., *Saints in Politics: 'The Clapham Sect' and the Growth of Freedom* (London, 1953)

Hudson, W. D., *Reason and Right: A Critical Examination of Richard Price's Moral Philosophy* (London, 1970)

Hughes, G. W., *Robert Hall* (London, 1943)
  With Freedom Fired: The Story of Robert Robinson, Cambridge Nonconformist (London, 1955)

Hulling, M., 'Patriarchalism and its Early Enemies', *PT*, 2 (1974), 410–19

Hunt, C. L., 'Religious Ideology as a Means of Social Control', *Sociology and Social Research*, 33 (1949), 191–205

Hunt, N. C., *Two Early Political Associations: The Quakers and the Dissenting Deputies in the Age of Sir Robert Walpole* (London, 1961)

Inglis, K. S., *Churches and the Working Classes in Victorian England* (London, 1963)

Innes, J., 'Jonathan Clark, Social History and England's "Ancien Regime"', *PP*, 115 (May 1987), 165–200

Ippel, H. P., 'British Sermons and the American Revolution', *The Journal of Religious History*, 12 (1982), 191–205

Itzkin, E. S., 'The Halévy Thesis – A Working Hypothesis? English Revivalism: Antidote for Revolution and Radicalism 1789–1815', *CH*, 44 (1975), 47–56

Jacob, J. R., *Henry Stubbe, Radical Protestantism and the Early Enlightenment* (Cambridge, 1983)

Jacob, M. C., 'The Church and the Formulation of the Newtonian World-View', *Journal of European Studies*, 1 (1971), 128–48
  'Millenarianism and Science in the Late Seventeenth Century', *JHI*, 37 (1976), 355–41
  The Newtonians and the English Revolution (Hassocks, 1976)

The Radical Enlightenment: Pantheists, Freemasons and Republicans (London, 1981)

James, F. G., 'The Bishops in Politics 1688–1714', in *Conflict in Stuart England*, edited by W. A. Aiken and B. D. Henning (London, 1960)

Jebb, H. H., *A Great Bishop of One Hundred Years Ago: Being a Sketch of the Life of Samuel Horsley, LL.D., Formerly Bishop of St David's, Rochester, and St Asaph, and Dean of Westminster* (London, 1909)

Jewson, C. B., *The Jacobin City: A Portrait of Norwich in its Reaction to the French Revolution 1788–1802* (Glasgow, 1975)

'Norwich Baptists and the French Revolution', *Baptist Quarterly*, 24 (1972), 209–15

Johnson, Richard, 'Educational Policy and Social Control in Early Victorian England', *PP*, 49 (1970), 96–119

Jones, M. G., *The Charity Schools Movement. A Study of 18th Century Puritanism in Action* (London, 1964)

Hannah More (Cambridge, 1952)

Kelly, Gary, *The English Jacobin Novel 1780–1805* (Oxford, 1976)

Kendrick, T. F. J., 'Sir Robert Walpole, the Old Whigs and the Bishops, 1733–1736: A Study in Eighteenth-Century Parliamentary Politics', *HJ*, 11 (1968), 421–45

Kent, J., *The Age of Disunity* (London, 1966)

Jabez Bunting, The Last Wesleyan: A Study in the Methodist Ministry after the Death of John Wesley (London, 1955)

'Methodism and Revolution', *Methodist History*, 12 (1973–4), 136–44

Kenyon, J. P., *Revolution Principles: The Politics of Party 1689–1720* (Cambridge, 1977)

Kiernan, V., 'Evangelicalism and the French Revolution'. *PP*, 1 (1952), 44–56

Kilcup, R. W., 'Burke's Historicism', *JMH*, 49 (1977), 394–410

Kitching, J., 'The Catholic Poor Schools 1800–1840', *Journal of Educational Administration and History*, 1 (1969), 1–8, and 2 (1969), 1–12

Knight, Frida, *University Rebel: The Life of William Frend (1757–1841)* (London, 1971)

Knights, Ben, *The Idea of Clerisy in the Nineteenth Century* (Cambridge, 1978)

Kramnick, Isaac, *The Rage of Edmund Burke, Portrait of an Ambivalent Conservative* (New York, 1977)

'Religion and Radicalism: English Political Theory in the Age of Revolution', *PT*, 5 (1977), 505–34

Kriegel, A. D., 'Liberty and Whiggery in Early Nineteenth-Century England', *JMH*, 52 (1980), 253–78

Landis, P. A., *Social Control: Social Organisation and Disorganisation in Process* (1939, revised edition, Chicago, 1956)

Laqueur, T. W., 'The Queen Caroline Affair: Politics as Art in the Reign of George IV', *JMH*, 54 (1982), 417–66

Religion and Respectability: Sunday Schools and Working Class Culture, 1780–1850 (New Haven, 1976)

Lee, Janice V., 'Political Antiquarianism Unmasked: The Conservative Attack on the Myth of the Ancient Constitution', *BIHR*, 15 (1982), 166–79

Le Mahieu, D. L., *The Mind of William Paley* (Lincoln, Nebraska, 1976)

Levack, A. P., 'Edmund Burke, his Friends and the Dawn of Irish Catholic Emancipation', *The Catholic Historical Review*, 37 (1952), 385–414

Lewis, G. K., *Slavery, Imperialism and Freedom: Studies in English Radical Thought* (New York, 1978)

Lincoln, A., *Some Political and Social Ideas of English Dissent 1763–1800* (1938, reprinted New York, 1971)

Lindsay, J., Introduction to *Autobiography of Joseph Priestley*, edited by J. Lindsay (Bath, 1970), pp. 11–66

Linker, R. W., 'English Catholics in the Eighteenth Century: An Interpretation', *CH*, 25 (1966), 288–310

'The English Roman Catholics and Emancipation, the Politics of Persuasion', *JEH*, 27 (1976), 151–80

Looker, S. J. (ed.), *Shelley, Trelawny and Henley: A Study of Three Titans* (Worthing, 1950)

Lovegrove, Deryck, 'English Evangelical Dissent and the European Conflict 1789–1815', *SCH*, 20 (1983), 263–76

Lowe, W. C., 'Bishops and Scottish Representative Peers in the House of Lords, 1760–1775', *JBS*, 18 (1978), 86–106

McCalman, Iain, 'Unrespectable Radicalism: Infidels and Pornography in Early Nineteenth-Century London', *PP*, 104 (1984), 74–110

McClatchey, D., *Oxfordshire Clergy 1777–1869: A Study of the Established Church and of the Role of its Clergy in Local Society* (Oxford, 1960)

MacCunn, J., *The Political Philosophy of Burke* (London, 1913)

MacDonagh, O., 'The Politicization of the Irish Catholic Bishops 1800–1850', *HJ*, 18 (1975), 37–53

McFarland, Thomas, *Coleridge and the Pantheist Tradition* (London, 1969)

Machin, G. I. T., 'Canning, Wellington and the Catholic Question 1822–1829', *EHR*, 99 (1984), 94–100

'The Catholic Emancipation Crisis of 1825', *EHR*, 306 (1963), 458–82

The Catholic Question in English Politics 1820–1830 (Oxford, 1964)

'The Duke of Wellington and Catholic Emancipation', *JEH*, 14 (1963), 190–208

'The No-Popery Movement in Britain in 1828–9', *HJ*, 6 (1963), 193–211

'Resistance to Repeal of the Test and Corporation Acts 1828', *HJ*, 22 (1979), 115–39

Mack, Mary P., *Jeremy Bentham: An Odyssey of Ideas 1748–1792* (London, 1962)

McKenzie, L. A., 'Rousseau's Debate with Machiavelli in the *Social Contract*', *JHI*, 2 (1982), 209–28

McLachlan, H., *English Education under the Test Acts: Being the History of the Non-Conformist Academies 1662–1820* (Manchester, 1931)

The Unitarian Movement in the Religious Life of England: Its Contribution to Thought and Learning 1700–1900 (London, 1934)

Maclear, J. F., 'The Idea of "American Protestantism" and British Nonconformity, 1829–1840', *JBS*, 21 (1981), 68–89

McManners, J., *Death and the Enlightenment: Changing Attitudes to Death among Christians and Unbelievers in Eighteenth Century France* (New York, 1981)

MacPherson, C. B., *Burke* (Oxford 1980)

Manning, B., *The Protestant Dissenting Deputies* (Cambridge, 1952)

Marmion, J. P., 'The Beginnings of the Catholic Poor Schools in England', *Recusant History*, 17 (1984), 67–83

Martin, R. H., *Evangelicals United: Ecumenical Stirrings in Pre-Victorian Britain 1795–1830*, Studies in Evangelicalism, 4 (London, 1983)

Mather, F. C., 'Georgian Churchmanship Reconsidered: Some Variations in Anglican Public Worship 1714–1830', *JEH*, 36 (1985), 255–83

Meacham, S., 'The Evangelical Inheritance', *JBS*, 3 (1963), 88–104

Mead, Sidney M., *The Lively Experiment: The Shaping of Christianity in America* (New York, 1963)

Miller, David, *Philosophy and Ideology in Hume's Political Thought* (Oxford, 1981)

Miller, G. T., 'Fear God and Honour the King: The Failure of Loyalist Civil Theology in the Revolutionary Crisis', *Historical Magazine of the Protestant Episcopalian Church*, 47 (1978), 221–42

Miller, N. C., 'John Cartwright and Radical Parliamentary Reform, 1808–1819', *EHR*, 83 (1968), 705–28

Milton-Smith, J., 'Earl Grey's Cabinet and the Objects of Parliamentary Reform', *HJ*, 15 (1972), 55–74

Mitchell, A., 'The Association Movement of 1792–3', *HJ*, 4 (1961), 56–77

Monro, D. H. (ed.), *A Guide to the British Moralists* (London, 1972)

Moon, N. S., 'Caleb Evans, Founder of the British Education Society', *The Baptist Quarterly*, 24 (1971), 175–90

Moore, D. C. 'Concession or Cure: The Sociological Premises of the First Reform Act', *HJ*, 9 (1966), 39–59

Morris, R. J., 'Voluntary Societies and British Urban Elites 1780–1850', *HJ*, 26 (1983), 95–118

Mossner, E. C., 'The Religion of David Hume', *JHI*, 39 (1978), 653–63

Mullett, C. F., 'A Case of Allegiance: William Sherlock and the Revolution of 1688', *Huntington Library Quarterly*, 10 (1946–7), 83–103

Namier, Lewis, *Crossroads of Power: Essays on Eighteenth Century England* (London, 1962)

   England in the Age of the American Revolution, second edition (London, 1961)

   The Structure of Politics at the Accession of George III, second edition (London, 1957)

Naphthine, D., and W. A. Speck, 'Clergymen and Conflict 1660–1763', *SCH*, 20 (1983), 231–51

Newan, S., 'A Note on *Common Sense* and Christian Eschatology', *PT*, 6 (1978), 101–8

Newton, Robert, *Eighteenth Century Exeter* (Exeter, 1984)

Nicholls, D., *Church and State in Britain since 1820* (London, 1967)

Niebuhr, H. R., *The Social Sources of Denominationalism* (Hamden, Connecticut, 1929)

Norman, E. R., *Anti-Catholicism in Victorian England* (London, 1968)

   Church and Society in England, 1770–1970 (Oxford, 1976)

   The English Catholic Church in the Nineteenth Century (Oxford, 1984)

O'Farrell, P., 'Historians and Religious Conviction', *Historical Studies*, 17 (1976–7), 279–98

O'Gorman, Frank, *Edmund Burke, his Political Philosophy* (London, 1973)

Parssinen, T. M., 'The Revolutionary Party in London 1816–20', *BIHR*, 45 (1972), 266–82

Patterson, A. T., *Radical Leicester: A History of Leicester 1780–1850* (Leicester, 1954)

Peach, Bernard (ed.), *Richard Price and the Ethical Foundations of the American*

Revolution: Selections from his Pamphlets (Durham, North Carolina, 1979)

Peaston, A. E., *The Prayer Book Reform Movement in the XVIIIth Century* (Oxford, 1940)

Pellew, George, *The Life and Correspondence of the Right Hon. Henry Addington, First Viscount Sidmouth*, 3 vols. (London, 1847)

Pelling, Henry, 'Religion and the Nineteenth-Century British Working Class', *PP*, 27 (1964), 128–33

Perkin, H., *The Origins of Modern English Society 1780–1880* (London, 1969)

Peterson, Susan R., 'Richard Price's Politics and his Ethics', *JHI*, 45 (1984), 537–47

Piggin, S., 'Halévy Revisited: The Origins of the Methodist Missionary Society: An Examination of Semmel's Thesis', *Journal of Imperial and Commonwealth History*, 9 (1980), 17–37

Plamenatz, John, *The English Unitarians* (Oxford, 1966)

Pocock, J. G. A., 'Burke and the Ancient Constitution – A Problem in the History of Ideas', *HJ*, 3 (1960), 125–43

'Gibbon's *Decline and Fall* and the World View of the Late Enlightenment', *ECS*, 10 (1977), 287–303

The Machiavellian Moment: Florentine Political Thought and the Atlantic Republican Tradition (Princeton, 1975)

'*The Machiavellian Moment* Revisited: A Study in History and Ideology', *JMH*, 53 (1981), 49–72

'The Political Economy of Burke's Analysis of the French Revolution', *HJ*, 25 (1982), 331–49

Politics, Language and Time: Essays in Political Thought and History (New York, 1971)

'Virtues, Rights and Manners: A Model for Historians of Political Thought', *Political Theory*, 9 (1981), 353–68

Prevs, J. S., 'Machiavelli's Functional Analysis of Religion: Context and Object', *JHI*, 40 (1979), 171–90

Prochaska, F. K., 'English State Trials in the 1790s: A Case Study', *JBS*, 13 (1973), 63–82

'Thomas Paine's *The Age of Reason* Revisited', *JHI*, 33 (1972), 561–76

Pym, David, *The Religious Thought of Samuel Taylor Coleridge* (Gerrards Cross, 1978)

Quinlan, M. J., *Victorian Prelude: A History of English Manners 1700–1830* (1941; reprinted London, 1965)

Quinton, A., *The Politics of Imperfection: The Religious and Secular Traditions of Conservative Thought in England from Hooker to Oakeshott* (London, 1978)

Rack, H. D., '"Christ's Kingdom Not of this World": The Case of Benjamin Hoadley versus William Law Reconsidered', *SCH*, 12 (1975), 275–91

Randall, H. W., 'The Rise and Fall of a Martyrology: Sermons on Charles I', *Huntington Library Quarterly*, 10 (1946–7), 135–67

Raphael, D. D., 'Review of Peach's *Richard Price and the Ethical Foundations of the American Revolution*', *PPN*, 4 (1980), 70–4

Rashid, S., '"He Startled . . . as if he saw a Spectre": Tucker's Proposals for American Independence', *JHI*, 43 (1982), 439–60

'Richard Whately and Christian Political Economy at Oxford and Dublin', *JHI*, 38 (1977), 147–55

'Richard Whately and the Struggle for Rational Christianity in the Mid Nineteenth

Century', *Historical Magazine of the Protestant Episcopal Church*, 47 (1978), 293–331

Ravitch, N., 'The Social Origins of French and English Bishops in the Eighteenth Century', *HJ*, 8 (1965), 309–25

Raymond, A., '"I fear God and honour the King": John Wesley and the American Revolution', *CH*, 45 (1976), 316–28

Read, D., *Peterloo: The 'Massacre' and its Background* (Manchester, 1958)

Redwood, J., *Reason, Ridicule and Religion; The Age of Enlightenment in England 1660–1750* (London, 1976)

Reynolds, R., *British Pamphleteers*; vol. 2, *From the French Revolution to the Nineteen Thirties* (London, 1951)

Richey, R. E., 'The Origins of British Radicalism: The Changing Rationale for Dissent', *ECS*, 7 (1973–4), 179–92

Richey, R. E., and D. G. Jones (eds), *American Civil Religion* (New York, 1974)

Rickword, E., *Radical Squibs and Loyal Ripostes* (Bath, 1971)

Robbins, C., *The Eighteenth-Century Commonwealthman* (Cambridge, Massachusetts, 1959)

    'Faith and Freedom (*c.* 1677–1729)', *JHI*, 36 (1975), 47–62

Roberts, J. M., *The Mythology of Secret Societies* (London, 1972)

    'The Origins of a Mythology: Freemasons, Protestants and the French Revolution', *BIHR*, 44 (1971), 78–97

Roberts, M. J. D., 'The Society for the Suppression of Vice and its Early Critics 1802–1812', *HJ*, 26 (1983), 159–76

Robinson, E., 'New Light on the Priestley Riots', *HJ*, 3 (1960) 73–5

Rose, R. B., 'The Priestley Riots of 1791', *PP*, 18 (1960), 68–88

Rosman, Doreen M., *Evangelicals and Culture* (London, 1984)

Ross, E. A., *Social Control: A Survey of the Foundations of Order* (New York, 1901; reprinted Cleveland, 1969)

    Social Control and the Foundations of Sociology, edited by E. F. Borgatta and H. J. Meyer (Boston, 1959)

Royle, E., *The Infidel Tradition from Paine to Bradlaugh* (London, 1975)

    Radical Politics 1790–1900: Religion and Unbelief (London, 1971)

    Victorian Infidels: The Origins of the British Secularist Movement 1791–1866 (Manchester, 1974)

Royle, E. and J. Walvin, *English Radicals and Reformers 1760–1848* (Brighton, 1982)

Rudé, George, *Paris and London in the Eighteenth Century* (London, 1974)

    Wilkes and Liberty: A Social Study of 1763 to 1774 (Oxford, 1962)

Russell, Anthony J., *The Clerical Profession* (London, 1980)

Schlatter, R., *The Social Ideas of Religious Leaders 1660–1688* (London, 1940)

Schneider, B. R., *Wordsworth's Cambridge Education* (Cambridge, 1959)

Schochet, G. J., *Patriarchalism and Political Thought* (Oxford, 1975)

Schofield, R. E., *The Lunar Society of Birmingham: A Social History of Provincial Science and Industry in Eighteenth-Century England* (Oxford, 1963)

    Mechanism and Materialism: British Natural Philosophy in an Age of Reason (Princeton, 1970,)

Schofield, R. E. (ed.), *A Scientific Autobiography of Joseph Priestley 1733–1804* (Cambridge, Massachusetts, 1966)

Schwartz, R. B., *Samuel Johnson and the Problem of Evil* (Wisconsin, 1975)

Scrivener, M., 'Godwin's Philosophy: A Revaluation', *JHI*, 39 (1978), 615–26

   Radical Shelley: The Philosophical Anarchism and Utopian Thought of Percy Bysshe Shelley (Princeton, 1982)

Sellers, I., *Nineteenth-Century Nonconformity* (London, 1977)

Semmel, Bernard, 'Élie Halévy, Methodism and Revolution', Introduction to É. Halévy, *The Birth of Methodism in England*, translated and edited by B. Semmel (Chicago, 1971), pp. 1–29

   The Methodist Revolution (London, 1974)

Shelley, P. B., *The Complete Poetical Works*, edited by Neville Rogers, 4 vols (Oxford, 1972–5)

Shelton, W. G., *Dean Tucker and Eighteenth-Century Economic and Political Thought* (London, 1981)

Short, K. R. M., 'The English Indemnity Acts 1726–1867', *CH*, 42 (1973), 366–76

   'The English Regium Donum', *EHR*, 330 (1969), 59–78

Silver, Harold, *The Concept of Popular Education* (London, 1965)

   English Education and the Radicals 1780–1850 (London, 1975)

Skinner, Q., *The Foundations of Modern Political Thought*, 2 vols. (Cambridge, 1978)

   'Meaning and Understanding in the History of Ideas', *History and Theory*, 8 (1969), 3–53

   'Motives, Intentions and the Interpretation of Texts', *New Literary History*, 3 (1972), 393–408

Smith, A. A., 'Nonconformity in Green Street, Cambridge', *Journal of the Presbyterian Historical Society of England*, 14 (1969), 59–66

Smith, A. W., 'Irish Rebels and English Radicals 1798–1820', *PP*, 7 (1955)

Smith, D. D., 'Gibbon in Church', *JEH*, 35 (1984), 452–63

Smith, Olivia, *The Politics of Language 1791–1819* (Oxford, 1984)

Soloway, R. A., *Prelates and People: Ecclesiastical Social Thought in England, 1783–1852* (London, 1969)

   'Reform or Ruin: English Moral Thought during the First French Republic', *Review of Politics*, 25 (1963), 110–28

Springborg, P., 'Leviathan and the Problem of Ecclesiastical Authority', *PT*, 3 (1975), 289–303

Stafford, W., 'Religion and the Doctrine of Nationalism in England at the Time of the French Revolution and Napoleonic Wars', *SCH*, 18 (1982), 381–95

Stanhope, Earl of, *Life of the Right Honourable William Pitt*, 4 vols., third edition (London, 1867)

Steintrager, James, *Bentham* (London, 1977)

   'Language and Politics: Bentham on Religion', *The Bentham Newsletter*, 4 (1980), 4–20

   'Morality and Belief: The Origin and Purpose of Bentham's Writings on Religion', *The Mill Newsletter*, 6 (1971), 3–15

Stephen, Leslie, *History of English Thought in the Eighteenth Century*, 2 vols. (1876; third edition 1902; reprinted New York, 1949)

Stephens, J., 'The London Ministers and Subscription, 1772–1779', *ED*, 1 (1982), 43–71

Stevenson, J., *Popular Disturbances in England 1700–1870* (London, 1979)

Stewart, B. S., 'The Cult of the Royal Martyr', *CH*, 38 (1969), 175–87

Stigant, P., 'Wesleyan Methodism and Working Class Radicalism in the North', *Northern History*, 6 (1971), 98–116

Straka, G. M., *The Anglican Reaction to the Revolution of 1688* (Madison, Wisconsin, 1962)

  'The Final Phase of the Divine Right Theory in England 1688–1702', *EHR*, 77 (1962), 638–58

Stromberg, R. N., *Religious Liberalism in Eighteenth-Century England* (London, 1954)

Strout, Cushing, *The New Heavens and New Earth: Political Religion in America* (New York, 1974)

Swanson, Guy, *Religion and Regime: A Sociological Account of the Reformation* (Ann Arbor, 1967)

Sykes, Norman, 'Benjamin Hoadley, Bishop of Bangor', in *The Social and Political Ideas of Some English Thinkers of the Augustan Age AD 1650–1750*, edited by F. J. C. Hearnshaw (London, 1928), pp. 112–55

  Church and State in England in the XVIIIth Century, Birkbeck Lectures, 1931–3 (Cambridge, 1934)

  From Sheldon to Secker, Aspects of English Church History, 1660–1768, The Ford Lectures 1958 (Cambridge, 1959)

Taylor, E. R., *Methodism and Politics 1791–1851* (Cambridge, 1935)

Thomas, D. O., *The Honest Mind: The Thought and Work of Richard Price* (Oxford, 1977)

  Richard Price 1723–1791 (Cardiff, 1976)

Thomas, William, *The Philosophical Radicals: Nine Studies in Theory and Practice 1817–1841* (Oxford, 1979)

Thompson, E. P., *The Making of the English Working Class* (London, 1963; revised edition, Harmondsworth, 1968)

Thompson, Kenneth A., *Bureaucracy and Church Reform: The Organisational Response of the Church of England to Social Change 1800–1965* (Oxford, 1970)

Thorpe, T. E., *Joseph Priestley* (London, 1906)

Tierney, B., *Religion, Law and the Growth of Constitutional Thought 1150–1650*, The Wiles Lectures (Cambridge, 1982)

Toon, P., *The Emergence of Hyper-Calvinism in English Nonconformity 1689–1765* (London, 1967)

Troeltsch, E., *The Social Teaching of the Christian Churches*, 2 vols. (1912), translated by O. Wyon (New York, 1931)

Turnbull, P., 'The "Supposed Infidelity" of Edward Gibbon', *HJ*, 25 (1982) 23–41

Turner, J. M., '"Of Methodists and Papists Compar'd"', *Proceedings of the Wesley Historical Society*, 41 (1977), 37–8

Vickers, John, *Thomas Coke, Apostle of Methodism* (London, 1969)

Viner, J., *Religious Thought and Economic Society: Four Chapters of an Unfinished Work*, edited by Jacques Melitz and Donald Winch (Durham, North Carolina, 1978)

  The Role of Providence in the Social Order: An Essay in Intellectual History, The Jayne Lectures for 1966 (Philadelphia, 1972)

Waddington, John, *Congregational History 1700–1800 in Relation to Contemporaneous*

Events, Education, the Eclipse of Faith, Revivals, and Christian Missions (London, 1876)

Wadsworth, A. P., 'The First Manchester Sunday Schools', *Bulletin of the John Rylands Library*, 33 (1951), 299–336

Walker, D. P., *The Decline of Hell; Seventeenth Century Discussions of Eternal Torment* (London, 1964)

Walmsley, Robert, *Peterloo: The Case Reopened* (Manchester, 1969)

Walsh, J. D., 'Élie Halévy and the Birth of Methodism', *TRHS*, fifth series, 25 (1975), 1–20

'Methodism and the Mob in the Eighteenth Century', *SCH*, 8 (1972), 213–27

'Methodism at the End of the Eighteenth Century', in *A History of the Methodist Church in Great Britain*, vol. 1, edited by R. Davies and G. Rupp (London, 1965), pp. 275–315

'Origins of the Evangelical Revival', in *Essays in Modern English Church History in Memory of Norman Sykes*, edited by G. V. Bennett and J. D. Walsh (London, 1966), pp. 132–62

Ward, B., *The Dawn of the Catholic Revival in England 1781–1803*, 2 vols. (London, 1909)

The Eve of Catholic Emancipation: Being the History of the English Catholics during the First Thirty Years of the Nineteenth Century, 3 vols. (London, 1911–12)

Sequel to Catholic Emancipation (to 1850), 2 vols. (London, 1915)

Ward, W. R., *Georgian Oxford, University Politics in the Eighteenth Century* (Oxford, 1958)

'Power and Piety: The Origins of Religious Revival in the Early Eighteenth Century', *Bulletin of the John Rylands University Library of Manchester*, 63 (1980), 231–52

'The Relations of Enlightenment and Religious Revival in Central Europe and in the English Speaking World', *SCH*, Subsidia 2 (1979), 281–305

Religion and Society in England 1790–1850 (London, 1972)

'The Religion of the People and the Problem of Control 1790–1830', *SCH*, 8 (1972), 237–57

'The Tithe Question in England in the Early Nineteenth Century', *JEH*, 16 (1965), 67–81

Wardroper, John, *Kings, Lords and Wicked Libellers: Satire and Protest 1760–1837* (London, 1973)

Warne, Arthur, *Church and Society in Eighteenth-Century Devon* (Newton Abbot, 1969)

Warner, W. J., *The Wesleyan Movement in the Industrial Revolution* (London, 1930)

Waterman, A. M. C., 'The Ideological Alliance of Political Economy and Christian Theology 1798–1833', *JEH*, 34 (1983), 231–44

Watkins, C. K., *Social Control* (London, 1975)

Watts, M. R., *The Dissenters: From the Reformation to the French Revolution* (Oxford, 1978)

Wearmouth, R. F., *Methodism and the Common People of the Eighteenth Century* (London, 1945)

Methodism and the Working Class Movements of England 1800–1850, second edition (London, 1947)

Webb, R. K., *The British Working Class Reader 1790–1848* (London, 1955)

Weber, M., *The Protestant Ethic and the Spirit of Capitalism*, translated by Talcott Parsons (London, 1930)

Webster, A. B., *Joshua Watson, the Story of a Layman 1771–1855* (London, 1954)

Whyte, J. H., 'The Influence of the Catholic Clergy on Elections in Nineteenth Century Ireland', *EHR*, 75 (1960), 239–59

Wiener, Joel H., *Radicalism and Free Thought in Nineteenth-Century Britain: The Life of Richard Carlile* (Wesport, Connecticut, 1983)

Wilbur, E. M., *A History of Unitarianism in Transylvania, England and America* (Cambridge, Massachusetts, 1952)

Williams, G. A., *Rowland Detrosier: A Working Class Infidel 1800–1834*, Borthwick Papers, 28 (York, 1965)

Wilson, B. R. (ed.), *Patterns of Sectarianism: Organisation and Ideology in Social and Religious Movements* (London, 1967)

Winch, D., *Adam Smith's Politics: An Essay in Historiographical Revision* (Cambridge, 1978)

Windstrup, G., 'Locke on Suicide', *PT*, 8 (1980), 169–82

Winstanley, D. E., *Unreformed Cambridge: A Study of Certain Aspects of the University in the Eighteenth Century*, second edition (London, 1952)

Woodring, C. R., *Politics in the Poetry of Coleridge* (Madison, Wisconsin, 1961)

Yeo, Eileen, 'Christianity in Chartist Struggle 1832–1842', *PP*, 91 (1981), 109–39

Yolton, J. W., *John Locke and the Way of Ideas* (Oxford, 1956)

Ziegler, Philip, *Addington: A Life of Henry Addington, First Viscount Sidmouth* (London, 1965)

Index

Index